AN INTRODUCTION TO

JAPANESE GRAMMAR
AND
COMMUNICATION STRATEGIES

AN INTRODUCTION TO
JAPANESE GRAMMAR AND COMMUNICATION STRATEGIES

日本語の文法とコミュニケーション・ストラテジー

Senko K. Maynard

The Japan Times

First edition: November 1990
3rd printing: May 1992

Jacket design: CADEC, Inc.

Published by The Japan Times, Ltd.
5-4, Shibaura 4-chome, Minato-ku, Tokyo 108, Japan

ISBN4-7890-0542-9

Printed in Japan

Preface

"I'm still not exactly sure," she said, "when to use *ga* and when to use *wa*."

She is not alone. Many students of Japanese have questions about the basic grammatical rules of the Japanese language. As a Japanese teacher who has taught in American universities for some 14 years, I've come to the conclusion that even the best student can benefit from a supplementary guide to the classroom instruction which comprehensively explains grammatical points and communication strategies. What the student who asked me about *ga* and *wa* needed was exactly such a book. Let's face it, since Japanese is the fastest growing foreign language learned in American universities today, large classes are often inevitable, and the pace of the classroom instruction can sometimes move faster or slower than an individual student's comprehension level.

That's why I wrote this book. To challenge the student who wants to learn more. To bring aid and comfort to many serious students of the Japanese language who really want to get the rules down cold and to study at their own pace. You may be enrolled in elementary, intermediate or in advanced courses and you need to organize bits of information you've accumulated into a comprehensive picture. Maybe you're a very advanced student and yet you feel that your knowledge of Japanese grammar is a little fuzzy, and you'd like to review those points that have always troubled you. Or perhaps you're planning to study the Japanese language and you'd like to supplement your primary text with this book. You may not have time to be enrolled in or have easy access to structured language courses and you need a guide for your self-study. Although I've directed this book primarily toward those whose goal is to reach the intermediate or advanced intermediate proficiency level, anyone interested in the Japanese language will find this book a good source for reference and review.

The purpose of this book is to explain in great detail not only how Japanese grammar operates, but how you should use it strategically in conversation so that you're both grammatically and socially correct. For as you know, learning a foreign language well requires that you learn the culture that goes with it. Whenever possible, I've included notes and commentary about customs, rituals and social standards you simply must know in order to be a proper member of the Japanese speaking society.

The ritual of inviting a guest to help himself/herself to another serving of food, for example, requires that you know that as the guest you *initially* refuse or at least hesitate. Your hostess will assure you that it's okay to have more. You may hesitate again. Once again the invitation will be extended. Finally, you accept. This is how Japanese people expect it to happen. If—as the guest—you accept the invitation too quickly and reach for the food in one swift motion, you will be denying an unspoken norm in Japanese social relations. No one will shoot you for your *faux pas*. Perhaps even worse, no one will ever tell you that you're coming across too strong for the sensibilities of the Japanese.

You need no prior knowledge of Japanese to learn from this book. I've deliberately structured the content to flow from easy-to-grasp material to more difficult topics and more refined grammatical points. Each successive entry builds upon all the information that comes before it, so that were you to study the book page by page from beginning to end your knowledge would be progressive.

Because this book is virtually an anthology of grammar and communication strategies, Japanese teachers may also find it a useful reference to add to their personal library.

In describing the Japanese language to English speakers I have incorporated the long-standing tradition of the National Language Study in Japan *(Kokugogaku)* as well as analyses made by many linguists outside of Japan. My reason for doing so is to as much as possible communicate to the English speaking world how Japanese themselves see the language. By preserving this internal point of view, I hope that the reader will gain unexpected insight into the thinking of Japanese people as it is reflected in language. Incorporating an external point of view based on the results of Japanese linguistics outside of Japan is also important because this book is written specifically for English speakers. Additionally, I have included some findings reached through Contrastive Analysis of Japanese and English.

As the saying goes, "We stand on the shoulders of those who came before us." So, too, I stand on the shoulders of many others who have come before me in having contributed to Japanese linguistics and language studies. Although I cannot list each and every work which has helped me in writing this book, I gratefully acknowledge the following which have directly influenced my writing in some of the entries: *Suru to Naru no Gengogaku* by Yoshihiko Ikegami, *Japanese Patterns of Behavior* by Takie Sugiyama Lebra, *Japanese and the Japanese* by Takao Suzuki, *A Dictionary of Basic Japanese Grammar* by Seiichi Makino and Michio Tsutsui, *Japanese: The Spoken Language* by Eleanor Jorden with Mari Noda, *Japanese Language Patterns* by Anthony

Alfonso and *Bunshooron Soosetsu* by Masaru Nagano. I should also mention that some results of my own research, particularly from my book *Japanese Conversation: Self-contextualization through Structure and Interactional Management* have found their way into the text.

Finally, I would like to express my sincere gratitude to Tazuko Monane for offering insightful commentary on the manuscript, to Chiaki Kaku of The Japan Times for her scrupulous attention to detail in editing the book, and to my husband, Michael, for proofreading and for offering assistance in every aspect of this project.

October, 1990
SKM

Table of Contents

List of Entries

Part One:

Preliminaries

1.1.   To the Reader

The main part of this book consists of Preliminaries, Entries and Sample texts. In the Preliminaries, some introductory remarks are made. Here I introduce ten basic grammatical and strategic characteristics of modern Japanese which will be referred to throughout the book whenever relevant. Presented in the Entries section are 130 main entries representing a mixture of categories. Some bear grammatical headings (such as "Negation of Verbs") while others are labeled with functional notions (such as "Requesting"). The rationale for this mixture of categories is simple. I believe a student of Japanese must possess a combination of at least these two related but different types of knowledge in order to become proficient. I have made an effort in this book to make connections between grammatical structures and communication strategies, both of which are necessary to realize various communicative functions.

When launching a project as serious as learning a foreign language so totally different from one's native language, one must know the concrete goal of such a project. In the Sample Texts section three language samples representing different genres and styles of modern Japanese are given. These are taken from real-life situations, from video recordings of casual conversations collected in Japan, and from publications written for mass consumption in Japan today. In writing this book, I have presented Japanese grammar and sociocultural strategies so that the reader, after studying the book carefully, will be able to understand how these sample texts mean what they mean. This, I hope, decreases the level of frustration among students concerning the gap between classroom Japanese and the authentic Japanese which students will encounter once they step out of the classroom.

Ultimately, as a student of Japanese, you must be able not only to comprehend Japanese but also to express your thoughts in Japanese. Language learning is not imitation, but creation. We should not end up simply memorizing a few "conversational expressions" without understanding how those expressions mean what they mean. We should also remind ourselves that just being able to order a cup of coffee in Japanese is not enough to thrive in today's complex world. To communicate in Japanese in a meaningful way, study of the basic grammar is indispensable, particularly for adult non-native speakers. Knowing the grammar will help you acquire Japanese since it makes comprehension easier and provides a basis on which you can judge the appropriateness of your own speech. But you need more than grammatical correctness to participate in real conversations. Understanding communication strategies introduced in this book will assist you in participating in crosscultural communication successfully.

Still, understanding grammar and knowing "about" the language is not enough to be proficient in a foreign language. Far from it. A variety of experiences, which ideally includes living in Japan and using the language in context, is necessary to become totally competent in Japanese. Participating in structured instruction is extremely important. This will offer the opportunity to learn the basics of the Japanese language as well as many opportunities to interact in Japanese. For language learning it is essential to actually use the language. Language cannot be mastered simply by reading about it. Beyond participating in structured instruction, since language is a part of the society and culture in which it is spoken, one must always remain curious and sensitive to the community as a whole. Knowing about various aspects of Japan is an important part of language education which should be incorporated into one's learning experience.

A book such as this one cannot possibly explain everything about Japanese. But this book can assist students of Japanese in learning many important grammatical structures and useful communication strategies in modern Japanese. Learning Japanese involves a variety of activities; learning through this book is only one part of a large project. But after having studied 130 entries discussed in this book, you will have taken an important step toward achieving your goal.

1.2. Sound System

Although it is best to actually hear the sound of spoken Japanese first-hand, the following information may be useful before reading the Romanized Japanese in this book. The following chart provides the single vowel, consonant-plus-vowel cluster, consonant-plus-semivowel [y]-plus-vowel cluster, and single consonant which form Japanese sounds. Each sound receives one beat (or mora) when pronouncing Japanese.

Note that a long vowel is considered a combination of single vowels and is spelled out *aa* or *oo* and so forth throughout this book. These vowels receive as many beats as represented by the number of single vowels. Consonants [k], [s], [p] and [t] receive one beat in a double consonant environment; the consonant [n], if it appears by itself, also receives a single beat. For example, *okaasan* is a five-mora word (*o-ka-a-sa-n*) and *hakkiri* is a four-mora word (*ha-k-ki-ri*). It should be pointed out that the consonant [g] is optionally nasalized in all environments except at the word-initial position.

The Sounds of Japanese

1	2	3	4	5	6	7	8	9	10	11	12	13	14	15
a	ka	ga	sa	za	ta	da	na	ha	ba	pa	ma	ya	ra	wa
i	ki	gi	shi	ji	chi	—	ni	hi	bi	pi	mi	—	ri	—
u	ku	gu	su	zu	tsu	—	nu	hu	bu	pu	mu	yu	ru	—
e	ke	ge	se	ze	te	de	ne	he	be	pe	me	—	re	—
o	ko	go	so	zo	to	do	no	ho	bo	po	mo	yo	ro	—
	kya	gya	sha	ja	cha	—	nya	hya	bya	pya	mya	—	rya	—
	kyu	gyu	shu	ju	chu	—	nyu	hyu	byu	pyu	myu	—	ryu	—
	kyo	gyo	sho	jo	cho	—	nyo	hyo	byo	pyo	myo	—	ryo	—

Consonants: *k, s, t, p,* and *n* (These sounds by themselves do not appear word-initially.)

Additionally, in transcribing foreign sounds not available in the Japanese sound system, other sound combinations are used. Some examples include: [fo] (as in *fo*rk,) [fi] (as in *Phi*ladel*phi*a), [ti] (as in par*ty*), [wo] (as in *vo*dka), [je] (as in *ja*ne) and [di] (as in *di*esel).

1.3. Writing System and Romanization

Japanese employs a combination of three different types of writing systems: *hiragana, katakana* and *kanji. Hiragana* is used for Japanese words for which *kanji* cannot be easily provided. Conjugating endings of verbs and adjectives, grammatical particles and auxiliary verbs are written in *hiragana. Katakana* is used similarly for transcribing foreign loan words (other than Chinese) and some onomatopoeic words. *Katakana* is also used for stylistic reasons; for example, to attract special attention from the reader. This book contains only the most frequently used kanji selected from *Jooyoo Kanji* characters. Depending on the textbook you use or the program you enroll in, you will learn these writing symbols at different stages and at different speeds. In this book, Japanese examples are accompanied with Japanese writing commonly used today, that is, a combination of all three systems.

The Romanization used in this textbook is of a modified Hepburn style. Long vowels are spelled out (for example as *aa, ii,* etc.) rather than marking them with a lengthening diacritical mark. The syllabic *n* is spelled as *n'* when followed by a vowel or a semivowel, *y.*

Although the Japanese writing system does not separate each word, in the Romanization presentation in this book, words are separated for convenience. Some hyphens are used to mark separation of morphological units (smallest meaningful units that form an individual word). Proper nouns are spelled with capital letters and interrogative sentences are punctuated with a question mark when the quotation marker *ka* is absent.

1.4. Characteristics of the Japanese Language

Japanese is spoken by more than 120 million people, most of whom live on the four main islands of Japan. Japanese is suggested to be distantly related to Korean, and therefore to the Altaic languages (among them, Mongolian and Turkish). Japanese is a topic-comment prominent language with a basic word order of the verb being placed at the final position, in contrast with English, a subject-predicate prominent language with a basic word order of subject-verb-object. Japanese has particles or postpositions that express not only grammatical relationship but also interpersonal feelings. Non-specification of topics, subjects, objects, and particles is common. It has a rich system of respectful and humble forms as well as a variety of polite expressions.

In what follows I list the ten most basic structural characteristics of modern Japanese. We will refer to them whenever these and other related characteristics become relevant throughout the book.

1. *Verb-final*
    The basic Japanese word order is verb-final.

2. *The I-type Adjective*
    The *i*-type adjective behaves like a verb in that it can constitute a predicate by itself.

3. *Topic-comment Prominence*
    The notion of topic plays a vital part in organizing information to form an utterance or a sentence. Topic is marked by the topic-marking particle *wa* (and *mo*).

4. *Not Saying the Obvious*
    Not specifying the elements which are obvious to the communication participants is frequent. As long as the information is recoverable, there is no need to specify. Little structural constraint blocks such deletion.

5. *Speech Style—formal/informal and honorifics*
    Japanese uses different devices to mark formal or informal styles. Additionally, a speaker shows reverence to those of higher social status

by using respectful and humble forms of the honorific system.

6. *Modifier Precedes the Modified*
   Beyond being verb-final, the basic word order in Japanese is that a modifier (such as adjectives and clausal modifiers) precedes the modified.

7. *Postpositional Particles*
   Two types of particles, grammatical and interactional, are used to show grammatical and interpersonal relations respectively. Particles are postposed to the element whose relation is defined.

8. *Verb/Adjective Conjugation*
   Verbs and adjectives change forms based on tense and on how the speaker views the event and the state.

9. *Numbers and Counters*
   Japanese does not make the distinction between grammatical singular and plural. When specifying quantity, Japanese employs a set of counters.

10. *Non-agent Orientation*
    Japanese tends to view and describe the world as a natural state or a change brought about by some force. Specification of subject or agent is not as prominent a concern as observed in English.

1.5. Simple and Complex Sentences

Each utterance or sentence may contain single or multiple propositional content. By simple sentences we mean sentences with a single predicate—regardless of whether or not it appears on the surface—and by complex sentences we mean the ones that contain more than one predicate.

All Japanese simple sentences end with one of the following structures: (1) Verb (including existential verbs), (2) Adj-*i*, (3) [Adj-*na* + *da*], and (4) [N + *da*], all optionally followed by auxiliary verbs and auxiliary adjectives.

When more than one predicate is incorporated into a sentence, the following methods are possible. I am not providing Japanese examples at this point. The following information is provided for general background knowledge only.

1. Continue by using the stem of the verb and the verb gerundive form.
2. Add another clause and connect it with a conjunction.
3. Add clausal modification or clausal explanation to modify the

noun—together they function as a noun.

4. Use a nominalizer *koto* or *no*; grammatical clauses become noun phrases.
5. What is quoted may consist of simple or complex sentences within a quoted sentence.

The relationship between two clauses is either "coordinate" or "subordinate." In a coordinate connection, two clauses are connected without subordinating one to the other. In a subordinate connection, a clause is incorporated within another (main) clause. Coordinate relationships are expressed by the "and" and "but" connection. In a subordinate relationship, there are three types. The first shows, among other things, relationships such as cause-effect, condition-result, duration or sequencing of time, and quotation. Second is noun modification, including both clausal modification and clausal explanation. Third is nominalization using the nominalizers *koto* and *no*.

Most of the complex sentence structures will be introduced in the second half of the book. In the beginning, attention should be paid to the structure of the simple sentence only.

1.6. Arrangement of Each Entry

Each entry is arranged to consist of some of the following: Items 1, 2, and 3 are arranged in that order. Items 4, 5, and 6 are ordered as they need to appear in the most appropriate order, not necessarily in the order presented here.

1. **Target Expression(s)**
   Target expressions are the main focus. We concentrate on these expressions and learn how they are structured and what they mean when used in communication. Some target expressions are formulaic, and are to be memorized as they are. Some target expressions are structural representations of grammatical patterns. For these entries it is important to understand the grammatical process explained.

2. **Grammatical** or **Strategic Explanation**
   Depending on the kind of entry, either a structural or strategic explanation is given. For the structural explanation, it is particularly important to understand how bits and pieces construct the whole of the expression learned. In the strategic explanation, how the target expression should or should not be used in an actual social setting is discussed. Cultural background information and relevant social knowledge

are also given here to substantiate the strategies chosen by Japanese speakers.

3. **Examples**

Expressions similar to the target expression(s) are given as examples. These additional expressions should help the student further understand the structure and the strategy of the target expression.

4. **Practice**

Upon familiarization with the Japanese expressions, the student is asked to perform several types of practice. This will help reinforce your understanding of each entry. This section may be skipped if it becomes too demanding or uncomfortable. You can always study the book a second time and try the practice section then. Only the type of practice that can be performed by oneself and can be corrected easily is selected.

5. **Additional Information**

No reader is required to learn everything in one reading. Information provided here is not necessarily crucial at each level. Therefore, the student may ignore this section first and then come back to it later.

6. **Warning**

In some entries, some warnings especially useful for beginning and intermediate students of Japanese are given. These warnings often originate from frequent errors made by students.

Additionally, in a few cases, a brief excerpt or a sample is taken from Japanese writings. These samples show how each expression being learned in an entry is used by Japanese novelists. There is no need to practice these examples: they are presented simply for your information. These examples are given, in part, to prepare the reader for the sample texts given toward the end of the book.

Whenever possible, items are listed alphabetically or in the *a-i-u-e-o* order depending on whether English or Japanese entries appear first. The *a-i-u-e-o* order is based on the list of Japanese sounds given in Section 1.2. Vowels starting from the top to bottom, i.e., *a, i, u, e, o* are first, followed by *ka, ki, ku, ke, ko* and so forth. For lines 3, 5, 7 and 10, voiced sounds follow voiceless counterparts: *ga* after *ka, gi* after *ki*, and so on. Sounds in line 11 follow voiced counterparts; i.e., *pa* follows *ba* and *bi* follows *pi* and so forth. *N* is the last mora in the *a-i-u-e-o* order.

In each entry, new vocabulary items are listed. Words which appear in earlier entries excluding those items in the Additional Information segment are not listed. Each new vocabulary item is listed in the order in which it appears in each section, not in alphabetical order. The word list containing all vocabulary items arranged in alphabetical order is provided in the Appendix. When necessary, example sentences are accompanied by glossing—a word-by-word translation—given immediately below the Japanese.

1.7. Abbreviations

The following list provides abbreviations in alphabetical order:

Adj basic	basic form of the adjective
Adj-*i*	*i*-type adjective
Adj-*na*	*na*-type adjective
Adj stem	stem of the adjective
Adj *te*	gerundive *te*-form of the adjective
Adv	adverb
AuxAdj	auxiliary adjective
AuxV	auxiliary verb
Conj	conjunction
Dem	demonstrative
F	feminine speech style
Int	interjection
IO	indirect object
IP	interactional particle
L	linker
lit.	literal translation
M	masculine speech style
N	noun (including noun phrases)
O	direct object
PN	proper noun
Q	question marker
QT	quotation marker
S	subject marker
T	topic marker
V	verb (including existential verbs and the be-verb)
Vbasic	basic form of the verb
Vformal	formal style of the verb

Vinformal	informal style of the verb
Vnon-past	non-past form of the verb
Vpast	past form of the verb
Vstem	stem of the verb
V*te*	gerundive *te*-form of the verb
☺	casual speech style
◆	written style
[ ]	grammatical pattern
*	non-existent, ungrammatical and unacceptable form
' '	English translation
/	alternative expression (Japanese language items that may be alternated are underlined.)
( )	optional or additional

See Appendix 1 for the definition of some grammatical terms listed above.

Part Two:

Entries

1. Greetings—1. Common Greetings

(1-3-97)

> *Good morning.*
>
> **Ohayoo gozaimasu.**
> おはようございます。
> **Ohayoo.** ☺
> おはよう。

Strategic Explanation

Typical Japanese greetings consist of a set of formulaic expressions. The following expressions are used when you see a person for the first time in a day, depending on the time of your encounter.

    a.   **Ohayoo (gozaimasu).** おはよう（ございます）。   'Good morning.'
       Gozaimasu makes the greeting formal and polite; when greeting your social superior, *gozaimasu* should be added. Among close colleagues and friends, *ohayoo* in a positive tone of voice suffices.

    b.   **Konnichiwa.** こんにちは。 'Good afternoon.'
       Remember that *n* is syllabic in Japanese. This word contains five syllables, pronounced as *ko-n-ni-chi-wa*. Be careful not to pronounce it as *ko-ni-chi-wa*.

    c.   **Konbanwa.** こんばんは。 (pronounced as *ko-n-ba-n-wa*)
       'Good evening.'

As in English, when greeted with these expressions, answering by identical greetings will suffice. If you bow—even slightly—as you say these greetings, you are adding a greater degree of politeness. If you can witness actual native speakers' behavior or watch it on videotape, observe how the Japanese move their heads and upper torsos when greeting each other.

Among complete strangers, greetings as introduced here are not customarily exchanged, unless you greet a person so that you can start a business interaction, or unless the environment defines some social relationship between you and the addressee. Although at least in some parts of the United States it is common to greet complete strangers in an elevator, such greeting exchanges are not customary in Japan. It is also considered impolite to offer these greetings when you are not facing your addressee, unless of course you are doing so over the phone. Especially when you greet someone as you approach the person on the street or in the hallway, do not use these greetings after you pass by your addressee. The greeting exchange should be completed before you pass each other. It is thought inconsiderate to continue the greeting once you have passed the addressee. Compare this with the sometimes-occurring American situations where by the time the greeting ritual—"Hi, how are you?" "Fine, and you?" "OK."—is completed, the two speakers may have passed each other.

Warning

Konnichiwa and *konbanwa* are not used among family members. Likewise, among familiar company employees, when meeting each other at the company, instead of *konnichiwa*, other brief greetings such as *aa doomo* or nodding are used to acknowledge each other.

Many Americans greet each other by saying "How are you?" Although it is possible to literally translate this phrase into Japanese *ikaga desu ka?* 'how are you?,' this expression is not normally used, unless you are specifically concerned about the physical condition of the other—asking a person how he or she feels after being sick, for example. Another possible translation of 'how are you?' is *(o)genki desu ka?* which is also rarely used by Japanese. *(O)genki desu ka?* is used when you meet your friend after a while and you are concerned about how he or she has been; this expression is similar to the English 'how have you been?' Instead of *how are you* the Japanese strategy of greeting requires, first, the appropriate greeting formula introduced here, and second, innocuous comments on the weather. Talking about the weather, or, really, any noncontroversial or universal topic is a widely exercised strategy (also in many parts of the world) to express the speaker's interest in the person addressed; such expressions show a friendly attitude.

Practice

What do you say in Japanese when:

1. you meet your friend in the morning;
2. you meet your superior in the morning;
3. you greet an acquaintance you run into at the store during the day;
4. you meet a member of your social club at an evening membership meeting;

——————— Answers ———————

1. *Ohayoo.* ☺ 　　おはよう。
2. *Ohayoo gozaimasu.*　おはようございます。
3. *Konnichiwa.*　　こんにちは。
4. *Konbanwa.*　　こんばんは。

2. Describing State—1. Adjectival Predicate

> *(It's) hot, isn't it?*
>
> **Atsui-desu ne.**
> あついですね。
>
> [Adj-*i*]

Grammatical Explanation

There are five ways of modifying nouns in Japanese: (1) the use of what is called *i*-type adjectives, [Adj-*i*], (2) using demonstratives, (3) modifying another noun connected with the particle *no*, [N + *no*], (4) using nominal adjectives, and (5) through clausal modifiers. Here we focus on the first type.

The *i*-type adjectives all end with -*i*. (Not all words ending with -*i* are adjectives, however.) They precede the nouns they modify (refer to characteristic 6). Thus, 'hot day' in Japanese is *atsui hi, atsui* 'hot' preceding *hi* 'day.'

Japanese adjectives differ from English adjectives in this respect: [Adj-*i*] may also be used as a predicate (refer to characteristic 2). That is to say, *atsui* is a predicate meaning '(it) is hot' and is used independently in casual or informal situations. [Adj-*i*], when used as a predicate, may be followed by -*desu*, a suffix to indicate a formal style. Thus, *atsui-desu* also means '(it) is hot' but it is a more formal expression of *atsui*. This is the safest style for beginning language learners since it is applicable to many social situations. It is better to be a little more formal than less formal—particularly when you are learning to speak Japanese.

Japanese has a rich system of particles—functional words normally consisting of only a few syllables—which function grammatically and interactionally. Japanese particles are "postpositional" (placed immediately after) to the element whose relation to other elements is being defined (refer to characteristic 7). Among interactional particles, *ne* and its lengthened version *nee* are most frequently used. *Ne* and *nee* roughly function, as English tag-questions (such as *don't you* in *you like to read, don't you?*) used when soliciting assurance and/or agreement from the listener. *Ne* and *nee* are attached to declarative sentences, both affirmative and negative. In general, interactional particles are used in spoken Japanese. When used in written discourse, it gives a flavor of being in a speaking-directly-to-the-reader style, as one finds in personal letters.

You may be wondering what happened to *it* in the English target expression, *(It's) hot, isn't it?* As will be explained later, pronouns are frequently not mentioned in Japanese, and therefore, there is no need to match each English word with its Japanese equivalent (refer to characteristic 4). Unlike English, the grammatical subject does not require overt expression in a Japanese sentence. A word-by-word translation is hardly a recommended strategy for learning Japanese. Note that the *it* in the target structure does not refer to something identified earlier—the "anaphoric" function of pronouns. The *it* is placed in English only because it is grammatically required.

Commentary on the weather is frequently used as a greeting. It is a safe subject to bring up to show that you are not a threat to the other person and to express your intention to maintain a friendly attitude. The best response to a comment like *atsui-desu nee*, is *soo desu nee* '(lit. that is so) yes, indeed'—regardless of whether you truly think so or not.

List of Commonly Used *I*-Type Adjectives

atarashii	新しい	new
atatakai	暖かい	(pleasantly) warm
atsui[*1]	暑い，熱い	hot
atsui[*1]	厚い	thick, heavy
isogashii	忙しい	busy
utsukushii	美しい	beautiful
oishii	おいしい	delicious
ooi[*2]	多い	many, much
ookii	大きい	large
osoi	遅い	late, slow
omoshiroi	おもしろい	interesting, funny
kibishii	きびしい	strict, demanding
kurai	暗い	dark
sabishii	寂しい	lonely
samui	寒い	cold (in reference to the atmosphere)
subarashii	すばらしい	splendid
sukunai[*2]	少ない	a few, little
semai	せまい	narrow
suzushii	涼しい	cool
takai[*3]	高い	tall
takai[*3]	高い	expensive
chiisai	小さい	small
chikai	近い	near
tsumetai	冷たい	cold (to touch)
tooi	遠い	distant

nagai	長い	long
hayai	早い, 速い	early, quick
hikui	低い	low
hiroi	広い	wide, spacious
hurui*4	古い	old
mazui	まずい	with bad taste
mijikai	短い	short
muzukashii	むずかしい	difficult
yasashii	やさしい	kind, easy
yasui	安い	inexpensive
yoi/ii	良い	good
wakai*5	若い	young
warui	悪い	bad

*1. The word *atsui* represents two separate adjectives. When the three morae *a-tsu-i* are pronounced with low/high/low pitch, *atsui* means 'hot'; when pronounced with low/high/high pitch it means 'thick, heavy.'

*2. *Ooi* and *sukunai* must not be used as direct modifiers of nouns. They are used as predicates only. [*Ooku no* + N] and [*sukoshi no* + N] are used for noun modification. It is possible to use *ooi* and *sukunai* as clause modifiers when *ooi* and *sukunai* are used as predicates, as in *chokin no sukunai hito* 'a person with little savings.' For the adjectives *chikai* and *tooi*, both forms (*chikai* and *chikaku no*, *tooi* and *tooku no*) are possible when used for noun modification.

*3. The adjective *takai* has two separate meanings, one meaning 'tall' as in tall person and tall building, the other meaning 'expensive.'

*4. The adjective *hurui* is not used to express a person's old age. 'Old (in age)' is expressed by an expression *toshi o totta* 'lit. gained age,' a clausal modifier preceding the noun.

*5. Adjective *wakai* normally refers to a young adult; *wakai hito*, for example, means a young or younger adult. *Wakai*, however, is never used with *kodomo* 'child.' Instead, *osanai* is used to refer to an infant.

Practice

Comment on the following items as shown in the example. For vocabulary, refer to the list of [Adj-*i*] provided earlier.

(Example: time: late → *Osoi-desu nee.*)

1. time: early
2. exam: easy, difficult, long, short
3. cake: delicious, expensive, inexpensive, small, large

——— Some sample answers ———
1. *Hayai-desu.* 　　早いです。
2. *Muzukashii-desu ne.* むずかしいですね。
3. *Oishii-desu ne.* 　おいしいですね。

3. Speech Style—1. Spoken, Written, Formal and Informal Styles

Target Expressions

> *(It's) early, isn't it?*
>
> **Hayai-desu ne.**
> 早いですね。
> **Hayai nee.** ☺
> 早いねえ。
>
> [Adj-*i* + -*desu*]

Strategic Explanation

Just as in English, Japanese has different language styles depending on the genre and the situational context in which the language is used. We concentrate on two fundamental feature differences here: written and spoken language on one hand and the formal and informal (casual) style on the other.

Written and Spoken Styles

The basic difference between the prototypical written and spoken style lies in the fact that in writing, we create a planned discourse addressed to a non-specific audience, while in spontaneous speaking we create unplanned discourse addressed directly to the interaction partner. This means that speech is featured by increased level of fragmentation with devices emotionally appealing to the listener. It encourages what Tannen (1984) calls personal and emotional "involvement." On the other hand, in written language you are more likely to see complex sentence structures into which information is richly packed—a process called "integration."

More specifically, we can note the following features of spoken Japanese.

In spoken Japanese:
1. Language is much more fragmented with shorter utterances and phrases.
2. Interactional particles are frequently used at the end of phrases and utterances.
3. Fillers and hesitation noises (*uh-huh, um. . .*), and interactional conjunctions occur frequently.
4. What is understood and obvious is not expressed to the extent it is expressed in written discourse.

5. Postposing fragments after the final verb is more frequently observed.
6. Verbs end with gerundive and other continuing forms at the end of utterances.
7. Remarks on communication itself (metacommunication) are made.
8. Utterances may be co-created by both speakers.

Formal and Informal Styles

Differences between formal and informal styles are important in Japanese. Just as it is the case in English, but more distinctly in Japanese, we find different speech styles depending on the social situation and the social status of the participants. Formal social situations such as school, business ceremonies or other public gatherings require formal and careful style. Formal style is also recommended toward social superiors even in less formal situations. Normally a higher social status is attributed to speakers who are older, or male, or higher in rank in the workplace, or who are considered in general to hold a higher social status—a holder of a more prestigious occupation, for example. The speech style chosen by a speaker who represents a different social level is not reciprocal. Friendly informal speech from a social superior does not mean that one should respond in the same style.

An informal, casual style is used among social equals; an extremely casual style is reserved for close friends. Even among speakers representing a socially different status, if the situation of speech is personal and informal, as during casual chatting while drinking *sake*, the style chosen is likely to be informal. Choosing the appropriate style in different social encounters, however, requires social sensitivity and experience. It is best to play it safe by using the formal style until you know when you are expected to use an informal speech style.

Closely related to the choice of speech style is the well-discussed tendency of a Japanese to identify himself or herself as a member of a group. An individual is simultaneously a member of various social groups—family, university from which one has graduated, or the company where one is employed. Depending on the situational context, one of these and other groups (or what Nakane [1970] calls "frames") is emphasized. Inside the group is called *uchi* 'inside,' whereas outside the group is referred to as *soto* 'outside,' and a different social orientation and behavior is observed in these two contrasting social territories. Within *uchi* a feeling of what Doi (1973) calls *amae* 'dependence' prevails. When the *amae* relationship is mutually recognized, the speech style becomes informal and casual. In fact, contrary to the common belief that Japanese are inherently formal and polite, Japanese enjoy casual and familiar relationships, and often expose an emotional vulnerability among *uchi* group members.

As a foreigner learning Japanese, an overly casual style is not recommended until a strong *amae* relationship is established. Foreign nationals are categorically excluded from membership in the most basic group recognized in Japan, that is, being Japanese. The style chosen by Japanese toward a foreigner, a person who belongs to *soto*, at least during initial encounters, is most likely to be formal. Viewed from the outside, this gives the impression that Japanese are always formal and polite—an image widely held outside Japan.

Choosing appropriate speech style is an important aspect of communication in any society. In Japanese, the distinction between these styles is somewhat clearer than it is in English, and Japanese society tends to penalize inappropriate speech style more severely than other societies do. Naturally speech styles vary in gradations. Some spoken styles are more careful and softer than others while other styles may be more or less blunt and straightforward. We all acquire a sensitivity to speech styles in our own culture. The key is to learn the meaning of different styles in a foreign language and to cultivate a sensitivity in accordance with the norms of that society.

At this point we should be aware of two styles, one formal and the other informal (or plain or casual). In using [Adj-*i*], when the *-desu* ending is added, it is formal, while the form without *-desu* is considered informal, plain, and casual. The plain, casual style will be marked by the symbol ☺ throughout the book.

Additional Information

Informal style is used in written Japanese in fiction, non-fiction, prose and modern poetry. In writing letters, however, formal style is used if the relationship and the situation call for it. Business letters are always written in a formal style. Personal letters exchanged between social intimates may be in formal or informal style reflecting the particular relationships between the parties.

Throughout this book we identify different styles by using the symbol ☺ for very casual speech and ♦ for sentences created specifically for written discourse and for what would be considered awkward in spoken style. Unmarked examples are neutral or formal and this is the basic style we will learn in this book.

4. Describing State—2. Adjectival Predicate with Topic

> *It's warm today, isn't it?*
> ***Kyoo wa atatakai-desu nee.***
> 今日は暖かいですねえ。
>
> [N + *wa*]

Grammatical Explanation

The target expression above contains a formal style of [Adj-*i*]; that is, *atatakai-desu* preceded by a noun *kyoo* 'today' and *wa*, a topic marker. *Wa* is a particle which marks the "topic" of an utterance/a sentence or a topic activated across several utterances/sentences (refer to characteristic 3). Topic is defined simply as "something that is being talked about." In the sentence *kyoo wa atatakai-desu nee*, *kyoo* is marked as a topic; the statement is about the topic; *kyoo* 'today' is something that is talked about. The remaining portion of the utterance, that is, *atatakai-desu nee* is called "comment" and provides information pertinent to the topic. The concepts of topic and comment are extremely important for understanding how Japanese organize sentences; we will return to this issue later.

On Japanese Nouns

Since this entry marks the first appearance of Japanese nouns, we must note one grammatical characteristic of Japanese nouns that is very different from English.

There is no grammatical distinction between singular and plural nouns in Japanese (refer to characteristic 9). Thus for both one apple and two apples, *ringo* suffices. Whether *ringo* is singular or plural depends on the context and is not marked in the noun form. Since a grammatical singular and plural distinction is not required in Japanese, learning whether or not an English noun is countable, that is, whether or not the plural -*s* should be attached, is difficult for Japanese students learning English. It is sometimes difficult to remember that the English noun *chalk* is uncountable (*two *chalks* is not acceptable in English when counting two pieces of chalk) while the noun *pencil* is (one must say two *pencils*).

Examples

---

eigo	英語	N	English
shigoto	仕事	N	work, job
ee	ええ	Int	yes
hontooni	本当に	Adv	really, indeed
ringo	りんご	N	apple

---

(1) *Eigo wa muzukashii-desu.*
英語はむずかしいです。
(English is difficult.)

(2) *Shigoto wa kibishii.* ☺
仕事はきびしい。
(The job is demanding.)

(3) A: *Kyoo wa samui-desu ne.*
今日は寒いですね。
(It's cold today, isn't it?)
B: *Ee, hontooni.*
ええ，本当に。
(Yes, indeed.)

(4) *Ringo wa oishii-desu.*
りんごはおいしいです。
(Apples are delicious.)

Practice

---

tempura	N	*tenpura* 天ぷら
		(fried vegetables and fish)
Tokyo	PN	*Tookyoo* 東京

Comment in Japanese about the following:

1. today: hot weather
2. tempura: delicious
3. Tokyo: far away
4. today: warm, cold ☺

—— Some Sample Answers ——
1. *Kyoo wa atsui-desu nee.*　今日は暑いですねえ。
2. *Tenpura wa oishii-desu.*　天ぷらはおいしいです。
3. *Tookyoo wa tooi-desu ne.*　東京は遠いですね。
4. *Kyoo wa atatakai ne.* ☺　今日は暖かいね。

Additional Information

Some Japanese proper nouns written in the conventional alphabet in Western literature are misrepresentations of original Japanese words. For example, Tokyo, so spelled in English literature worldwide, is pronounced with four beats or morae *To-o-kyo-o* in Japanese. In this book when Japanese transliteration is given, it is given in such a manner as to reflect the actual mora structure and the pronunciation of each word.

5. Loan Words

> *coffee, hamburgers, personal computers*
> **koohii, hanbaagaa, pasokon**
> コーヒー, ハンバーガー, パソコン

Grammatical Explanation

Throughout history the Japanese language has borrowed many words from foreign countries, first, from China as early as the Nara period (710-794 A.D.). During the Heian and the Edo periods (8th through 19th century) Chinese words continued to enter into the Japanese language, and many were integrated into Japanese to the extent that they are no longer considered foreign "loan" words. Today, most Chinese words are written in *kanji* compounds and carry the Chinese reading (*on*-reading).

Around 1600 A.D., the Japanese language began to borrow many Western words particularly from Portuguese and Dutch (during the Edo period). Additionally, German, French, and most of all, English loan words have been introduced since the beginning of the Meiji era (1868 A.D.). Western loan words are written in *katakana* and are pronounced according to the Japanese phonological rules, mostly in the form of available Japanese morae. Therefore, the sounds you hear for English words in Japanese may be very different from the original English, and may in fact be incomprehensible.

Sometimes a homonym in English may be introduced in Japanese as words with two distinct pronunciations. For instance, the word "strike" has been borrowed in two distinct ways: *sutoraiku* to mean 'strike' as in baseball, and *sutoraiki* to mean 'strike' as in the labor movement. A loan word may be specialized in meaning in such a way as to share the same semantic field with a related Japanese word. For example, the word *biru*, a shortened version of the English word 'building' normally refers to Western style tall buildings only, while the Japanese word *tatemono* 'building' refers to other types of buildings. As shown here in the case of *biru* and others (*hankachi* for handkerchief, *maiku* for microphone), long foreign words are often shortened. Multiple words may be shortened also, often into four syllable words; *pasokon* for *perso*nal *com*puter.

A loan word can be generative. It can be combined with Japanese or other foreign words to produce a compound noun. The word *pan* 'bread'—from Portuguese pão—for example, is combined with several morphemes (smallest meaningful units that constitute a word) and other words to form the following:

shokupan	食パン	loaf of bread
baagaapan	バーガーパン	hamburger buns
huransupan	フランスパン	French bread
raimugipan	ライ麦パン	rye bread
roorupan	ロールパン	rolls

Most loan words are integrated into Japanese as nouns and may make morphological changes accordingly. Drive, *doraibu* in Japanese, is combined with the verb *suru* 'do,' as in *doraibu-suru*, to mean the verb 'to drive' (as in *to drive a car*). English adjectives are normally loaned as adjectives which end with *-na*. For example, unique, *yuniiku* in Japanese, is used as *yuniikuna hito* 'a unique person' (Adjectives are discussed later).

There are also pseudo-loan words made in Japan. These are foreign words but they are created by Japanese with meanings different from the original language. For example, *naitaa* made of the English word "night" followed by a morpheme "-er" meaning baseball night games. In today's Japanese writing, Roman letters of the alphabet are also used. The nationwide Japanese railway network is called JR-*sen* (pronounced *jeiaaru-sen*), with the Roman letters as its authentic written symbols. You may also find foreign words appearing in Japanese writing with the original writing symbols. These are "foreign words" and are not considered "loan words" which constitute a part of Japanese vocabulary.

List of Common Loan Words and Foreign Proper Nouns

Country names

Amerika	アメリカ	America (United States of)
Igirisu	イギリス	England
Itaria	イタリア	Italy
Oranda	オランダ	Holland
Kanada	カナダ	Canada
Supein	スペイン	Spain
Doitsu	ドイツ	Germany
Huransu	フランス	France

City names

Sanhuranshisuko	サンフランシスコ	San Francisco
Shikago	シカゴ	Chicago
Toronto	トロント	Toronto
Nyuuyooku	ニューヨーク	New York
Honoruru	ホノルル	Honolulu
Pari	パリ	Paris
Bosuton	ボストン	Boston
Rondon	ロンドン	London
Rosanzerusu	ロサンゼルス	Los Angeles

Personal names

Sumisu	スミス	Smith
Jon	ジョン	John
Taanaa	ターナー	Turner
Nanshii	ナンシー	Nancy
Biru	ビル	Bill
Buraun	ブラウン	Brown

Drinks

uisukii	ウイスキー	whiskey
koohii	コーヒー	coffee
koora	コーラ	coke
juusu	ジュース	juice, fruit drinks
biiru	ビール	beer
miruku	ミルク	milk
wain	ワイン	wine

Food

aisukuriimu	アイスクリーム	ice cream
kasutera	カステラ	sponge cake [from *pão de Castella*]
keeki	ケーキ	cake

sandoitchi	サンドイッチ	sandwich
suteeki	ステーキ	steak
hanbaagaa	ハンバーガー	hamburger [served with hamburger buns]
hanbaagu	ハンバーグ	hamburger [served with food items other than hamburger buns, like Salisbury steak]
pan	パン	bread [from Portuguese *pāo*]

Sports

goruhu	ゴルフ	golf
sukeeto	スケート	skate
sukii	スキー	ski
jogingu	ジョギング	jogging
dansu	ダンス	dance
tenisu	テニス	tennis
basukettobooru	バスケットボール	basketball
booringu	ボウリング	bowling

Transportation

takushii	タクシー	taxi
basu	バス	bus
monoreeru	モノレール	monorail
rimujin	リムジン	limousine

Others

arubaito	アルバイト	part-time job [from German *Arbeit*]
kamera	カメラ	camera
suupaa	スーパー	supermarket
depaato	デパート	department store
terebi	テレビ	television
baa	バー	bar
pasokon	パソコン	personal computer
hoteru	ホテル	hotel
manshon	マンション	upscale apartment or condominium [from English word *mansion*]
rajikase	ラジカセ	radio-cassette player
rajio	ラジオ	radio
resutoran	レストラン	restaurant
waapuro	ワープロ	word-processor
waishatsu	ワイシャツ	solid colored dress shirt [from *white shirt*]

Additional Information

The nationality of a person is expressed by adding *-jin* 'lit. person' after the country name. *Amerika-jin* 'American,' *Igirisu-jin* 'English person,' *nihon-jin* 'Japanese,' and so forth.

More recently, in mass communication, especially in advertising, English words (or, only their pronunciation or meaning) and Japanese words are combined in order to create new words, sometimes with an intended pun. For example, in an advertisement for a resort called Izu, a headline goes "This Izu." The intended pun is that "This Izu" sounds like English "this is," and it emphasizes the meaning of "this is it!" (the ultimate resort). Another example is a word *okushon* made from Japanese *oku* 'one hundred million' and the second syllable of the English word "mansion." The English loan word *manshon* means an upscale apartment or condominium in Japanese. It just happens that the first syllable *man* means ten thousand in Japanese; in order to express the outrageous price of residential units in Japan, instead of being priced in *man* 'ten thousands of yen,' they are priced in *oku* 'one hundred millions of yen.' For this reason, the new word *okushon* was coined to mean an outrageously expensive residential unit.

With today's marketing, many American brand names have joined Japanese proper nouns. You may have your coffee and doughnut at *Misutaa-doonatsu* and eat lunch at *Makudonarudo*, or *Kentakkii-huraido-chikin*. You may fly to Japan by *Yunaiteddo-kookuu* (United Airlines) or *Noosu-Uesuto-kookuu* (Northwest Airlines).

For those who are interested in learning loan word in Japanese, there are loan word dictionaries. See for example, *Kadokawa Gairaigo Jiten* published by Kadokawa Shoten in Tokyo.

6. Personal Names and Occupations

Target Expressions

> *Ms. Yamada, Mr. Jones*
> **Yamada-san, Joonzu-san**
> 山田さん, ジョーンズさん
>
> [-san]

Strategic Explanation

In most cases Japanese prefer to address a person by his or her last name plus *-san*. *-San* applies to both genders and all marital statuses. There is no distinction between Miss, Mrs., Ms., and Mr. (In the English translation appearing in this book, one of these titles is chosen for convenience.) In Japanese, surnames appear first and the given names follow. Most Japanese do not have middle names. Thus, Taro Yamada (*Yamada Taroo* in Japanese) is most often addressed and referred to as *Yamada-san*. In reference to foreign names, there is no need to reverse the order. Bill Johnson will be *(Biru) Jonson-san*. Other similar suffixes include: *-sama* (polite and formal), *-chan* (familiar) and *-kun* (primarily used by male in reference to younger males, and used by young schoolgirls in reference to male classmates). In familiar situations first names with *-san* may be used. For example, *Taroo-san* or *Biru-san*. Although some names are nearly impossible to classify as male or female, the following tips may be helpful. Most three-syllable first names which end with *-ko* are female names. Most four-syllable names which end with *-hiko*, *-hito*, *-hiro*, and *-kazu* are male first names.

Japanese may address others by referring to the occupational title, for example, *sensei* 'teacher' as in *Tanaka-sensei* 'Professor Tanaka.' This is used both as referential and addressing terms. Some occupations may be used with *-san*, as in *moderu-san*, when referring to the occupation and when addressing a fashion model, particularly when personal names are not known. These include *kangohu-san* 'nurse,' and *untenshu-san* 'driver' or 'chauffeur.' Some occupational titles are used for self-address when communicating with social inferiors. For example, a teacher may refer to himself or herself by saying *sensei* toward students, or a female nurse referring to herself as *kangohu-san* toward a child patient. (The term for university professors *kyooju* is not used for self-addressing purposes, however.)

Warning

Do not use *-san* when referring to yourself. Although in English it is possible to say 'I'm Ms. Jones,' in Japanese *-san* should not be attached for self-referencing. This also applies to the situation when you are referring to a member of your *uchi* group toward the member of your *soto* group. This is because in-group members are considered so close to oneself that they should be treated as one treats oneself, that is, without *-san*.

List of Common Last Names

Ichikawa	市川	Takahashi	高橋
Itoo	伊藤	Tanaka	田中
Ueda	上田	Nakagawa	中川
Ogawa	小川	Hara	原
Katoo	加藤	Matsumoto	松本
Kobayashi	小林	Yamada	山田
Saitoo	斉藤	Yamanaka	山中
Satoo	佐藤	Yamashita	山下
Suzuki	鈴木	Watanabe	渡辺

List of Common Occupations

isha	医者	medical doctor
enjinia	エンジニア	engineer
(daigaku) kyooju	（大学）教授	university professor
kaishain	会社員	company employee
kangohu	看護婦	female nurse
kashu	歌手	singer
gakusei	学生	student
gakusha	学者	scholar
ginkooin	銀行員	banker, bank employee
kenchikuka	建築家	architect
koomuin	公務員	public servant, government employee
sakanaya	魚屋	fish store owner/worker
sarariiman	サラリーマン	salaried employee
seijika	政治家	politician
sensei	先生	teacher, professor
shuhu	主婦	housewife
ten'in	店員	store attendant
hisho	秘書	secretary
pianisuto	ピアニスト	pianist
moderu	モデル	(fashion) model
yaoya	八百屋	greengrocer

7. Self-identification by *Da*

Target Expression

I'm Anderson.

Andaason desu.
アンダーソンです。

[*da*]

Grammatical Explanation

The verb *be* in Japanese is *da* (its formal counterpart is *desu*). There is no grammatical subject-verb agreement in Japanese. *Da* is used for the present tense of the be-verb regardless of the person and number of the subject, i.e., in place of English *am*, *is*, as well as *are*.

In expressing 'I'm Brown' in Japanese, since whom 'I' refers to is obvious, there is no need to specify it (refer to characteristic 4). Japanese is a verb-final language, and therefore, *desu* is placed after the personal name "Anderson" (refer to characteristic 1). We construct an utterance *Andaason desu* 'I'm Anderson.'

When considering the structure of a Japanese sentence, think of it as verb-centered; the most important part of the sentence is the verbal element, and all other aspects are specified only when necessary, all added before the verbal element. Contrast this with English sentence structure in which one is required to identify the grammatical subject, verb and sometimes object.

So far, we have studied two predicate types: (1) [Adj-*i*], and (2) *da*. It is important to recognize here that the suffix *-desu* attached to [Adj-*i*] is different from the verb *da* discussed here. *-Desu* attached to [Adj-*i*] does not function as a verbal predicate 'be'; it only assigns a stylistic feature. Remember that while the verb 'be' takes either *da* or *desu*, [Adj-*i*] predicate takes only *-desu* (*takai-da). When *-desu* is used for stylistic purposes, we mark it with a hyphen to indicate that it is a suffix, rather than an independent verb.

Practice

1. Assume you are an American (medical) doctor named Miller. Describe yourself in Japanese.

2. Describe Ms. Takahashi as given below:
    her name: Sachiko Takahashi

her occupation: a public servant
her nationality: Japanese

—— Answers ——
1. *Miraa desu. Isha desu. Amerika-jin desu.*
   ミラーです。医者です。アメリカ人です。
2. *Takahashi Sachiko-san desu. (Takahashi-san wa) koomuin desu. Nihon-jin desu.*
   高橋幸子さんです。(高橋さんは)公務員です。日本人です。

Warning

The informal form *da* is often deleted completely. In spoken language, the informal form of *nihon-jin desu* 'I'm Japanese' is simply *nihon-jin.*

8. Deictic Expression—1. The *Ko-so-a-do* System

Target Expressions

> *this book, that book*
>
> **kono hon, ano hon**
> この本，あの本
>
> [*kono, sono, ano, dono*]
> [*kore, sore, are, dore*]

Grammatical Explanation

Japanese demonstratives and pronouns are marked by prefixes *ko-, so-, a-,* and *do-*. Depending on how the speaker views the referent in terms of physical or psychological distance from where the speaker is situated, references such as *this, it,* and *that* (these are called deictic expressions) are assigned. *Ko-* is assigned when referring to an item closest to the participants, especially to the one closest to the speaker. *So-* is assigned when an item is closest to the listener, while *a-* is used to identify those items that are away from both the speaker and the listener. *Do-* is used when making interrogative (question) words.

The *ko-so-a-do* system is useful in distinguishing items in a defined conceptual universe of discourse. When a new item is introduced within a frame of reference and when it is anaphorically referred to (i.e., referred back to an element identified earlier), the *so-* reference is used. On the other hand, if the referent is assumed to be known by both participants and can be recalled into the current frame of reference or discourse, the *a-* reference is used. Thus, for example, if you introduce Tracy first in conversation and then refer back to her, you would use *sono* reference as in 'There's this person called Tracy and that person (*sono hito*). . . .' If you know that the listener already knows about the person you are going to talk about, *ano* reference is used, as in 'Is that person (*ano hito*) well? You know, that person (*ano hito*) we met in Kyoto last month.' In fact, by using *a-* series, you communicate an assumed knowledge and an experience in common with your companion. This strategy may be used to create empathy based on shared information.

List of *Ko-so-a-do* Words

Demonstratives		(used as in *kono hon* 'this book')
kono	この	this (close to the speaker)
sono	その	that (close to the listener)
ano	あの	that (away from but identified by both speakers)
dono	どの	which

Pronouns		
kore	これ	this one
sore	それ	that one
are	あれ	that one over there
dore	どれ	which one

The *ko-so-a-do* system generates additional sets:

Locative nouns		
koko	ここ	this place (here)
soko	そこ	that place (there)
asoko	あそこ	that place over there (over there)
doko	どこ	which place (where)

Directional nouns		
kochira	こちら	this way
sochira	そちら	that way
achira	あちら	direction toward that way over there
dochira	どちら	which way, which one

Directional nouns are also used as polite versions of personal pronouns; *kochira* meaning 'this person,' *dochira* meaning 'which person,' etc.

Adjective

kooyuu	こういう	such as this
sooyuu	そういう	such as that
aayuu	ああいう	such as that
dooyuu	どういう	such as what, of what kind

Manner adverbs

koo	こう	this way
soo	そう	that way
aa	ああ	that way
doo	どう	what way, which way

Examples

| Asagaya 阿佐ケ谷 | PN | a place name (in Tokyo) |
| Asagaya Apaato 阿佐ケ谷アパート | PN | a name of an apartment building |

(1) *Kochira wa Yamanaka-san desu.*
こちらは山中さんです。
(This is Ms. Yamanaka.)

(2) *Kono hon wa muzukashii-desu ne.*
この本はむずかしいですね。
(This book is difficult, isn't it?)

(3) *Asagaya Apaato wa ano biru desu.*
阿佐ケ谷アパートはあのビルです。
(Asagaya Apartment is that building over there.)

Practice

newspaper	N	shinbun	新聞
house	N	uchi	家
book	N	hon	本

What would you say in Japanese when you want to describe:

1. the place you are is cool (in temperature)

2. you find a newspaper over there and want to point it out to your friend
3. you are standing next to the house and want to describe it as being new
4. you are looking at a book and want to describe it as being old

--------- Answers ---------

1. *Koko wa suzushii-desu ne.*　　ここは涼しいですね。
2. *Shinbun wa asoko desu.*　　　新聞はあそこです。
3. *Kono uchi wa atarashii-desu.*　この家は新しいです。
4. *Kore wa hurui hon desu ne.*　これは古い本ですね。
   or *Kono hon wa hurui-desu ne.*　この本は古いですね。

9. Introducing—Expressions for Social Introduction

Target Expressions

I'm Smith. How do you do?
Sumisu desu. Hajimemashite, doozo yoroshiku.
スミスです。はじめまして，どうぞよろしく。

Strategic Explanation

When introducing people at social gatherings and meetings, formulaic expressions are used. *Hajimemashite* '(lit. for the first time) how do you do,' *doozo yoroshiku* '(lit. please be favorable to me) how do you do' are prototypical examples. For formal occasions, a politer version, *doozo yoroshiku onegai-shimasu* should be used.

Study the following interaction.

Asada:　　*Aa, Sumisu-san, kochira wa Nakagawa-san desu.*
浅田：　　ああ，スミスさん，こちらは中川さんです。
　　　　　(Oh, Mr. Smith, this is Ms. Nakagawa.)

Nakagawa:　*Nakagawa desu. Hajimemashite, doozo yoroshiku.*
中川：　　中川です。はじめまして，どうぞよろしく。
　　　　　(I am Nakagawa. How do you do?)

Smith:	*Sumisu desu. Kochira koso doozo yoroshiku.*
スミス：	スミスです。こちらこそどうぞよろしく。
	(I am Smith. How do you do?)

Kochira koso (lit. this side also) is used by Smith to express the greeting from her side also; this expression is used when someone already gives the greeting and you wish to return the same, similar to the English expression 'same here,' or 'same to you.'

Utterances *hajimemashite* and *doozo yoroshiku* should be accompanied by bowing. Bowing expresses sincerity and goodwill; it is important to bow, particularly when you are introduced to a social superior. The timing to raise your head when bowing can be tricky. Theoretically a social subordinate should not raise his or her head before the superior does. Check the height of your superior's bowing before you raise your head completely. You can also perform multiple bowings if needed.

When introduced for the first time to a person at a social occasion, people engage in non-offensive small talk. A favored strategy among Japanese for "breaking the ice," is to mention common acquaintances or common backgrounds, leading to questions such as 'do you know so-and-so?' or 'have you worked with so-and-so?' 'where are you from?' and so forth.

Additional Information

With increasing encounters with Westerners, Japanese expect to shake hands when introduced. Hand-shaking is appropriate particularly when introductions are conducted in English without an interpreter. However, if you are introduced to a Japanese superior in Japanese under formal circumstances, it is best to express your respect by following the custom of the superior, and bow respectfully. If the other party offers their hand, you should, of course, shake hands. You may also notice that Japanese bow and shake hands simultaneously, a behavior perhaps peculiar to Westerners. Japanese are only trying to adopt the Western way, while expressing greetings in a Japanese style.

In business meetings, *meishi* 'business cards' are often exchanged. Hand the card to whomever you meet so that the writing faces toward him or her. As you hand your business card, bow slightly to show respect; as you receive the business card, bow slightly again to express gratitude. Silently read the title and the name carefully. This shows respect; the information you gain by reading the business card is useful for defining the person's relative social status and, therefore, for deciding on what speech style you should choose.

10. Verbal Predicate—1. Common Verbs: Non-past

> *A friend will come.*
> **Tomodachi ga kimasu.**
> 友だちが来ます。
>
> [Vnon-past]

Grammatical Explanation

We already learned the be-verb, that is, *da/desu*. All other verbs in Japanese end with the vowel *-u*. (Needless to say, not all words that end with *-u* are verbs, however.) The verbs change ending forms in Japanese according to features associated with the verb, and they take specific forms when the auxiliary verbs are attached (refer to characteristic 8). For example, verb endings are changed to indicate past tense, negation, as well as causative and passive features. Here we focus on the non-past tense, so called since it expresses English equivalents of both present and future tenses. In other words the basic purpose of non-past tense is to convey that the action or the state referred to has not yet occurred. Verb forms are considered by many students of Japanese to be a rather difficult aspect to learn. Although it requires a certain amount of memorization, the system itself is rather simple. Unlike the more complex verb conjugation of Romance and some Germanic languages, in Japanese there is no correspondence between the person (such as the first-, second-, and third-person), the number (singular and plural) and the verb form. In fact, since the changing process of verb forms differs substantially from Romance and Germanic languages, "conjugation" may be a misnomer; we use this term only for convenience sake.

Three Verb Conjugation Types

Verb conjugation follows rules specific to the types of verbs, and for that reason verbs are categorized into three types based on the endings of the "basic" ([Vbasic]) or "dictionary" form. (There are different ways to explain Japanese verbs—some categorize verbs into five groups instead—, but here we use one of the simplest.) The three groups are: *U*-verbs, *RU*-verbs and Irregular verbs. *U*-verbs include all verbs that are neither *RU*- nor Irregular verbs. *RU*-verbs end with *-iru*, and *-eru* in their basic forms. There are only two irregular verbs, the verb *suru* 'to do' and *kuru* 'to come.' There are some special honorific verbs ending with *-aru*. These are special irregular verbs and will be studied in Entry 86.

The basic form is the form listed in the dictionary, and is the informal, non-past affirmative form of the verb. For deriving the formal version from the basic form, the following rules apply.

U-verbs: Delete final *-u* and add *-imasu*.

           nomu (to drink) → *nomimasu*

RU-verbs: Delete final *-ru* and add *-masu*.

           taberu (to eat) → *tabemasu*

Irregular Verbs: **suru** (to do) → **shimasu**

                  kuru (to come) → **kimasu**

There are a few exceptions to the basic rules of verb categorization. The following verbs, although ending with *-iru* and *-eru* forms, are *U*-verbs and are conjugated likewise.

hairu (to enter)	入る	*hairimasu*
heru (to decrease)	減る	*herimasu*
iru (to need)	要る	*irimasu*
kaeru (to return)	帰る	*kaerimasu*
kiru (to cut)	切る	*kirimasu*
mairu (to go [humble])	参る	*mairimasu*
shaberu (to chat)	しゃべる	*shaberimasu*
shimeru (to dampen)	しめる	*shimerimasu*
suberu (to slide, to slip)	すべる	*suberimasu*

In cases of *iru*, *kaeru*, *kiru*, and *shimeru*, there are *RU*-verbs with identical mora structure: *iru* 'to be, to exist,' *kaeru* 'to change, to exchange,' *kiru* 'to wear,' and *shimeru* 'to close.'

Japanese verbs are further categorized based on their tendency to describe either a state or a dynamic action. The prototypical stative verbs are the existential verbs *iru* and *aru*, both meaning 'there exists.' The *i*-type adjective predicates are also stative. Prototypical active verbs are *iku* 'go,' *oyogu* 'swim,' and *nomu* 'drink.'

The Meanings of Non-past Form

When a non-past form of the verb is used, it means the following:

1.   *Description of the present state* (for stative verbs):

     (1a)   <u>*Kodomo*</u>   <u>*ga*</u>   **<u>*imasu*</u>.**

            child   S   there is

            子供がいます。

            (There is a child.)

2. *Description of definite future* (for active verbs):

(2a)   <u>Kaigi</u>   <u>wa</u> <u>juu-ji</u>   <u>ni</u> <u>**hajimarimasu.**</u>
meeting   T   ten o'clock   at begin

会議は十時に**始まります**。

(The meeting will start at ten.)

3. *Personal will* (for active verbs when the subject is 'I'):

(3a)   <u>Atarashii</u> <u>kaisha</u>   <u>de</u> <u>isshookenmei</u>   <u>**hatarakimasu.**</u>
new   company at   hard   work

新しい会社でいっしょうけんめい**働きます**。

(I will work hard at the new company.)

4. *Pointing out principles or the nature of things* (for both stative and active verbs):

(4a)   <u>Mizu</u> <u>wa</u> <u>sesshi</u>   <u>reido</u>   <u>de</u> <u>**koorimasu.**</u>
water T   centigrade   zero degree   at   freeze

水は摂氏零度で**凍ります**。

(Water freezes at zero degree centigrade.)

5. *Description of rules, regulations and habits:*

(5a)   <u>Maiasa</u>   <u>hachi-ji</u>   <u>ni</u> <u>kaisha</u>   <u>e</u> <u>**ikimasu.**</u>
every morning eight o'clock at company to go

毎朝八時に会社へ**行きます**。

(Every morning I go to the office at eight.)

6. *Description of procedures:*

(6a)   <u>Tamanegi</u> <u>wa</u> <u>usuku</u> <u>**kirimasu.**</u>
onion   T   thinly slice

玉ねぎは薄く**切ります**。

(Onions are sliced thin. [as in a cookbook])

Japanese verbs tend to have an abstract and more generalized meaning when used in non-past tense as shown in categories numbered 4, 5 and 6 above. In order to express the present tense of the action verbs, the present progressive tense (to be discussed under Entry 51) is used.

Other Notes on Verbs

The formal non-past verb form is also called *masu*-form due to the obvious reason of ending with *-masu*. *Masu*-form minus *-masu* is the "stem" of the verb, [Vstem]. The verb stems become useful later when we learn to attach to them other grammatical elements. It is useful to know that the stem of the *RU*-verb is the same as the informal non-past form (for example *taberu* 'eat') minus *-ru*, that is, *tabe*.

Note the verb position in a sentence. In normal situations, it appears at the end of the sentence (refer to characteristic 1). You may consider this phenomenon as an extension of characteristic 6 in that verbs are modified by all preceding modifying elements, including subjects, objects, and other adverbial phrases.

At this point, we note two additional grammatical particles, namely, the subject-marker *ga* and the object-marker *o*, both of which will be discussed in detail later.

Examples

(1) *Tomodachi ga*[*1] *kimasu.*
友だちが来ます。
(A friend is coming.)

(2) *Katoo-san wa*[*1] *sandoitchi o tabemasu.*
加藤さんはサンドイッチを食べます。
(Ms. Kato will eat sandwiches.)

> *1. It is important to note that case-marking grammatical particles follow the nouns whose case the particles assign. These are postpositions in contrast with English prepositions which precede nouns.

List of Common Verbs

Basic form		English	Formal form
U-verbs:			
au	会う	to meet	*aimasu*
aku	開く	to open	*akimasu*
asobu	遊ぶ	to play	*asobimasu*
arau	洗う	to wash	*araimasu*
utau	歌う	to sing	*utaimasu*
okuru	送る	to send	*okurimasu*
okoru	おこる	to be angry	*okorimasu*
otosu	落とす	to drop	*otoshimasu*[*2]
odoroku	おどろく	to be surprised	*odorokimasu*
odoru	踊る	to dance	*odorimasu*
owaru	終わる	to end	*owarimasu*
kau	買う	to buy	*kaimasu*
kaeru	帰る	to return	*kaerimasu*
kiku	聞く	to hear	*kikimasu*

shimaru	閉まる	to close [intransitive]	*shimarimasu*
suwaru	すわる	to sit down	*suwarimasu*
shaberu	しゃべる	to chatter	*shaberimasu*
naku	泣く	to cry	*nakimasu*
nugu	ぬぐ	to take off (clothes, etc.)	*nugimasu*
nomu	飲む	to drink	*nomimasu*
hataraku	働く	to work	*hatarakimasu*
matsu	待つ	to wait	*machimasu*[2]
motsu	持つ	to possess	*mochimasu*[2]
morau	もらう	to receive	*moraimasu*
yuu	言う	to say	*iimasu*[3]
yomu	読む	to read	*yomimasu*
warau	笑う	to laugh	*waraimasu*

RU-verbs:

-iru ending verbs:

iru	いる	to exist	*imasu*
ochiru	落ちる	to drop [intransitive]	*ochimasu*
okiru	起きる	to get up	*okimasu*
kiru	着る	to wear	*kimasu*
shinjiru	信じる	to believe	*shinjimasu*
dekiru	できる	can do	*dekimasu*
miru	見る	to see	*mimasu*

-eru ending verbs:

akeru	開ける	to open [transitive]	*akemasu*
ageru	上げる	to give	*agemasu*
ireru	入れる	to pour in	*iremasu*
oshieru	教える	to teach	*oshiemasu*
kotaeru	答える	to answer	*kotaemasu*
shimeru	閉める	to close [transitive]	*shimemasu*
suteru	捨てる	to throw away	*sutemasu*
deru	出る	to go out	*demasu*
neru	寝る	to sleep, to go to bed	*nemasu*

---

[2]. There is a phonological (sound) change to be noted when conjugating verbs. For verbs that end with *-su* and *-tsu* in their basic forms, the formal non-past forms are *-shimasu* and *-chimasu* respectively. There is no 'si' or 'ti' sound in Japanese, except in some special case of loan words as in *paatii*.

[3]. When handling conjugation of the verb *yuu* 'to say,' think of it spelled '*iu*,' (which is the way it is actually written in Japanese, but nonetheless pronounced as '*yuu*'). Thus, the formal version of *yuu (iu)* is *iimasu*.

Practice

```
------------------------------------------------------------
novel      N     shoosetsu      小説
Turner     PN    Taanaa         ターナー
to travel  V     ryokoo-suru    旅行する
------------------------------------------------------------
```

By combining the words chosen from each group given below, create Japanese sentences.

1. read   (I)   novel
2. travel   Mr. Turner
3. drink   coke ☺
4. eat   Ms. Tanaka   cake

——— Answers ———

1. *Shoosetsu o yomimasu.*   小説を読みます。
2. *Taanaa-san wa ryokoo-shimasu.*   ターナーさんは旅行します。
3. *Koora o nomu.* ☺   コーラを飲む。
4. *Tanaka-san wa keeki o tabemasu.* 田中さんはケーキを食べます。

Additional Information

The irregular verb *suru* is very productive. It is combined with nouns (of Chinese origin) to make a noun into a verb. For example:

kenkyuu (research) *-suru*	研究する	to conduct research
nyuuyoku (taking a bath) *-suru*	入浴する	to take a bath
hanbai (sale) *-suru*	販売する	to sell
benkyoo (study) *-suru*	勉強する	to study
rokuon (recording) *-suru*	録音する	to record
ryokoo (trip) *-suru*	旅行する	to travel
yushutsu (export) *-suru*	輸出する	to export

Additionally, foreign loan words become verbs by adding *-suru*; for example, *fookasu* (focus) *-suru* 'to focus,' and *shanpuu* (shampoo) *-suru* 'to shampoo.'

Recently in Japan, the verb *suru* has been added to all types of nouns, including those of Japanese origin. In conversational Japanese, new verbs are created which sometimes require expanded semantic interpretation. *Hurusato* (hometown) *-suru*, for example, means to enjoy the feeling of association with or visiting one's hometown. These words are in colloquial use only; they are to be avoided especially in formal writing.

11. Verbal Predicate—2. Existential Verbs: Non-past

> *Mrs. Yamada is there.*
>
> **Yamada-san ga imasu.**
>
> 山田さんがいます。
>
> [*aru, iru*]

Grammatical Explanation

We have learned two kinds of verbs, 1) the be-verb, *da*, and 2) common verbs ending with the *-u* sound. Additionally, we have noted that in Japanese [Adj-*i*] may be used as an independent predicate. The existential verbs, *iru* and *aru* constitute another Japanese verb predicate type. The verbs *iru* and *aru*, both of which can be translated into English 'there is/are,' are called existential verbs—their basic meaning is to state that something exists. The verb *iru* conjugates according to the *RU*-verb conjugation rules, *aru* which is a *U*-verb does not follow the *U*-verb rules entirely. At this point, we will learn four forms only: *aru*, *arimasu* (the formal non-past of *aru*) and *iru*, *imasu* (the formal non-past of *iru*). The meaning and the usage surrounding these two verbs differ from those of the English existential verb, *there is/are*, and deserve special attention.

There are basic and extended meanings in these stative verbs, and in some cases, a preference for one or the other, as described below.

1. *Physical existence:*

   For expressing physical existence, as shown in the target expression, if what exists is animate, *iru* is used; if inanimate, *aru*. Thus we have:

   (1a) *Neko ga imasu.*
         cat   S   there is
         ねこがいます。
         (There is a cat.)

   (1b) *Teeburu ga arimasu.*
         table   S   there is
         テーブルがあります。
         (There is a table.)

If the cat is dead, *neko no shigai ga arimasu* 'there is a cat's body is used.

In some cases for expressing the existence of a person, both *aru* and *iru* are used, with *iru* implying a person's concrete existence (sometimes in a certain location) and *aru* implying more abstract existence. For example:

(1c) <u>Ano</u>   <u>hito</u>   <u>wa</u> <u>teki</u>   <u>ga</u> <u>iru.</u>
      that   person T   enemy S   there
      あの人は敵がいる。
      ([lit. As for that person there are enemies.] He has some enemies.)

(1d) *Ano hito wa teki ga aru.*
      あの人は敵がある。
      (There are enemies against him.)

2. *Possession:*

Both *iru* and *aru* are used to express possession. *Aru* and *iru* are used for animate possession, and *aru* is used for inanimate possession.

(2a) <u>*Tanaka-san*</u>   <u>*(ni)*</u>   <u>*wa*</u> <u>*(o)kane*</u>   <u>*ga*</u> <u>*arimasu (*imasu).*</u>
      Ms. Tanaka   for   T   money   S   there is
      田中さん(に)は(お)金があります。
      (Ms. Tanaka has money.)

(2b) <u>*(Watashi [ni] wa)*</u> <u>*otooto*</u>   <u>*ga*</u> <u>*arimasu/imasu.*</u>
      (I)   younger brother   S   there is
      (私[に]は)弟が<u>あります</u>/<u>います</u>。
      (I have a younger brother.)

In the examples above, what exists and what is possessed are marked by the subject marker *ga*. One may wonder about this characterization; as shown in the English translation, the money is not the "subject"; it is rather the object that Ms. Tanaka possesses. We will return to this point later. For now, just note that what exists and what is possessed are marked by *ga*, unless of course it is a topic, in which case it is marked by *wa*. The possessor is marked by the topic marker *wa*, optionally preceded by another particle *ni*. *Ni* indicates location in this usage. We will discuss many functions of the particle *ni* later.

Practice

```
-------------------------------------------------------------
cookies    N    kukkii    クッキー
tree       N    ki        木
dog        N    inu       犬
-------------------------------------------------------------
```

1. Using existential verbs, describe in Japanese the existence of the
   following:
   a. delicious cookies
   b. a tall tree
   c. young person
   d. a dog

2. Using existential verbs, describe the possession of the following:
   a. Ms. Sakai, money
   b. I, children
   c. Mr. Johnson, a car

Answers

1a. *Oishii kukkii ga arimasu.*   おいしいクッキーがあります。
 b. *Takai ki ga arimasu.*   高い木があります。
 c. *Wakai hito ga imasu.*   若い人がいます。
 d. *Inu ga imasu.*   犬がいます。
2a. *Sakai-san (ni) wa (o)kane ga arimasu.*
   酒井さん(に)は(お)金があります。
 b. *(Watashi ni wa) kodomo ga arimasu/imasu.*
   (私には)子供があります/います。
 c. *Jonson-san (ni) wa kuruma ga arimasu.*
   ジョンソンさん(に)は車があります。

Additional Information

As extended meanings of *iru/aru*, the following points should be noted.

1. *Occurrence of incidents:*
   Aru is used to express occurrence of incidents. (In this use, the locative
   particle *de*—instead of another locative particle *ni* which is normally
   used—co-occurs.)

   (1a) *Kono heya de paatii ga arimasu.*
        this   room in party S   there is
        この部屋でパーティーがあります。
        (There is a party in this room.)

(1b) *Tookyoo de/ni jishin   ga atta.*
Tokyo   in   earthquake S there was
東京で/に地震があった。
(There was an earthquake in Tokyo.)

(*Atta* is an informal past tense form of *aru*.)

2. *Existence of parts of a whole:*
Both *aru* and *iru* are used for the animate subject.

(2a) *Onaka ga suita hito   wa arimasen ka.*
be hungry   person T there is   Q
おなかがすいた人はありませんか。
(Isn't there anyone who is hungry?)

(*Ka* is a question marker.)

3. *Existence in narratives:*
Both *aru* and *iru* are used for the animate subject when the subject
is introduced in a narrative. *Aru* is more frequently used to let the
reader know the existence of narrative characters while *iru* is used
when the location of the characters is emphasized.

(3a) *Mukashi mukashi,   ojiisan to obaasan   ga arimashita.*
once upon a time   old man and old woman S there were
むかしむかし，おじいさんとおばあさんがありました。
(Once upon a time, there were [lived] an old man and an old
woman.)

(*Arimashita* is the formal past tense form of *aru*.)

Another expression associated with the existential verb *aru* should be mentioned in passing. The expression *dearu* 'to be,' may be used in place of *da*
in written Japanese. For example, a well known novel by Soseki Natsume is
titled *Wagahai wa neko dearu* (I am a cat). The conjugation of *dearu*
follows that of *aru*.

(a) *Nihon-jin wa hatarakimono dearu.* ♦
Japanese T hard worker   are
日本人は働き者である。
(Japanese are industrious.)

12. Deictic Expression—2. Personal Pronouns

> *I, we*
>
> **watashi, watashi-tachi**
> わたし, わたしたち

Strategic Explanation

The use of personal pronouns in Japanese is far more restricted than in English. Although a variety of pronoun-like forms are used in Japanese depending on the gender of the speaker and the referent, or on the speech style chosen, in reality there is a tendency to avoid their use. First, however, let us look at the system.

Personal Pronouns

	first person 'I'	second person 'you'
Very formal	*watakushi* わたくし	*otaku(-sama)*, *sochira(-sama)* おたく(さま) そちら(さま)
Formal	*watashi* わたし *atakushi* [female] あたくし	*anata* あなた
Informal	*boku* [male] 僕 *atashi* [female] あたし	*kimi* 君
Very informal	*ore* [male] おれ	*omae* [male], *anta* お前 あんた

For the third person, limited use of *kare* 'he (often meaning boyfriend or male lover),' and *kanojo* 'she (often meaning girlfriend or female lover),' are used. A frequently used form for the third person is *ano hito* 'that person,' meaning either 'he' or 'she.'

Learning how to use Japanese personal pronouns is important, but more important is to understand how *not* to use them. First, since pronouns are anaphoric expressions referring to referents uniquely identifiable among speech participants, they are normally avoided (refer to characteristic 4).

Recall that in Japanese there is no strict requirement in grammar as in the case of English for every sentence to have a grammatical subject. Simply put, whatever is assumed to be known is easily left unsaid. This is why earlier we introduced an expression *Andaason desu* without the grammatical subject *watashi* 'I' (see Entry 7).

Second, if there is a need to use the second-person personal pronoun *anata*, it should be avoided when addressing your superior. Normally it is safer to address the listener by name. Instead of asking Mr. Anderson by saying *Anata wa gakusei desu ka?* 'Are you a student?,' *Andaason-san wa gakusei desu ka* is preferred. If the name of the listener is not known, use the politer version of *anata*, namely, *otaku (-sama).*

Third, the pronoun *anata* is widely used by wives as a vocative when they address their husbands. Husbands address their wives by their first name without -*san*, or by a very informal version of the second-person pronoun, *omae*. The pronominal address terms chosen by husbands and wives are not reciprocal.

The plural form of personal pronouns are made by adding a suffix -*tachi*; *watakushi-tachi, watashi-tachi, boku-tachi, kimi-tachi, atashi-tachi, ore-tachi, omae-tachi* and *anta-tachi*. For *anata*, -*gata* may also be added, that is, *anata-gata*. The suffix, -*tachi*, can be added to some other nouns referring to persons as well. For instance, *kodomo-tachi* meaning 'children.' *Yamamoto-san-tachi* is also possible. This refers not to a group of people with the same last name, Yamamoto, but to 'Yamamoto and others.' For 'they,' plural of *ano hito*, that is, *ano hito-tachi* is often used.

13. Particles—1. Basic Case Markers

Target Expression

> *Mr. Araki drinks beer.*
> **Araki-san ga biiru o nomimasu.**
> 荒木さんがビールを飲みます。
>
> [ga] [o] [ni]

Grammatical Explanation

One major difference between English and Japanese sentence structure is the word order. Japanese has a basic topic-comment and subject-object-verb order in contrast with English subject-verb-object order (refer to characteristic 1). In Japanese, word order is relatively free, although there is a preferred word order which we will study later. In English the position in relation to the verb defines the grammatical case of the noun. In Japanese, instead of word order, particles are used to mark cases. Consider the difference in meaning between the following sentences.

(a)   Mary kills John.
    Mearii ga Jon o korosu. / Jon o Mearii ga korosu.
    メアリーがジョンを殺す。 ジョンをメアリーが殺す。

(b)   John kills Mary.
    Jon ga Mearii o korosu. / Mearii o Jon ga korosu.
    ジョンがメアリーを殺す。 メアリーをジョンが殺す。

As shown in the Japanese translation, different particles mark the subject and object case; the position of the noun does not assign cases. Three particles which we concentrate on are:

ga	subject marker (abbreviated as S)
o	object marker (abbreviated as O)
ni	indirect object marker (abbreviated as IO)

At this point we must go back to the question posed earlier about the notion of "subject" in Japanese, in contrast with that of English. In Japanese, the subject, not in a strict grammatical sense (as in "*subject*-verb agreement"), refers to the element that is most prominent and focused upon, and is directly associated with and predicated by the verb in active (not passive) sentences. We will refer to this subject as an element of "primary predicate focus." *Ga* identifies the element in primary predicate focus defined by the specific verbal predicate. For action verbs introduced earlier, subject is the agent or the performer of the action. For a group of verbs that express a direct sensory perception, the primary predicate focus is placed on the items that cause such perception. These expressions will be learned in time. For stative verbs, the noun marked by subject marker *ga* is the element whose state is described. For existential sentences the subject is what exists, for an existential possessive sentence a subject is what is possessed.

There are four possible ways in which different types of verbs interact with the concept of "subject," as shown below.

Verb types:	N + *ga*
1. Active transitive	N is the doer, the agent (N + *o* designates object). ***Tomodachi ga*** *hon o yomu.* 友だちが本を読む。 (My friend reads a book.)
2. Active intransitive	N is the doer, the agent (N + *o* is not used). ***Tomodachi ga*** *kuru.* 友だちが来る。 (My friend comes.)
3. Stative	N is what is described. ***Ano hito ga*** *sensei desu.* あの人が先生です。 (That person is the teacher) ***Tatemono ga*** *aru.* 建物がある。 (There is a building.)
4. Reactive	N is the source for response and reaction. ***Aisukuriimu ga*** *suki da.* ice cream S like アイスクリームが好きだ。 (I like ice cream.)

In the first case, the agent or the doer of the action is the subject and what is acted on is the object. In the second type, the agent of the intransitive verb is the subject. In sentences with stative verbs, what is described is the subject, i.e., the element of primary predicate focus. In the fourth type, which will be called "reactive" description, the source that causes reaction or response in the experiencer (the person who experiences this response process) is the subject. Only a limited number of verbal and adjectival predicates fall into this category (see Appendix 5 for the listing of predicates for "reactive" description. The reactive predicate may be active or stative. In a broad sense *aru* and *iru* are considered to be reactive stative). In all types noun phrases are marked by *ga*, unless the noun becomes the topic in which case it is marked by *wa*.

In some "reactive" structures it is possible to add another dimension; the experiencer of the event described may appear in a sentence or an utterance by N followed by *ga*. For example:

(c) ***Watashi ga*** *aisukuriimu ga suki da.*
私がアイスクリームが好きだ。
(I like ice cream.)

The term "reactive" is chosen because the [N + *ga* + reactive predicate] structure primarily postulates that something existing out there causes the experiencer's response and reaction. We will learn more about the predicates of "reactive" description in Entry 46.

Remember, not all *ga*-marked noun phrases appear on the surface of the sentence. If they are topics and/or assumed to be known among participants, they are likely to be left unsaid. When the element of primary predicate focus is chosen to become the topic of utterance or across several utterances, *ga* is taken over by *wa*, the topic marker. Thus, it is possible to say, for example, *hon wa arimasu*, in which case, *hon* conveys shared information and becomes the topic.

Examples

(1) *Tomodachi ga kimasu.*
    friend   S   come
    友だちが来ます。
    (A friend will come.)

(2) *Tomodachi ni hon o agemasu.*
    friend   IO book O give
    友だちに本をあげます。
    (I will give my friend a book.)

(3) *Ookii tatemono ga arimasu.*
    large building   S there is
    大きい建物があります。
    (There is a large building.)

(4) *(O)kane ga arimasu.*
    （お）金があります。
    (There is money.)

Note that in all examples, case-marking particles are placed immediately after the nouns whose cases are defined. In sentence (2), it is possible to change the order of case-marked phrases. *Hon o tomodachi ni agemasu* is a grammatical sentence, with identical cases assigned as in sentence (2).

Practice

---

someone	N	*dare-ka*	誰か
car	N	*kuruma*	車
present, gift	N	*purezento*	プレゼント

Mix words from each category and create Japanese sentences by adding appropriate case-marking particles.

someone	read	newspaper
Mr. Tanaka	buy	coffee
friend	give	new car
Jim	drink	book
		present

—————— Some Sample Answers ——————

1. *Dare-ka ga koohii o nomimasu.*　　誰かがコーヒーを飲みます。
2. *Shinbun o yomu.*　　　　　　　　新聞を読む。
3. *Jimu-san ga atarashii kuruma o kaimasu.*
   ジムさんが新しい車を買います。
   (*Jimu-san wa*, if 'Jim' is presented as a topic.)
4. *Tomodachi ni purezento o agemasu.*
   友だちにプレゼントをあげます。

Additional Information

For many nouns of Chinese origin, the following choice regarding the use of object marker *o* should be noted. For the word *benkyoo* 'study,' either *benkyoo o suru* or *benkyoo-suru* is acceptable. If, however, the noun is modified by [N + *no*], adjectives, or adjectival clauses, only the [*benkyoo o suru*] pattern is acceptable. Note that sentence (a) is correct while sentence (b) is not. It is of course possible to use *benkyoo-suru* as a single verb preceded by its object [N + *o*], as shown in (c). When the [N + *o*] phrase appears as an object of the verb, the verb cannot take another noun marked by *o*, as shown in the ungrammatical example sentence (d).

(a)　*Nihongo no benkyoo o suru.*
(b)　**Nihongo no benkyoo-suru.*
(c)　*Nihongo o benkyoo-suru.*
(d)　**Nihongo o benkyoo o suru.*

14.　Not Saying the Obvious

Strategic Explanation

In this section we examine our characteristic 4. Generally speaking, in Japanese any and all elements are left unsaid as long as what is unsaid is generally "understood." Nouns, verbs, and even particles are frequently deleted particularly in spoken style. In Japanese, expressions are more closely tied to the surrounding situation than in English. The subject-predicate axis is not as rigid or as strongly felt in Japanese. Instead of following the rule of subject-verb-object as it is the case in English, only what needs to be mentioned in a specific context is added before the sentence-final verbal elements. Mentioning unnecessary bits of information is in fact a sign of clumsiness in Japanese conversation; it only indicates a lack of conversational skill. The guideline provided below should be followed when leaving things unsaid.

1. *Topic of the sentence and discourse:*
   Once a topic marked with the particle *wa* is introduced in discourse, it normally remains unmentioned unless a specific need arises. For example, when the topic continues in a new conversation segment or a new paragraph, it may be restated to signal that the same topic is still active.

2. *Answer to a question:*
   In an answer to a question, what is already stated in the question is often not repeated.

3. *Information situationally interpretable:*
   Pronouns which are situationally interpretable are often unmentioned; the 'I' and 'you' are self-evident.

4. *Culturally and socially shared information:*
   There is no need to explain the already shared knowledge of one's culture and society.

5. *Grammatical particles:*
   Deletion of grammatical particles is normally restricted to informal spoken language only.

Additional Information

In spoken Japanese, even the main clause may be left unsaid. This is possible when participants readily understand the context.

(a) *Kaettara (doo desu ka)?*
   return   how about
   帰ったら(どうですか)？
   ([How about] returning?)

(b) <u>Takai</u>   <u>kara</u>   (kaimasen).
    expensive because
    高いから（買いません）。

(Because it is expensive [I don't buy].)

Emphasis on not mentioning the obvious does not exclude repetition or redundancy in conversation. In fact, repetition occurs frequently in spoken Japanese. What is emphasized here is that compared to English, Japanese has less grammatical constraints that block this "tendency to mention less," and this is much more extensively observed than in English.

The tendency for mentioning less is exercised in the process of word-formation as well. Long noun phrases tend to be shortened into four syllable words, often combining the initial two syllables from two words. See, for example:

Toodai	東大	**Too**kyoo **Dai**gaku	東京大学
		'Tokyo University'	
sotsuron	卒論	**sotsu**gyoo **ron**bun	卒業論文
		'graduation thesis, dissertation'	
natsumero	ナツメロ	**natsu**kashi no **mero**dii	なつかしのメロディー
		'nostalgic melody'	
masukomi	マスコミ	**masu** **komyu**nikeeshon	マスコミュニケーション
		'mass communication'	
Nichigin	日銀	**Ni**hon **Gin**koo	日本銀行
		'The Bank of Japan'	

As shown in the case of *masukomi*, when shortening phonological change may occur. Note that in the last example, *nichi*, another reading of the same *kanji* is used for *ni* of *nihon*.

15. Structure of the Japanese Sentence—1. Topic and Comment

Grammmatical Explanation

We are already familiar with the terms "topic" and "comment." But what are they really? Why are they important in Japanese? How do they interact with another structural relation, that is, subject and predicate?

First, as we defined earlier, topic is what is being talked about. It can be the subject, object or any other grammatical element. Topic and comment themselves are not strictly grammatical notions. The topic-comment relation is based on how information is structured in communication. It is an overall umbrella-like system of distinguishing what is being talked about (topic) in actual communication, and what is being introduced as information added (comment) to the topic.

The comment consists of a subject and a predicate. In Japanese as we have already seen, subject is interpreted broadly. We defined subject as an item of primary predicate focus directly associated with the verb. Predicate consists of the verb, which is located at the end of an utterance, preceded by other elements such as adverbs, adjectives and nouns.

Topic-comment and Subject-predicate Structures

In order to understand how topic-comment and subject-predicate relate to each other, examine the schematization presented below. The elements in square brackets become the topics in the example sentences; these phrases are no longer mentioned.

OVERALL ORGANIZATION OF
SENTENCE OR UTTERANCE

TOPIC   COMMENT

SUBJECT   PREDICATE

(1) *Koko ni wa*   *kudamono ga*   [*koko ni*] *arimasu.*
ここには   くだものが   [ここに]あります。

(2)	Tanaka-san wa 田中さんは	[Tanaka-san ga] [田中さんが]	nihon-jin desu. 日本人です。
(3a)	(No topic selected)	Tomodachi ga 友だちが	kimasu. 来ます。
(3b)	Sono tomodachi wa その友だちは	[tomodachi ga] [友だちが]	Amerika-jin desu. アメリカ人です。
(3c)	[Tomodachi wa] [友だちは]	[tomodachi ga] [友だちが]	Terebi o mimasu. テレビを見ます。

In sentence (1), the topic chosen is the locative phrase *koko ni* 'here.' The subject, locative phrases, and verb constitute the predicate, with the subject being *kudamono* 'fruit,' marked by *ga*. In this sentence the focus is placed on what exists there, namely, *kudamono*, which is the subject of the sentence. What is introduced as topic (that is, locative phrase *koko ni*) defines the general framework into which the information described by comment is incorporated. Once the locative phrase is promoted to be the topic, it becomes defunct within the predicate framework. In sentence (2), *Tanaka-san* is identified as topic, which coincides with the subject of the sentence. When topic and subject coincide, topic takes over the subject phrase which becomes defunct and is no longer mentioned. Of course, the topic itself is also deletable, as shown in sentence (3c). Only grammatical particles *ga* and *o* only are overridden by *wa* (and another topic marker *mo*); other particles remain with *wa* attached to them, as in *ni wa*, *to wa*, *de wa* and so forth.

Imagine a situation where you describe your friend to a listener. In sentence (3a), the subject *tomodachi* is introduced into discourse with *ga*, and no topic is yet assigned. When a piece of information new to the listener is introduced, it does not yet constitute a topic. But in sentence (3b), *sono tomodachi* anaphorically refers to the same individual and it is marked with *wa*, now becoming the topic. Further, in sentence (3c) the topic which coincides with the subject is deleted. This process follows a three-step progression:

1. The new information is introduced as subject [N + *ga*].
2. The topic is established [N + *wa*].
3. The established topic is deleted [Ø (zero)].

Although not all cases of topic establishment follow this sequence, it represents a prototypical case. (Especially in narratives, the dramatic characters may be introduced with *wa*, although they appear for the first time in the story. By virtue of introducing a character as if consisting of already given information, the character is accepted as the topicalized main character of the story.)

Think of topic as a framework or notion shared by the interactants. Into this framework, information provided by the subject-predicate axis which constitutes comment, is incorporated. Whereas in English, this process is not normally reflected in sentential structures, in Japanese we have an overt topic marker *wa* to do precisely that. Hence Japanese is known as a topic-comment prominent language. The topic-comment structure may roughly be translated into English 'as for X/speaking of X, it is Y,' meaning that there is a special relationship between X and Y.

Japanese prefer the topic-comment structure when describing events. Instead of saying 'John speaks Japanese well,' Japanese would say 'as for John, his Japanese is good,' *Jon-san wa nihongo ga joozu desu*; *joozu desu* means 'be good at.' (Note here that *joozu da* is a "reactive" predicate with the element of primary predicate focus marked by *ga*.) What *wa* marks creates an overall informational framework, and what *ga* marks identifies the element of primary predicate focus.

In spoken English the topic-comment structure may appear as in:

    (a)   Ryan's Cafe . . . I won't go there. It's too expensive.

    (b)   John. I don't know about him.

In these utterances topics are placed in the initial position. Phrases *Ryan's Cafe* and *John* are announced as something about which comments follow. Although this type of topicalized utterance structure has restricted usage in English, in Japanese, topic-comment is the predominant structure.

Contrasting *Wa* and *Ga*

A related fact regarding the subject marker *ga* should be mentioned at this point. Imagine a situation where you are interested in knowing which one is Mr. Smith among a group of people in the room. In this case, the utterance you make is something like:

    (c)   *Dono hito ga Sumisu-san desu ka.* (*Ka* is a question marker.)

          どの人がスミスさんですか。

          (Which person is Mr. Smith?)

In providing an answer to such a question, your friend would point to Mr. Smith and answer by using the [X *ga* Y *da*] pattern.

(d) *Ano hito ga Sumisu-san desu.*
     あの人がスミスさんです。
     (That person is Mr. Smith.)

Since *ano hito* 'that person' provides new information and points out an item that satisfies the condition of being Mr. Smith exhaustively (that person and that person alone), this use of *ga* is called *ga* for "exhaustive listing." [X *ga*] in this pattern carries with it a connotation of "X and only X is the Y in question." A special feature of exhaustive listing *ga* is that the item marked with *ga* normally receives phonological prominence.

You might be wondering about another possible way of asking a question in the situation described above. By making *Sumisu-san* the topic, you may ask a question:

(e) *Sumisu-san wa dono hito desu ka.*
     スミスさんはどの人ですか。
     (As for Mr. Smith, which person is he?)

An answer to this question may take the form:

(f) *(Sumisu-san wa) ano hito desu.*
     (スミスさんは)あの人です。
     (Mr. Smith is that person over there.)

Sumisu is the topic marked by *wa*, *ano hito desu* provides comment, a piece of new information. Different strategies of questioning and answering occur depending on how a speaker chooses the topic, that is, how a speaker organizes given and new information.

16. Identifying Topics—Topic Marker *Wa*

Target Expression

> *Mr. Takagi goes to Osaka every week.*
> **Takagi-san wa maishuu Oosaka e ikimasu.**
> 高木さんは毎週大阪へ行きます。
>
> [wa] [mo]

Grammatical Explanation

The topic, being that which is talked about, can be a grammatical subject, object, locative and so forth. In the example sentence above, *Takagi-san* 'Mr. Takagi' is a subject as well as a topic marked by *wa*.

Going a step further, theoretically there could be sentences containing two separate items, one a topic and the other a subject. For example, examine the following sentence.

(a) *Kono hoteru wa saabisu ga ii   desu   yo.*
    this hotel   T   service   S good   IP
    このホテルはサービスがいいですよ。
    ([lit. As for this hotel, service is good.] The service of this hotel is good.)

Here we have a topic *kono hoteru* which offers the framework, and the comment, *saabisu ga ii* which in turn consists of subject *saabisu* and predicate *ii*. Topic defines the "whole" and subject focuses on its "part." This example leads us to one of the most well-known (among grammarians) Japanese sentences:

(b) *Zoo   wa hana   ga   nagai.*
    elephant   T   trunk   S   long
    ぞうは鼻が長い。
    ([lit. As for elephants, trunks are long]) Elephants' trunks are long.)

Again, this sentence makes sense when you know that topic can be practically any element of the sentence and it exists outside the subject-predicate axis. The relationship between the topic and the subject in this sentence is also that of whole-part.

Going even a step further, we can conceive of sentences with multiple topics. For example:

(c) *Watanabe-san   wa ashita   wa kaisha   o   yasumimasu.*
    Ms. Watanabe   T tomorrow T   company O will be absent
    渡辺さんはあしたは会社を休みます。
    (Ms. Watanabe will be absent from the company tomorrow.)

In this case, the topic framework is a combination of *Watanabe-san* and the temporal phrase *ashita*.

An additional topic marking particle should be introduced at this point. *Mo* which signals topic with the meaning of 'also' and 'in addition' functions similarly with *wa*. (*Mo* takes over particles *ga* and *o* as in the case of *wa*.) For example:

(d) *Sasaki-san mo yasumimasu.*
    佐々木さんも休みます。
    (Ms. Sasaki will also be absent.)

The particle *mo* will be discussed in detail in Entry 97.

Before proceeding, an issue concerning the topic marker in relation to subordinate clauses needs to be discussed. Since the topic is what is being talked about, it does not normally occur in a subordinate clause. This is because a subordinate clause is less important than the main clause in terms of its contribution to the overall information structure. When a noun phrase appears in subordinate clauses, the use of *wa* is normally avoided and the noun phrase is marked by another appropriate grammatical particle. Even when that noun phrase conveys information shared by participants, the topic marker *wa* is avoided. This usage of particles other than *wa* is best described as non-topicalization, that is, avoidance of topic marker due to the structure of the relevant information. Among subordinate clauses, there are some types in which this change is not obligatory, that is, subordinate clauses marked by *noni* 'despite,' and *keredomo* 'although.'

A phenomenon closely associated with the topic marker *wa* is a special use of it, often called "contrastive *wa*." When a *wa*-marked phrase together with *wa* is pronounced with phonological prominence, it implies contrast, regardless of whether the contrastive item is specified or not. When there are multiple topics within an utterance or a sentence, it is often the case that some in fact carry a contrastive meaning. In example (e), *Bosuton e wa* is pronounced prominently (in a higher tone and with more volume than normal), and it carries the contrastive meaning as described below.

(e) *Yamakawa-san wa Bosuton e wa ikimasu.*
山川さんはボストンへは行きます。
(Mr. Yamakawa goes to Boston.)

Here the intended message is that Mr. Yamakawa goes at least to Boston, although he may not go to the contrasted implied place, for example, New York City.

Practice

Sunday	N	*nichiyoobi*	日曜日
room	N	*heya*	部屋
busy	Adj	*isogashii*	忙しい

Express the following in Japanese by selecting underlined phrases as topics.

1. I am a Japanese.
2. On Sunday, (I) stay in my room.[*1] [use the existential verb]
3. Tomorrow Mrs. Sasaki is busy.

── Answers ──

1. *(Watashi wa) nihon-jin desu.* （私は）日本人です。
2. *Nichiyoobi wa heya ni imasu.* 日曜日は部屋にいます。
3. *Ashita wa Sasaki-san wa isogashii-desu.*
   あしたは佐々木さんは忙しいです。

---

*1. Possessive pronouns in Japanese are deleted unless there is need for emphasis. In sentence 2., it is assumed to be ''my'' room unless otherwise noted. There is no need to translate each and every word into Japanese. The key is to convey as closely as possible in appropriate Japanese what you mean in English.

17. Particles—2. Markers for Time, Location, Methods, etc.

Target Expression

I'm going back to the United States at Christmas.
Kurisumasu ni Amerika e kaerimasu.
クリスマスにアメリカへ帰ります。

[*ni*] [*e*] [*de*] [*to*] [*made*]

Grammatical Explanation

We spend some time here familiarizing ourselves with a number of frequently used grammatical particles. These are attached to nouns and define grammatical relationships between that noun and other elements. Recall that we have studied subject marker *ga*, object marker *o*, and indirect object marker *ni* earlier.

---

hachi-ji	八時	N	eight o'clock
gakkoo	学校	N	school
toosuto	トースト	N	toast
hamueggu	ハムエッグ	N	ham-and-eggs
koocha	紅茶	N	(black) tea
natsuyasumi	夏休み	N	summer vacation
tegami	手紙	N	letter

(a) *ni* Locative marker (*in, at*), also directional
　　　　(O)kane wa koko ni arimasu yo.
　　　　（お）金はここにありますよ。
　　　　(There is money here.)

(b) *ni* Temporal marker—point of time (*at*)
　　　　Hachi-ji ni ikimasu.
　　　　八時に行きます。
　　　　(I'll go at eight o'clock.)

(c) *ni* Marker of source (*from*)
　　　　Tomodachi ni karimasu.
　　　　友だちに借ります。
　　　　(I'll borrow from my friend.)

(d) *e* Directional marker (*to, toward*)
　　　　Gakkoo e ikimasu.
　　　　学校へ行きます。
　　　　(I'm going to school.)

(e) *de* Locative marker—place of dynamic action (*in, at*)
　　　　Koko de benkyoo-shimasu.
　　　　ここで勉強します。
　　　　(I'll study here.)

(f) *de* Instrumental marker (*by, through*)
　　　　Kore de kirimasu.
　　　　これで切ります。
　　　　(I'll cut (it) with this.)

(g) *to* Joint action (*with*)
　　　　Sasaki-san to ikimasu.
　　　　佐々木さんと行きます。
　　　　(I'll go with Ms. Sasaki.)

(h) *to* Enumerative (*and*)
　　　　Toosuto to hamueggu o tabemasu.
　　　　トーストとハムエッグを食べます。
　　　　(I will have toast and ham-and-eggs.)

(i) *ka* Alternative (*or*)
　　　　Koohii ka koocha o nomimasu.
　　　　コーヒーか紅茶を飲みます。
　　　　(I'll drink coffee or tea.)

(j) **kara**   Starting point (*from*)
     Ashita kara natsuyasumi desu.
     あしたから夏休みです。
     (It's summer vacation from tomorrow.)

(k) **made**   Ending point (*till, up to, to*)
     Ashita made machimasu.
     あしたまで待ちます。
     (I'll wait until tomorrow.)

(l) **made ni** Deadline (*by*)
     Ashita made ni tegami o kakimasu.
     あしたまでに手紙を書きます。
     (I'll write a letter by tomorrow.)

The explanations that follow are given to help you distinguish between some of the particles, particularly that ubiquitous *ni*, which can be used to mark indirect object, location, direction, time, goal, and so forth.

1. *Directional e and ni:*
    The differences between the two directional markers *e* and *ni*, which are interchangeable in many cases, are the following. *E* is used to express the direction associated with an action and is used when emphasizing its process. The verbs such as *iku* 'to go,' *kuru* 'to come,' and *kaeru* 'to return' can be and often are used to focus on the process of the actions referred to. For example, *Tookyoo-eki e iku* 'to go to Tokyo station.'

    Ni, on the other hand, is used when emphasizing the result of the action. The verbs such as *hairu* 'to enter,' *ireru* 'to put in,' *tsukeru* 'to attach,' *tsuku* 'to arrive' and *atsumaru* 'to gather' can be and often are used to focus on the result of the action and are preferably marked by *ni*. For example, *heya ni hairu* 'to enter a room.'

    Parenthetically, *made* which can also be used for direction, describes the destination of the action focusing on the goal. The verbs such as *hakobu* 'to carry,' and *aruku* 'to walk' often co-occur with *made*, for example, *uchi made aruku* 'walk (to) home.'

2. *Locative de and ni:*
    The difference between the two locatives *de* and *ni* should also be mentioned. When describing the location where the dynamic action takes place, *de* is obligatory. On the other hand when the stative verb is used, the location in which that state exists is described by *ni*. The verbs that co-occur with the locative *ni* are limited. Frequently used examples are; *iru, aru, sumu* 'to live,' and *oku* 'to place (something).' Locative par-

ticles introduced here may be followed by topic markers *wa* and *mo*. For example:

(2a) *Amerika de benkyoo-shimasu. Nihon **de mo** shimasu.*
アメリカで勉強します。日本でもします。
(I'll study in America. I'll also study in Japan.)

(2b) *Heya **ni wa** tomodachi ga imasu.*
部屋には友だちがいます。
(In the room there is my friend.)

3. *Ni for 'source' and kara for 'starting point':*
As we already discussed, *ni* is a particle of location. Location here is to be interpreted in a broad sense; it could indicate various points of locations involved in an action. Depending on the verb, *ni* can indicate the location from where the source of action is sought. In this case, it is interchangeable with *kara*.

(3a) *Tomodachi **ni** kikimashita yo.*[1]
友だちに聞きましたよ。
(I heard from a friend.)

(3b) *Tomodachi **kara** kikimashita yo.*[1]
友だちから聞きましたよ。
(I heard from a friend.)

[1]. *Kikimashita* is the formal past-tense form of the verb *kiku. Yo* is an interactional particle which marks introduction of new information often with emphasis.

Examples

Jonson	ジョンソン	PN	Johnson
kurisumasu	クリスマス	N	Christmas
Nyuujaajii	ニュージャージー	PN	New Jersey
nishuukan	二週間	N	two weeks
mise	店	N	store
mikan	みかん	N	tangerine
----

(1) *Jonson-san wa kurisumasu ni Nyuujaajii e kaerimasu.*
ジョンソンはクリスマスにニュージャージーへ帰ります。
(Mr. Johnson will return to New Jersey for Christmas.)

(2) *Tomodachi to kuruma de Nyuuyooku e ikimasu.*
友だちと車でニューヨークへ行きます。
(He will go to New York by car with his friend.)

(3) *Depaato de purezento o kaimasu.*
デパートでプレゼントを買います。
(He will buy some presents at a department store.)

(4) *Jonson-san wa nishuukan Nyuujaajii ni imasu.*
ジョンソンさんは二週間ニュージャージーにいます。
(Mr. Johnson will be in New Jersey for two weeks.)

(5) *Mise de ringo to mikan o kaimasu.*
店でりんごとみかんを買います。
(I'll buy some apples and tangerines at the store.)

Practice

```
----------------------------------------------------------
postage stamp   N   kitte          切手
post office      N   yuubinkyoku    郵便局
children         N   kodomo-tachi   子供たち
----------------------------------------------------------
```

1. Express the following in Japanese:
    a. Mr. Kondo goes to France with his friends.
    b. I read a book in a bright room.
    c. I buy stamps at the post office.
    d. Children watch TV in a spacious room.
    e. I'll write a letter by tomorrow.

2. Describe what you do on Sundays.

——— Answers ———
1a. *Kondoo-san wa tomodachi to Huransu e ikimasu.*
近藤さんは友だちとフランスへ行きます。
  b. *Akarui heya de hon o yomimasu.* 明るい部屋で本を読みます。
  c. *Yuubinkyoku de kitte o kaimasu.* 郵便局で切手を買います。
  d. *Kodomo-tachi wa hiroi heya de terebi o miru.*
子供たちは広い部屋でテレビを見る。
  e. *Ashita made ni tegami o kakimasu.*
あしたまでに手紙を書きます。
——— Some Sample Answers ———
2. *Shinbun o yomimasu.* 新聞を読みます。
   Terebi o mimasu. テレビを見ます。

Additional Information

Concerning locative particles, the following should be noted. For verbs of motion (such as *tooru* 'to pass through,' *aruku* 'to walk,' *noboru* 'to climb,' *magaru* 'to turn,' *tobu* 'to fly' and *yokogiru* 'to cross'—often with the meaning of English 'on,' 'across,' and 'through') the relevant location is expressed by the object marker *o*. A similar phenomenon is observed in English; *crossing the street*—where 'the street' does not take a locative preposition. Compare this with *working in the room*—where *the room* is preceded by the preposition *in* indicating location.

With some active verbs, both *o* and *de* can co-occur; but they convey different meanings. For example:

(a) *Kodomo-tachi wa kawa **o** oyoide mukoo gishi ni iku.*
子供たちは川を泳いで向こう岸に行く。
(Children swim across the river and reach the other side.)

(b) *Kodomotachi wa kawa **de** oyogu.*
子供たちは川で泳ぐ。
(Children swim in the river.)

When one swims across the river following basically a straight line, the object marker *o* is used, while when the swimming takes place in the river at various locations between the two banks, *de* is used.

Warning

The enumerative *to* connects only nouns and noun phrases. Do not use it to connect verbs, adjectives and clauses.

18. Word Order—1. Preferred Word Order

Target Expression

> *Ms. Turner will go to Hakata by Bullet Train.*
> **Taanaa-san wa Shinkansen de Hakata e ikimasu.**
> ターナーさんは新幹線で博多へ行きます。

Grammatical Explanation

Although the grammatical word order in Japanese is relatively free, there is a preferred order of elements within the sentence. First, topics, if they appear, come in the initial position. This is because by identifying a topic, both the speaker and listener align themselves to appreciate a common starting point. Recall the two characteristics regarding basic word order in Japanese, characteristics 1 (verb-final) and 6 (modifier precedes the modified). Under normal circumstances, verbal elements always come at the very end of the utterance. The preferred order is schematized below. Numbers under the column Roman Numeral II show the preferred order of elements within that slot.

I	II	III	IV
Topic +	1. temporal 2. locative 3. subject 4. joint action (*to*) 5. method (*de*) 6. starting point (*kara*) 7. direction (*ni, e*) 8. object (*o*)	+ Verbal/ Adjectival Predicate	+ Interactional Particles

Examples

(1) *Hara-san   wa   ashita   kodomo-tachi   to   densha   de*
      Ms. Hara   T   tomorrow   children   with   train   by

    Tookyoo   e   ikimasu   ne.
    Tokyo   to   go   IP

原さんはあした子供たちと電車で東京へ行きますね。
(Ms. Hara goes to Tokyo tomorrow with her children, doesn't she?)

(2) *Kodomo-tachi   wa   sensei   to   toshokan   ni   imasu   ne.*
      children   T   teacher with   library   at   there are   IP
子供たちは先生と図書館にいますね。
(Children are at the library with the teacher, aren't they?)

Again, the best strategy here is to memorize a few sentences which contain various correctly-ordered elements, and to use these sentences as reference points. Examples (1) and (2) will serve as a good start.

Practice

----
pianist   N   *pianisuto*   ピアニスト

By putting grammatical elements in a preferred order in Japanese, express the following.

1. Mr. Inoue is in that room. ☺ (In response to the question— "Where is Mr. Inoue?")
2. Bill will buy some fruit at the new supermarket.
3. A wonderful pianist will come to Tokyo from New York.

─────── Answers ───────

1. *Inoue-san wa ano heya ni iru yo.* ☺
   井上さんはあの部屋にいるよ。
2. *Biru-san wa atarashii suupaa de kudamono o kaimasu.*
   ビルさんは新しいスーパーでくだものを買います。
3. *Subarashii pianisuto ga Nyuuyooku kara Tookyoo e kimasu.* すばらしいピアニストがニューヨークから東京へ来ます。

Additional Information

As we have seen, the order of elements in the Japanese sentence is quite different from that of English. The difference in order is not limited to syntactic elements alone. Recall that in Japanese the family name (a more general group identification) precedes the given name (a more specific individual identification). In specifying addresses, Japanese starts from a larger area to a specific area, while in English the reverse is true. For example, *Tookyoo no Oota-ku* 'Tokyo's Ota Ward' versus Los Angeles, California. Likewise, addresses written on the envelopes and cards follow this basic principle. In Japanese, the larger area designation precedes the smaller area designation.

19. Temporal Expressions

Target Expressions

> *morning, today, this week*
>
> ### *asa, kyoo, konshuu*
> 朝，今日，今週

Grammatical Explanation

A host of time-indicating nouns can be used as adverbs modifying the verbs. A parallel phenomenon is observed in English where a time-indicating phrase such as *today* may be used as a noun in *today is Sunday*, as well as an adverb in *today I must work all day*. These phrases are mostly deictic, that is to say, they are specified by the speaker's relation to the here-and-now world.

List of Useful Temporal Expressions

1. *General*

asa	朝	morning
ima	今	now
itsumo	いつも	always
kesa	今朝	this morning
kon'ya	今夜	tonight
gogo	午後	afternoon
gozenchuu	午前中	morning, before noon
yuube	夕べ	last night
sakuban ◆	昨晩	last night
sakki	さっき	shortly before
soochoo ◆	早朝	early morning
hiruma	昼間	daytime
mayonaka	真夜中	midnight
yuugata	夕方	evening
yoru	夜	night

2. *A systematized list of temporal phrases*

The list below shows past, present and future phrases for (a) day, (b) week, (c) month and (d) year. For example, *ototoi* 'the day before yesterday,' *kinoo* 'yesterday,' *kyoo* 'today,' *ashita* 'tomorrow,' *asatte* 'the day after tomorrow.' The last column lists words 'every . . .' as in *mainichi* 'every day.' For the word 'tomorrow,' both *ashita* and *asu* are used with the former being more colloquial.

	−2	−1	now	+ 1	+ 2	every
(a)	ototoi	kinoo	kyoo	ashita/asu	asatte	mainichi
	おととい	きのう	今日	あした/あす	あさって	毎日
(b)	sensenshuu	senshuu	konshuu	raishuu	saraishuu	maishuu
	先々週	先週	今週	来週	さ来週	毎週

頁番号

68

(c)	sensengetsu	sengetsu	kongetsu	raigetsu	saraigetsu	maitsuki
	先々月	先月	今月	来月	さ来月	毎月
(d)	ototoshi	kyonen	kotoshi	rainen	sarainen	mainen
	おととし	去年	今年	来年	さ来年	毎年

3. _Four Seasons_ (may take temporal particle _ni_)

haru	春	spring
natsu	夏	summer
aki	秋	fall
huyu	冬	winter

4. _Days of the week_ (normally takes temporal particle _ni_)

getsuyoobi	月曜日	Monday
kayoobi	火曜日	Tuesday
suiyoobi	水曜日	Wednesday
mokuyoobi	木曜日	Thursday
kin'yoobi	金曜日	Friday
doyoobi	土曜日	Saturday
nichiyoobi	日曜日	Sunday

Examples

hayaku	早く	Adv	early
iroirona	いろいろな	Adj	various
koto	こと	N	thing(s)
au	会う	V	to see (a person)

(1) _Sasaki-san wa asa hayaku okimasu._
佐々木さんは，朝早く起きます。
(Mr. Sasaki gets up early in the morning.)

(2) _Itsumo koohii o nomimasu._
いつもコーヒーを飲みます。
(He always drinks coffee.)

(3) _Asa kara benkyoo-shimasu._
朝から勉強します。
(He begins studying in the morning.)

(4) _Gogo wa iroirona koto o shimasu._
午後はいろいろなことをします。
(In the afternoon he does various things.)

(5) *Getsuyoobi wa tenisu o shimasu.*
月曜日はテニスをします。
(On Mondays he plays tennis.)

(6) *Suiyoobi wa yuugata tomodachi ni aimasu.*[1]
水曜日は夕方友だちに会います。
(On Wednesdays he meets his friends in the evening.)

(7) *Kin'yoobi wa uchi ni imasu.*
金曜日は家にいます。
(On Fridays he stays home.)

[1]. The verb *au* 'to see someone, to meet someone,' takes *ni* as an object marker. This usage is idiomatic; the use of *ni* will be explained again in Entry 29.

Practice

Patricia	PN	*Patorishia*	パトリシア
church	N	*kyookai*	教会
to go on	V	*shutchoo-*	出張する
a business trip		*suru*	

Using the temporal phrases and placing them in the preferred position, describe the following.

1. Patricia goes to church every week.
2. I eat ham-and-eggs with toast every morning.
3. Ms. Sasaki is in that store now.
4. I am going to Kyoto on business two weeks from now.

——— Answers ———

1. *Patorishia-san wa maishuu kyookai e ikimasu.*
パトリシアさんは毎週教会へ行きます。
2. *(Watashi wa) maiasa toosuto to hamueggu o tabemasu.*
(私は)毎朝トーストとハムエッグを食べます。
3. *Sasaki-san wa ima ano mise ni imasu.*
佐々木さんは今あの店にいます。
4. *Saraishuu Kyooto e shutchoo-shimasu.*
さ来週京都へ出張します。

Warning

Although some of the temporal expressions introduced here do not normally take the temporal particle *ni*, there are some cases where they must, as in days of the week. As will be mentioned later, when a temporal expression contains numerals (as in the date of the month and time of the day), the temporal particle *ni* is required. Some temporal phrases have slightly different meanings depending on whether or not they are followed by temporal particles. For example, *san-nen kan* 'for three years' points to the whole duration of three years, while *san-nen kan ni* 'in three years/within three years' may point to a specific time within those three years. Among temporal nouns without numerals, some may be optionally accompanied by *ni*, as in *haru ni*, in which case the time defined by the expression is in focus or in contrast with other possibilities (for example, in contrast with winter).

20. Modifying—1. Nominal Modifiers with *No*

Target Expressions

> *a Japanese car, the author of this book*
> **nihon no kuruma, kono hon no chosha**
> 日本の車，この本の著者
>
> [N + *no*]

Grammatical Explanation

Regarding the modification of nouns, we have already learned [Adj-*i*] in Japanese. Here is another way to modify or explain about a noun phrase. Place a [N + *no*] before the noun to be modified (refer to characteristic 6). *No* is a particle; we will call *no* used in this way as a linker (abbreviated as L) which links nouns. In the target expression *nihon* 'Japan' and *no* are placed before the noun *kuruma* 'car.' The phrase *nihon no* describes what kind of car it is. *Kono hon no chosha* 'the author of this book' is a combination of a phrase *kono hon* (which consists of a demonstrative *kono* specifying *hon*) plus *no* which in turn specifies *chosha* 'author.'

To go a step further, we can generate phrases with multiple linkers. For example:

(a)

Nihon	no	kudamono	no	hinshu	no	namae
Japan	L	fruit	L	variety	L	name

日本の果物の品種の名前

(names of the varieties of fruits of Japan)

Again, it is important to remember that the order of nouns in Japanese is the reverse of the English [noun + *of* + noun] structure. The literal translation may be something like "Japan's fruits' varieties' names" in which case the order is identical. Thinking of the [N + *no*] pattern as equivalent to the English [N + possessive marker (')] may be helpful in confirming the order of nouns, as in "Japan's fruits' varieties' names."

The use of *no* discussed here applies to pronouns as well; for example, *watashi no hon* '(lit. I's book) my book,' *kare no otoosan* 'his father.' Again, pronoun forms are not as frequently used in Japanese. Recall that where we translated 'my room' earlier, we used only *heya* without *watashi no*. Unless there is a special need, these pronominal forms are avoided in Japanese. It is also possible to add *no* to a noun phrase which already has particles attached. For example, *Tookyoo kara no tegami* 'a letter from Tokyo,' where *Tookyoo kara* 'from Tokyo' is linked to *tegami* 'letter' by the linker *no*. The [N + *no*] structure can modify noun phrases which are already modified by adjectives; for example, *Yamada-san no atarashii kuruma* 'Yamada's new car,' and *Tookyoo no atarashii depaato* 'Tokyo's new department store.'

The [N + *no*] phrase is also used to express apposition, that is, in an expression such as *musume no Yooko* which means 'my daughter, Yoko.' In a broader perspective, we see a common semantic origin in this use of *no* as the one we already noted above in that the phrase *musume no* specifies and adds information to *Yooko*.

Examples

Sarii	サリー	PN	Sally

(1) *Kore wa Watanabe-san no heya desu ne.*

これは渡辺さんの部屋ですね。

(This is Mr. Watanabe's room, isn't it?)

(2)

Amerika-jin	no	tomodachi	no	Sarii-san	to
American	L	friend	L	Sally	with

depaato		e	ikimasu.
department store		to	go

アメリカ人の友だちのサリーさんとデパートへ行きます。

(I'm going to a department store with my American friend, Sally.)

(3) *Huransu no wain wa oishii ne.* ☺
フランスのワインはおいしいね。

(French wine is delicious, isn't it?)

Practice

----
shachoo	社長	**N**	company president
ojoosan	お嬢さん	**N**	(someone's) daughter
Yooroppa	ヨーロッパ	**PN**	Europe
totemo	とても	**Adv**	very, extremely

Fill in the blanks with appropriate particles so that the Japanese sentence will correspond to the English version provided.

1. *Kono kaisha (   ) shachoo (   ) Amerika-jin desu.*
   この会社　　　　社長　　　　　アメリカ人です。
   (The president of this company is American.)[*1]

2. *Sasaki-san (   ) ojoosan wa rainen (   ) aki Yooroppa (   )*
   佐々木さん　　　お嬢さんは　来年　　　　秋　ヨーロッパ
   ikimasu.
   行きます。
   (Mrs. Sasaki's daughter goes to Europe next fall.)

3. *Nihongo (   ) sensei wa totemo kibishii-desu.*
   日本語　　　　先生はとてもきびしいです。
   (The Japanese language teacher is very strict.)

4. *Ano hito (   ) namae wa Tamiya-san desu.*
   あの人　　　　名前は　　　田宮さんです。
   (That person's name is Ms. Tamiya.)

```
───── Answers ─────
1. no, wa    2. no, no, e   3. no    4. no
   の、は        の、の、へ      の        の
```

[*1.] The word order of modification in this English sentence is different from sentences 2 and 3. In English modification, some modifying elements precede the modified. These include adjectives, possessive pronouns, and noun modification. When the [N + *of* + N] structure is used as in 1, what is modified precedes the modifying [*of* + N] In 1, *of this company* modifies *the president*. In Japanese all modifying elements precede the modified,

and therefore, in 1. there is a discrepancy regarding the order of the modifying and the modified in the original English and Japanese translation
(refer to characteristic 6). What is important is to discover which modifies
what in English and then to create a Japanese expression that corresponds
to it, regardless of the English surface word order.

Additional Information

There are some conventionalized uses and non-uses of the linking particle
no, which are exceptions to the phenomenon mentioned above. First, there
are groups of words that can appear either as [N + *no* + N] or as complex
nominals; for example, *seiyoo* 'Western world' and *bunka* 'culture' may
appear as *seiyoo no bunka* or as a complex nominal *seiyoobunka*. There
are some cases where the linking *no* cannot be used. For example, a complex noun *nyuugakushiken* (combination of *nyuugaku* 'entrance' and
shiken 'examination') but not *⃰nyuugaku no shiken*; and *shakaishugi*
'socialism' (combination of *shakai* 'society' and *shugi* 'ideology') but not
⃰shakai no shugi. In some cases *no*-linked nouns and complex nominals differ in meaning: *Tookyoo Daigaku* 'Tokyo University,' and *Tookyoo no
daigaku* 'university in Tokyo,' for example. These conventions must be
learned one by one.

21. Inquiring—1. Questions and Interrogative Words

Target Expressions

> *Do you go? (Are you going?)*
> > **Ikimasu ka.**
> > 行きますか。
>
> *When is the exam?*
> > **Shiken wa itsu desu ka.**
> > 試験はいつですか。
>
> *Which one is Mr. Yamada's book?*
> > **Dore ga Yamada-san no hon desu ka.**
> > どれが山田さんの本ですか。

Grammatical Explanation

In phrasing a formal question, the particles *ka* (glossed as Q) is added at the end of the sentence. *Ka* may follow both formal and informal endings of verbs, existential verbs and [Adj-*i*]. The [V/Adj informal + *ka*] combination, however, is extremely blunt. For practical purposes, only use the [V/Adj formal + *ka*] combination. For the be-verb *da*, only the [*desu* + *ka*] combination is possible; *da ka* is an incorrect form. The interrogative particle *ka* receives a slight rising intonation.

When an interrogative word (question words equivalent to English 'what,' 'when,' 'where,' and so forth) is inserted, unlike English, it is inserted in the place where its answer would normally appear. For example, in *shiken wa ashita desu* 'the exam is tomorrow,' the word *itsu* 'when' is inserted in the same place where the temporal phrase *ashita* 'tomorrow' appears. In Japanese, there is no need to start questions with interrogative words. Simply follow the principle of the preferred word order studied earlier (Entry 18).

In conversation when asking a question, a rising intonation at the end of the utterance—without *ka*—may be used. Thus *iku* or *ikimasu* with rising intonation (on the last mora only) means 'do you go?' For sentences with *da*, delete *da* and just use rising intonation, *shiken wa ashita?* suffices as a plain version of *shiken wa ashita desu ka?* *Shiken wa ashita da?* must be avoided. For [Adj-*i*], *takai?* and *takai-desu?* may be used, the latter being a more gentle style used predominantly by female speakers.

At this point let's look more closely at the two target sentences *shiken wa itsu desu ka?* and *dore ga Yamada-san no hon desu ka?* Notice that in these sentences we find the topic marker *wa* and subject marker *ga*. In the question *shiken wa itsu desu ka?*, new information (the time of the exam) is sought about the topic, that is, *shiken* 'exam.' Therefore *shiken* is marked as a topic. In other words, exam is the starting point of this question, a piece of information assumed to be shared between the speaker and the listener. In the question *dore ga Yamada-san no hon desu ka?*, the information sought is the identification of Yamada's book. Therefore *dore* is not marked with a topic marker; the information corresponding to *dore* is the information sought. *Dore* is marked with a case marker appropriate to the case defined in the sentence structure, in this case the subject marker *ga*. The answer to this question is constructed with *ga*; *kore ga Yamada-san no hon desu* 'this is Mr. Yamada's book.' Again this is because *kore* 'this' constitutes a new piece of information, a newly provided answer. Although *kore* itself is a deictic expression and therefore has potential to become the topic marked with *wa*, *kore* is given as a piece of new information in this specific context.

List of Interrogative Words

Pronouns

ikutsu	いくつ	how many
ikura	いくら	how much
dare	誰	who
doko	どこ	which place, where
dochira	どちら	which one (of the two), where [politer than *doko*]
dore	どれ	which one (among many)
nani	何	what

Adverbs

doo	どう	how
ikaga	いかが	how [polite]
naze/dooshite	なぜ/どうして	why
nande ☺	なんで	why

For forming a question to ask which of the two, use the pattern [N + *to* + N + *to* + *dochira ga*]. For instance:

(a) <u>*Kore*</u> <u>*to*</u> <u>*sore*</u> <u>*to*</u> <u>*dochira*</u> <u>*ga*</u> <u>*oishii-desu*</u> <u>*ka.*</u>
    <u>this</u> <u>and</u> <u>that</u> <u>and</u> <u>which</u> <u>S</u> <u>delicious</u> <u>Q</u>
    これとそれとどちらがおいしいですか。
    (Which is delicious, this or that?)

For forming alternate questions, simply repeat single questions.

(b) A: *Takai-desu ka. Yasui-desu ka.*
        高いですか。安いですか。
        (Is it expensive or inexpensive?)
    B: *Takai-desu.*
        高いです。
        (It is expensive.)

(c) A: *Kyoo ikimasu ka. Ashita ikimasu ka.*
        今日行きますか。あした行きますか。
        (Do you go today or tomorrow?)
    B: *Ashita ikimasu.*
        あした行きます。
        (I'll go tomorrow.)

Examples

---
byooin	病院	N	hospital
yo	よ	IP	[emphatic interactional particle]
---

(1) A:
Hara-san	wa	itsu	dare to	doko	e
Mr. Hara	T	when	who with	where	to

ikimasu	ka.
go	Q

原さんはいつ誰とどこへ行きますか。

(As for Mr. Hara, when, with whom, and where is he going?)

B: *Raishuu Sumisu-san to Igirisu e ikimasu.*
来週スミスさんとイギリスへ行きます。
(I will go to England with Mr. Smith next week.)

(2) A: *Are wa nan desu ka.*
あれは何ですか。
(What is that?)

B: *Aa, are wa byooin desu yo.*
ああ、あれは病院ですよ。
(Ah, that is a hospital.)

A: *Soo desu ka. Ookii byooin desu ne.*
そうですか。大きい病院ですね。
(Is that so? It's a large hospital, isn't it?)

Practice

---
dictionary	N	jisho	辞書
Narita airport	PN	Narita kuukoo	成田空港
breakfast	N	asagohan	朝ごはん
---

1. Ask your friend about the following; provide possible answers to questions b, d and e.
   a. the price of this large dictionary
   b. what your friend buys at the department store
   c. with whom your friend goes to Narita airport
   d. where your friend has breakfast
   e. whether your friend goes to San Francisco next month ☺

2. Ask your friend what he/she does at the following times. How will he/she answer?
   a. tomorrow
   b. Thursdays
   c. tonight
   d. next week ☺

Answers

1a.   *Kono ookii jisho wa ikura desu ka.*
      この大きい辞書はいくらですか。

b. A: *Depaato de nani o kaimasu ka.*
        デパートで何を買いますか。

   B: *Atarashii jisho o kaimasu.* 新しい辞書を買います。

c.   *Dare to Narita kuukoo e ikimasu ka.*
      誰と成田空港へ行きますか。

d. A: *Doko de asagohan o tabemasu ka.*^{*1}
        どこで朝ごはんを食べますか。

   B: *Hoteru de tabemasu.* ホテルで食べます。

e. A: *Raigetsu Sanhuranshisuko iku?* ☺
        来月サンフランシスコ行く？

   B: *Iku yo.* ☺ 行くよ。

--- Some Sample Answers ---

2a. A: *Ashita nani o shimasu ka.*   あした何をしますか。

   B: *Tookyoo e ikimasu.*   東京へ行きます。

b. A: *Mokuyoobi wa nani o shimasu ka.*
       木曜日は何をしますか。

   B: *Piano no renshuu o shimasu*   ピアノの練習をします。

c. A: *Kon'ya nani o shimasu ka.*   今夜何をしますか。

   B: *Tomodachi ni aimasu.*   友だちに会います。

d. A: *Raishuu nani suru?* ☺   来週何する？

   B: *Shinkansen de Kyooto iku.* ☺   新幹線で京都行く。

---

*1.   It is possible to say *asagohan wa doko de tabemasu ka?* for this question. This question is more appropriate when you wish to make *asagohan* the topic. If not, *doko de asagohan o tabemasu ka* is fine, in which case the unmentioned topic phrase *anata wa* constitutes the latent topic.

Additional Information

Other informal questions are used in casual conversation. Among males, *kai* and *no kai* are used for yes/no questions, and *n dai* are used for questions with interrogative words. *Kai, no kai* and *n dai* follow informal verb forms as in (a) and (b). The be-verb (*da*) preceding these forms is deleted as in (c). For gentle style used predominantly by females, the particle *no* is sometimes added to informal or formal verb forms, transforming the statements into questions. For sentences ending with informal *da*, instead of *＊da no*, *na no* is used.

(a) *Iku no kai?* ☺ M
   行くのかい？
   (Are you going?)

(b) *Itsu iku n dai?* ☺ M
   いつ行くんだい？
   (When are you going?)

(c) *Ano hito dare dai?* ☺ M
   あの人誰だい？
   (Who's that?)

(d) *Iku no?* ☺ F
   行くの？
   (Are you going?)

(e) *Kore nan na no?* ☺ F
   これ何なの？
   (What's this?)

(f) *Moo odekake desu no?* ☺ F
   もうお出かけですの？
   ([lit. Already leaving, is it?] Are you going out?)

Another point to be remembered: when the question marker *ka* appears with falling intonation, it marks a statement which acknowledges something curious not known before. For example:

(g) *Aa, Tajima-san desu ka.* ↘
   ああ，田島さんですか。
   (Oh, you are Ms. Tajima, I see.)

22.   Verbal Predicate—3.   Past

> Ms. Kasai went to the art museum yesterday.
> **Kasai-san wa kinoo bijutsukan e ikimashita.**
> 河西さんはきのう美術館へ行きました。
>
> [Vpast]

Grammatical Explanation

The verb form we have studied so far primarily refers to the description of present and future events and states. Although some argue that Japanese does not have a strict "tense system," the form to be introduced here is best understood as the past tense form of the verb since it functions similarly to English past and (past) perfect tenses (refer to characteristic 8). Formal and informal past tense forms are derived as follows:

U-verbs

formal: replace -u with -imashita
informal: verbs ending with -ku, replace -ku with -ita
verbs ending with -gu, replace -gu with -ida
verbs ending with -u, -tsu and -ru, replace them with -tta.
verbs ending with -nu, -bu, and -mu, replace them with -nda
verbs ending with -su, replace -su with -shita

RU-verbs

formal: take off -ru, and add -mashita
informal: take off -ru, and add -ta

Irregular Verbs

formal: suru takes shimashita, kuru takes kimashita
informal: suru takes shita, kuru takes kita

Existential Verbs

formal: iru takes imashita, aru takes arimashita
informal: iru takes ita, aru takes atta

Be-verb

da takes deshita (formal) and datta (informal)

"*Ta*" Song

It is easiest to memorize the conjugation of [Vinformal past] forms if you put it to the tune of "John Brown's Body" —what I call the "*Ta*" song. (For gerundive forms, change *ta* and *da* to *te* and *de*, respectively.)

(1) *taberu—tabeta*; *miru—mita*;
(2) *-tsu, -ru, -u—-tta*; *-su—-shita*;
(3) *-ku, -gu—-ita, -ida*;
(4) *-mu, -bu, -nu—-nda*;
(5) *suru—shita, kuru—kita.*

Line (1) shows *RU*-verb changes, and lines (2) through (4) show verb final changes for *U*-verbs. Line (5) lists irregular verb changes for *suru* and *kuru*.

Purposes of the Past Tense Form

The past tense form is generally used for the following purposes:

1. *Descriptions of past events:*

(1a) <u>Kinoo</u> <u>wa</u> <u>ame</u> <u>ga</u> **hurimashita**. (*hurimashita* is past
yesterday T rain S fell   tense of *huru* 'to fall')
きのうは雨が**降りました**。
(It rained yesterday.)

2. *Commentary on fulfillment of a wish or desire:*

(2a) *Basu ga* **kita***!* (*kita* is past tense of *kuru* 'to come')
バスが**来た**！
(The bus came!)

This expression implies that you were waiting for the bus, and finally you see the bus coming. It refers to the current realization of a wish.

(2a) *Hontooni yoku* **hareta***!*
本当によく**晴れた**！ (*hareta* is past tense of *hareru* 'to clear up')
([lit. It cleared up completely.] How nice, it has cleared up!)

3. *Reaffirmation of an assumption:*

(3a) *Tanaka-san* **deshita** *ne.* (*deshita* is past tense of *da*)
田中さんでしたね。
(You are [lit. were] Mrs. Tanaka, right?)

4. *Expressions of urging someone to act or to perform*—used only in situations which allow for manipulation (only in past informal forms):

(4a) *Saa, **katta, katta**!* (*katta* is past tense of *kau* 'to buy')
さあ，買った，買った！
(Come on, buy these!)

(4b) *Kodomo-tachi wa **kaetta, kaetta**!* (*kaetta* is past tense of *kaeru*
子供たちは帰った，帰った！　　　 'to return')
(Children, come on, go home!)

Examples

Howaito-san	ホワイトさん	PN	Mr. White
yoku	よく	Adv	often, a lot, well
ichinichijuu	一日中	Adv	all day long
soo da	そうだ	V	that's right
hurusato	ふるさと	N	hometown
Yamanashi	山梨	PN	Yamanashi, name of prefecture

----

(1) A: *Kinoo wa nani o shimashita ka.*
きのうは何をしましたか。
(What did you do yesterday?)

　　 B: *Hon o yomimashita.*
本を読みました。
(I read a book.)

(2) *Howaito-san wa ototoi kara kinoo made Kyooto ni imashita.*
ホワイトさんはおとといからきのうまで京都にいました。
(Mr. White was in Kyoto from the day before yesterday until yesterday.)

(3) A: *Kinoo wa yoku hurimashita nee.*
きのうはよく降りましたねえ。
(It rained a lot yesterday, didn't it?)

　　 B: *Ee, hontooni. Ichinichijuu uchi ni imashita yo.*
ええ，本当に。一日中家にいましたよ。
(Yes, indeed. I was at home all day.)

(4) *Aa, soo da, Kanai-san no hurusato wa Yamanashi deshita ne.*
ああ，そうだ，金井さんのふるさとは山梨でしたね。
(Oh, that's right, Mr. Kanai, your hometown is Yamanashi, right?)

Additional Information

The [Vpast] has different meanings depending on whether the verb is active or stative, especially when the verb appears in subordinate clauses. When the active [Vpast] appears in a subordinate clause, it expresses the completion of action prior to the tense defined by the main verb, while the active [Vnon-past] indicates an action not yet completed prior to the tense defined by the main verb.

(a) <u>*Ano*</u>   <u>*hito*</u>   <u>*ni*</u> ***atta*** <u>*kara*</u>   <u>*chichi*</u>   <u>*ni*</u>   <u>*denwa-shita.*</u>
that   person   O   met because   my father   IO   called
あの人に**会った**から父に電話した。
(Because I met him, I called my father.)

(b) *Ano hito ni **au** kara chichi ni denwa-shita.*
あの人に**会う**から父に電話した。
(Because I was going to meet him, I called my father.)

Additional information regarding the tense in subordinate clauses will be given when necessary throughout this book.

Mainly because of the phenomenon observed in examples above, some grammarians call the Japanese [Vpast] a "perfective." We will continue to call it [Vpast] because in case of stative verbs, [Vpast] does not carry a strong sense of "perfectiveness." Note also that although [Vpast] in simple sentences can carry a strong perfective sense—particularly when accompanied by an adverb *moo* 'already'—as shown in (c), it can also refer to a straightforward past-tense event as in (d).

(c) *Moo tabeta?*
もう食べた？
([lit. Did you eat?] Have you eaten already?)

(d) *Kinoo ikimashita.*
きのう行きました。
(I went yesterday.)

Practice

1. Describe in Japanese the following activities that took place in the past.
   a. your drinking sake with Mr. Sakuma last night
   b. your eating some delicious chocolate ☺
   c. your staying late at the company

2. You are talking to Mr. Sasaki and are wondering when he came to the United States. How will you ask a question? Also provide an answer.

3. Ask your friend what he/she did at the following times. How will he/she respond?
   a. yesterday
   b. last week
   c. this morning
   d. last summer

--------- Answers ---------

1a. *Yuube Sakuma-san to sake o nomimashita.*
   夕べ佐久間さんと酒を飲みました。

b. *Oishii chokoreeto tabeta.* ☺ おいしいチョコレート食べた。

c. *Osoku made kaisha ni imashita.* おそくまで会社にいました。

2. A: *Sasaki-san wa itsu Amerika e kimashita ka.*
      佐々木さんはいつアメリカへ来ましたか。

   B: *Kyonen kimashita.* 去年来ました。

--------- Some Sample Answers ---------

3a A: *Kinoo nani o shimashita ka.* きのう何をしましたか。
   B: *Goruhu o shimashita.* ゴルフをしました。

b. A: *Senshuu doko e ikimashita ka.* 先週どこへ行きましたか。
   B: *Kyooto no daigaku e ikimashita.* 京都の大学へ行きました。

c. A: *Kesa nani o tabemashita ka.* 今朝何を食べましたか。
   B: *Meron o tabemashita.* メロンを食べました。

d. A: *Kyonen no natsu wa nani o shimashita ka.*
      去年の夏は何をしましたか。

   B: *Yooroppa e ikimashita.* ヨーロッパへ行きました。

23. Verbal Predicate—4. Future

Target Expression

I'll go to Japan next year.

Rainen nihon e ikimasu.
来年日本へ行きます。

[Vnon-past]

Grammatical Explanation

As mentioned earlier, the non-past verb form is used not only to express the present tense but also to indicate definite future events and actions. This is why we prefer the term, "non-past," which describes both present and future tenses. Here we examine this and other ways to express the future tense in Japanese.

First, the [Vnon-past] form describes definite future. It expresses the speaker's strong belief that those events are likely to occur. When the subject is in the first-person, it also expresses the speaker's intentions.

For expressing the speaker's uncertainty about future events and states, use [Vbasic] followed by auxiliary verb [AuxV] -*daroo* or its formal version -*deshoo*. For formal style, use [Vformal non-past] followed by -*deshoo*. -*Daroo* (-*deshoo*) expresses uncertainty. When combined with [Vnon-past] (including existential verbs *iru* and *aru*), this strategy expresses one's doubt about the future events and states described. For the be-verb, replace *da* with *daroo/deshoo* for expressing uncertainty. We will study -*daroo*/ -*deshoo* in detail in Entry 99.

Other future expressions are also used, such as *rainen nihon e iku tsumori/yotei desu* 'I intend to go to Japan next year,' but these expressions will be learned later.

Practice

later	Adv	*ato de*	あとで
to clean	V	*katazukeru*	かたづける

1. Describe your intentions to do the following in the future and specify when:
   a. eat a hamburger
   b. watch television
   c. clean your room

2. You are uncertain of tomorrow's weather, but you feel it will probably clear up. How will you express this to your colleague?

─────── Answers ───────

1a. *Ato de hanbaagaa o tabemasu.* あとでハンバーガーを食べます。
  b. *Kon'ya terebi o mimasu.* 今夜テレビを見ます。
  c. *Ato de heya o katazukemasu.* あとで部屋をかたづけます。
   Ashita heya o katazukemasu. あした部屋をかたづけます。
2. *Ashita wa hareru-deshoo.* あしたは晴れるでしょう。

Additional Information

The auxiliary verb -*daroo* is also used for making the conversation go more smoothly and comfortably. By expressing some doubt, -*daroo* gives a hesitant and therefore less domineering flavor to one's comments and opinions. Instead of asking, for example, *Shinjuku eki wa doko desu ka?* 'where is Shinjuku station?,' *Shinjuku eki wa doko deshoo ka?* may be used. This is less straightforward and shows the speaker's consideration toward others. Another extended use of -*daroo* is to show sympathy toward or understanding of another's feelings. Instead of saying *isogashii-desu ne* 'you are busy,' *isogashii-deshoo ne* is preferred to mean something like 'oh, you must be busy. . .' showing sympathy. This contrasts with American English in which softness and sympathy are primarily communicated by intonation and tone of voice.

*   *   *   *   *

"Keisatsu no mono desu."　「警察の者です。」
"Donna goyoo deshoo ka."　「どんなご用でしょうか。」
([lit. I'm from the Police] Police.)
([lit. What kind of business is it?] What can I do for you?)
　　　　　　　　　　　　　　　　—Tanikawa, 1982, p.55.

In this example, *deshoo ka* is used in a question sentence; it functions to make the question less straightforward, and therefore, softer.

24. Expressions of Location

Target Expressions

> *in front of the bank, inside the room*
> ***ginkoo no mae, heya no naka***
> 銀行の前，部屋の中

Grammatical Explanation

Noun phrases linked with *no* and locative particles are used to describe locations. For example, a noun *naka* 'inside' is modified by an [N + *no*] struc-

86

ture. For expressing 'inside the box,' *hako no naka* is used (be warned of the word-order here). Here is a list of common locative noun phrases.

List of Locative Expressions

tsukue	机	N	desk
eki	駅	N	station
hako	箱	N	box
kawa	川	N	river

aida	間	*biru no* **aida** (between the buildings)	ビルの**間**
ue	上	*tsukue no* **ue** (on [top of] the desk)	机の**上**
ushiro	うしろ	*tatemono no* **ushiro** (behind the building)	建物の**うしろ**
saki	先	*kono* **saki** (up ahead)	この**先**
shita	下	*tsukue no* **shita** (under the desk)	机の**下**
soba	そば	*eki no* **soba** (near the station)	駅の**そば**
chikaku	近く	*eki no* **chikaku** (near the station)	駅の**近く**
tonari	となり	*uchi no* **tonari** (next door to my house)	家の**となり**
naka	中	*hako no* **naka** (inside the box)	箱の**中**
mae	前	*uchi no* **mae** ([in] front of the house)	家の**前**
mukoo	向こう	*kawa no* **mukoo** (beyond the river)	川の**向こう**
yoko	横	*tatemono no* **yoko** (beside the building)	建物の**横**

Both *naka* and *hako no naka* are noun phrases. Depending on how the location functions in a predicate, *hako no naka* takes any of the grammatical particles. Thus, we have *hako no naka ni* 'inside the box,' *hako no naka e* 'into the box,' and *hako no naka kara* 'from inside the box.' *Hako no naka* can also become the grammatical topic, subject or object as in *hako no naka o miru* 'to look inside the box.'

The locative phrase can also appear preceding the be-verb *da* as in *naihu to fooku wa hikidashi no naka desu* 'knives and forks are inside the drawer.' Note that in this use, the locative particle *ni* is not used. In other words, in Japanese there are two ways for describing locations, although the English translation is identical. Recall the concept of topic in interpreting this example. Here 'knives and forks' are not the location 'inside the drawer.' The topic-comment relation requires extended interpretation as discussed in Entry 15.

(a) <u>Naihu</u> <u>to</u> <u>fooku</u> <u>wa</u> <u>hikidashi</u> <u>no</u> <u>naka</u> **ni** **arimasu**.
    knife and fork T drawer L inside there are
ナイフとフォークは引き出しの中にあります。
(Knives and forks are in the drawer.—This is closer to 'there are knives and forks in the drawer.')

(b) *Naihu to fooku wa hikidashi no naka* **desu**.
ナイフとフォークは引き出しの中です。
(Knives and forks are in the drawer.)

Examples

oku	置く	V	to put
hon'ya(-san)	本屋(さん)	N	bookstore
Jimu-san	ジムさん	PN	Jim
au	会う	V	to meet, to see

(1)   *Tsukue no ue ni waapuro o okimasu.*
机の上にワープロを置きます。
(I put a word processor on the desk.)

Tsukue no shita ni wa waapuro no hako o okimasu.
机の下にはワープロの箱を置きます。
(I will put the box of the word processor under the desk.)

(2) A: *Asoko ni hon'ya-san ga arimasu ne.*
あそこに本屋さんがありますね。
(There is a bookstore over there, right?)

   B: *Doko desu ka.*
どこですか。
(Where is it?)

   A: <u>Ano</u> <u>ookii</u> <u>biru</u> <u>no</u> <u>tonari</u> <u>desu.</u>
      that large building L next to is
あの大きいビルのとなりです。
(Next to that large building.)

B: *Aa, arimasu.*
ああ、あります。
(Ah, there is.)

A: *Ano hon'ya-san de kinoo Jimu-san ni aimashita yo.*
あの本屋さんできのうジムさんに会いましたよ。
(I saw Jim at that bookstore yesterday.)

B: *Hontoo desu ka.*
本当ですか。
(Really?)

Practice

```
-------------------------------------------------------------
telephone         N     denwa          電話
Nakano station    PN    Nakano-eki     中野駅
lobby             N     robii          ロビー
-------------------------------------------------------------
```

Based on the sketch, make a question-answer pair to identify the location of the items listed below.

Items:
1. telephone
2. post office
3. department store
4. children
5. restaurant in the hotel

—— Some Sample Answers ——
1. A: *Denwa wa doko ni arimasu ka.* 電話はどこにありますか。
   B: *Nakano-eki no mae desu.* 中野駅の前です。

2. A: *Yuubinkyoku wa doko desu ka.* 郵便局はどこですか。

   B: *Depaato no tonari desu yo.* デパートのとなりですよ。

3. A: *Depaato wa hoteru no tonari desu ka.*
   デパートはホテルのとなりですか。

   B: *Iie. Yuubinkyoku no tonari desu.*
   いいえ，郵便局のとなりです。

4. A: *Kodomo-tachi wa doko ni imasu ka.*
   子供たちはどこにいますか。

   B: *Yuubinkyoku no mae ni imasu.* 郵便局の前にいます。

5. A: *Hoteru no resutoran wa doko desu ka.*
   ホテルのレストランはどこですか。

   B: *Robii no ue desu.* ロビーの上です。

25. Indefinite Pronoun *No*

Target Expression

> *I bought the expensive one.*
> ***Takai no o kaimashita.***
> 高いのを買いました。
>
> [modifier + *no*]

Grammatical Explanation

The indefinite pronoun *no* (different from the linker *no*) functions like the English indefinite pronoun "one," and "ones." *No* cannot be used alone, nor with demonstratives alone; it must be accompanied by a modifier. As shown in the target expression, *takai no* 'expensive one' may be used when specification of what is expensive is already shared among interactants. Therefore it is unnecessary and is considered redundant to specify it with a regular noun, for example, *takai kuruma*.

No, when combined with personal pronouns and nouns indicating possessor, adds the meaning of possession in two ways. For example, first, *watashi no* is used independently to mean 'mine.' Second, *watashi no* means 'my' when it precedes a noun, for example, *watashi no okane* 'my money' (in this case *no* is a linker). Note other examples of the indefinite pronoun *no*; *ano hito no* 'his,' *Yamada-san no* 'Ms. Yamada's,' and so

90

forth. When the indefinite pronoun *no* is preceded by demonstratives such as *kono*, instead of *kono no, kore* must be used.

Examples

(1)　*Koko ni ookii no ga arimasu yo.*
　　ここに大きいのがありますよ。
　　(Here is the large one.)

(2) A:　*Akai no to shiroi no to dochira ga ii-desu ka.*
　　　赤いのと白いのとどちらがいいですか。
　　　(Which one is better, the red one or the white one?)
　　B:　*Akai no ga ii-desu.*
　　　赤いのがいいです。
　　　(The red one is good [for me].)

(3) A:　*Dare no desu ka.* (holding a book)
　　　誰のですか。
　　　(Whose is this?)
　　B:　*Sumisu-san no desu.*
　　　スミスさんのです。
　　　(That is Mr. Smith's.)

Practice

Create a question-response pair for each situation.

1. There were two melons (*meron*) on the kitchen counter. This morning you find only the smaller one. Your roommate gave the large one to her friend next door. You are wondering where the large one is, and you ask:

2. You have two balls, one red and the other white. You want to give your friend whichever one she likes, and you ask: ☺

3. At a family get-together, food is served. Your nephew is wondering where his (share) of the dessert is on the table, and he asks: ☺

―――― Some Example Answers ――――
1. A: *Ookii meron wa doko desu ka.* 大きいメロンはどこですか。
   B: *Ookii no wa tomodachi ni agemashita.*
      大きいのは友だちにあげました。
2. A: *Akai no to shiroi no to dochira ga ii.* ☺F
      赤いのと白いのとどちらがいい？
   B: *Shiroi no ga ii wa.*[1] ☺F　白いのがいいわ。
3. A: *Boku no dore?* 僕のどれ？ (or *Boku no doko?* 僕のどこ？)
      ☺M

B: *Kore yo.* これよ。(or *Koko yo.* ここよ。) ☺F
Kore da yo. これだよ。(or *Koko da yo.* ここだよ。) ☺M

---

*1. The sentence-final *wa* pronounced in a high tone is an interactional particle used by female speakers. It adds a mild confirmation to the statement and characterizes the speech as being feminine. *Wa* may be used by males to add mild confirmation if it is pronounced in a low tone although this use is much less frequent.

26. Negating—1. Negation of Verbs

Target Expression

> *I'm not going to the office today.*
> **Kyoo wa kaisha e ikimasen.**
> 今日は会社へ行きません。

Grammatical Explanation

To form negation in Japanese, verb endings are changed into negative forms (refer to characteristic 8). Japanese does not operate like English, which negates with [auxiliary verbs + *not*] as in *do/does/did not*. Negation in Japanese is somewhat similar to the English process of adding negative prefixes such as *discourage*, and *uncover*, except that in Japanese, the endings of the verbs are changed to form the negative. Negative verb forms in Japanese are as follows:

U-verbs

informal non-past:	replace the final vowel with -*anai*
	(For *U*-verbs ending in a [vowel + -*u*],
	replace the final verb by -*wanai*.)
formal non-past:	replace -*masu* of -*masu* form with -*masen*
informal past:	replace -*nai* of -*anai* form by -*nakatta*
formal past:	add -*deshita* to -*masen* form

RU-verbs

informal non-past:	replace -ru by -nai
formal non-past:	replace -masu of -masu form by -masen
informal past:	replace -nai by -nakatta
formal past:	add -deshita immediately after -masen

Existential Verbs

Iru follows RU-verb conjugation. For aru:

informal non-past:	nai (There is no form *aranai.)
formal non-past:	arimasen
informal past:	nakatta
formal past:	arimasen-deshita

Irregular Verbs

informal non-past:	suru takes shinai, kuru takes konai
formal non-past:	suru takes shimasen, kuru takes kimasen
informal past:	suru takes shita, kuru takes kita
formal past:	suru takes shimashita, kuru takes kimashita

Be-verb

informal non-past:	dewa-nai, ja-nai (contracted form)
formal non-past:	dewa-arimasen, ja-arimasen (contracted form)
informal past:	dewa-nakatta, ja-nakatta (contracted form)
formal past:	dewa-arimasen-deshita, ja-arimasen-deshita (contracted form)

Note that the negative of da has alternative formal forms: ja-nai desu (non-past) and ja-nakatta desu (past).

Sample Verb Negative Forms

[Vbasic]	informal non-past	formal non-past	informal past	formal past
U-verb:				
kaku	kakanai	kakimasen	kakanakatta	kakimasen-deshita
asobu	asobanai	asobimasen	asobanakatta	asobimasen-deshita
RU-verb:				
taberu	tabenai	tabemasen	tabenakatta	tabemasen-deshita
Be-verb:				
da	dewa-nai	dewa-arimasen	dewa-nakatta	dewa-arimasen-deshita
	ja-nai	ja-arimasen	ja-nakatta	ja-arimasen-deshita

The topic marker *wa* in the target sentence *kyoo wa kaisha e ikimasen* must now be explained in the context of negation. When we negate a statement, we negate what is known. In this sense, *wa* appearing in negative sentences is a special case of topic marking. In fact *wa* defines what we are negating. It defines the negative scope. This usage of *wa* is often called "negative *wa*." Negative *wa* also implies contrastiveness, another quality associated with the topic marker *wa* as mentioned earlier (Entry 16). Negation implies a contrast with the assumed affirmative statement. Note that qualities associated with *wa*, namely, contrastiveness and negation, are simply consequences of the fundamental function of *wa*, that is, the identification of topic in communication.

In fact we can create another version of the target sentence by adding *wa* to another noun phrase as in *kyoo wa kaisha e wa ikimasen*. This sentence defines the negative scope one step further than the original target sentence. It implies 'I don't go to the office today, although I may go somewhere else.' It negates the possibility of going specifically to the office, but not necessarily the possibility of going somewhere else. *Wa* in negative sentences then is a useful tool for defining what exactly a speaker wishes to negate.

We noted that for negative sentences of the be-verb, *dewa-nai/dewa-arimasen* are used. Consider that in these negative expressions, *wa* also appears. It literally negates what precedes *wa*, that is, *de*, the gerundive form of the verb *da*. In the sentence *nihon-jin dewa-arimasen*, what is negated is 'being Japanese,' implying that the person is of some other nationality. *Dewa-nai* and *dewa-arimasen* have contracted versions used in casual speech, i.e., *ja-nai* and *ja-arimasen*.

A point of caution: the reader is reminded that the discussion above does not exclude the possibility of negating without *wa*. It is possible to negate with other case markers without *wa* in the context where the relevant phrase does not constitute topic. Consider the following. Speaker A at least knows that someone else is not coming; A asks a question as shown in (a). In response to this question, B answers in (b).

(a)　*Dare ga kimasen ka.*
　　誰が来ませんか。
　　(Who isn't coming?)

(b)　*Yamada-san ga kimasen.*
　　山田さんが来ません。
　　(Mr. Yamada is not coming.)

Here (b) provides an answer by marking with *ga* the piece of new information—the name of the person who is not coming. In this case what is known is the fact that someone is not coming; Yamada-san cannot be marked by *wa*, since it is not a piece of shared information.

Another important point to be studied in relation to negative sentences; the interrogative words in negative statements take the [interrogative word + *mo*] structure. *Dore-mo, dare-mo, nani-mo,* and *doko e mo* are frequently used. These are equivalent to 'any one,' 'anyone,' 'anything,' and 'anywhere,' meaning total negation. (When the [interrogative word + *mo*] combination is used for affirmative sentences it adds the meaning of total positiveness 'all' and 'every.') (See Appendix 6 for the list regarding this point.)

In rapid colloquial speech, *ra* in *-ranai* and *-ranakatta* becomes *n*, creating *wakannai* (instead of *wakaranai*) and *wakannakatta* (instead of *wakaranakatta*). Also in an extremely casual male speech, *-nai* in informal negative endings changes to *-nee*. This creates forms such as *ikanee* instead of *ikanai*, *tabenee* instead of *tabenai*. These expressions are considered extremely colloquial and often rude; they should be avoided under normal circumstances.

Examples

```
---------------------------------------------------------
kooen      公園      N      park
amari      あまり    Adv    (not) so much
tenki      天気      N      weather
hontoo     本当      N      truth
---------------------------------------------------------
```

(1) *Kinoo chikaku no kooen e ikimashita.*
きのう近くの公園へ行きました。
(Yesterday I went to a nearby park.)

Kinoo wa amari ii tenki ja-arimasen-deshita.
きのうはあまりいい天気じゃありませんでした。
(Yesterday the weather was not so good.)

Totemo samukatta-desu.
とても寒かったです。
(It was very cold.)

Kooen ni wa dare-mo imasen-deshita.
公園には誰もいませんでした。
(There was no one [else] in the park.)

(2) A: *Ano hito wa Itaria-jin ja-arimasen yo.*
あの人はイタリア人じゃありませんよ。
(He is not an Italian.)

B: *Soo desu ka. Shirimasen-deshita.*
そうですか。知りませんでした。
(Is that so? I didn't know that.)

(3) A: *Kawamura-san wa ikimasen-deshita yo.*
川村さんは行きませんでしたよ。
(Ms. Kawamura didn't go.)

B: *Hontoo desu ka.*
本当ですか。
(Really?)

Practice

Make negative statements in Japanese for the following:

1. (I), watch TV, last night ☺
2. (I), Japanese
3. American, there is, anyone, in this building
4. Jack, eat, breakfast
5. (I), went, anywhere, last Saturday

——— Answers ———

1. *Yuube (wa) terebi minakatta yo.* ☺
ゆうべ(は)テレビ見なかったよ。
2. *(Watashi wa) nihon-jin ja-arimasen.*
(私は)日本人じゃありません。
3. *Kono tatemono no naka ni (wa) Amerika-jin wa dare-mo imasen yo.*
この建物の中に(は)アメリカ人は誰もいませんよ。
4. *Jakku-san wa asagohan o tabemasen.*
ジャックさんは朝ごはんを食べません。
5. *Senshuu no doyoobi (ni) (wa) doko e mo ikimasen-deshita.*
先週の土曜日(に)(は)どこへも行きませんでした。

Additional Information

Although less frequently used and in use primarily in written discourse, another negative ending *-mai* should be mentioned in passing. *-Mai* expresses the negative intention of the speaker, and is attached to the [Vnonpast] form, and optionally to [Vstem] of the *RU*-verb. For existential verbs *aru* and *iru*, *arumai* and *imai* are used. For the verbs *kuru* and *suru*, *kurumai* and *surumai* (as well as *kimasumai* and *shimasumai*) are used. For the verb *da/desu*, *dewa-arumai* is used; for [Adj-*i*], *-ku(wa)-arumai* is used. For example:

(a) *Sonna koto wa yuumai.* ♦
そんなことは言うまい。
(I won't say such a thing.)

(b) *Moo sake wa nomumai.*
もう酒は飲むまい。
(I won't drink sake any more.)

(c) *Amai mono wa tabe(ru)mai.*
甘い物は食べ(る)まい。
(I won't eat sweet things.)

In spoken Japanese, *to omou* 'think' is added to create the expression *mai to omou* 'to think not to.'

Another negative form used primarily in the written style is *-nu*. To obtain *-nu* and its gerundive form *-zu*, replace *-nai* of negative verb forms with *-nu* or *-zu*.

For the *i*-type adjective, replace the final *-i* with *-karazu(da)*.

(d) *Sore wa wakaranu.* ♦
それはわからぬ。
(I don't know that.)

(e) *Kyoo wa samukarazu, atsukarazu da.* ♦
今日は寒からず，暑からずだ。
(Today is neither hot nor cold.)

Warning

It is a good idea to remind ourselves that not all negative expressions mean negation of a statement. Two main exceptions are: (1) negation used for the purpose of invitation as in (a), and (2) negative endings used in exclamatory expressions as in (b).

(a) <u>*Kaimono*</u> <u>*ni*</u> <u>*ikanai?*</u>
shopping   for   don't go
買い物に行かない？
(Don't you want to go shopping?)

(b) *Ara, Kawamura-san ja-nai!*
あら，川村さんじゃない！
(Oh, isn't that Ms. Kawamura!)

27. Quantity—1. Quantifiers of Adverbial Phrases

> *many, a little, not at all*
> **takusan, sukoshi, zenzen**
> たくさん, すこし, ぜんぜん

Grammatical Explanation

Quantifiers, or degree words, are used as adverbial phrases, and are normally placed immediately after the noun whose quantity is described. For example, *ringo o takusan kaimashita* 'I bought many apples.' Note in English the quantifier *many* precedes the noun, *apples*.

When degree words are used to modify adjectives, they immediately precede them, as in *taihen muzukashii* 'very difficult.' Here is a list of frequently used adverbial quantifiers.

oozei	大勢	many (only in reference to people)
kanari	かなり	considerably
sukoshi	少し	a few, a little
zuibun	ずいぶん	very much
taihen	大変	much
takusan	たくさん	many, much
chotto	ちょっと	a little
choppiri	ちょっぴり	very little, a wee bit

There are some adverbial quantifiers used with negative statements only, similar to the English *at all* which are always used in negative statements. These include:

amari	あまり	(not) so
sukoshimo	少しも	(not) at all
zenzen	全然	(not) at all
chittomo	ちっとも	(not) at all

Another useful quantifying strategy is to express 'only' and 'no more than.' For example, *dake* 'only' as in *mikan wa sukoshi dake kaimashita* 'I bought only a few tangerines,' and *shika* in negative sentences as in *mikan wa sukoshi shika kaimasen-deshita* 'I didn't buy more than a few oranges,' or 'I bought only a few oranges.'

Warning

Adverbial quantifiers *takusan* and *oozei* cannot be used to modify adjectives (*takusan ookii*).

Examples

```
---------------------------------------------------------------
sake    酒    N    sake (rice wine)
---------------------------------------------------------------
```

(1) A: *Osoku narimasu ka.*
　　　　遅くなりますか。
　　　　(Will you be late?)

　　B: *Ee, sukoshi.*
　　　　ええ，少し。
　　　　(Yes, a little.)

(2)　　*Sake wa amari nomimasen. Biiru wa takusan nomimasu.*
　　　　酒はあまり飲みません。ビールはたくさん飲みます。
　　　　(I don't drink too much sake. I drink a lot of beer.)

(3) A: *Kono kamera wa chotto takai nee.* ☺
　　　　このカメラはちょっと高いねえ。
　　　　(This camera is a bit expensive, isn't it?)

　　B: *Soo desu ka. Kochira no kamera wa ikaga desu ka.*
　　　　そうですか。こちらのカメラはいかがですか。
　　　　(Is that so? How about this camera over here?)

Practice

```
---------------------------------------------------------------
white wine    N    shiro wain        白ワイン
shopper       N    kaimonokyaku      買い物客
---------------------------------------------------------------
```

1. Comment on the following by adding quantifiers of your choice.
    a. your drinking of white wine
    b. there being shoppers
    c. John (not) studying

2. You know Sakai went drinking last night. You suspect that he drank a lot. What question/answer interaction could take place?

3. Comment to your landlord about today's weather being very or a bit cold. How will she respond?

―――― Some Sample Answers ――――――――――
1a.   *Shiro wain o <u>sukoshi</u>/<u>takusan</u> nomimashita.*

      白ワインを<u>少し</u>/<u>たくさん</u>飲みました。

  b.   *Kaimonokyaku ga <u>takusan</u>/<u>oozei</u> imashita.*

      買い物客が<u>たくさん</u>/<u>大勢</u>いました。

  c.   *Jon-san wa chittomo benkyoo-shimasen.*

      ジョンさんはちっとも勉強しません。

2. A: *Yuube takusan nonda?* ☺ ゆうべたくさん飲んだ？

   B: *Sukoshi ne.* ☺   少しね。

3. A: *Kesa wa <u>sukoshi</u>/<u>zuibun</u> samui-desu ne.*

     今朝は<u>少し</u>/<u>ずいぶん</u>寒いですね。

   B: *Hontooni nee.* 本当にねえ。

―――――――――――――――――――――――

Additional Information

The quantifier *chotto* has additional functions; (1) vocative phrase 'excuse me!' or 'hey' to catch the attention of someone, and (2) when making a request, to add the meaning of 'just' in, for example, 'could I just borrow this?' *kore chotto karite mo ii-desu ka?* These expressions will be discusssed later.

The difference between the *dake* and the *shika* sentences lies in the speaker's intention as to whether she/he emphasizes that there *is* something, or there *isn't* as much as there should be. See for example:

(a)
<u>Sen-en</u>	**shika**	<u>arimasen</u>	<u>kara</u>	<u>resutoran</u>
one thousand yen	only	there isn't	because	restaurant

<u>e</u>	<u>wa</u>	<u>ikemasen</u>	<u>yo.</u>
to	T	cannot go	IP

千円**しか**ありませんからレストランへは行けませんよ。

(Since I have only one thousand yen, I can't go to a restaurant.)

(b)
<u>Sen-en</u>	**dake**	<u>arimasu</u>	<u>kara</u>	<u>koohii</u>
one thousand yen	only	there is	because	coffee

<u>gurai</u>	<u>wa</u>	<u>nomemasu</u>	<u>yo.</u>
such as	T	can drink	IP

千円**だけ**ありますからコーヒーぐらいは飲めますよ。

(Since I have at least one thousand yen, I can go have a cup of coffee.)

But not:

(c)   **Sen-en dake arimasu kara, resutoran e wa ikemasen.*

28. Quantity—2. Numerals and the Number System

Target Expressions

> one, ten, one hundred
>
> **ichi, juu, hyaku**
>
> 一, 十, 百

Grammatical Explanation

Here is the number system in Japanese. There are two number systems up to number 10, one originally Japanese and the other of Chinese origin. The number system consisting of indigenous Japanese vocabulary is limited in its use; it is used for counting objects without counters (to be explained later), and for describing ages up to 10 years old; its variation is also used for dates up to the 10th of the month, as well as for a few other combinations. The number system of Chinese origin is more extensively used. It is used for mathematical calculation, for combinations that make higher numbers, and in combination with various counters.

		Japanese Origin		Chinese Origin	
1	one	hitotsu	ひとつ	ichi	いち
2	two	hutatsu	ふたつ	ni	に
3	three	mittsu	みっつ	san	さん
4	four	yottsu	よっつ	shi (yon)	し（よん）
5	five	itsutsu	いつつ	go	ご
6	six	muttsu	むっつ	roku	ろく
7	seven	nanatsu	ななつ	shichi (nana)	しち（なな）
8	eight	yattsu	やっつ	hachi	はち
9	nine	kokonotsu	ここのつ	kyuu (ku)	きゅう（く）
10	ten	too	とお	juu	じゅう

For combining numbers higher than 10, use the Chinese origin numbering system according to the following rules:

1. For number 11, add one to the word for 10, for number 12, add two to the word for 10, and so forth:

> *juu ichi, juu ni, juu san, juu shi (juu yon), juu go, juu roku, juu shichi (juu nana), juu hachi, juu kyu (juu ku)*

2. For numbers in ten's, numbers one to nine plus *juu* are used:

> *ni-juu, san-juu, yon-juu, go-juu, roku-juu, shichi-juu (nana-juu),*
> *hachi-juu, kyuu-juu; nan-juu* (how many tens)

3. Continue to use the number 20 for numbers in twenties such as *ni-juu hachi* for 28, and the number 30 for numbers in thirties, and so forth until 100 *hyaku*:

4. For numbers beyond 100, start with the word for 100; the numbers from 1 to 10 and then to 99 should follow until you reach 200 (*ni-hyaku*); then repeat the process until you reach 1,000 (*sen*):

> *hyaku, ni-hyaku, san-byaku, yon-hyaku, go-hyaku, rop-pyaku,*
> *nana-hyaku, hap-pyaku, kyuu-hyaku; nan-byaku* (how many hundreds)
> ex. 253—*ni-hyaku go-juu san*; 368—*san-byaku roku-juu hachi*

Note that after *san* and *nan*, *byaku* is used (instead of *hyaku*). For *roku* and *hachi*, *rop-pyaku* and *hap-pyaku* combinations are used.

5. For numbers beyond 1,000, start with the word for 1,000, and work downward in units of 100 and 10 until you reach 10,000 (*man*):

> *sen, ni-sen, san-zen, yon-sen, go-sen, roku-sen, nana-sen, has-sen,*
> *kyuu-sen; nan-zen* (how many thousands)
> ex. 1,508—*sen go-hyaku hachi*; 7,945—*nana-sen kyuu-hyaku*
> *yon-juu go*

Note the sound change in *san-zen, nan-zen* and *has-sen*.

6. For numbers beyond 10,000, start with 10,000, then 1,000 and so on until 100,000 (*juu-man*):

> *ichi-man, ni-man, san-man, yon-man, go-man, roku-man, nana-man (shichi-man), hachi-man, kyuu-man; nan-man* (how many ten thousands)
> ex. 84,321—*hachi-man yon-sen san-byaku ni-juu ichi*

7. *Man* is combined with numbers up until 9,999. Thus *kyuu-sen kyuu-hyaku kyuu-juu kyuu-man* is 99,990,000. 100,000,000 is *ichi-oku*:

> ex. 28,410,763—*ni-sen hap-pyaku yon-juu ichi-man nana-hyaku*
> *roku-juu san*

Note that from 1 through 9,999 Japanese and English have equivalent expressions. At the 10,000 mark, however, Japanese counts in units of *man*, thus 20,000 is "two"-*man*, 30,000, "three"-*man*, etc. The same holds true for the unit *oku* which designates 100,000,000.

100,000,000,000	*is-sen-oku*	one hundred billion
10,000,000,000	*hyaku-oku*	ten billion
1,000,000,000	*juu-oku*	one billion
100,000,000	*ichi-oku*	one hundred million
10,000,000	*is-sen-man*	ten million
1,000,000	*hyaku-man*	one million
100,000	*juu-man*	one hundred thousand
10,000	*ichi-man*	ten thousand
1,000	*sen*	one thousand
100	*hyaku*	one hundred
10	*juu*	ten
1	*ichi*	one
0	*rei, zero*	zero

[Example Numbers]

48	*yon-juu hachi* (or *shi-juu hachi*)
105	*hyaku go*
136	*hyaku san-juu roku*
3,792	*san-zen nana-hyaku kyuu-juu ni*
756,248	*nana-juu go-man roku-sen ni-hyaku yon-juu hachi*

Useful Phrases Using the Number System

Date of the Month

(from the 1st to the 10th)

tsuitachi 一日 , hutsuka 二日 , mikka 三日 , yokka 四日 , itsuka 五日 , muika 六日 , nanoka 七日 , yooka 八日 , kokonoka 九日 , tooka 十日

For dates beyond the 10th, add the number and *nichi*; *juu go-nichi* '15th,' *ni-juu san-nichi* '23rd.' Exceptions are *juu yokka* '14th,' *hatsuka* '20th,' and *ni-juu yokka* '24th.' For 'which date,' use *nan-nichi*.

Duration of Days

For the duration of one day, use *ichi-nichi*. For the duration of more than one day, forms identical to dates of the month are used op-

tionally followed by -kan, as in *juu go-nichi-kan* 'for fifteen days.'
Nan-nichi can also mean 'how many days.'

Month

Add *gatsu* to the numbers of Chinese origin up to 12.

> *ichi-gatsu* 一月 , *ni-gatsu* 二月 , *san-gatsu* 三月 , *shi-gatsu* 四月 ,
> *go-gatsu* 五月 , *roku-gatsu* 六月 , *shichi-gatsu* 七月 ,
> *hachi-gatsu* 八月 , *ku-gatsu* 九月 , *juu-gatsu* 十月 ,
> *juu ichi-gatsu* 十一月 , and *juu ni-gatsu* 十二月

Only these combinations are used. For 'which month,' use *nan-gatsu*.

Time

byoo	秒	seconds
hun (-pun)	分	minutes
ji	時	hours
jikan	時間	duration of hours
han	半	thirty minutes

For *hun,* a phonological change occurs as shown below:

ip-pun	一分	one minute
san-pun	三分	three minutes
rop-pun	六分	six minutes
hap-pun	八分	eight minutes
jup-pun/jip-pun	十分	ten minutes

Additional useful phrases for time indication is *sugi* 'past,' and *mae* 'before.'

[Example Times]

10:30	*juu-ji han*	十時半
3:57	*san-ji go-juu nana-hun (sugi)*	三後五十七分(すぎ)
	yo-ji san-pun mae	四時三分前
2:00 p.m.	*gogo ni-ji*	午後二時
7:05 a.m.	*gozen shichi-ji go-hun (sugi)*	午前七時五分(すぎ)

Remember to attach the particle *ni* when indicating specific time, as in *san-ji ni* 'at three o'clock.'

Examples

(1) A: *Shikago wa ima nan-ji desu ka.*
シカゴは今何時ですか。
(What time is it in Chicago now?)

B: *Ni-ji desu.*
二時です。
(Two o'clock.)

A: *Gozen ni-ji desu ka.*
午前二時ですか。
(Two a.m.?)

B: *Iie, gogo ni-ji desu.*
いいえ，午後二時です。
(No, two p.m.)

(2) *San-ji han ni densha ga kimasu.*
三時半に電車が来ます。
(The train comes at three thirty.)

Practice

---
birthday   N   *tanjoobi*   誕生日

Comment on the following by adding appropriate numerals. For numbers 3, 4 and 5, create a question-answer pair.

1. your birthday
2. your friend's age
3. your friend's birthday
4. birthday of your friend, Sachiko, being July 13th
5. time you usually get up

——— Some Sample Answers ———

1. *Tanjoobi wa go-gatsu itsuka desu.* 誕生日は五月五日です。
2. *Ni-juu san desu.* 二十三です。
3. A: *Jon-san no tanjoobi wa itsu desu ka.*
ジョンさんの誕生日はいつですか。
B: *Juu ni-gatsu yooka desu.* 十二月八日です。
4. A: *Sachiko-san no tanjoobi wa itsu desu ka.*
幸子さんの誕生日はいつですか。
B: *Shichi-gatsu juu san-nichi desu.* 七月十三日です。
5. A: *Nanji ni okimasu ka.* 何時に起きますか。
B: *Shichi-ji han ni okimasu.* 七時半に起きます。

Additional Information

For phone numbers, just as in English, each number is read as a single digit number. For example, 832-5601 will be read, *hachi san ni no go roku zero ichi.* The particle *no* is added at the hyphen. The area code (*kyokuban*) is also read as a single digit number. Tokyo's area code is 03, *kyokuban zero san.*

29. Particles—3. More about Particles

Both Ms. Sasaki and I are university students.
Sasaki-san mo watashi mo daigakusei desu.
佐々木さんも私も大学生です。

[*mo*] [*to*] [*ni*] [*ka*]
[*kara*] [o]

Grammatical Explanation

Beyond the particles we have studied so far, we should make note of some others (refer to characteristic 7). Here we focus on specifics of some frequently used particles and patterns.

1. *Enumerative particles, mo, to, ya, yara, toka and dano*
   For the expression of enumeration of nouns:

[A *mo* B *mo*]*1	both A and B
[A *to* B *to* C]	A and B and C
[A *ya* B (*ya* C) *nado*]	A and B (and C) and others
[A *ni* B *ni* C]	A, additionally B, additionally C
[A *yara* B *yara*]	A and B and perhaps others also
[A *ka* B]*2	A or B
[A *toka* B *toka*]	such things as A and B (perhaps)
[A *dano* B *dano*]	such things as A and B

   *1. The negation of [A *mo* B *mo*] pattern negates both. Thus:
   Biiru mo uisukii mo dame desu. '(lit. Both beer and whiskey are not good.) I drink neither beer nor whiskey.'
   *2. [A *ka* B] may be used for listing alternatives, which will be discussed later in Entry 102.

---
daigakusei	大学生	N	college student
omoshiroi	おもしろい	Adj	interesting
mono	物	N	thing(s)

(1a)   *Sasaki-san mo Mikami-san mo daigakusei desu.*
佐々木さんも三上さんも大学生です。
(Both Ms. Sasaki and Ms. Mikami are university students.)

(1b) A: *Kinoo hon'ya de kono hon to sono hon o kaimashita.*
きのう本屋でこの本とその本を買いました。
(I bought this and that book at the bookstore yesterday.)

    B: *Sono hon omoshiroi-desu ka.*
その本おもしろいですか。
(Is that book interesting?)

(1c)   *Koohii toka koocha toka iroirona mono ga arimashita.*
コーヒーとか紅茶とかいろいろな物がありました。
(There were various things such as tea and coffee.)

(1d)   *Kono hon ka ano hon o kaimasu.*
この本かあの本を買います。
(I'm going to buy this book or that book.)

2. *Use of particle* ni
Beyond the locative, directive and source-indicating use of *ni* discussed in Entry 17, the following points should be taken into consideration.

  A. *Ni* is used to show the goal, location and grammatical object of some verbs; these are considered idiomatic:

> *noru* as in *basu ni noru* 'to get on the bus'
> *kotaeru* as in *shitsumon ni kotaeru* 'answer the question'
> *au* as in *tomodachi ni au* 'see a friend'
> *niru* as in *chichioya ni niru* 'resemble one's father'

  B. *Ni* marks what one emotionally responds to when using a group of intransitive verbs that express feelings and emotions.

akiru	あきる	to get bored, to get tired of
akireru	あきれる	to be surprised, be astounded
akogareru	あこがれる	to long for, pine for
amaeru	甘える	to be dependent upon

kizuku	気づく	to notice
kodawaru	こだわる	to be bothered
komaru	困る	to be troubled
koriru	こりる	to learn by experience
natsuku	なつく	to become attached to
haradatsu ♦	腹立つ	to get angry
horeru	ほれる	to fall in love, to be infatuated
mayou	迷う	to be puzzled

(2a) *Benkyoo ni akita.* ☺
勉強にあきた。
(I'm tired of studying.)

(2b) *Iroirona koto ni yoku kizukimasu nee.*
いろいろなことによく気づきますねえ。
(You [lit. notice things well, don't you] are rather perceptive, aren't you?)

C. *Ni* co-occurs with some of the [Adj-*i*] predicates as shown below. In these examples, similarly to the case in B above, *ni* identifies the specific item that the adjective predicate applies to, i.e., 'resistant (specifically) to heat.'

atsusa ni tsuyoi	暑さに強い	resistant to heat
shigen ni toboshii	資源に乏しい	poor in resources
eki ni chikai	駅に近い	close to the station

3. *Use of particle o*
Let's sum up the usage of the particle *o*.

A. Marks direct object:
(3a) *Miruku o nomimasu.*
ミルクを飲みます。
(I drink milk.)

B. Indicates directional movement—along, across or through:
(3b) *Ekimae no toori o aruita.*
駅前の通りを歩いた。
(I walked along the street in front of the station.)

C. Indicates the starting point of an action:
(3c) *Kaisha o nan-ji ni demasu ka.*
会社を何時に出ますか。
(What time do you leave the company?)

4. *Locative* kara *and* o

When using *kara* and *o* for indicating location (meaning 'from'), the following distinctions are made. *Kara* means 'from a certain physical location,' while *o* may also indicate an abstract source, and it is sometimes used idiomatically.

(4a) *Daigaku kara denaide-kudasai.*
      大学から出ないでください。
      (Please do not leave the [university] campus.)

(4b) *Nannen ni daigaku o demashita ka.*
      何年に大学を出ましたか。
      (In what year did you graduate from the university?)

(4c) *Kodomo ga uchi o demashita.*
      子供が家を出ました。
      (My child left home. [i.e., ran away from home or married into some other family])

5. *Use of particle* de

Beyond the locative and instrumental use of *de* studied earlier, *de* is used for the following purposes.

A.   Amount of time or money:
     (5a) *Go-sen-en de kono hon o kaimashita.*
           五千円でこの本を買いました。
           (I bought this book for 5,000 yen.)

B.   Cause or reason:
     (5b) *Kaze   de   kaisha   o   yasumimashita.*
           cold   due to   company   O   was absent
           かぜで会社を休みました。
           (I was absent from the office due to a cold.)

C.   Limit or extent of something:
     (5c) *Kaigi   wa   ato   juu go-hun   de owarimasu.*
           meeting T   more   fifteen minutes in be over
           会議はあと十五分で終わります。
           (The meeting will be over in fifteen minutes.)

     (5d) *Tookyoo de ichiban yuumeina resutoran e ikimashita.*
           Tokyo   in most famous   restaurant to went
           東京で一番有名なレストランへ行きました。
           (We went to the most famous restaurant in Tokyo.)

Practice

----
amai	甘い	Adj	sweet
kurai	暗い	Adj	dark
michi	道	N	road
aruku	歩く	V	to walk
yokogiru	横切る	V	to go across
taihuu	台風	N	typhoon
yasumi	休み	N	day(s) off
Jurii-san	ジュリーさん	PN	Julie
Pegii-san	ペギーさん	PN	Peggy

What particles should we use for the following expressions? Fill in the blanks with appropriate particles.

1. I ate a lot of sweets, such as cake and cookies.
   Keeki (   ) kukkii (   ) amai mono o takusan tabemashita.
   ケーキ　　　クッキー　　　甘い物をたくさん食べました。

2. I walked along the dark road.
   Kurai michi (   ) arukimashita.
   暗い道　　　　歩きました。

3. I left the room.
   Heya (   ) demashita.
   部屋　　　出ました。

4. Which one is better, this or that? (or, Which one do you like, this or that?)
   Kore (   ) sore (   ) dochira (   ) ii-desu ka.
   これ　　　それ　　　どちら　　　いいですか。

5. I will cross the park. ('To cross' in Japanese is a motion verb that implies 'to pass through.')
   Kooen (   ) yokogirimasu.
   公園　　　　横切ります。

6. I bought this car for two million yen.
   Kono kuruma wa ni-hyaku-man-en (   ) kaimashita.
   この車は　　　　二百万円　　　　買いました。

7. I met my friend at three o'clock.
   Tomodachi (   ) san-ji (   ) aimashita.[*3]
   友だち　　　三時　　　会いました。

8. I was absent from school due to the typhoon.
   Taihuu (   ) gakkoo wa yasumi desu.
   台風　　　　　学校は休みです。

9. Both Julie and Peggy are American.
   Jurii-san (   ) Pegii-san (   ) Amerika-jin desu.
   ジュリーさん　ペギーさん　　　アメリカ人です。

──────── Answers ────────
1. *ya, nado* や，など (or *yara, yara* やら，やら)
2. *o* を　3. *o* を　4. *to, to, ga* と，と，が
5. *o* を　6. *de* で　7. *to, ni* と，に
8. *de* で　9. *mo, mo* も，も (or *to, wa* と，は)

---

*3. *Tomodachi to au* is also possible; this carries the meaning of 'meet with a friend.'

30. Requesting—1. Asking for Items and Services

Target Expression

> *Please (take me) to the airport.* (said to a taxi driver)
> **Kuukoo made onegai-shimasu.**
> 空港までお願いします。

Strategic Explanation

There are two formulaic expressions in asking for items and services. First, *onegai-shimasu* 'I make a request' for the addressee's services, and second, *kudasai* 'please give (or hand over),' primarily used in the transaction of objects and things, requesting specific items. When handing in forms at a bank or at public service offices for example, *onegai-shimasu* should be used since you are requesting their service. When purchasing some items, *kore o kudasai* is frequently used although the politer expression *kore o onegaishimasu* may also be used. When asking for someone on the phone as in 'Masako, please' or 'May I speak to Masako?' *Masako-san onegai-shimasu* is used. For making requests that involve action (for example, 'please read this'), another form is used, which we will learn later (Entry 40).

One point to be noted regarding requests. Normally one should avoid making straightforward requests to social superiors. A more polite way of making requests is to turn it into a question, something similar to English 'could you . . . ?' or 'would it be possible for you to . . . ?' Imagine a situation where you want to obtain an information packet from your professor. Instead of saying *kore kudasai*, one should say *kore itadaite mo yoroshii deshoo ka?* 'would it be all right if I received this?' This form will be studied later (Entry 110).

Examples

kokusai denwa 国際電話	N	overseas telephone call
remon レモン	N	lemon

(1) *Tookyoo eki e/made onegai-shimasu.* (to a taxi driver)
   東京駅へ/までお願いします。

   (Please [take me] to Tokyo station.)

(2) *Kore onegai-shimasu.* (at a bank)
   これお願いします。

   (Please take care of this.)

(3) *Kokusai denwa onegai-shimasu.* (on the phone)
   国際電話お願いします。

   (Overseas telephone call, please.)

(4) *Kore kudasai.* (at a store)
   これください。

   (I'll take this.)

(5) *Sono remon mittsu kudasai.* (at a greengrocer)
   そのレモン三つください。

   (I'll take three of the lemons.)

Practice

magazine	N	*zasshi*	雑誌
package	N	*kozutsumi*	小包み
front desk	N	*huronto*	フロント
Shinjuku station	PN	*Shinjuku-eki*	新宿駅

How would you express your request for the following:

1. to purchase this magazine (at a store)
2. to handle this package (at a post office)
3. to connect me to the front desk (at a hotel)
4. to drive me up to Shinjuku station (to a taxi driver)

───────── Answers ─────────

1. *Kono zasshi (o) kudasai.*　　　　この雑誌(を)ください。
2. *Kono kozutsumi onegai-shimasu.*　この小包みお願いします。
3. *Huronto onegai-shimasu.*　　　　フロントお願いします。
4. *Shinjuku-eki made onegai-shimasu.*　新宿駅までお願いします。

31.　Negating—2.　Past Tense and Negation of the *I*-type Adjective

Target Expression

> *This book wasn't so interesting.*
> **Kono hon wa amari omoshirokunakatta-desu.**
> この本はあまりおもしろくなかったです。

Grammatical Explanation

As we have already learned, [Adj-*i*] behaves like a verb. That is to say, adjectives conjugate just like verbs (refer to characteristic 8). Here we concentrate on the past tense and the negative forms of [Adj-*i*].

Past tense forms:
　informal past　　　　　replace the final -*i* with -*katta*
　formal past　　　　　　add -*desu* to informal past
Negative forms:
　informal non-past　　　replace -*i* with -*kunai*

formal non-past	add -*desu* to informal non-past
informal past	replace -*i* with -*kunakatta*
formal past	add -*desu* to informal past

The negative affix -*nai* which was introduced for the negation of verbs is in fact an *i*-type adjective, and therefore it is essential that you master how [Adj-*i*] conjugates.

There is also a variation in the formal negative forms of [Adj-*i*].

| formal non-past | replace -*i* with -*kuarimasen* |
| formal past | add -*deshita* to -*kuarimasen* |

The -*kuarimasen* negation is considered slightly more polite than the -*kunai-desu* negation.

It should be noted that optionally *wa* is inserted to form the negative expression -*ku(wa)-nai*. The conjugation with the particle *wa* inserted focuses on what is negated slightly more than the conjugation without. For example, *takakuwa-arimasen* has an interpretation of not being expensive similar to the English expression 'at least it's not expensive.'

Sample *I*-Type Adjective Conjugation

[Affirmative]

	non-past	past
informal	*hiroi*	*hirokatta*
formal	*hiroi-desu*	*hirokatta-desu*

[Negative]

	non-past	past
informal	*hirokunai*	*hirokunakatta*
formal	*hirokunai-desu*	*hirokunakatta-desu*
	hirokuarimasen	*hirokuarimasen-deshita*

Examples

ga	が	Conj	but
Kyuushuu	九州	PN	the island of Kyushu (part of Japan)
Tekisasu	テキサス	PN	Texas

(1)　A: *Kono resutoran wa takai-desu ka. Yasui-desu ka.*
　　　このレストランは高いですか。安いですか。
　　　(Is this restaurant expensive? Is it inexpensive?)

B: *Senshuu koko de tabemashita ga, totemo takakatta-desu yo.*
先週ここで食べましたが，とても高かったですよ。
(I ate here last week, but it was quite expensive.)

A: *Soo desu ka. Oishikatta-desu ka.*
そうですか。おいしかったですか。
(I see. Was it good?)

B: *Amari oishikunakatta-desu ne.*
あまりおいしくなかったですね。
(It wasn't very delicious.)

(2) A: *Kyuushuu no huyu wa amari samukuarimasen. Tekisasu no huyu wa ikaga desu ka.*
九州の冬はあまり寒くありません。テキサスの冬はいかがですか。
(Kyushu's winter is not too cold. How is it in Texas?)

B: *Tekisasu mo amari samukunai-desu yo.*
テキサスもあまり寒くないですよ。
(It isn't so cold in Texas either.)

Warning

The informal non-past negative form of the adjective *ii* 'good' is *yokunai*. Other forms follow; *yokunai-desu, yokuarimasen-deshita, yokunakatta, yokunakatta-desu.*

Practice

sushi	N	*sushi* すし	(vinegared rice served with fish)
movie	N	*eiga* 映画	

Comment on the following using the negative form of *i*-type adjectives.

1. sushi: not so delicious
2. New York: not far from here
3. that movie: not good at all ☺
4. Yesterday: not warm

──── Answers ────

1. *Kono sushi wa amari oishikunai-desu ne.*
このすしはあまりおいしくないですね。
(or *oishiku[wa]-arimasen ne* おいしく(は)ありませんね)

2. *Nyuuyooku wa koko kara tookunai-desu.*
ニューヨークはここから遠くないです。
(or *tooku[wa]-arimasen* 遠く(は)ありません)

3. *Sono eiga wa zenzen yokunakatta yo.* ☺
   その映画は全然よくなかったよ。
4. *Kinoo wa atatakaku(wa-)arimasen-deshita.*
   きのうは暖かく（は）ありませんでした。
   (or *atatakakunakatta-desu* 暖かくなかったです)

32. Responding to Questions—1. Answering Yes/No Questions

Target Expressions

yes, no, yeah, nope

hai, iie, un, uun
はい, いいえ, うん, ううん

Strategic Explanation

In answering questions, *hai, ee* and *un* are used to indicate agreement. Although each is a way of saying 'yes,' one should be aware of the different situations in which each is optimally used. *Hai* is most neutral; *ee* is conversational; *un* is casual and restricted to communication among familiar *uchi* (in-group) members. Another interjection *haa* 'yes' is formal and polite, often used as a humble form toward social superiors. For negative answers, *iie, iiya* (or *iya*) and *uun* are used. *Iie* is most neutral; *iiya* (or *iya*) is conversational and frequently preferred by males; the use of *uun* is casual and is restricted to usage among familiar *uchi* members under informal circumstances.

Examples

(1) A: *Nihongo wa muzukashii-desu ka.*
      日本語はむずかしいですか。
      (Is Japanese difficult?)
   B: *Ee, totemo./Iie, zenzen.*
      ええ, とても。/いいえ, ぜんぜん。
      (Yes, very much so./No, not at all.)

(2)　A: *Koohii nomu?* ☺
コーヒー飲む？
([lit. Do you drink coffee?] Do you want to drink coffee?)
　　B: *Un.* ☺
うん。
(Yeah.)

(3)　A: *Yamada-san desu ka.*
山田さんですか。
(Are you Ms. Yamada?)
　　B: *Hai, soo desu.*
はい，そうです。
(Yes, I am.)

It is possible to answer question (1) with *hai, nihongo wa totemo muzukashii-desu*. However, in real conversation there is no need to repeat. Short answers are perfectly acceptable (refer to characteristic 4) and in fact are preferred. When answering a question with the verb *be* as in question (3), *soo desu* is preferred to an answer in a complete sentence. *Hai, Yamada desu* would not be used unless there was a need for repeating. For the *be*-verb sentences, answer with *hai soo desu* 'yes, it is so,' or *iie soo dewa-arimasen* 'no, it isn't so.' (Warning: Even when the sentence has a *da/desu* expression, if it is an adjective, *soo da* and *soo dewa-nai* forms are not normally used. For example, in answering the question *takai-desu ka?*, *hai, takai-desu* is used. Likewise, in answer to the question *benri desu ka?*, *hai, benri desu* is appropriate but not **hai soo desu*. *Benri desu* is a formal version of *benri da*, another type of adjectival predicate, which we will learn in Entry 37.)

Practice

shinseki	親戚	N	relative
daigaku	大学	N	university

Answer the following questions both affirmatively and negatively.

1.　*Ashita dekakemasu ka.*
あした出かけますか。

2.　*Jonson-san desu ka.*
ジョンソンさんですか。

3.　*Ano hito wa Yamamoto-san no shinseki desu ka.*
あの人は山本さんの親戚ですか。

4. *Kono daigaku no toshokan, atarashii?*
この大学の図書館，新しい？

(Answer in both formal and informal styles.)

—————— Some Sample Answers ——————

1. *Iie, dekakemasen.*   いいえ，出かけません。
2. *Iie. Andaason desu.*   いいえ。アンダーソンです。
3. *Hai, soo desu yo.*   はい，そうですよ。
4. *Un, atarashii yo.* ☺   うん，新しいよ。
   Ee, atarashii-desu.   ええ，新しいです。

Additional Information

You may hear Japanese people saying *hai* quite frequently in conversations. If you were to interpret every *hai* as agreement and affirmation, these conversations would sound quite silly. But as we will discuss later, *hai* does not always nor simply mean 'yes.' Actually *hai* has a very important social function. It is a respectful listener response (called *aizuchi* 'back-channel' responses), which is equivalent to English *uh-huh* and *yeah*. Additionally, *hai* has ritualistic functions; it is the preferred utterance (1) as when responding to your name in a roll-call, equivalent to answering ''here,'' (2) as a movement-accompanying utterance when you hand something to someone, equivalent to ''here you go,'' or ''here it is,'' and (3) as an energetic signal to get something started, equivalent to the English ''go.'' When conversing with a Japanese person you should understand that the *hai* you hear, more often than not, means 'I hear what you're saying. And?' It would be unwise to interpret every *hai* and *ee* as an affirmative answer.

33. Quantity—3. Counters

Target Expressions

three hours, ten dollars, two pairs (of shoes)
san-jikan, juu-doru, ni-soku
三時間，十ドル，二足

Grammatical Explanation

Each language provides different ways for counting objects. Just as Japanese people learning English must simply memorize things like "an ear of corn," "a kernel of corn," or "a litter of kittens," one must learn a set of counters (or classifiers) when counting in Japanese. These counters are used for a set group of items and are attached immediately following the number. Here are some examples:

Objects

kai	階	for the stories of a building
ko	個	used for a broad category of small and compact objects, including round fruit, balls, boxes, etc.
satsu	冊	for bound objects such as books, notebooks, magazines, etc.
soku	足	for pairs of shoes, socks, stockings, etc.
dai	台	for vehicles, machines and things such as bicycles and television sets
tsuu	通	for letters and documents
hai	杯	for liquid in cups, glasses, bowls, buckets, etc.
hon	本	for long, cylindrical objects including trees, sticks, pens, bananas, fingers, etc.
mai	枚	flat, thin objects including paper, dishes, stamps, blankets, boards, etc.

Currency

en	円	yen
sento	セント	cent
Doitsu maruku	ドイツマルク	German mark
doru	ドル	dollar
pondo	ポンド	pound

Measuring units

kiro	キロ	used for both kilometers and kilograms
guramu	グラム	gram
senchi	センチ	centimeter
meetoru	メートル	meter
rittoru	リットル	litter

Animal world

hiki	匹	for insects, fish, small animals such as cats and dogs

too	頭	for large animals such as horses, bears, deer, etc.
wa	羽	for birds

Frequency

kai	回	times, as in *ik-kai* 'once'
do	度	times, as in *ichi-do* 'once'

Order

ban	番	as in *ni-ban* 'number two, second place'
too	等	as in *san-too* 'third place'

Duration

jikan	時間	hour, as in *yo-jikan* 'four hours'
shuukan	週間	week, as in *ni-shuukan* 'for two weeks'
hun	分	minute, as in *hap-pun* 'eight minutes'
byoo	秒	second, as in *go-juu-byoo* 'fifty seconds'
nen kan	年間	year, as in *juu-nen kan* 'for ten years'

People

hitori 一人 and *hutari* 二人 for one and two persons. When there are more than two people, use the appropriate number and add -*nin*; *san-nin*三人, *yo-nin*四人, *go-nin*五人, *roku-nin*六人, *shichi-nin*七人 (or *nana-nin*), *hachi-nin*八人, *ku-nin*九人, *juu-nin*十人, *juu ichi-nin* 十一人 , and so forth.

In combining numbers with classifiers, phonological changes may occur. Some examples are given below.

	mai:	*hiki:*	*hon:*	*satsu:*
1	*ichi-mai* 一枚	*ip-piki* 一匹	*ip-pon* 一本	*is-satsu* 一冊
2	*ni-mai* 二枚	*ni-hiki* 二匹	*ni-hon* 二本	*ni-satsu* 二冊
3	*san-mai* 三枚	*san-biki* 三匹	*san-bon* 三本	*san-satsu* 三冊
4	*yon-mai (yo-mai)* 四枚	*yon-hiki* 四匹	*yon-hon* 四本	*yon-satsu* 四冊
5	*go-mai* 五枚	*go-hiki* 五匹	*go-hon* 五本	*go-satsu* 五冊
6	*roku-mai* 六枚	*rop-piki* 六匹	*rop-pon* 六本	*roku-satsu* 六冊

7	shichi-mai	shichi-hiki	shichi-hon	shichi-satsu
	(nana-mai)	(nana-hiki)	(nana-hon)	(nana-satsu)
	七枚	七匹	七本	七冊
8	hachi-mai	hap-piki	hap-pon	has-satsu
	八枚	八匹	八本	八冊
9	kyuu-mai	kyuu-hiki	kyuu-hon	kyuu-satsu
	九枚	九匹	九本	九冊
10	juu-mai	jup-piki	jup-pon	jus-satsu
		(jip-piki)	(jip-pon)	(jis-satsu)
	十枚	十匹	十本	十冊
	nan-mai	nan-biki	nan-bon	nan-satsu
	何枚	何匹	何本	何冊

For expressing frequency, a pattern, [duration of time + *ni* + frequency] is used; *ichi-nichi ni ichi-do* 'once a day,' *mikka ni ichi-do* 'once in three days,' *is-shuukan ni san-jikan* 'three hours in a week,' etc.

Additional Information

Useful phrases which specify quantity are those which express approximation. The phrases *hodo, kurai, gurai, bakari* and *yaku* all express approximation of quantity equivalent to the English 'about.' The phrase *yaku* precedes the quantifier while all others follow it. The phrase *goro* is used only to express approximation of a point in time meaning 'approximately the time (when).' Another strategy is to use two consecutive numbers which limit the quantity to somewhere between the two numbers; *ni-san-nin* 'two to three people,' *go-rop-pun* 'five to six minutes.' Approximations bring forth ambiguity which is advantageous in certain situations. Particularly when one is making a request, approximation is preferred; it is easier for the listener to accept the request when it is made in approximation. For example:

(a) *Jaa sore **ichi-jikan gurai** kashite-kudasai.*
じゃあそれ**一時間ぐらい**貸してください。

(Well then, please loan that to me for about one hour.)

Examples

(1) *Kitte o juu-mai kudasai.*
切手を十枚ください。

(I'd like ten stamps.)

(2) *Koko kara daigaku made yaku yon-kiro desu.*
ここから大学まで約四キロです。

(It is about four kilometers from here to the university.)

(3) A: *Kore ikura?* ☺
これいくら？
(How much is this?)

B: *San-zen-en desu.*
三千円です。
(It's three thousand yen.)

A: *Kore mo san-zen-en?* ☺
これも三千円？
(Is this also three thousand yen?)

B: *Iie, sore wa san-zen go-hyaku-en desu.*
いいえ，それは三千五百円です。
(No, that is three thousand and five hundred yen.)

Practice

----
pork   N   *butaniku* ぶた肉
----

1. Express the following quantity and price in Japanese by using appropriate counters, and create sentences.
   a. five sheets of paper
   b. two notebooks
   c. 12 letters (of correspondence)
   d. approximately one thousand dollars
   e. seven minutes

   f.
   ¥5,800

   g.
   $29.00

   h.
   ¥13,700

2. You are addicted to coffee, and are curious to find out about how many cups of coffee your friend drinks a day. Ask this question. How will you answer if you were asked the same question? ☺

3. You need some pork for cooking dinner tonight. Your roommate wants to ask you how many grams of pork you bought. You bought 400 grams. What dialogue might follow? ☺

4. Your friend asks you how many books are in this room. Can you give an approximate number?

5. You look in your wallet and discover there are only two one-thousand yen bills. How would you convey this to your friend?

6. You are standing by a brand new car. Ask the price of this car. The salesman gives you a price in yen.

─────── Some Sample Answers ───────

1. a. *Konna kami go-mai kudasai.*　こんな紙五枚ください。
   b. *Nooto o ni-satsu kaimashita.*　ノートを二冊買いました。
   c. *Tegami ga juu ni-tsuu kimashita.* 手紙が十二通来ました。
   d. A: *Ikura gurai arimasu ka.*　いくらぐらいありますか。
      B: *Sen-doru gurai desu.*　千ドルぐらいです。
   e. A: *Koko kara eki made nan-pun gurai desu ka.*
         ここから駅まで何分ぐらいですか。
      B: *Nana-hun gurai desu.* 七分ぐらいです。
   f. *Kono hon wa go-sen hap-pyaku-en desu.*
      この本は五千八百円です。
   g. A: *Kono kasa ikura deshita ka.* この傘いくらでしたか。
      B: *Ni-juu kyuu-doru deshita.*　二十九ドルでした。
   h. *Kono uisukii wa ip-pon ichi-man san-zen nana-hyaku-en desu.* このウイスキーは一本一万三千七百円です。

2. A: *Koohii ichinichi ni nan-bai gurai nomu?* ☺
      コーヒー一日に何杯ぐらい飲む？
   B: *Hap-pai gurai.* ☺　八杯ぐらい。

3. A: *Butaniku nan-guramu gurai katta?* ☺
      ぶた肉何グラムぐらい買った？
   B: *Yon-hyaku-guramu.* ☺ 四百グラム。

4. A: *Kono heya ni wa hon wa nan-satsu gurai arimasu ka.* この部屋には本は何冊ぐらいありますか。
   B: *Go-hyaku-satsu gurai arimasu yo.*
      五百冊ぐらいありますよ。

5. *Ni-sen-en shika arimasen.*　二千円しかありません。

6. A: *Kono kuruma wa ikura desu ka.* この車はいくらですか。
   B: *Ni-hyaku nana-juu-man-en desu.* 二百七十万円です。

34. Inviting and Suggesting—1. Inviting and Suggesting Items

> *How about some coffee?*
> **Koohii demo ikaga desu ka.**
> コーヒーでもいかがですか。
>
> [*ikaga desu ka*]

Strategic Explanation

Ikaga desu ka 'how about it' or its informal version *doo desu ka* are useful for making suggestions and invitations by specifying items. *Ikaga deshoo ka*, a more polite version is also used for people one must be polite toward. When suggesting or inviting, the items you specify are often followed by the particle *demo*. *Demo* is used when other choices are expected to exist and the speaker lists only one of the possible alternatives. *Demo* adds the English meaning of 'or something,' making the suggestion less specific, and therefore less imposing because it doesn't confine the partner to only the choice offered. Such usage of a particle expresses interpersonal sensitivity and consideration toward the listener, and it is preferred among Japanese.

Examples

shokuji	食事	N	meal
isshoni	いっしょに	Adv	together
ip-pai	一杯	N	(lit. one cup), idiomatically *ip-pai doo*, is an invitation for drinking
anoo	あのう	Int	(hesitation marker "uh . . . well . . .")
nomimono	飲みもの	N	drink

(1) A: *Shokuji isshoni ikaga desu ka.*
　　　食事いっしょにいかがですか。
　　　(How about eating together?)

B: *Ee, ii-desu nee.*
ええ、いいですねえ。
(Yes, that will be nice.)

(2) A: *Kon'ya ip-pai doo?* ☺
今度一杯どう？
(How about drinking tonight?)

B: *Ii nee.*
いいねえ。
(That will be nice.)

(3) A: *Anoo, nomimono demo ikaga desu ka.*
あのう、飲みものでもいかがですか。
(How about something to drink?)

B: *Ee, onegai-shimasu.*
ええ、お願いします。
(Yes, please.)

Practice

1. You are working as a salesclerk at a major department store. You ask your customer whether she likes the item you are holding in your hand.

2. Your friend wants to buy a new suitcase. Both of you are at a store looking at this and that suitcase. How will you ask your friend about the one right next to you? ☺

3. How will you ask whether your close friend would like some coffee? ☺

4. How will you formally suggest to your colleague that the two of you have dinner together? How should your colleague respond?

─────── Answers ───────

1. *Kore wa ikaga desu ka.* これはいかがですか。
2. *Kore doo?* ☺ これどう？
3. *Koohii demo doo?* ☺ コーヒーでもどう？
4. A: *Shokuji demo isshoni ikaga desu ka.*
食事でもいっしょにいかがですか。
   B: *Ii-desu nee.* いいですねえ。

35. Appealing to the Listener—1. Interactional Particles

Mr. Johnson, right?
Jonson-san desu ne.
ジョンソンさんですね。

Strategic Explanation

We have already learned the interactional particles *ne* and *yo*. *Ne* is a confirmation seeker similar to English expressions 'right?' and 'don't you agree?,' normally tagged at the end of an utterance. *Yo* is a particle of assertion which adds moderate emphasis especially useful when the speaker provides a new piece of information. Several other particles convey the speaker's attitude and feelings toward the content of the statement and toward one's partner. Frequently attached in the sentence-final position, they are also called sentence-final particles (refer to characteristic 7). In spoken language, however, some of these particles may occur at the end of phrases within an utterance.

The list below provides characteristics relevant to the use of these particles.

The Use of Interactional Particles

	Gender of speaker	Relative social status	Style	Implications and effects	Combination with others
ne (*nee*)	M/F		FO/INF	confirmation and friendliness	*yo ne, wa ne, no yo ne, wa yo ne*
na (*naa*)	M/F	S higher than L	INF	confirmation often self-addressed	
yo	M/F	S higher than L	FO/INF	assertion providing new information while adding moderate emphasis	*yo ne, wa yo, wa yo ne, no yo ne*

sa	M/F	S higher than L ☺		insistence of obviousness	
wa (with high rising tone:)					
	F		FO/INF	femininity mild insistence	*wa yo, wa ne, wa yo ne*
(with low tone:)					
	M		FO/INF	mild insistence	
ze	M	among friends, S higher ☺		strong insistence	
na	M	S higher than L ☺		negative imperative	*na yo*
no	M/F		FO/INF familiar	question empathy	*no ne no yo ne*

M = Male, F = Female, S = Speaker, L = Listener, FO = Formal style, INF = Informal style

Ka could be considered an interactional particle since it appears sentence-finally and expresses the speaker's interrogative attitude toward the statement.

As shown in the list above, interactional particles make interaction more expressive. Of the particles listed here, *ne* is the most frequently used, often appearing not only sentence-finally but also within an utterance boundary at locations where some type of feedback expression is requested.

It is important to note that some of the particles are restricted in terms of the verb-ending forms that immediately precede them. *Ne* and *yo* can be attached to all informal and formal verb and adjective endings as well as immediately after a noun. *Wa* can be used with both formal and informal endings but not with a noun immediately preceding it. *Sa* is used primarily for informal endings as well as immediately after a noun. *Ze* is used with informal forms and cannot co-occur with nouns immediately preceding them. *Na* and *naa* are used with informal endings, but not used immediately following a noun. When *no* is used, the preceding informal *be*-verb, *da*, changes to *na*; *Nihon-jin na no?*

There are also cases where multiple particles are attached for combined effects as shown below.

(a)	*Ima*	*no*	*shigoto*	*wa*	*muzukashii*	*desu*	*yo*	*ne.*
	now	L	work	T	difficult	be	IP	IP

今の仕事はむずかしいです**よね**。

(Your present job is difficult, isn't it?)

Additional Information

As a variation of the interactional particle, you may hear *desu ne* inserted many times. For example:

(a) *Sore de **desu ne**, ashita made ni **desu ne**, onegai-shimasu yo.*
それで**ですね**，あしたまでに**ですね**，お願いしますよ。
(So, by tomorrow, could you take care of it?)

Desu ne carries a slightly more formal flavor than *ne*; it is used for similarly to *ne* and *nee*.

Examples

```
------------------------------------------------------------
onegai    お願い    N      request
saa       さあ      Int    well, let's see . . .
------------------------------------------------------------
```

(1) *Anoo, chotto onegai ga arimashite ne . . .*
well a little request S exist . . .
あのう，ちょっとお願いがありましてね……
(Well to be frank, I have some request to make . . .)

(2) *Ano ne, chotto ne, onegai ga atte ne . . .* ☺
well IP a little IP request S exist IP
あのね，ちょっとね，お願いがあってね……
(Well, uhh . . . I have a request . . .)

(3) *Asa kara nee, denwa ga takusan arimashita yo.*
朝からねえ，電話がたくさんありましたよ。
(There were many phone calls since morning.)

(4) A: *Ano onna no ko ne, dare no kodomo na no?* ☺
あの女の子ね，誰の子供なの？
(Whose child is that girl?)

B: *Saa, dare no kodomo desu ka ne.*
さあ，誰の子供ですかね。
(Well, whose child is she?)

Warning

When used sentence-internally, interpersonal particles add a more colloquial flavor to speech. One should refrain from overly frequent insertion of particles in formal speech and in situations where politeness is expected.

Since *yo* appears frequently, some caution is necessary. Because *yo* is used in statements to provide new bits of information while asserting an opinion, claim, advice, warning, etc., one should avoid using it with one's social superior. This is because the presumption of one's social superior's lack of knowledge is unadvisable.

Note that particles under normal circumstances receive no phonological stress. For example, although *yo* is used to express slight emphasis in that the speaker focuses on the information that the listener does not yet know by adding *yo*, *yo* itself does not receive stress. Interactional particles *ne(e)* and *sa(a)* may sometimes appear independently to solicit listener responses or as conversational filler.

36. More about Interrogative Words

Target Expressions

Is anyone there?

Dare-ka imasu ka.
誰かいますか。

No one is there.

Dare-mo imasen.
誰もいません。

[*dare-ka*]
[*nani-mo*]

Grammatical Explanation

Although we have already learned interrogative words, the use of these words needs re-examination because they have special meanings when combined with different particles.

First, when interrogative words are followed by *mo* in affirmative sentences, they add the meaning of 'every.' Therefore, *dare* 'who' plus *mo* means 'everybody,' *dore-mo* 'everything,' *dochira-mo* 'both,' and so forth. (Note that *nani-mo* does not occur in affirmative sentences, however.) When the [interrogative word + *mo*] pattern appears in negative sentences, it adds a meaning of total negation, as in *doko-mo* 'anywhere,' *doko e mo* 'to anywhere' *itsu-mo* 'any time,' and *nani-mo* 'anything,' and so forth. In

Japanese, unlike English, negation must be completed by the negative verb ending as well. Thus, *nani-mo arimasen* 'there isn't anything' or 'there is nothing.'

Second, when interrogative words are followed by *de mo*, the meaning of 'any' is added. *Dare de mo* means 'any person,' in a sentence such as *dare de mo ii-desu* 'any person is good (fine).'

Third, when an interrogative word is followed by the particle *ka*, it adds the meaning of 'some' in, for example, *doko-ka e ikimashita* 'He went somewhere.' In English, however, in question sentences 'any' is preferred. So when the [interrogative word + *ka*] is used in question sentences, it is best to say that it adds the meaning of the English 'any.' See for example, *nani-ka arimasu ka* 'Is there anything?' Although the basic meaning added by the use of [interrogative word + *ka*] is that of 'some,' different interrogative words bear slightly different meanings. We will study them in example sentences. See Appendix 6 for the complete listing of these forms discussed here.

Examples

```
-----------------------------------------------------------------
Ahurika   アフリカ       PN       Africa
-----------------------------------------------------------------
```

(1)   A: *Dare-ka kimasu ka.*
　　　　誰か来ますか。
　　　　(Is someone coming?)
　　　B: *Iie, dare-mo kimasen yo.*
　　　　いいえ，誰も来ませんよ。
　　　　(No, no one will come.)

(2)　　*Doko-ka ii resutoran wa arimasen ka.*
　　　どこかいいレストランはありませんか。
　　　(Is there any nice restaurant?)

(3)　　*Itsu-ka Ahurika e ikimasu.*
　　　いつかアフリカへ行きます。
　　　(Someday I will go to Africa.)

(4)　　*Kinoo wa ikura-ka ame ga hurimashita.*
　　　きのうはいくらか雨が降りました。
　　　(Yesterday it rained somewhat.)

Additional Information

The interrogative pronoun *nan-ka* is used further for two other purposes. First, it appears as a filler in conversation; second, it is used to introduce a topic emphatically. For an example of a filler, see Sample Text 1. An example below shows an emphatic topic introduction by *nan-ka*, which has a similar function of "such as" in English.

(a) *Tokai **nan-ka** kiken de, kitanakute, daikirai da.*
都会**なんか**危険で，きたなくて，大きらいだ。
(Places such as large cities are dangerous and filthy, I hate them.)

37. Describing State—3. *Na*-type Adjectives

Target Expression

> *It's quiet, isn't it?*
>
> ***Shizuka desu ne.***
> 静かですね。
>
> [Adj-*na*]

Grammatical Explanation

We have studied two ways to modify nouns so far. The first by [Adj-*i*] and the second modifying by the [N + *no*] structure. The third method is to use a group of adjectives called nominal adjectives, or "*na*-type adjectives," [Adj-*na*], that modify nouns that follow (refer to characteristic 7). They are sometimes called nominal adjectives because although they function as adjectives, grammatically they behave similarly to nouns, although not totally. Unlike [Adj-*i*], [Adj-*na*] cannot be used as they are as predicates. They are obligatorily followed by either *da* or its formal version, *desu*, when used as predicates. They are called *na*-type adjectives because *na* obligatorily marks this group of phrases when directly modifying nouns. (All nominal adjectives end with *na* but not all words ending with *na* are nominal adjectives.) In short, when modifying a noun, the *na*-ending basic form is used, while when used as a predicate, *na* is deleted and *da* co-occurs. The stem of [Adj-*na*] is reached by taking away *na* from the basic form of the *na*-type adjective. Conjugation of nominal adjectives follows that of the verb *da*, including past tense. Here is a list of common nominal adjectives. (For conjugation of [Adj-*na*], see the list provided in Entry 38.)

List of Na-type Adjectives

atatakana	暖かな	warm
awarena	あわれな	pitiful
idaina	偉大な	great
ijiwaruna	いじわるな	mean
iyana	いやな	distasteful
kantanna	簡単な	simple[*1]
kasukana	かすかな	faint
kikenna	危険な	dangerous
kiraina	きらいな	distasteful
kireina	きれいな	pretty, clean
kookana	高価な	expensive
gankona	がんこな	stubborn
shizukana	静かな	quiet
sukina	好きな	preferred, favorite
zeitakuna	ぜいたくな	extravagant
joozuna	上手な	skillful
teineina	ていねいな	polite
hadena	派手な	showy
hubenna	不便な	inconvenient
heibonna	平凡な	commonplace
benrina	便利な	convenient, useful
nigiyakana	にぎやかな	bustling
yukaina	ゆかいな	pleasant, funny
reiseina	冷静な	cool (in disposition)

[*1]. Simple here means easy to solve, not in the sense of simple life which is translated with another nominal adjective, as *shissona seikatsu*.

Examples

```
-----------------------------------------------------------
mondai    問題     N     question
jinsei    人生     N     life, lifetime
-----------------------------------------------------------
```

(1) A: *Kono mondai wa kantan desu ne.*
　　　　この問題は簡単ですね。
　　　　(This question is simple, isn't it?)

　　　B: *Soo desu ka.*
　　　　そうですか。
　　　　(Is it?)

A: *Totemo kantanna mondai desu yo.*
とても簡単な問題ですよ。
(It's a very simple question.)

B: *Soo desu ka nee. Kantan ja-arimasen yo.*
そうですかねえ。簡単じゃありませんよ。
(Is it [really] so? It's not simple.)

(2) *Tanaka-san wa kaisha de iroirona shigoto o suru.* ♦
田中さんは会社でいろいろな仕事をする。
(Mr. Tanaka performs various kinds of jobs at his company.)

(3) *Ano hito no jinsei wa amari heibon dewa-arimasen-deshita.*
あの人の人生はあまり平凡ではありませんでした。
(That person's life was not so ordinary.)

Kikenna koto mo takusan arimashita.
危険なこともたくさんありました。
([lit. There were many dangerous things] He faced many dangers.)

(4) A: *Kyoo ichinichijuu kodomo-tachi wa shizuka deshita yo.*
今日一日中子供たちは静かでしたよ。
(The children were quiet all day long today.)

B: *Soo desu ka. Kinoo wa shizuka ja-arimasen-deshita ga . . .* *²
そうですか。きのうは静かじゃありませんでしたが……
(Really? They weren't quiet yesterday . . .)

*2. The conjunction *ga* used at the end of an utterance makes the expression less abrupt and therefore encourages a softer and more comfortable interaction. See Entry 57 for further explanation.

Practice

| tool | N | *doogu* | 道具 |
| singer | N | *kashu* | 歌手 |

Comment on the following in Japanese.

1. this tool: convenient, useful
2. that red flower: was really pretty
3. she: distasteful person
4. that singer's life: not ordinary ♦
5. this question: simple? ☺

─────── Answers ───────

1. *Kore wa benrina doogu desu ne.*　これは便利な道具ですね。
2. *Sono akai hana wa hontooni kirei-deshita.*
　その赤い花は本当にきれいでした。
3. *Iyana hito desu nee.*　いやな人ですねえ。
4. *Ano kashu no jinsei wa heibon dewanai.* ♦
　あの歌手の人生は平凡ではない。
5. *Kono mondai kantan?* ☺　この問題簡単？

Additional Information

Some grammarians treat [Adj-*na*] as a nominal or a noun and it is sometimes called "*na* nominal." Although [Adj-*na*] behaves in part like a nominal, it cannot become the sentential topic, subject, or object by itself. Due to this and other reasons I prefer to categorize it as an adjective. Note, however, that dictionaries normally list [Adj-*na*] without *na*.

When faced with a phrase, such as *byooki no hito* 'a sick person' and *kenkoona hito* 'a healthy person,' you may wonder how you handle the choice between *no* or *na*. There is no way to predict which one is correct; you must learn case by case as to which is a noun and which is [Adj-*na*].

In this case *byooki* is a noun and *kenkoo* is a *na*-type adjective, and therefore, when modifying the noun *hito*, *byooki* requires the linker *no* while *genki* requires the *genkina* form. It might be helpful to know that only *na*-type adjectives can be modified by adverbs; *kenkoona* can be modified to form *motto kenkoona*. (*Motto byooki no* is a wrong structure.) But of course, to use the modifier correctly you must first know whether a phrase is a noun or a *na*-type adjective.

38.　Modifying—2.　More about Adjectives

Target Expressions

a new house, not-new house
　　　　atarashii uchi, atarashikunai uchi
　　　　新しい家，新しくない家

134

Grammatical Explanation

Here we summarize the use of the two types of adjectives. As shown below, when immediately preceding nouns both adjectives take the basic form; the *i*-ending form for the [Adj-*i*] and *na*-ending form for the [Adj-*na*]. Unlike English adjectives, Japanese adjectives themselves can take negative and past tense forms. For example, *wakakatta sensei* '(lit. was-young teacher) the teacher who was young' and *wakakunai hito* '(lit. not-young person) a person who is not young,' and so on. The list below exemplifies such use.

Adjective Pre-nominal Forms

[Adj-*i*]	[Adj-*na*]
atarashii uchi 新しい家 (new house)	*kantanna mondai* 簡単な問題 (simple question)
atarashikunai uchi 新しくない家 (not-new house)	*kantan dewa-nai mondai* 簡単ではない問題 (not-simple question)
atarashikatta uchi 新しかった家 (house that was new)	*kantan datta mondai* 簡単だった問題 (question that was simple)
atarashikunakatta uchi 新しくなかった家 (house that was not new)	*kantan dewa-nakatta mondai* 簡単ではなかった問題 (question that was not simple)

Adjective Forms Used as Predicates

	[Adj-*i*]	[Adj-*na*]
INF	*Kono uchi wa atarashii.* この家は新しい。	*Kono mondai wa kantan da.* この問題は簡単だ。
FO	*Kono uchi wa atarashii-desu.* この家は新しいです。 (This house is new.)	*Kono mondai wa kantan desu.* この問題は簡単です。 (This question is simple.)
INF	*Kono uchi wa atrarashikunai.* この家は新しくない。	*Kono mondai wa kantan dewa-nai.* この問題は簡単ではない。 *(Kono mondai wa kantan ja-nai.)* （この問題は簡単じゃない。）

FO	*Kono uchi wa atarashikunai-desu.* この家は新しくないです。	*Kono mondai wa kantan dewa-arimasen.* この問題は簡単ではありません。 (*Kono mondai wa kantan ja-arimasen.*) （この問題は簡単じゃありません。）
	Kono uchi wa atarashiku (wa-) arimasen. この家は新しく（は）ありません。 (This house is not new.)	*Kono mondai wa kantan dewa-nai-desu.* この問題は簡単ではないです。 (This question is not simple.)
INF	*Kono uchi wa atarashikatta.* この家は新しかった。	*Kono mondai wa kantan datta.* この問題は簡単だった。
FO	*Kono uchi wa atarashikatta-desu.* この家は新しかったです。 (This house was new.)	*Kono mondai wa kantan deshita.* この問題は簡単でした。 (This question was simple.)
INF	*Kono uchi wa atarashiku-nakatta.* この家は新しくなかった。	*Kono mondai wa kantan dewa-nakatta.* この問題は簡単ではなかった。 (*Kono mondai wa kantan ja-nakatta.*) （この問題は簡単じゃなかった。）
FO	*Kono uchi wa atarashiku (wa-) nakatta-desu.* この家は新しく（は）なかったです。	*Kono mondai wa kantan dewa-arimasen-deshita.* この問題は簡単ではありませんでした。 (*Kono mondai wa kantan ja-arimasen-deshita.*) （この問題は簡単じゃありませんでした。）
	Kono uchi wa atarashiku (wa-) arimasen-deshita. この家は新しく（は）ありませんでした。 (This house was not new.)	*Kono mondai wa kantan dewa-nakatta desu.* この問題は簡単ではなかったです。 (This question was not simple.)

FO = Formal style, INF = Informal style

When multiple adjectives are used, all but the last one take the gerundive form. The gerundive form of the *i*-type adjective is made by replacing the final *-i* with *-kute*; the gerundive form of the *na*-type adjective is reached by replacing *na* with *de*, which is the gerundive form of *da*.

It is also possible to use multiple negative adjective forms. In such cases, since the negative ending -*nai* is an *i*-type adjective, the gerundive form -*nakute* is used for both *i*-type and nominal adjectives. For example, *benri dewa-nakute, yasukunakute, shizuka dewa-nai apaato* 'not-convenient, not-cheap, not-quiet apartment.'

Examples

```
-----------------------------------------------------------------
sorega . . .   それが…   Int     hesitation marker
                                 (before presenting
                                 unfavorable
                                 information)
shinsenna      新鮮な    Adj     fresh
sakana         魚        N       fish
-----------------------------------------------------------------
```

(1) A: *Tanaka-san wa donna hito desu ka.*
     田中さんはどんな人ですか。
     (What [kind of] person is Ms. Tanaka?)
     B: *Tanaka-san nee . . . soo desu nee . . . ijiwaruna hito desu ne.*
     田中さんねえ…そうですねえ……いじわるな人ですね。
     (Ms. Tanaka . . . well . . . she's a mean person.)

(2) A: *Kinoo no shiken wa doo deshita ka.*
     きのうの試験はどうでしたか。
     (How was yesterday's exam?)
     B: *Sorega . . . kantan dewa-nai mondai ga takusan arimashite nee . . .*
     それが……簡単ではない問題がたくさんありましてねえ……
     (Uhh . . . there were many difficult questions . . .)

(3) *Oishikute yasukute shinsenna sakana nai?* ☺
     おいしくて安くて新鮮な魚ない？
     (Do you have any delicious, inexpensive and fresh fish?)

(4) *Tomodachi no Sano-san wa mainichi benri de nigiyakana suupaa de kaimono o shimasu.*
     友だちの佐野さんは毎日便利でにぎやかなスーパーで買物をします。
     (My friend, Ms. Sano, shops every day at a convenient and bustling supermarket.)

Additional Information

Using adjectives in different tenses can create a semantic difference worth noting. Examine the pair of sentences below, for example.

(a) *Otoko* *wa* **hageshii** *ame no naka o* *isoide*   *aruita.* ◆
man   T   pouring   rain   in   hurriedly   walked
男は**はげしい**雨の中を急いで歩いた。
(The man hurried through the pouring rain.)

(b) *Otoko wa* **hageshikatta** *ame no naka o isoide aruita.* ◆
男は**はげしかった**雨の中を急いで歩いた。
(The man hurried through the rain that came pouring down then.)

Expression (a) implies that it was a pouring rain, and not a quiet, soft rain.
Expression (b), however, implies that the rain may have been light at times,
but when the man hurried through, the rain came pouring down at that very
moment.

Practice

polite	Adj	*teineina*	ていねいな
place	N	*tokoro*	ところ
accurate	Adj	*seikakuna*	正確な
watch, clock	N	*tokei*	時計

Create sentences that contain the following [Adj + N] phrases.

1. words: polite
2. day: not warm
3. sandwich: was not delicious
4. place: not convenient
5. watch: small and accurate

―――― Some Sample Answers ――――

1. *Teineina kotoba mo wakarimasu ka.*
   ていねいなことばもわかりますか。
2. *Atatakakunai hi wa goruhu wa shimasen.*
   暖かくない日はゴルフはしません。
3. *Oishikunakatta sandoitchi wa doo shimashita ka.*
   おいしくなかったサンドイッチはどうしましたか。
4. *Watashi no uchi wa amari benridewa-nai tokoro ni*
   arimasu. 私の家はあまり便利ではないところにあります。
5. *Chiisakute seikakuna tokei wa takai-desu yo ne.*
   小さくて正確な時計は高いですよね。

39. Speech Style—2. Masculine and Feminine Speech

Target Expressions

> *It's already three o'clock.*
> Male: ***Moo san-ji da ne.***
>   もう三時だね。
> Female: ***Moo san-ji ne.***
>   もう三時ね。

Strategic Explanation

Although the differences between masculine and feminine speech style in formal Japanese are few, in casual Japanese there are a number of differences. (It is best to study with tutors and instructors representing both genders when studying Japanese. When you have access to Japanese drama and documentaries or actual interaction of Japanese male and female speakers, pay attention to the different manner of communication between male and female speakers.)

In the choice of vocabulary, men use pronouns such as *boku* and *kimi* for 'I' and 'you,' while women prefer *watashi* and *anata*. With certain words, women use the respectful prefixes *o-* and *go-* more readily. As a rule, *o-* is added to words which originated in Japan, while *go-* is added to words of Chinese origin. Although the basic function of these respectful prefixes is to show politeness and/or to show respect to the addressee and therefore may be used by both sexes, for some words the prefix *o-* is used predominantly by female speakers. Since respectful prefixes are attached to nouns associated with one's social superior in formal situations, one must not use them in reference to actions related to oneself or to one's *uchi* members.

Examples of Respectful Prefixes (1)
Used by Both Male and Female Speakers

gosotsugyoo	ご卒業	graduation
gokekkon	ご結婚	marriage
goryokoo	ご旅行	travel
onamae	お名前	name
ohanashi	お話	talk

Examples of Respectful Prefixes (2)
Used Predominantly by Female Speakers

*o*sushi	おすし	sushi
*o*tomodachi	お友だち	friend
*o*benkyoo	お勉強	study

It is best for beginners not to overuse respectful prefixes. Not all nouns are readily prefixed with these affixes, so one should exercise restraint and caution when using them.

The difference between masculine and feminine speech style under discussion here should be understood in the broader category of more or less blunt versus more or less gentle style. Female speakers may sometimes choose to use a rather blunt style and male speakers may choose the gentle style when a gentle quality is favorably evaluated. However, in this book we use the term masculine and feminine speech style since masculine speech is representatively blunt and feminine speech more gentle in casual conversational interaction.

The informal casual verb *da* is used predominantly in blunt style by males. In gentle speech predominantly used by females, *da* is deleted totally. For example, while a male speaker may utter *moo san-ji da* 'oh, it's three o'clock,' a female speaker is likely to use *ara, moo san-ji* 'oh, it's already three o'clock.' Similarly, for exclamatory expressions, while a male may use *benri da naa* 'how convenient!,' a female speaker is more likely to say *benri nee*, again without *da*.

Perhaps the most prominent feature of the masculine and feminine speech difference is seen in the use of different interactional particles. While both male and female speakers may use *wa* with a low falling tone, *wa* with a high rising tone is exclusively used by female speakers. Female speakers frequently add *wa* alone or in combination with other particles at the end of utterances. While a male speaker may say *iku yo* 'I'm going,' a female speaker expresses the similar feeling by saying *iku wa yo*.

Some exclamatory interjections are restricted to female use only (or when impersonating a female). These include *ara* and *maa*, both expressing surprise.

Over all, women tend to use more extensive polite expressions in both, formal and informal situations. It should also be noted that there is a noticeable pitch difference between masculine and feminine speech. Listen carefully for features pointed out here when you have an opportunity to encounter both male and female speakers of Japanese. When we use M and F in this book, we mean by M a blunt style predominantly, but not necessarily exclusively, used by male speakers, and by F, the gentler feminine style.

40. Requesting—2. Requesting to Do or Not to Do

Target Expressions

> *Please open the window.*
> **Mado o akete-kudasai.**
> 窓を開けてください。
>
> *Don't smoke, please.*
> **Tabako o suwanaide-kudasai.**
> タバコをすわないでください。
>
> [Vte + -kudasai]

Grammatical Explanation

Earlier we learned the phrase *kudasai* for requesting the transfer of items. Here we extend that use by replacing the object noun phrases with the gerundive forms of the verb. The gerundive form of the verb takes *-te* (or *-de*) endings, and therefore it is sometimes called *-te* form, which is transcribed as [Vte] throughout this book. Deriving *-te* forms is simple. Replace the final *-ta* of the informal past tense of the verb with *-te*, and *-da* with *-de*. (Use the "*Ta*" song [given in Entry 22] if you need to refresh your memory in obtaining [Vinformal past] forms.) For making a negative request, add *-de* to the negative informal non-past form. In informal familiar style, *-kudasai* may be deleted altogether. Some sample gerundive forms are given below.

Verbs	Gerundive te-form	Negative	Gerundive negative
iku (to go)	*itte*	*ikanai*	*ikanaide*
行く	行って	行かない	行かないで
oyogu (to swim)	*oyoide*	*oyoganai*	*oyoganaide*
泳ぐ	泳いで	泳がない	泳がないで
taberu (to eat)	*tabete*	*tabenai*	*tabenaide*
食べる	食べて	食べない	食べないで
suru (to do)	*shite*	*shinai*	*shinaide*
する	して	しない	しないで
kuru (to come)	*kite*	*konai*	*konaide*
来る	来て	来ない	来ないで

One important point to be noted is that the [V*te + -kudasai*] structure is not normally used toward one's social superiors. Since this form clearly spells out the request without much consideration given to the requested, however politely it is delivered, it conveys the feeling of a mild command. The [V*te + -kudasai*] expresses a request or command made politely or casually toward social equals or subordinates. In fact public notices and announcements which prohibit smoking are expressed in a formal style as in: *(o) tabako wa goenryo kudasai* 'Please refrain from smoking.' If one wants to request something from one's social superior, interrogative sentences with respectful forms, that is, [V*te + -itadakemasu ka*], [V*te + -itadake-masu-deshoo ka*] and [V*te + -itadakemasen-deshoo ka*] are preferred. (This will be discussed later again.)

Additional Information

The negative gerundive may also be formed by the negative expression of *nai*, i.e., *nakute*. For example, *iwanakute*, instead of *iwanaide*. There are some restrictions in using these forms. See Entry 76 for differences between *-naide* and *-nakute*. The [V*te + -kudasai*] structure requires *-naide* endings.

Examples

```
-----------------------------------------------------------------
denwa-suru  電話する   V    to make a phone call
wasureru    忘れる     V    to forget
isogu       急ぐ       V    to hurry
oshieru     教える     V    to teach
-----------------------------------------------------------------
```

(1) *Denwa-shite-kudasai.*
     電話してください。
     (Please call.)

(2) *Wasurenaide-kudasai.*
     忘れないでください。
     (Please don't forget.)

(3) *Isoide!* ☺
     急いで！
     (Hurry!)

(4) *Oshiete ne.* ☺
     教えてね。
     (Tell me, will you?)

Practice

---

to lend	V	*kasu*	貸す
right away	Adv	*sugu*	すぐ
to enter	V	*hairu*	入る
to fill (in the form)	V	*kinyuu-suru*	記入する
pen	N	*pen*	ペン
to rescue	V	*tasukeru*	助ける

Make the following requests to your colleagues and friends.

1. to lend (me) this book
2. to come right away
3. not to enter
4. to fill in the form by pen
5. to rescue (me) ☺

─────── Answers ───────
1. *Kono hon kashite-kudasai.* この本貸してください。
2. *Ima sugu kite-kudasai.* 今すぐ来てください。
3. *Hairanaide-kudasai.* 入らないでください。
4. *Pen de kinyuushite-kudasai.* ペンで記入してください。
5. *Tasukete!* ☺ 助けて！

41. Appealing to the Listener—2. Tagged Auxiliary Verbs

Target Expression

You saw Kazuko today, didn't you?
> ***Kyoo Kazuko-san ni atta-deshoo?***
> 今日 和子さんに会ったでしょう？

Grammatical Explanation

Auxiliary verb forms, *-daro(o)* and *-desho(o)*, when pronounced with rising intonation, may be added immediately following the verb and adjectives to appeal to the listener. When *-daro(o)/-desho(o)* are tagged, similarly to the interactional particle *ne*, a meaning of 'isn't it right?' and 'don't you agree?' is added. It is a question requesting confirmation and/or agreement. The form immediately preceding *-daro(o)* is what I call "pre-auxiliary form." There are several cases where [pre-Aux] forms precede items including [AuxV] and auxiliary adjective [AuxAdj] forms, and therefore it is useful to learn this set of V/Adj forms for the combinations we will learn later. First, let us find out what these forms are.

Pre-aux Forms

Verbs	non-past, affirmative	*oyogu*
	non-past, negative	*oyoganai*
	past, affirmative	*oyoida*
	past, negative	*oyoganakatta*
Existential	non-past, affirmative	*aru, iru*
Verbs	non-past, negative	*nai, inai*
	past, affirmative	*atta, ita*
	past, negative	*nakatta, inakatta*
Be-verb	non-past, affirmative	(deleted totally)
	non-past, negative	*dewa-nai, ja-nai*
	past, affirmative	*datta*
	past, negative	*dewa-nakatta, ja-nakatta*
Adj-*i*	non-past, affirmative	*akai*
	non-past, negative	*akakunai*
	past, affirmative	*akakatta*
	past, negative	*akakunakatta*
Adj-*na*	non-past, affirmative	*kantan*
	non-past, negative	*kantandewa-nai, kantanja-nai*
	past, affirmative	*kantandatta*
	past, negative	*kantandewa-nakatta, kantanja-nakatta*

Although *-daroo* and *-deshoo* were introduced earlier as expressions of uncertainty, they are introduced here again since they function differently when used as tagged [AuxV]. Note that *-daro(o)/-desho(o)* discussed here are always pronounced with rising intonation. *-Deshoo* is normally used by females, and *-daroo* by males in casual conversation; these expressions are used primarily in spoken discourse. The shorter versions *-desho* and *-daro* are used among *uchi* members in casual situations only. These expressions encourage friendliness and closeness among speakers and listeners. In extremely colloquial situations *-jan* is used for the same purpose, but this form should be avoided; it carries colloquialism lacking in education and/or maturity. Since both *-deshoo* and *-daroo* request confirmation or agreement, the listener normally sends feedback responses such as *un* or *hun*.

The use of *-daroo* and *-deshoo* should be avoided when speaking to one's social superior. This is because these phrases ask for confirmation of something that your superior is assumed to already know. Using these phrases gives the impression that you are challenging the depth and the extent of your superior's knowledge; it carries a condescending tone.

Examples

```
-------------------------------------------------------------
hora    ほら     Int    interjection requesting
                        attention
toki    時      N      time
-------------------------------------------------------------
```

(1) A: *Hora, kyoo Tanaka-san ni atta-desho?* ☺**F**
　　　ほら，今日 田中さんに会ったでしょ？
　　　(See, I saw Ms. Tanaka today, right?)
　　B: *Un.*
　　　うん。
　　　(Uh huh.)
　　A: *Ano toki ne, moo ku-ji han datta-desho?* ☺**F**
　　　あの時ね，もう九時半だったでしょ？
　　　(At that time, it was already 9:30, wasn't it?)
　　B: *Un.*
　　　うん。
　　　(Yeah.)

(2) 　*Moo takusan tabeta-daro?* ☺**M**
　　　もうたくさん食べただろ？
　　　(You already ate enough, didn't you?)

(3) 　*Asoko ni bijutsukan ga aru-deshoo?* **F**
　　　あそこに美術館があるでしょう？
　　　(There is an art museum over there, isn't there?)

Practice

By adding tagged auxiliary verbs, express the following in either male or female style according to your gender.

1.   Your teacher is strict, right? ☺
2. A: You are going to see our (company) president at the Ginza
       tonight, right? ☺
    B: Yeah, I am. ☺

─────── Answers ───────
1.   *Sensei kibishii-daro?* ☺ **M**   先生きびしいだろ？
     Sensei kibishii-deshoo? ☺ **F**   先生きびしいでしょう？
2. A: *Kon'ya Ginza de shachoo ni au-daro?* ☺**M**
      今夜銀座で社長に会うだろ？
      Kon'ya Ginza de shachoo ni au-desho? ☺ **F**
      今夜銀座で社長に会うでしょ？
   B: *Aa, au yo.* ☺**M**   ああ，会うよ。
      Ee, au wa yo. ☺ **F**   ええ，会うわよ。

42. Inquiring—2. Negative Questions

> *Didn't Mr. Yamada come to the company yesterday?*
> **Yamada-san wa kinoo kaisha ni kimasen-deshita ka.**
> 山田さんはきのう会社に来ませんでしたか。

Grammatical Explanation

Placing the question marker *ka* immediately after a negative verb ending
creates a negative question. Negative questions are also produced by slightly
raising the last syllable of formal or informal negative statements;
ikimasen-deshita? and *ikanakatta?*, for example. In addition to this type of
negative question, there are two other possibilities for expressing questions
which strongly assume negation. One is the utterance with the tagged
[AuxV] form *-desho(o)/-daro(o)* added after the negative verb ending. For
example, 'you didn't go to a concert yesterday, did you?' can be expressed
in Japanese *kinoo ongakukai ni ikanakatta-desho?* The other is adding *ne*
for confirmation; *ikimasen-deshita ne* 'you didn't go, did you?'

One point of interest regarding the negative question; present tense negative questions addressed directly to the listener may be used to invite or request, as shown in example (3).

Examples

taipuraitaa	タイプライター	N	typewriter
tsukau	使う	V	to use
yuushoku	夕食	N	dinner
minna	みんな	N	everyone
kaigi	会議	N	meeting
shusseki-suru	出席する	V	to attend

(1)　　*Kazuko-san, watashi no taipuraitaa tsukawanakatta?*
　　　和子さん, 私のタイプライター使わなかった？
　　　(Kazuko, didn't you use my typewriter?)

(2)　　*Yamada-san konakatta-desho?*
　　　山田さん来なかったでしょ？
　　　(Mr. Yamada didn't come, did he?)

(3) A:　*Yuushoku isshoni shimasen ka.*
　　　夕食いっしょにしませんか。
　　　(Won't you have dinner with me?)
　　B:　*Ii-desu nee.*
　　　いいですねえ。
　　　(That will be nice.)

(4) A:　*Minna kaigi ni shusseki-shimashita ka.*[1]
　　　みんな会議に出席しましたか。
　　　(Did everyone attend the meeting?)
　　B:　*Iie.*
　　　いいえ。
　　　(No.)
　　A:　*Dare ga imasen-deshita ka.*
　　　誰がいませんでしたか。
　　　(Who wasn't there?)
　　B:　*Koyama-san ga shusseki-shimasen-deshita ga. . . .*
　　　小山さんが出席しませんでしたが……
　　　(Ms. Koyama didn't attend.)

[1].　The verb *shusseki-suru* takes *ni* as a direct object marker.

43. Responding to Questions—2. Answering Negative Questions

Target Expressions

> *Didn't Mr. Yamada come to the company yesterday?*
> **Yamada-san wa kinoo kaisha ni kimasen-deshita ka.**
> 山田さんはきのう会社に来ませんでしたか。
> *No, he didn't.*
> **Ee, kimasen-deshita ga. . .**
> ええ，来ませんでしたが……

Strategic Explanation

When answering a negative question, what is assumed by the questioner plays a major role. If the assumption is negative, answering *yes* or *no* depends on whether that negative assumption is agreeable (yes) or not (no). Thus in the target expression, unlike English, the listener responds that the questioner's assumption is correct by *ee* 'yes,' although the content of the answer itself is negative as shown above in *kimasen-deshita ga. . . .*

Even in negative questions, if the assumption is positive—as when they are used for invitation and request, the use of *ee/iie* is similar to the use for affirmative questions, that is, *ee* (or *hai*) indicates agreement to the positiveness, whereas *iie* is used to make a negative answer. Negative questions may also be used for politeness and indirectness. For example, *denwa wa arimasen ka* instead of *denwa wa arimasu ka* is a politer way of asking for the same information. In this case even though the construction is negative, the speaker's assumption is not.

If you get confused about the usage of *ee* (or *hai*) and *iie* when answering (negative) questions, one way to avoid any misunderstandings is to avoid saying *ee* or *iie* altogether. Simply answer with a verb, either in the affirmative or negative form. For example, when asked *ikimasen-deshita ka?*, by answering with *ikimashita yo* or *ikimasen-deshita yo*, you will communicate clearly.

Examples

```
------------------------------------------------------------
imooto     妹      N    (my) younger sister
kissaten   喫茶店   N    coffee shop
------------------------------------------------------------
```

(1) A: *Imooto ni awanakatta-desho?* ☺**F**
妹に会わなかったでしょ？

(You didn't see my younger sister, did you?)

B: *Un, awanakatta wa yo.* ☺**F**
うん，会わなかったわよ。

(No, I didn't see [her].)

(2) A: *Kinoo Sakai-san to isshoni Shinjuku e ikimasen-deshita ne.*
きのう酒井さんといっしょに新宿へ行きませんでしたね。

(Didn't you go to Shinjuku yesterday with Mr. Sakai?)

B: *Ee, ikimasen-deshita.*
ええ，行きませんでした。

(No, I didn't go.)

(3) A: *Nihongo no waapuro wa arimasen ka.*
日本語のワープロはありませんか。

(Is there a Japanese language word processer?)

B: *Ee, arimasu yo.*
ええ，ありますよ。

(Sure, there is.)

(4) A: *Atode kissaten e ikimasen ka.*
あとで喫茶店へ行きませんか。

(Won't you go to a coffee shop later?)

B: *Kyoo wa chotto . . .*[*1]
今日はちょっと……

(Not today . . .)

*1. When responding to an invitation, if the answer is negative, an expression such as *kyoo wa chotto* '(lit. today a bit . . .) perhaps not today . . .' is useful. There is no need to elaborate why you cannot accept the invitation. Just let your speech trail off after saying *chotto. . . .*

Practice

Ginza　銀座　　**PN**　Ginza (place name in
　　　　　　　　　　　　Tokyo)

Provide a question-answer pair or a brief conversation for the following situations.

1. Your friend didn't go to the library today. You suspect she didn't go there yesterday either.

2. Last night you heard the telephone ringing as you opened the door to your apartment. By the time you got to the phone, it stopped ringing. This morning you meet Kayoko whom you suspect might have

called you the night before. How will you find out if it was indeed her who called? Use negative question for indirectness. ☺

3. You suspect that your friend didn't study at all when he was in college. How will you find out the truth? ☺

4. You politely ask your colleague whether she would like to go to the Ginza with you next Sunday.

———— Some Sample Answers ————

1. A: *Kinoo mo ikimasen-deshita ka.* きのうも行きませんでしたか。
   B: *Ee, ikimasen-deshita.* ええ，行きませんでした。

2. A: *Kayoko-san, yuube denwa shinakatta?* ☺
   加代子さん，ゆうべ電話しなかった？
   B: *(Un,) shinakatta wa yo.* ☺ （うん，）しなかったわよ。

3. A: *Zenzen benkyoo-shinakattadesho?* ☺
   全然勉強しなかったでしょ？
   B: *Uun, shita yo.* ☺ ううん，したよ。
   A: *Itsu?* ☺ いつ？
   B: *Yuube. San-jikan.* ☺ ゆうべ。三時間。
   A: *Uso desho?* ☺ うそでしょ？
   B: *Uso ja-nai yo.* ☺ うそじゃないよ。

4. A: *Raishuu no nichiyoobi isshoni Ginza e ikimasen ka.*
   来週の日曜日いっしょに銀座へ行きませんか。
   B: *Ee, Nanji goro?* ええ。何時ごろ？
   A: *Juu-ji wa doo desu ka.* 十時はどうですか。
   B: *Ii-desu yo. Juu-ji ne.* いいですよ。十時ね。

44. Inviting and Suggesting—2. Inviting and Suggesting to Do Something Together

Target Expressions

Shall we eat?

Let's eat.

Tabemashoo ka.
食べましょうか。

Tabemashoo.
食べましょう。

[Vstem + *mashoo (ka)*]

[V + *(y)oo (ka)*]

Strategic Explanation

When inviting and suggesting to do something, use non-past negative verb forms; for example, *tabemasen (ka)?* 'shall we eat?' There is an additional form, the "volitional" form, used for invitation and suggestion. Volitional forms are available for verbs that describe humanly controllable action only. Invitation expressed by volitional forms is direct, and should not be used toward social superiors. For the purpose of inviting social superiors, *ikaga deshoo ka* and other respectful strategies are required. In order to reach volitional forms, the following operation is necessary.

Volitional

Formal:	All verbs	change *-masu* of formal non-past form to *-mashoo* (i.e., [Vstem + *mashoo*])
Informal:	*U*-verbs	change the last vowel *-u* to *-oo*
	RU-verbs	change the final *-ru* to *-yoo*
	Irregular verbs	*suru* takes *shiyoo*
		kuru takes *koyoo*

For existential verbs, only *iru* meaning 'to stay' takes the form *iyoo* and *imashoo*. Inviting and suggesting by using volitional forms is similar to the English expression of "let's . . ." or "let's not . . ." Volitional forms may also be used with the interrogative particle *ka*. Use *naide-iyoo, naide-imashoo, naide-okoo* and *naide-okimashoo* for the negative invitation and suggestion; for example, *ikanaide-imashoo* 'let's not go,' *tabenaide-iyoo* 'let's not eat,' *kakanaide-okoo* 'let's not write it (and leave it as is)' and *tabenaide-okimashoo* 'let's not eat it (and leave it as is).'

Additional Information

When the subject of the volitional form is the first-person singular, it expresses the will and intention of the speaker. This expression normally appears in the form *-(y)oo to omotte-iru* (lit. thinking to do), for example, *ikoo to omotte-imasu* 'I think I will go.' Depending on the context, the first-person *ikoo* and *ikimashoo* may also function as formal expression of the speaker's will, meaning 'I will go.' When volitional forms are used for interrogative purposes with the first person subject, they function as "consultative." For example, *ikoo ka?* or *ikimashoo ka?* 'shall I go?'

Examples

(1) A: *Doo desu ka, koohii demo nomimashoo ka.*
どうですか，コーヒーでも飲みましょうか。
(How about . . . shall we have coffee or something?)

B: *Ee, depaato no soba no kissaten e ikimashoo.*
ええ，デパートのそばの喫茶店へ行きましょう。
(Yes, let's go to a coffee shop near the department store.)

(2) *Saa, ikimashoo.*
さあ，行きましょう。
(OK, let's go.)

Saa, ikoo. ☺
さあ，行こう。
(OK, let's go.)

(3) A: *Jaa, hairimashoo ka.*
じゃあ，入りましょうか。
(Well, shall we enter?)

B: *Ee, soo shimashoo.*
ええ，そうしましょう。
(Yes, let's do that.)

(4) *Hayaku ikoo.* ☺
早く行こう。
(Let's go now.)

(5) A: *Tetsudaimashoo ka.*
手伝いましょうか。
(Shall I assist you?)

B: *Ee, onegai-shimasu.*
ええ，お願いします。
(Yes, please.)

(6) A: *Kyoo wa samui-desu nee. Ikanaide-imashoo.*
今日は寒いですねえ。行かないでいましょう。

(It's cold today, isn't it? Let's not go.)

B: *Ee, soo desu ne.*
ええ，そうですね。

(Yes, I guess so.)

(7) A: *Watashi ga ikimashoo.*
私が行きましょう。

(I will go.)

B: *Soo desu ka. Onegai-shimasu.*
そうですか。お願いします。

(All right. Please take care of it.)

Practice

```
------------------------------------------------------------
door          N  to        戸
to close      V  shimeru   閉める
------------------------------------------------------------
```

1. Invite your friend to do the following:
   a. make a trip together this summer
   b. have coffee or something at the coffee shop ☺
   c. play tennis tomorrow
   d. go out for dinner together

2. Ask your superior if you should do the following for him or her:
   a. open the package
   b. close the door
   c. call Ms. Kato (on the phone)

―――― Some Sample Answers ――――

1a. *Kotoshi no natsu isshoni ryokoo-shimashoo yo.*
今年の夏いっしょに旅行しましょうよ。

b. *Kissaten de koohii demo nomoo.* ☺
喫茶店でコーヒーでも飲もう。

c. *Ashita tenisu demo shimasen ka.*
あしたテニスでもしませんか。

d. *Kon'ya yuushoku isshoni ikaga desu ka.*
今夜夕食いっしょにいかがですか。

2a. *Sono kozutsumi akemashoo ka.* その小包み開けましょうか。

b. *To o shimemashoo ka.* 戸を閉めましょうか。

c. *Katoo-san ni denwa-shimashoo ka.*
加藤さんに電話しましょうか。

45. Responding to Invitations and Suggestions

Target Expression

Yes, let's do that.

Ee, soo shimashoo.
ええ，そうしましょう。

Strategic Explanation

When suggestions and invitations are offered, there are formulaic responses that will prove quite useful. When invited, for example, by the expression *ikimashoo* 'let's go,' the following responses are available.

1. *Positive:*

   (1a) *Ee, ii-desu nee.*
   ええ，いいですねえ。
   (Yes, that will be nice.)

   (1b) *Ee, soo shimashoo ka.*
   ええ，そうしましょうか。
   (Yes, shall we do that then?)

   (1c) *Ee, soo shimashoo.*
   ええ，そうしましょう。
   (Yes, let's do so.)

   (1d) *Un, soo shiyoo.* ☺
   うん，そうしよう。
   (Yeah, let's do so.)

   (1e) *Ee, yorokonde.*
   ええ，よろこんで。
   (With pleasure.)

   (1f) *Ee, zehi.*
   ええ，ぜひ。
   (Yes, by all means.)

2. *Negative:*

   (2a) *Soo desu nee. Chotto . . .*
   そうですねえ。ちょっと……
   (Let me see. Uhh . . .)

(2b) *Kon'ya wa chotto . . .*
今夜はちょっと……
(Tonight isn't the best time . . .)

3. *Undecided:*

(3a) *Soo desu nee . . .*
そうですねえ……
(Well . . .)

(3b) *Soo da naa . . .* ☺**M**
そうだなあ……
Soo nee . . . ☺**F**
そうねえ……
(Well . . .)

Examples

---

juusho	住所	**N**	address
iie, kekkoo desu			no, thank you
いいえ，結構です			no, there's no need to do so
ohiru	お昼	**N**	(lit. noon) lunch

---

(1) A: *Juusho o kakimashoo ka.*
住所を書きましょうか。
(Shall I write the address?)
B: *Ee, onegai-shimasu.*
ええ，お願いします。
(Yes, please.)
C: *Iie, kekkoo desu.*
いいえ，結構です。
(No, there is no need to do that.)

(2) A: *Ohiru demo isshoni doo desu ka.*
お昼でもいっしょにどうですか。
(How about having lunch together?)
B: *Ee, yorokonde.*
ええ，よろこんで。
(Yes, I'll be glad to.)
C: *Watashi wa chotto . . .*
私はちょっと……
(I'm tied up with something . . .)

Practice

Answer the following invitations and suggestions positively and negatively.

1. *Atode isshoni shokuji (o) shimasen ka.*
   あとでいっしょに食事(を)しませんか。
2. *Sorosoro kaerimashoo ka.*
   そろそろ帰りましょうか。
3. *Ashita denwa-shimashoo ka.*
   あした電話しましょうか。

--------- Some Sample Answers ---------

1. *Ee, zehi.*　　　　　　　　　　ええ，ぜひ。
   Kyoo wa chotto . . .　　　　　今日はちょっと……
2. *Soo desu ne. Soo shimashoo.*　そうですね。そうしましょう。
   Soo desu nee, mada chotto . . . そうですねえ，まだちょっと……
3. *Ee, onegai-shimasu.*　ええ，お願いします。
   Iie, kekkoo desu. Kochira kara denwa-shimasu.
   いいえ，結構です。こちらから電話します。
   (No, there's no need. I will call you.)

46.　Verbal Predicate—5.　Transitive and Intransitive Verbs

Target Expressions

Please open the door.
> **Doa o akete-kudasai.**
> ドアを開けてください。

The library opens at eight.
> **Toshokan wa hachi-ji ni akimasu.**
> 図書館は八時に開きます。

[Vt]
[Vint]

Grammatical Explanation

There are two basic ways an event may be described in language. The first is the type, "agent-operates-on-another-entity." For example, in the sentence

John eats an apple, the agent (John) operates (eats) on another entity (an apple). The second is the type "agent-conducts-itself." For example, in the sentence *John sleeps,* the agent (John) conducts itself (sleeps). The verbs that prototypically co-occur with the first and the second type are transitive and intransitive, respectively.

Having said this, a more important point must be raised. In Japanese, there is a strong tendency to view and describe an event as something happening by itself—often beyond the control of an agent. In short, the language is skewed to favor intransitive description. The transitive/intransitive distinction in English, therefore, is not reflected fully in Japanese. For Japanese, to view the world as "agent-operates-on-another-entity" is not a required axis as observed in English. Recall that Japanese is not under strict grammatical constraint as in English to create a sentence to fit this mold. The structure of the Japanese sentence is fluid and remains sensitive to the context in which it is used. This does not mean that Japanese do not describe events in the first type; in fact transitive verbs, or the use of verbs as transitive verbs, occur substantially. Nonetheless, orientation toward intransitiveness is a strong general undercurrent in Japanese.

Four Types of Verb Forms

In Japanese there are four types of transitive/intransitive verb forms as described below.

1. *Absolute intransitive verbs:*
   (Used solely as intransitive verbs)

shinu	死ぬ	to die
naku	泣く	to cry
aruku	歩く	to walk

2. *Transitive/intransitive pairs:*
   A number of transitive/intransitive verb pairs with similar roots including those that will be listed later.

3. *Absolute transitive verbs:*
   (Used solely as transitive verbs)

korosu	殺す	to kill
taberu	食べる	to eat
kiru	切る	to cut

4. *Verbs with both transitive and intransitive use:*
   (An identical verb used either as transitive or intransitive)

hiraku	開く	to open, to be opened
tojiru	閉じる	to close, to be closed

List of Transitive/Intransitive Pairs

	[Vt]	[Vint]
-u/-aru	husagu (to clog up) ふさぐ	husagaru (to be clogged up) ふさがる
-eru/-aru	mitsukeru (to find) 見つける	mitsukaru (to be found) 見つかる
-eru/-u	akeru (to open) 開ける	aku (to be opened) 開く
-su/-ru	naosu (to correct) 直す	naoru (to be corrected) 直る
-osu/-iru	okosu (to wake) 起こす	okiru (to get up) 起きる
-asu/-eru	samasu (to cool) さます	sameru (to become cool) さめる
-asu/-iru	tozasu (to shut) 閉ざす	tojiru (to be shut) 閉じる
-asu/-u	kawakasu (to dry) かわかす	kawaku (to be dried up) かわく
-esu/-ieru	kesu (to extinguish) 消す	kieru (to be extinguished) 消える

Note that these changes occur only among transitive/intransitive paired verbs. The changes described are not applicable to non-paired verbs.

In order to understand the difference between transitive and intransitive verbs, let us imagine a situation where an agent (Ms. Kanai) opened the door. This incident can be viewed in at least two following ways.

(a) **Kanai-san ga doa o akemashita.**
金井さんがドアを開けました。
(Ms. Kanai opened the door.)

The observer notices that someone (Ms. Kanai) acts toward another entity. The primary information derived from this view is that the agent performs an act on something or someone that experiences that act. The action is interpreted as dynamic, in that by performing an act, something (or someone) else becomes directly involved. In this view Kanai's action makes a physical impact on an object, door, which changes the general state of the event.

(b) **Doa ga akimashita.**
ドアが開きました。
(The door opened.)

The observer describes the event focusing upon the door and what happened to the door. The observer may not have access to information as to who or what opened the door. Or, it could be that he or she simply wishes to concentrate on the door, although he or she knows who or what (in this case Ms. Kanai) opened the door. Imagine, for example, a situation where Ms. Kanai had several keys and she is uncertain as to which one fits the door. After trying several, she finally succeeds. An observer may utter, *aa, doa ga aita!* defocusing on who or which key opened the door.

"Reactive" Descriptions and Transitive/Intransitive Verbs

An important issue closely related to transitive and intransitive verbs must be raised here. The predisposition not to mention the agent in Japanese is closely related to the way some Japanese sentence patterns follow. Earlier we defined subject in a broad sense—as an element of primary predicate focus. The person who directly experiences a phenomenon and who immediately reports this phenomenon is the experiencer and can be, but not necessarily, expressed with the [N + *ga*] structure.

It is important to identify the sentences which contain the source for the experiencer's reaction (sentences of "reactive" description) in light of transitive and intransitive verbs. Here are other verbal and adjectival predicates which are used for "reactive" description (see Appendix 5 for the full list of these predicates). Further explanation will be given in separate entries as indicated. Remembering these types of sentences is important. This is because the *ga*-marked subjects in these structures do not correspond to the grammatical subjects in English and therefore they sometimes cause confusion. The easiest way to master these special sentence structures is to memorize some representative sentences and use them for future reference points.

1. *Natural phenomena:*

   (1a) *Ame ga hutte-iru.*
   雨が降っている。
   (It is raining.)

2. *Sense and perception:*

   (2a) *Ii nioi ga suru.*　　　　　(See Entry 128)
   いいにおいがする。
   (It smells good.)

3. *Emotional response:*

   (3a) *Ano hito ga suki da.*　　　(See Entry 68)
   あの人が好きだ。
   (I like him.)

(3b) *Kodomo no koro   ga   natsukashii.*
child   L   time   S   nostalgic
子供の頃がなつかしい。
(I feel nostalgic about my childhood.)

4. *Spontaneous occurrence:*

(4a) *Yama ga mieru.*   (See Entry 67)
山が見える。
(The mountain is seen.)

5. *Physical condition:*

(5a) *Seki ga deru.*   (See Entry 66)
せきが出る。
([lit. Coughs appear.] I cough.)

6. *Others:*

(6a) *Nihongo ga wakarimasu.*   (See Entry 53)
日本語がわかります。
([lit. Japanese is understood.] I understand Japanese.)

(6b) *Kaigairyokoo   no tame   no   okane   ga   irimasu.*
overseas travel   for   L   money   S   need
海外旅行のためのお金がいります。
([lit. Money for overseas travel is needed.] I need money for overseas travel.)

Note that some grammarians treat sentences such as *ano hito ga suki da* 'I like that person' in a way different from the way it is explained here. They view that *ano hito* is an object of the adjectival predicate *suki da*, although it is marked by *ga*. According to this view, *ga* is explained as marking subjects as well as objects in some special cases (as this one).

Examples

(1) a. *Ashita no asa wa roku-ji ni okoshite kudasai ne.*
あしたの朝は六時に起こしてくださいね。
(Please wake me up at six o'clock tomorrow morning.)

b. *Maiasa nan-ji ni okimasu ka.*
毎朝何時に起きますか。
(What time do you get up every morning?)

(2) a. *Machigai o naoshimashoo ka.*
まちがいを直しましょうか。
(Shall I correct the mistake?)

b. *Machigai wa moo naorimashita yo.*
まちがいはもう直りましたよ。
(The mistake is already corrected.)

Additional Information

Other ways to describe a door being opened include: (1) *Doa ga akerareta.* 'The door was opened,' (2) *Doa ga aite-iru.* 'The door is open,' and (3) *Doa ga akete-aru.* '(Someone opened the door, and as a result) the door is open.' These expressions will be discussed later under separate entries.

Although in English an instrument can become the subject of the verb *open*, as in *this key opened the door*, in Japanese an inanimate object normally cannot perform dynamic action. In Japanese then, *kono kagi de doa o akemashita* 'with this key, (I) opened the door' must be used.

The morphological changes listed above between transitive and its intransitive counterpart show an interesting feature; transitive verbs tend to have -*su* (as in -*asu*, -*osu*, -*su*) while intransitive verbs have -*aru*, -*eru*, -*iru* and -*ru* endings. This is associated with the fact that in Japanese, causative takes -*(s)aseru* ending, and the passive takes -*(r)areru* ending, as we will learn later.

47. Common Apologies

Target Expression

> *I'm sorry.*
>
> **Sumimasen.**
> すみません。

Strategic Explanation

Typically Japanese apologize far more frequently than Americans. Apologies convey that a person recognizes one's own responsibility and the failure to meet the expectations of others. This in turn relieves the blame on others, and therefore shows thoughtfulness and kindness toward others. Apology is considered a virtue in Japan. When one apologizes and shows regret, Japanese are often emotionally moved and are more willing to forgive.

While Japanese are ready to apologize frequently, Americans seem reluctant to admit their own failures, much less to apologize. Apologizing, since theoretically it admits one's failure, may not be the best route to take if the problem is to be resolved in a court of law. Admitting guilt is interpreted as a confession of wrongdoing. But for Japanese, apologizing, sometimes profusely, is a sign of humility and admittance of one's own weakness which deserves understanding and sympathy. This contrast in apology phenomena is clearly observable in service encounters. Japanese merchants and service providers are ready to apologize for the slightest inconveniences their customers may encounter.

The formulaic phrases for apology are the following:

Sumimasen. すみません。	I'm sorry.
Mooshiwake arimasen. 申しわけありません。	I'm sorry. (polite)
Gomennasai. ごめんなさい。	I'm sorry, please forgive me.
Gomen. ☺ ごめん。	Sorry, excuse me. (casual)
Shitsurei. ☺ 失礼。	Sorry, excuse me. (frequently used by males)

We should be warned that *sumimasen* and *mooshiwake arimasen* are used for the purpose of expressing gratitude as well, which will be discussed later. Depending on circumstances, it is important to interpret some of these as expressions of gratitude, and not as apologies.

When apologizing, it is important that you give non-verbal signals along with your words. The more deeply felt your apology, the more slowly and deeply you bow. During the apology, one is normally expected to cast one's eyes downward and to assume an apologetic and humble stance.

There is a widely told episode (or different versions of the similar episode) which involves the apologetic attitude of Japanese which a foreigner in Japan failed to understand (see Kindaichi [1985]). A foreign maid said to her Japanese employer, *koppu ga kowaremashita* 'the glass broke.' This expression does not imply that the maid broke the glass. The expression *koppu o kowashimashita* 'I broke the glass,' however, implies that the blame is hers, since the transitive verb *kowasu* is used instead of the intransitive *kowareru*. Although the glass might have been old, and possibly it had a crack in it anyway so it may not necessarily have been the case that the maid caused it to break, Japanese prefer to hear *koppu o kowashite-shimaimashita*, an expression to willingly take the blame. This expression, normally coupled with an apology, something like *sumimasen, koppu o kowashite-shimaimashita*, is a formulaic strategy for apology. The use of transitive and intransitive verbs can convey very different social meanings, indeed.

As a student of Japanese, you may not feel comfortable to readily apologize for the smallest things for which theoretically you may not even be responsible for. There is no need to imitate Japanese behavior to the extent that you feel uncomfortable. It is useful, however, to know the different social meanings attached to the behavior of apology in Japan and in your native country.

I should also warn you that what deserves an apology differs from society to society. For example, during Tokyo's morning rush hour, it is practically impossible to apologize to everyone you bump into or whom you inadvertently touch. There are some occasions where allegedly polite Japanese do not apologize for what you think deserves an apology, and vice versa. Learning intricacies of these social rules is a part of the education we continue to receive by living in any society whether you are a native or a non-native speaker.

48. Adverbs—1. Common Adverbs

Target Expression

> *Please get up early tomorrow.*
> **Ashita hayaku okite-kudasai.**
> あした早く起きてください。

Grammatical Explanation

Just as adverbs may be formed by adding a suffix -*ly* to some adjectives in English (happy-happily), Japanese is equipped with two such processes. One is to generate adverbs from [Adj-*i*] by changing the final -*i* to -*ku*, that is, *oishii* (adjective) and *oishiku* (adverb). The other method is to form adverbs from [Adj-*na*] by changing the final -*na* to -*ni*, that is, *kireina* (adjective) and *kireini* (adverb). Additional examples are:

[Adj-*i*]		[Adv]	
atarashii	新しい	atarashiku	新しく
atatakai	暖かい	atatakaku	暖かく
atsui	暑い	atsuku	暑く
samui	寒い	samuku	寒く

[Adj-*na*]		[Adv]	
kantanna	簡単な	kantanni	簡単に
benrina	便利な	benrini	便利に

Adverbs are placed according to the word-order preference studied earlier (Entry 18). Among adverbs, temporal and locative adverbs precede other adverbs. Other commonly used adverbs, including adverbial quantifiers we learned earlier, are listed below:

sugu	すぐ	right away, soon
moo	もう	already, more (when used with degree words as in *moo sukoshi* 'a little more')
ato de	あとで	later
ittai	いったい	in the world (emphatic as in *what in the world*)
itsumo	いつも	always
guuzen	偶然	unexpectedly, coincidentally
kondo	今度	this time, next time
sakki	さっき	a while ago
tsuini	ついに	finally, at last
tokidoki	ときどき	sometimes
tamani	たまに	occasionally
nakanaka	なかなか	with difficulty
hinpanni	ひんぱんに	frequently
mamonaku	間もなく	soon, in no time
motto	もっと	more (*motto muzukashii* 'more difficult')
mottomo	最も	most (*mottomo muzukashii* 'most difficult')
yukkuri	ゆっくり	slowly, leisurely
yoku	よく	frequently, well
yooyaku	ようやく	with toil

Some adverbs expressing manners of action optionally take *to*, as in *hakkiri/hakkiri to* 'clearly,' *yukkuri/yukkuri to* 'slowly,' and so forth.

Examples

----
yoku	よく	Adv	well
tsuku	着く	V	to arrive

bubun	部分	N	part, section
tsukuru	作る	V	to make
naru	なる	V	to become

----

(1)　　*Yoku benkyoo-shimashita ne.*
　　　よく勉強しましたね。
　　　(You studied well.)

(2) A: *Densha wa itsu tsukimasu ka.*
　　　電車はいつ着きますか。
　　　(When will the train arrive?)

　　B: *Sugu tsukimasu yo.*
　　　すぐ着きますよ。
　　　(It should be here any moment!)

(3) A: *Kono bubun wa atarashiku tsukurimashita.*
　　　この部分は新しく作りました。
　　　(I newly made this section.)

　　B: *Koko wa?*
　　　ここは？
　　　(How about here?)

　　A: *Aa, soko wa atode shimasu.*
　　　ああ、そこはあとでします。
　　　(Oh, I'll do that later.)

(4) A: *Samuku narimashita nee.*
　　　寒くなりましたねえ。
　　　(It has become cold, hasn't it?)

　　B: *Ee, hontooni.*
　　　ええ、本当に。
　　　(Yes, it sure has.)

Practice

----

there is a 　　phone call	(idiomatic)	*denwa ga aru* 電話がある

Paying special attention to the underlined adverbs, express the following in Japanese.

1. Suggest your friend to go to the coffee shop <u>later</u>.
2. Tell your friend that there was a phone call <u>a while ago</u>. ☺
3. Tell your friend her sister became <u>really pretty</u>.
4. Request to your friend to come <u>right away</u>. ☺

—————— Answers ——————

1. *Atode kissaten e ikimashoo.*　あとで喫茶店へ行きましょう。
2. *Sakki denwa ga atta yo.* ☺　さっき電話があったよ。
3. *Hontooni kireini narimashita ne.*　本当にきれいになりましたね。
4. *Sugu kite.* ☺　すぐ来て。

Additional Information

Some adverbs are used almost like nouns. For example, the adverb *itsumo* 'always' may be used like a noun as shown below:

(a) 　**Itsumo** *no tabemono o chuumon-shimashita.*
いつもの食べ物を注文しました。

(I ordered the usual [food].)

(b) A: *Chichi wa maiasa roku-ji goro sanpo-shimasu.*
父は毎朝六時頃散歩します。

(My father always takes a walk about six o'clock every morning.)

B: **Itsumo** *desu ka.*
いつもですか。

(Always?)

A: *Ee,* **itsumo.**
ええ，いつも。

(Yes, always.)

Some manner adverbs are combined with the verb *suru* to form verbs. For example, *yukkuri-suru* means 'to take it easy, to spend time leisurely.'

49. Offering and Accepting Assistance

Target Expressions

Shall I help you?

　　　Tetsudaimashoo ka.
　　　手伝いましょうか。

Yes, thanks.

　　　Sumimasen, onegai-shimasu.
　　　すみません，お願いします。

Strategic Explanation

Earlier we have studied the consultative use of the volitional forms -(y)oo (ka) and the [Vstem + mashoo (ka)] construction. These expressions function to offer activity favorable or beneficial to the addressee. *Tetsudai-mashoo ka?* 'shall I help you?' for example, is used to offer assistance. How should one accept assistance offered from others?

The concept of *enryo*, a refusal of receiving another's favor for fear of the inconvenience it may cause, often discussed in literature on Japanese culture and society, plays a major part in the process of accepting a favor or assistance. Naturally, if one does not wish to accept assistance for one reason or another, *iie, kekkoo desu* 'no, thank you,' said in a definite tone of voice will suffice. A less defiant refusal is to add expressions such as *iie daijoobu desu kara* 'I'll be fine, so . . .' Informal refusal *uun, ii yo,* or *iie, ii-desu* 'no that's OK' are also useful. Even when one does wish to accept assistance, Japanese tend to refuse it at first. Study the following interaction.

motsu	持つ	V	to carry, to hold
daijoobu	大丈夫	N	all right
doomo sumimasen			thank you
どうもすみません			(This phrase can also be used for apology.)

A: *(O)nimotsu mochimashoo ka.*
　(お)荷物持ちましょうか。
　(The luggage, shall I carry [it for you]?)

B: *Iie, diajoobu desu kara . . .*
　いいえ，大丈夫ですから……
　(No, thank you, I'll be fine . . .)

A: *Demo omoi-deshoo.*
　でも重いでしょう。
　(But it must be heavy.)

B: *Soo desu ka. Doomo sumimasen.*
　そうですか。どうもすみません。
　(Well. . . . Thanks.)

In this interaction speaker B first refuses assistance. Speaker A continues to show sympathy and B finally accepts it. For a Japanese, to accept assistance right away is felt to be a bit too imposing. After all, the other person is offering to go through some trouble; so one feels somewhat guilty for accepting the kindness right away; a too quick and ready acceptance would suggest that one has expected assistance as a natural consequence. It is almost like taking advantage of someone's good will without consideration for him or her. Sensing that assistance is indeed needed, however, speaker A insists on offering assistance, and is accepted in the second round.

When accepting an offer, *ee, onegai-shimasu* is used in formal situations and/or toward your social superior; the informal counterpart toward social equals or subordinates is *un, tanomu yo* (normally used by male speakers), or *ee, tanomu wa* (used predominantly by female speakers).

Of course, depending on the situation as well as the interpersonal relations between the participants, Japanese may accept the offer without expressing *enryo* and without first refusing it. In fact the tendency not to show *enryo* is prevalent among young Japanese. *Enryo* is more frequently expressed when the offer comes from a social superior. It is useful to know that accepting assistance may sometimes take more than a single turn exchange in Japan.

Examples

```
---------------------------------------------------------------
okuru    送る    V    to take someone home
                       to see someone off
---------------------------------------------------------------
```

(1) A: *Tetsudaimashoo ka.*
　　　手伝いましょうか。
　　　(Shall I help you?)
　　B: *Iie, daijoobu desu.*
　　　いいえ，大丈夫です。
　　　(No, it's OK.)

(2) A: *Okuroo ka.* ☺ **M**
　　　送ろうか。
　　　(Shall I take you home?)
　　B: *Ja, sekkaku dakara onegai-suru wa.*[*1] ☺ **F**
　　　じゃ，せっかくだからお願いするわ。
　　　(Well, thanks, will you?)

(3) A: *Odenwa-shimashoo ka.*
　　　お電話しましょうか。
　　　(Shall I give you a call?)
　　B: *Ee, onegai-shimasu.*
　　　ええ，お願いします。
　　　(Yes, please.)

*1. The adverb *sekkaku* means 'especially, purposely' and 'kindly'; *sekkaku dakara* means 'since you are offering a special favor.' *Sekkaku* is often used to express the regret that the desired result was not achieved although a special, purposeful effort was made. This will be studied later in Entry 70.

Practice

---
to place, to put   V   *noseru*   のせる

Provide a suggestion/offer and response pair for the following situation.

1. You see an old man carrying a large item of luggage. You offer assistance.
2. You notice a woman having difficulty putting her luggage on the overhead rack in the train. You offer assistance.
3. Tonight is your turn to cook. You are busy with last-minute preparations. Your roommate offers to help. ☺
4. Your friend seemingly needs to talk to someone. You offer to call her later. ☺

——— Some Sample Answers ———

1. A: *Nimotsu mochimashoo ka.*　荷物持ちましょうか。
   B: *Sumimasen nee.*　すみませんねえ。
2. A: *Sore ue ni nosemashoo ka.*　それ上にのせましょうか。
   B: *Ee, sumimasen nee, onegaishimasu.*
   ええ，すみませんねえ。お願いします。
3. A: *Tetsudaoo ka.* ☺　手伝おうか。
   B: *Soo nee. Tetsudatte.* ☺ **F**　そうねえ，手伝って。
4. A: *Kon'ya denwa-shiyoo ka.* ☺　今夜電話しようか。
   B: *Ee, onegai.* ☺ **F**　ええ，お願い。

50. Verbal Predicate—6. Verb Categories (Stative and Durative Verbs)

Grammatical Explanation

Depending on whether or not a Japanese verb describes action or state, and whether or not the action or state is durative, the following verb categorization is made. Understanding the differences among categories is important and particularly useful when the progressive forms of the verb are studied. Here we learn the verb categorization in preparation for the next entry. At this point we concern ourselves with four basic verb types as shown below:

Stative:	1.	Stative	*iru* 'there exists'
	2.	Stative durative	*niru* 'to resemble'
Active:	3.	Active durative	*utau* 'to sing'
	4.	Active non-durative	*shinu* 'to die'

Stative verbs describe the state or condition of facts and objects. They do not represent concrete actions. Among stative verbs, the first type does not have progressive forms. The second type, stative durative, however, can take the progressive form. Active verbs are those that describe dynamic and concrete physical, often observable, action. Among them are durative and non-durative active verbs. An active durative verb refers to action that can be performed for a certain duration of time, such as singing, working, etc. An active non-durative verb describes an action or event that occurs in an instant and cannot be performed for a duration of time. For example, *shinu* 'die' occurs in an instant and is a non-durative verb.

Partial List of Verbs in Four Categories

1. *Stative*

aru	ある	there exists
iru	いる	there exists

2. *Stative durative*

chigau	ちがう	to differ
niru	似る	to resemble
wakaru	わかる	to understand

3. *Active durative*

asobu	遊ぶ	to play
arau	洗う	to wash
taberu	食べる	to eat
hashiru	走る	to run
benkyoo-suru	勉強する	to study
matsu	待つ	to wait
warau	笑う	to laugh

4. *Active non-durative*

aku	開く	to open
kekkon-suru	結婚する	to get married

shinu	死ぬ	to die
tomaru	止まる	to stop
wasureru	忘れる	to forget

There are a few verbs that are both active durative and active non-durative which include *kiru* 'to wear,' and *kiku* 'to listen to/to hear about.' These verbs have two different meanings, one of which becomes significant in a specific context.

51. The Progressive Form—Action in Progress and State of Completed Action

Target Expressions

> *(He) is singing a song.*
>
> > **Uta o utatte-imasu.**
> > 歌を歌っています。
>
> *The train is stopped.*
>
> > **Densha ga tomatte-imasu.**
> > 電車が止まっています。
>
> [Vte + -iru]

Grammatical Explanation

Earlier we have studied the gerundive or the *-te* form of the verb in the context of [Vte + -kudasai]. The gerundive form of the verb in essence refers to the realization of the action (as in the English *-ing* form), and although it alone cannot function grammatically as an independent verb, semantically it has the meaning of the verb. The [Vte] form in Japanese is used in combination with several grammatical forms, one of the most important of which is the progressive form.

-Te form of the verb and the existential verb *iru*, [Vte + -iru], constitutes progressive tense. The progressive tense structure has three related but distinct meanings.

1. For active durative verbs, the progressive tense expresses the progression of the action.

   (1a) *Suujii-san wa ima uta o **utatte-imasu**.*
   スージーさんは今歌を**歌っています**。
   (Susie is now singing a song.)

2. For active non-durative verbs, it refers to the continuation of a present state resulting from the already completed action.

   (2a) ***Kekkon-shite-imasu**.*
   結婚しています。
   (I am married.)

The verb *kekkon-suru* 'to get married' describes non-durative action (getting married is achieved in an instant); *kekkon-shite-iru* means 'be married, the result of getting married.'

   The negation of this type of progressive tense means an unachieved result, in a way similar to the negative statement in English perfect tense as shown in this translation.

   (2b) *Densha wa mada **kite-imasen**.*
   電車はまだ**来ていません**。
   (The train hasn't arrived yet.)

3. For some active verbs, progressive tense refers to an action repeated for a certain duration of time.

   (3a) *Daigaku   ni   **kayotte-imasu**.*
   university to   commute
   大学に**通っています**。
   (I am commuting to the university.)

This expression is used not to mean that the speaker is in the middle of commuting—such as riding in the train on his way to the university—, but is used to refer to the habitual, repeated action of commuting. Verb *sumu* 'live' expresses habitual action and is always used in the form *sunde-iru* to mean the English equivalent of 'live'; for example, *Tookyoo ni sunde-imasu* 'I live in Tokyo.' By changing *iru/imasu* to *ita/imashita*, we have access to the past progressive tense.

4. For a stative (non-durative) verb there is no [V*te* + *-iru*] combination. For a stative durative verb, the [V*te* + *-iru*] structure describes the continued state. In case of the *be*-verb, *de-iru* is possible as in;

   (4a) *Ii ko **de-imasu**.*
   いい子で**います**。
   (I continue to be a good kid.)

Note that for the verb that has both active durative and non-durative interpretation, the meaning differs depending on how it is used in an utterance. See examples to follow in which (a) expresses the continuation of action, while (b) expresses the state of completed action.

(a) *Sono toki chichi wa rajio no ongaku o **kiite-ita**.* ♦
その時父はラジオの音楽を聞いていた。
(My father was listening to the music on the radio then.)

(b) *Chichi wa moo sono nyuusu o **kiite-ita**.* ♦
父はもうそのニュースを聞いていた。
(My father had already heard that news.)

For negating the [V*te* + *-iru*] structure, two strategies are available; *utatteimasen*, and *utawanaide-imasu*. *Utatte-imasen* 'I'm not singing' is the straightforward negation of *utatte imasu*, while *utawanaide-imasu* 'I remain not singing' describes the continuation of the state of not singing.

Additional Information

There are two additional extended uses of the present progressive tense. First is to refer to an experience:

(a) *Ano hito wa yoku gaikoku e **itte-iru**.*
あの人はよく外国へ行っている。
(He has traveled to foreign countries often.)

Depending on the context *itte-iru* may be interpreted as the second case discussed earlier, i.e., *iku* is an active non-durative verb and therefore *itteiru* means the continuation of a present state (of being there) resulting from the already complete action (of going there). Thus for example:

(b) *Oji wa Kanada e **itte-imasu**.*
おじはカナダへ行っています。
(My uncle [went to Canada and still] is in Canada.)

Second, the use of a certain group of verbs is restricted to the progressive tense only and they merely describe the state or the quality of things.

(c) *Me no mae ni takai yama ga **sobiete-ita**.*
目の前に高い山がそびえていた。
(In front of my eyes, the tall mountain rose.)

Other verbs that fall under this group include *sugureru* 'to excel,' *arihureru* 'to be common,' and a specific use of the verb *suru*, as in *kawaii kao o suru* 'to have a cute face.'

In colloquial Japanese [V*te* + *-iru*] is contracted to [V*te* + *-ru*].

Examples

kankei	関係	N	relationship
sono koro	その頃	Adv	about that time
Keioo Daigaku 慶応大学		PN	Keio University

(1) *Koyama-san wa Tookyoo ni sunde-imasu.*
　　小山さんは東京に住んでいます。
　　(Ms. Koyama lives in Tokyo.)

(2) A: *Donna shigoto o shite-imasu ka.*
　　どんな仕事をしていますか。
　　(What line of work are you in?)

　B: *Ginkoo kankei no shigoto o shite-imasu.*
　　銀行関係の仕事をしています。
　　(I work in a banking related business.)

(3) A: *Taroo-kun ima nani shite-iru?* ☺
　　太郎君今何している？
　　(What's Taro doing now?)

　B: *Aa, ima terebi mite-ru yo.* ☺
　　ああ，今テレビ見てるよ。
　　(Oh, he's watching TV now.)

(4) *Sono koro chichi wa Keioo Daigaku de oshiete-imashita.*
　　その頃父は慶応大学で教えていました。
　　(My father was teaching at Keio University around that time.)

(5) *San-nen mae wa kekkon-shite-imasen-deshita.*
　　三年前は結婚していませんでした。
　　(Three years ago I wasn't married yet.)

Practice

economics	N	*keizaigaku*	経済学
history	N	*rekishi*	歴史
English literature	N	*eibungaku*	英文学

Provide a question/response pair for the following.

1. You ask whether your mutual friend Kayoko still lives in Nakano.
2. Your roommate comes home late at night. You want to find out what she was up to. ☺

3. You want to find out for whom the stranger standing in front of your office door is waiting for. How will you ask him?

4. You meet a new foreign student at college. You ask what he or she is studying.

--- Some Sample Answers ---

1. A: *Kayoko-san wa ima mo Nakano ni sunde-imasu ka.*
加代子さんは今も中野に住んでいますか。
   B: *Ee.* ええ。

2. A: *Nani shite-ta (no)?* ☺ 何してた(の)？
   B: *Toshokan de benkyoo-shiteta.* ☺ 図書館で勉強してた。

3. A: *Anoo, dare o matte-imasu ka.* あのう、誰を待っていますか。
   B: *Tabata-san desu ga . . .* [*1] 田畑さんですが……

4. A: *Nani o benkyoo-shite-imasu ka.* 何を勉強していますか。
   B: *Keizaigaku/rekishi/eibungaku desu.* 経済学/歴史/英文学です。

[*1]. It is possible to answer in a full sentence as in *Tabata-san o matte-imasu. Da* may be used to replace other verbs much as the verb *do* is used in English. In the above context, *Tabata-san desu* suffices. In casual conversation, it is also possible to shorten it to *Tabata-san.*

* * * * *

"Bancha demo, iremashoo ka." 「番茶でも、いれましょうか？」
Toguchi ni onna ga tatte-ita. 戸口に女が立っていた。
—Abe, 1981, p. 151.

"Shall I fix you some tea?" The woman was standing in the doorway.
—Saunders, 1967, p. 157.

The present progressive tense is used in this example to express 'was standing.' Note the use of *demo* and the consultative use of *iremashoo ka* explained in Entries 34 and 44, respectively.

52. Adverbs—2. Onomatopoeic and Mimicry Words

Target Expression

> *It is raining quietly and steadily.*
> **Ame ga shitoshito hutte-imasu.**
> 雨がしとしと降っています。

Grammatical Explanation

Japanese has a rich system of words describing sound or action directly and vividly. There are two categories; (1) *giseigo*, sound-imitating words, or onomatopoeic words, and (2) *gitaigo*, action-imitating words, or mimicry words. For example, the adverb *shitoshito* expresses the quiet and steady rhythm of the falling rain. English also has onomatopoeic words (for example "pitter-patter" to describe the falling rain) but their use is limited. Although in English the use of onomatopoeic words may connote childishness, Japanese *giseigo* and *gitaigo* are frequently used by great writers of Japanese literature and their use is not considered childish in the least.

Laughing may be described in English by different verbs; in Japanese both *giseigo* and *gitaigo* are attached as adverbs in order to describe the various ways to *warau* 'laugh.'

giseigo:	**geragera** *warau* げらげら笑う	to laugh boisterously
	kusukusu *warau* くすくす笑う	to giggle
	herahera *warau* へらへら笑う	to laugh condescendingly
gitaigo:	**nikoniko** *suru* にこにこする	to smile
	niyaniya *suru* にやにやする	to grin

Other frequently used *giseigo* and *gitaigo* include:

gabugabu がぶがぶ	*Mizu o **gabugabu** nomu.* 水を**がぶがぶ**飲む。 ([He/She] drinks water thirstily in big gulps.)
kirakira きらきら	*Hoshi ga **kirakira** kagayaite-iru.* 星が**きらきら**輝いている。 (The stars are shining and glittering.)
sarasara さらさら	*Kawa no mizu ga **sarasara** nagareru.* 川の水が**さらさら**流れる。 (The river [water] flows smoothly.)

Giseigo and *gitaigo* are often four mora words, formed with two two-mora pairs. There are a remarkable number of these words in the Japanese vocabulary. For those who are interested in sound symbolism in Japan, *Giongo Gitaigo Jiten* (published by Kadokawa Shoten in Tokyo, 1978) is available.

53. Expressions Meaning "I Don't Know"

Target Expressions

> *Do you understand?*
>
> > **Wakarimasu ka.**
> > わかりますか。
>
> *I don't understand.*
>
> > **Wakarimasen.**
> > わかりません。
>
> *Do you know?*
>
> > **Shitte-imasu ka.**
> > 知っていますか。
>
> *I don't know.*
>
> > **Shirimasen.**
> > 知りません。

Strategic Explanation

Although the target expressions listed above seem too specific to warrant an independent entry in this book, I decided to do precisely that. This is because when learning a foreign language it is useful to be able to express whether or not you understand the point being made. It is frustrating when one cannot convey that one does not understand, and worse, it is embarrassing when a student does this incorrectly. Here are some tips.

The basic distinction between *shiru* 'to know' and *wakaru* 'to be understood' is the following. *Wakaru* refers to an understanding of various aspects related to an object whose existence is already recognized. *Shiru* denotes recognition of an object and a familiarization with it. *Wakaru* is a verb for "reactive" description, which takes the form, *nihongo ga wakarimasu* '(lit. Japanese is understood) I understand Japanese.' Thus, the question form is, *nihongo ga wakarimasu ka?* The answer to this question takes the form *hai, wakarimasu* or *iie, wakarimasen.* On the other hand *shiru* is a transitive verb which takes object maker *o.* When asking *do you know Mrs. Tanaka?* always use *shitte-iru* form; thus *Tanaka-san o shitte-imasu ka?* The answer to this question takes either *hai, shitte-imasu* or *iie, shirimasen.*

Examples

imi	意味	N	meaning
shiten	支店	N	branch office

(1) A: *Kono kotoba no imi wakaru?* ☺
 この言葉の意味わかる？
 (Do you understand the meaning of this word?)

 B: *Un, wakaru yo.* ☺
 うん，わかるよ。
 (Yeah, I do.)

(2) A: *Nyuuyooku shiten no Sakai-san o yoku shitte-imasu ka.*
 ニューヨーク支店の酒井さんをよく知っていますか。
 (Do you know Mr. Sakai at the New York office well?)

 B: *Iie, shirimasen ga . . .*
 いいえ，知りませんが……
 (No. I don't know him, I'm afraid.)

Practice

feelings	N	*kimochi*	気持ち

Express that you don't know/understand the following items. Ask your friend formally whether he or she knows/understands them.

1. this kanji
2. Mr. Sasaki
3. feelings of your teacher Yamamoto
4. the meaning of the letter ☺

——— Answers ———

1. *Kono kanji ga/wa wakarimasen.* この漢字が/はわかりません。

 Kono kanji wakarimasu ka. この漢字わかりますか。

2. *Sasaki-san wa shirimasen.*　佐々木さんは知りません。
Sasaki-san o shitte-imasu ka.　佐々木さんを知っていますか。
3. *Yamamoto-sensei no kimochi ga wakarimasen.*
山本先生の気持ちがわかりません。
Yamamoto-sensei no kimochi ga wakarimasu ka.
山本先生の気持ちがわかりますか。
4. *Sono tegami no imi, yoku wakaranai yo.* ☺
その手紙の意味，よくわからないよ。
Sono tegami no imi, wakaru? ☺　その手紙の意味，わかる？

54. Structure of the Japanese Sentence—2.　Proposition and Modality

Target Expressions

(Regrettably) I lost my passport.
Pasupooto o nakushite-shimaimashita.
パスポートをなくしてしまいました。

[V*te* + *-shimau*]

Grammatical Explanation

As for Japanese sentence construction, we have learned earlier about the structural axis of topic-comment and subject-predicate. We look once more at the internal structure of the sentence, but with a different focus. A sentence (or an utterance) can be considered a combination consisting of "proposition"—logical propositional information (that is, who does what to whom, and so forth), and "modality"—expression of personal and emotional commitment the speaker makes toward that proposition. In fact we already studied various strategies for expressing modality in Japanese, such as negation, suggestion and invitation. Among modality, we can see two related but distinct types, "aspects" and "mood." Aspect means specific focus placed on different parts of action described by the verb, in relation to its tense and manner. For example, if one focuses on the fact that the action is in progress, [V*te* + *-iru*] is used for the active durative verb. The progressive form is one good example of aspect. By mood, we mean psychological and emotional judgments one makes toward the statement, such as speculation and suggestion.

For the expression of modality, the [V + (Aux)V] construction, [AuxV], auxiliary adjectives [AuxAdj], and the [N + da] structure, among other strategies, are used. I list here important devices for expressing aspects and mood in Japanese. We will study the meaning and use of these expressions later under separate headings as indicated in parentheses.

Aspects: **[V*te* + V] construction**

V*te-iru*	(Entry 51)
V*te-aru*	(Entry 95)
V*te-shimau*	(Entry 54)
V*te-oku*	(Entry 95)
V*te-iku*	(Entry 55)
V*te-kuru*	(Entry 55)

[Vstem + AuxV] construction
(All these expressions appear in Entry 121.)
Vstem-*hajimeru*
Vstem-*dasu*
Vstem-*kakeru*
Vstem-*kaesu*
Vstem-*sugiru*
Vstem-*naosu*

[N + *da*] construction

tokoro da	(Entry 129)

Mood: **[AuxV] and [AuxAdj]**

kamoshirenai	(Entry 99)
nakereba naranai	(Entry 107)
chigainai	(Entry 108)
-daroo/-deshoo	(Entry 99)
rashii	(Entry 91)
soona	(Entry 87)
mitaina	(Entry 89)
yoona	(Entry 89)

[N + *da*] construction

koto da	(Entry 120) ([Nominalizer + *da*] structure)
hazu da	(Entry 104)

beki da	(Entry 106)
mono da	(Entry 120)
wake da	(Entry 74)
no da	(Entry 74) ([Nominalizer + *da*] structure)

At this point we concentrate on only one of the aspects, namely [V*te* + *-shimau*]. The verb *shimau* means 'to put away,' and 'to store.' When using [V*te* + *-shimau*] combination, it indicates "completion" and "finality." The speaker emphasizes that the event is completed, expressing a sense of fatalism in that what is done once cannot be undone. It focuses on the completion of action and event meaning 'end up doing,' and 'finish doing.'

Because [V*te* + *-shimau*] emphasizes the aspect of an event or incident being totally completed (and irreversible), it is often used when one wishes to express a sense of regret.

(a) *Neko ga shinde-shimatta.*
ねこが死んでしまった。
(The cat died [and we cannot change this reality . . .].)

Naturally there are cases where the [V*te* + *-shimau*] construction does not imply a sense of regret; for example, *sono hon wa moo yonde-shimatta* 'as for that book, I've read it already,' or *shukudai wa moo shite-shimatta yo* 'as for my homework, I've finished it already.'

For an example of mood, review *-daroo/-deshoo* attached to the verb to express the speaker's doubt and uncertainty. Other examples of mood will be introduced later.

Examples

```
-----------------------------------------------------------
okureru   遅れる   V   to be late for
zenbu     全部     N   everything, every part
-----------------------------------------------------------
```

(1) *Densha ni okurete-shimatta.*
電車に遅れてしまった。
(I missed the train.)

(2) *Imooto ga keeki o zenbu tabete-shimaimashita.*
妹がケーキを全部食べてしまいました。
(My sister ate the whole cake.)

Additional Information

A colloquial version of [V*te* + -*shimau*] is created by replacing *te-shimau* with -*chau* (and *de-shimau* with -*jau*), and it sometimes indicates joy over unexpected good fortune. In example (a) *atatchatta* is a contracted version of *atatte-shimatta*, the verb *ataru* meaning 'win (a lottery).'

(a) *Takarakuji   ni   atatchatta.* ☺
lottery   at   won
宝くじにあたっちゃった。
(I won the lottery.)

55. Actions Involving Directions—Come and Go

Target Expression

I borrowed the book (and came back).
Hon o karite-kimashita.
本を借りてきました。

[V*te* + -*iku*]
[V*te* + -*kuru*]

Grammatical Explanation

When the action described is associated with movement between two points of space or time, that is, when it involves direction, the verbs of coming and going are attached to the [V*te*] form. These directional markers are obligatory; without them they sound incomplete. Since [V*te* + -*iku*] and [V*te* + -*kuru*] emphasize direction of the verb, they express an aspect of the verb. Although *iku* and *kuru* are independent verbs, when used in combination with [V*te*] forms, they add aspectual meaning to the preceding verb and this fact is indicated by a hyphen. For the verb *hashiru* 'to run' we obtain the following:

hashitte-iku   (when the speaker views the action of running from the location close-to-self toward the location away-from-self) *hashitte-kuru* (when the speaker views the action from the location away-from-self to the location close-to-self)

Based on this primary meaning, there are extended uses of [V*te* + *-iku*] and [V*te* + *-kuru*] to express the following aspects.

hikooki	飛行機	N	airplane
sora	空	N	sky
kanata	かなた	N	beyond
kieru	消える	V	to disappear
dandan	だんだん	Adv	gradually
mazushii	貧しい	Adj	poor
ganbaru	がんばる	V	to do one's best, to try hard
kangae	考え	N	idea
ukabu	うかぶ	V	appear
warui	悪い	Adj	bad
kaze	風	N	wind
huku	吹く	V	to blow

[V*te* + *-iku*]

1. Process of disappearance:
   (1a) *Hikooki wa sora no kanata e kiete-ikimashita.*
   飛行機は空のかなたへ消えていきました。
   (The airplane disappeared into the distance of the sky.)

2. Process of change within others:
   (2a) *Sono otoko wa dandan mazushikunatte-ikimashita.*
   その男はだんだん貧しくなっていきました。
   (The man became increasingly poorer.)

3. Continuation of process into the future:
   (3a) *Korekara mo ganbatte-ikimashoo.*
   これからもがんばっていきましょう。
   (Let's continue to keep on doing our best.)

[V*te* + *-kuru*]

1. Process of appearance:
   (1a) *Ii kangae ga ukande-kimashita.*
   いい考えがうかんできました。
   ([lit. Good ideas appeared.] I hit upon some good ideas.)

2. Process of change that takes place in self and those close to self:
   (2a) *Kimochi ga waruku natte-kimashita.*
   気持ちが悪くなって**きました**。
   (I began to feel ill.)

3. Beginning of process:
   (3a) *Tsumetai kaze ga huite-kimashita.*
   冷たい風が吹いて**きました**。
   (A cold wind began to blow.)

   (3b) *Ano hito no kimochi ga wakatte-kimashita.*
   あの人の気持ちがわかって**きました**。
   (I began to understand his or her feelings.)
   (Compare this with the English expression 'come to understand.')

4. Continuation of process to a certain point of past or up to the present:
   (4a) *Ima made ganbatte-kimashita.*
   今までがんばって**きました**。
   (I've done my best up until now.)

When the verb preceding *iku* and *kuru* does not describe a process of event or action, a slightly different interpretation is possible. For example, *katte-kuru* means either 'to go out to buy' or 'having bought and then to come back.' In the latter reading *kuru* operates as a main verb rather than simply adding an aspectual meaning to the verb.

Examples

```
---------------------------------------------------------------
wataridori  渡り鳥      N    migratory birds
minami      南         N    south
kuni        国         N    country
asaban      朝晩        N    mornings and
                              evenings
jugyoo      授業        N    class, lecture
kyooshitsu  教室        N    classroom
motte-kuru  持ってくる   V    to bring
---------------------------------------------------------------
```

(1) *Tookyoo de wa kugatsu ni wa suzushii hi ga ooku narimasu.*
東京では九月には涼しい日が多くなります。
(In Tokyo in September the days become cooler.)

Juugatsu ni wa wataridori ga minami no kuni e kaette-ikimasu.
十月には渡り鳥が南の国へ帰っていきます。
(In October migratory birds go back to southern countries.)

Juuichigatsu ni wa asaban kanari samuku natte-kimasu.
十一月には朝晩かなり寒くなってきます。
(In November mornings and evenings become rather cold.)

(2)　*Ima ku-ji san-pun mae desu.*
今九時三分前です。
(It is three minutes before nine now.)

Sugu nihongo no jugyoo ga hajimarimasu.
すぐ日本語の授業がはじまります。
(Soon the Japanese language class starts.)

Tomodachi no Andaason-san ga kyooshitsu ni haitte-kimashita.
友だちのアンダーソンさんが教室に入ってきました。
(Mr. Anderson, a friend, came into the classroom.)

Andaason-san wa atarashii jisho o motte-kimashita.
アンダーソンさんは新しい辞書を持ってきました。
(Mr. Anderson brought [with him] a new dictionary.)

Andaason-san no tomodachi no Guriin-san mo haitte-kimashita.
アンダーソンさんの友だちのグリーンさんも入ってきました。
(Mr. Anderson's friend, Mr. Green, also came [into the room].)

Guriin-san wa kesa nihongo no shinbun o katte-kimashita.
グリーンさんは今朝日本語の新聞を買ってきました。
(This morning Mr. Green bought and brought [with him] a Japanese newspaper.)

Practice

For the following verbs, create short sentences by using [V*te* + *-iku*] and [V*te* + *-kuru*] patterns.

1.	*tsurete-iku*	連れていく	(to take someone along)
	tsurete-kuru	連れてくる	(to bring someone along)
2.	*motte-iku*	持っていく	(to bring something to others)
	motte-kuru	持ってくる	(to bring something to one's self)
3.	*katte-iku*	買っていく	(to buy something and go)
	katte-kuru	買ってくる	(to buy something and come back)

—— Some Sample Answers ——

1. *Paatii ni tomodachi o tsurete-ikimashita.*
   パーティーに友だちを連れていきました。
   (I took my friend along to the party.)
   Ashita no paatii ni tomodachi o tsurete-kite-kudasai.
   明日のパーティーに友だちを連れてきてください。
   (Please bring your friends to the party tomorrow.)
2. *Kasa motte-itte ne.* ☺ かさ持っていってね。
   (Make sure to bring your umbrella.)
   Hon wa motte-kimashita ka. 本は持ってきましたか。
   (Did you bring your books with you?)
3. *Omiyage o takusan katte-ikimashoo yo.*
   おみやげをたくさん買っていきましょうよ。
   ([lit. Let's buy a lot of souvenirs and go back] Let's bring back
   a lot of souvenirs.)
   Omiyage katte-kimashita yo. おみやげ買ってきましたよ。
   (I bought a lot of souvenirs [and came back].)

56. Conjunctions—1. Common Conjunctions

Target Expressions

> *Although I read the book, I didn't understand it.*
> **Hon o yonda keredomo wakarimasen-deshita.**
> 本を読んだけれどもわかりませんでした。
> **Hon yonda kedo wakaranakatta.** ☺
> 本読んだけどわからなかった。
>
> [V*te*] [Adj *te*]
> [*soshite*] [*keredomo*]

Grammatical Explanation

So far we have focused primarily on simple sentences containing one main
verb. Now we proceed to complex sentences with multiple clauses. Here are
ways to connect clauses in Japanese.

1. *By the gerundive* [V/Adj *te*] *form:*
It is possible to end each clause by [V/Adj *te*] in order to continue with consequent clauses. This structure connects different clauses with the basic meaning of 'and.' In certain extended interpretations, however, a meaning of cause may be added depending on the context in which it appears.

(1a)

Sushi	*o*	**tabete**,	*sake*	*o*	**nonde**,	*tanoshii*	*paatii*
sushi	O	eat	sake	O	drink	enjoyable	party

deshita	*yo.*
was	IP

すしを**食**べて，酒を**飲**んで，楽しいパーティーでしたよ。

(We ate sushi, drank sake, and it was an enjoyable party.)

(1b) *Tanaka-san wa nihon-jin **de**, Buraun-san wa Amerika-jin desu.*
田中さんは日本人で，ブラウンさんはアメリカ人です。
(Mrs. Tanaka is Japanese, and Mrs. Brown is American.)

(1c)

Asaneboo	*o*	**shite**,	*okuremashita.*
oversleep	O	do	was late

朝ねぼうをして，遅れました。

(I overslept, and so I was late.)

2. *By using a number of conjunctions:*

soshite 'and,' *sorekara* 'then':

(2a) *Yuugohan o tabemashita. Soshite/Sorekara nemashita.*
夕ごはんを食べました。そして/それから寝ました。
(I ate supper. And then went to bed.)

keredomo, keredo, shikashi, demo, 'but':

(2b) *Imooto no apaato e ikimashita. Keredomo/Shikashi/Demo imasen-deshita.*
妹のアパートへ行きました。けれども/しかし/でもいませんでした。
(I went to my younger sister's apartment. But she wasn't there.)

dakara, desukara (polite version of *dakara*), *sorede, de* 'and so':

(2c)

Ashita	*kaigi*	*ga*	*arimasu.*	*Dakara/Desukara/Sorede*
tomorrow	meeting	S	there is	therefore

sono	*junbi*	*o*	*shite-imasu.*
that	preparation	O	do

あした会議があります。*だから/ですから/それで*その準備をしてい
ます。

(There is a meeting tomorrow. Therefore/So I am preparing
for it.)

kedo, ga 'although':

(2d)　*Kono hon wa nando-mo yomimashita kedo/ga yoku
wakarimasen.*
この本は何度も読みました*けど/が*よくわかりません。
(I read this book many times, but I cannot understand it well.)

noni 'in spite of':

(2e)　*Ano hito wa ame ga hutte-iru noni jogingu o shite-imasu.*
あの人は雨が降っているのにジョギングをしています。
(In spite of the rain, he is jogging.)

node 'since':

(2f)　Ashita　　gekkyuu　　o　morau　node　tanoshimi　desu.
tomorrow　monthly pay　O　receive　since　pleasure　is
あした月給をもらうので楽しみです。
(Since I will receive my [monthly] paycheck tomorrow, I look
forward to it [lit. it is a pleasure].)

Regarding where the conjunctions appear in relation to the clauses, the
following should be noted. First, *shoshite, sorekara, shikashi, demo,
dakara, desukara, sorede,* and *de* appear utterance initially, connecting the
preceding statement with the one starting with the conjunction. On the
other hand, *kedo, ga, noni,* and *node* must appear immediately following a
clause; they cannot start a new utterance. *keredomo* and *tokoroga* can appear in either position.

When using *noni* and *node,* if preceded by *da,* you must replace *da* with
na. For example, *nihon-jin na noni eigo ga joozu desu* 'despite being
Japanese, he or she is good at English' and *kore wa benrina noni
Yamakawa-san wa kaimasen-deshita* 'although this is convenient, Mr.
Yamakawa didn't buy.'

When conjunctions connect two clauses, the predicate in the subordinate
clause is normally, but not exclusively, in the informal form. As a basic rule
the style of the sentence is expressed by the ending of the main verb. When a
formal ending is used in a subordinate clause along with the formal ending
in the main clause, the utterance is considered to be highly formal.

Additional Information

Another way of connecting clauses to make multiple-clause sentences is to use the stem of the verb, [Vstem]. Conjoining clauses with [Vstem] is frequently used in written Japanese and formal speech, but limited in casual speech. For example:

(a) *Roku-ji ni oki, roku-ji han ni ie o deta.* ♦
六時に起き，六時半に家を出た。
(I got up at six and left home at six-thirty.)

Examples

```
---------------------------------------------------------------
dewa       では     Conj   then
repooto    レポート   N      report
perapera   ペラペラ  Adv    fluent (in language)
isshookenmei         Adv    hard, diligently
  いっしょうけんめい
kekkyoku 結局        Adv    in the end, after all
tsubureru つぶれる    V      to go bankrupt
---------------------------------------------------------------
```

(1) A: *Dewa sono repooto wa ashita motte-ikimasu.*
ではそのレポートはあした持っていきます。
(Well then, I will bring that report tomorrow.)

 B: *Ashita wa isogashii node asatte motte-kite-kudasaimasen ka.*
あしたは忙しいのであさって持ってきてくださいませんか。
(Since I am busy tomorrow, could you bring it the day after tomorrow?)

 A: *San-ji goro wa ikaga desu ka.*
三時ごろはいかがですか。
(How about around three o'clock?)

(2) A: *Taanaa-san wa nihon ni go-nenkan sunde-imashita.*
ターナーさんは日本に五年間住んでいました。
Desukara nihongo wa perapera desu.
ですから日本語はペラペラです。
(Mr. Turner lived in Japan for five years. Therefore he is fluent in Japanese.)

 B: *Soo desu ka.*
そうですか。
(Is that so?)

(3) *Isshookenmei hataraita noni kekkyoku kaisha wa tsuburete-shimaimashita.*
いっしょうけんめい働いたのに結局会社はつぶれてしまいました。

(Despite the fact that I worked hard, in the end the company went bankrupt.)

Practice

```
------------------------------------------------------------
kondo        今度      N    next time
shuumatsu    週末      N    weekend
enkai        宴会      N    banquet
supiichi     スピーチ   N    speech
taihenna     大変な    Adj  serious
machigai     まちがい   N    mistake
------------------------------------------------------------
```

How would you connect the following clauses?

1. *Ame ga hurimashita. Hito ga takusan kimashita.*
   雨が降りました。人がたくさん来ました。
2. *Shinjuku ni tsukimashita. Takushii ni norimashita.*
   新宿に着きました。タクシーに乗りました。
3. *Kondo no shuumatsu ni paatii ga arimasu. Biiru o takusan kaimashita.*
   今度の週末にパーティーがあります。ビールをたくさん買いました。
4. *Enkai wa roku-ji ni hajimarimasu. Go-ji yon-juu go-hun made ni hoteru no robii ni kite-kudasai.*
   宴会は六時にはじまります。五時四十五分までにホテルのロビーに来てください。
5. *Yoku renshuu-shimashita. Supiichi de taihenna machigai o shite-shimaimashita.* ☺
   よく練習しました。スピーチで大変なまちがいをしてしまいました。

────── Some Sample Answers ──────

1. *Ame ga hutta noni/keredomo hito ga takusan kimashita.*
   雨が降った<u>のに</u>/けれども人がたくさん来ました。
2. *Shinjuku ni tsuite takushii ni norimashita.*
   新宿に着いてタクシーに乗りました。
   Shinjuku ni tsuite sorekara takushii ni norimashita.
   新宿に着いてそれからタクシーに乗りました。
   Shinjuku ni tsuki takushii ni norimashita.
   新宿に着きタクシーに乗りました。
3. *Kondo no shuumatsu ni paatii ga aru kara/node biiru o takusan kaimashita.*
   今度の週末にパーティーがある<u>から</u>/のでビールをたくさん買いました。

4. *Enkai wa roku-ji ni hajimarimasu kara go-ji yon-juu go-hun made ni hoteru no robii ni kite-kudasai.*

宴会は六時にはじまりますから五時四十五分までにホテルのロビーに来てください。

5. *Yoku renshuushita <u>noni/keredo</u> supiichi de taihenna machigai o shite-shimatta.* ☺

よく練習した<u>のに/けれど</u>スピーチで大変なまちがいをしてしまった。

57. Conjunctions—2. Conjunctions for Interactional Appeal

Target Expression

Excuse me, but . . .

Sumimasen ga . . .
すみませんが……

Strategic Explanation

Some Japanese conjunctions do not neccessarily connect clauses logically. As in the use of the English *but* in the expression ''excuse me, but . . .,'' Japanese conjunctions often function to convey meanings useful in facilitating interaction. In spoken Japanese conjunctions are added at utterance-final positions with the deleted main clause being either implied or suggested. Since ending an utterance with a conjunction leaves the expectation of continuation, the listener has a feeling that the thought is unfinished. The feeling of incompleteness expresses a less imposing and therefore more considerate attitude. For example, by saying *soo wa omoimasen ga . . .* 'I don't think so (but) . . .,' the speaker softens his or her opposing statement and thereby minimizes disruption and ensures the maintenance of interpersonal harmony.

Imagine a situation where you hear an announcement at a department store requesting you to come to the reception desk. When you see the receptionist, you might say, *Watanabe* (your name) *desu ga . . .* 'I'm Watanabe.' The *ga* added at the end implies that something is to continue;

it conveys the speaker's desire to solicit the addressee, and therefore it expresses receptiveness.

Conjunctions *ga, kedo, keredo* are also used to introduce a topic of conversation. For example, *haru no ryokoo desu ga* 'it's about the spring trip, but . . .' An expression *yoku wakarimasen ga* 'I don't understand well (I'm not sure) but' is frequently used as a prefix to stating one's opinion. By appealing to the listener with a statement that disclaims authority, the speaker leaves room for further discussion and negotiation. Especially when one's opinion opposes another's, prefixing of this kind is considered useful and tactful.

Examples

koojoo	工場	N	factory
tokorode	ところで	Conj	by the way
kono aida	この間	Adv	recently

(1) *Yoku wakarimasen ga . . .*
よくわかりませんが……
(I don't understand it well, but . . .)

(2) A: *Sumimasen ga, kore o Yokohama koojoo e todokete-kudasai-masen ka.*
すみませんが，これを横浜工場へ届けてくださいませんか。
(Sorry to bother you, but could you please deliver this to the Yokohama factory?)

B: *Hai. San-ji goro ni narimasu ga . . .*
はい。三時頃になりますが……
(Sure. It will be about three o'clock . . .)

A: *Ii-desu yo. Onegai-shimasu.*
いいですよ。お願いします。
(Fine. Please take care of it.)

(3) *Yoku wakarimasen ga, sore wa achira no machigai ja-nai-deshoo ka.*
よくわかりませんが，それはあちらのまちがいじゃないでしょうか。
(I'm not sure, but isn't it their mistake?)

(4) *Tokorode, kono aida no chuumon no koto desu kedo . . .*
ところで，この間の注文のことですけど……
(By the way, it's about the order [made] the other day . . .)

Practice

```
to think      V      omou            思う
so            Adv    soo             そう
to explain    V      setsumei-suru   説明する
```

Use conjunctions for making the following expressions interactionally appealing.

1.   I think so but . . .
2.   It's about next month's trip . . .
3. A: Did you see (meet) John yesterday? ☺
      B: Yes, I did see him . . . ☺
4.   Excuse me, but please explain this one more time.

Answers

1.   *Soo omoimasu ga . . .*   そう思いますが……
2.   *Raigetsu no ryokoo no koto desu ga . . .*
       来月の旅行のことですが……
3. A: *Kinoo Jon ni atta?* ☺ きのうジョンに会った？
     B: *Atta kedo . . .* ☺   会ったけど……
4.   *Sumimasen ga, kore moo ichido setsumei-shite-kudasaimasen ka.*
       すみませんが，これもう一度説明してくださいませんか。

Additional Information

In general there is a tendency to use conjunctions more freely in Japanese than in English. In written discourse conjunctions and conjunctive phrases such as *shitagatte* 'therefore,' *sarani* 'furthermore,' *mata* 'additionally,' *ijoo nobeta yoo ni* 'as stated above,' and *yuu made mo naku* 'needless to mention' are frequently inserted merely to connect clauses. These conjunctions may not imply a logical connection, such as statement/conclusion; they are used to signal general connectedness between statements.

The use of the conjunction *ga* in the example below may be best called a transition word rather than a conjunction connecting opposing statements.

(a) *Sasaki-san to wa yoku kaigi de aimasu **ga**, nakanaka yarite desu ne.*
     佐々木さんとはよく会議で会います**が**，なかなかやり手ですね。
     (I see Sasaki often at meetings; [but] she is quite an achiever.)

Warning

It is absolutely crucial to pronounce conjunctions for interactional appeal in a falling tone, gradually fading and trailing. If the conjunction receives a rising tone, the listener is likely to wait for you to continue. In order to signal that you are yielding your turn, make sure to pronounce *kedo*, for example, in a falling tone.

58. Getting Attention from Friends and Strangers

Target Expression

> *Uh, excuse me . . .*
>
> *Anoo, sumimasen ga . . .*
> あのう, すみませんが……

Strategic Explanation

When you want to attract your friends' attention, you can simply use their names, as in *nee, Akiko-san* 'say, Akiko.' *Nee* functions as an attention getting phrase among in-group members. When you don't know the name, or cannot recall the name of the person, the following phrases are useful.

(a) *Anoo, sumimasen (ga) . . .*
    あのう, すみません(が)……
    (Uh, excuse me [but] . . .)

(b) *Anoo, shitsurei desu ga . . .*
    あのう, 失礼ですが……
    (Uh, sorry to be rude . . .)

(c) *Anoo . . .*
    あのう……
    (Uhhh . . .)

The phrase *anoo* is pronounced hesitantly. The hesitation marker *anoo* is useful to express your unwillingness (with even a sense of guilt) to bother strangers for your need. Thus, hesitation shows a respect for and consideration toward others. In casual situations, the interactional particle *nee* (often used by females) or an adverb *chotto* may be used as a pre-announcement of address terms toward in-group members, for example, *nee okaasan* 'say, mom.'

If you need to catch the attention of someone far away from you, use *sumimaseeen!* 'excuse me!' in a loud voice. When you are visiting someone or entering a mom-and-pop store, you can call attention to the fact that you are there by saying *gomenkudasai* 'hello.'

Warning

The expression *ano ne* is used between in-group members only. *Ano ne* has an intimate, friendly and somewhat condescending tone, and therefore should be avoided toward your superiors.

Practice

----
platform no.14   N   *juu yon-bansen no hoomu*   14番線のホーム
restroom   N   *otearai*   お手洗い

Assume that you need assistance from strangers (numbers 1, 2 and 3 below) and your friend, Sally (numbers 4 and 5). How would you start your utterance?

1. to find out the whereabouts of platform number 14
2. to find out the present time
3. to find out location of the restrooms
4. to request permission to borrow this dictionary from your friend Sally ☺
5. to request your friend Sally to bring you today's newspaper ☺

——— Some Sample Answers ———

1. *Sumimasen ga juu yon-bansen no hoomu wa doko desu ka.*
   すみませんが14番線のホームはどこですか。
2. *Anoo, sumimasen ga ima nan-ji deshoo ka.*
   あのう，すみませんが今何時でしょうか。
3. *Anoo, sumimasen kedo, otearai wa doko deshoo ka.*
   あのう，すみませんけど，お手洗いはどこでしょうか。
4. *Nee, Sarii-san, kono jisho kashite.* ☺
   ねえ，サリーさん，この辞書貸して。
5. *Chotto, Sarii-san, kyoo no shinbun motte-kite.* ☺
   ちょっと，サリーさん，今日の新聞持ってきて。

59. Family Terms

> *my mother, my younger brother*
> ### haha, otooto
> 母, 弟
> *(someone else's) mother, (someone else's) younger brother*
> ### okaasan, otootosan
> お母さん, 弟さん

Grammatical Explanation

One important feature in Japanese family terms shows a striking contrast with English. Japanese provides two distinct sets of terms depending on whether you are referring to the family among *uchi* group, or *soto* group members. This system reflects the fact that Japanese make a clear distinction between the members of *uchi* versus *soto*; and this is particularly so when they make reference to *uchi* members.

Family Terms

	Referential terms: one's own	Referential terms: someone's	Address terms: one's own	Address terms: someone's
grandfather	sohu 祖父	ojiisan おじいさん	ojiisan おじいさん	ojiisan おじいさん
grandmother	sobo 祖母	obaasan おばあさん	obaasan おばあさん	obaasan おばあさん
father	chichi 父	otoosan お父さん	(o)toosan/papa (お)父さん/パパ	otoosan お父さん
mother	haha 母	okaasan お母さん	(o)kaasan/mama (お)母さん/ママ	okaasan お母さん
elder brother	ani 兄	oniisan お兄さん	(o)niisan (お)兄さん	FN[*1] + -san
elder sister	ane 姉	oneesan お姉さん	(o)neesan (お)姉さん	FN + -san
younger brother	otooto 弟	otootosan 弟さん	FN	FN + -san
younger sister	imooto 妹	imootosan 妹さん	FN	FN + -san
uncle	oji おじ	ojisan おじさん	ojisan おじさん	ojisan おじさん

aunt	oba	obasan	obasan	obasan
	おば	おばさん	おばさん	おばさん
daughter	musume	ojoosan	FN	FN + -san
	娘	おじょうさん		
son	musuko	musukosan	FN	FN + -san
	息子	息子さん		
wife	tsuma/kanai	okusan	omae/ FN	okusan
	妻/家内	奥さん	おまえ	奥さん
husband	shujin	goshujin(sama)	anata	goshujinsama
	主人	ご主人(さま)	あなた	ご主人さま
				(LN[*1] + -san)
child	kodomo	kodomosan		
	子供	子供さん		
sibling	kyoodai	gokyoodai		
	兄弟	ご兄弟		
family	kazoku	gokazoku		
	家族	ご家族		

*1. FN/LN are abbreviations of first name/last name.

Practice

Describe things about your family members and relatives. Make at least one statement about each of your family members and relatives.

─────── Some Sample Answers ───────
Haha wa go-juu go desu.   母は五十五です。
Otooto wa daigakusei da kedo / na noni zenzen benkyoo-
　　shinai wa yo. ☺F   弟は大学生だけど/なのに全然勉強しないわよ。
Ane wa ima Nyuuyooku desu.   姉は今ニューヨークです。

Additional Information

The use of family terms is extended to the fictive use—what is called "other-oriented self-designation (Suzuki 1978)." In this use, a husband may be called *otoosan* by his wife. Here the wife views her husband as a "father" from the child's point of view. Obviously the wife is not the husband's biological mother. In fact the husband calls himself "father" when facing a child, another case of other-oriented self-designation—identifying self in relation to the weaker or the weakest among relevant members. This is also observed in the United States but its use is much more limited. Similar referential terms are used by children, or adults taking the children's point of view, to identify man and woman by using *oniisan*, *ojisan* and *ojiisan* or *oneesan*, *obasan* and *obaasan*, respectively, depending on the age of the person. A younger male resembles a "brother," a middle-aged man is like an "uncle," an older man is described as "grandfather," even when there is no biological link. You can imagine the unpleasant shock a woman might feel when she is called *obasan*, instead of *oneesan*, and *obaasan* instead of *obasan* from neighborhood children. Compare this with English; although uncle and aunt are used for family friends who are about the age of the child's uncle and aunt, when a person addresses a stranger, general address terms such as "Mr." and "Miss" are used regardless of the age.

60. Description of Possession

Target Expression

> *Do you have the ticket?*
> **Kippu o motte-imasu ka.**
> 切符を持っていますか。
>
> [N + *o* + *motte-iru*]

Grammatical Explanation

Earlier we have studied that *aru* and *iru* can be used to express possession. Another strategy is to use the verb *motsu* 'to possess.' The verb *motsu* is used in the present progressive tense and it expresses the state of possessing or the state of in possession of something. To be noted is that when what is possessed is animate, *motte-iru* cannot be used; either *aru* or *iru* must be chosen.

Examples

(1) *Jisho wa nan-satsu gurai motte-imasu ka.*
辞書は何冊ぐらい持っていますか。
(About how many dictionaries do you possess?)

(2) *Kyoo wa okane o takusan motte-imasu.*
今日はお金をたくさん持っています。
(I have a lot of money [on me] today.)

(3) *Tomodachi ga takusan imasu.*
友だちがたくさんいます。
(I have many friends.)

(4) <u>Watashi</u> <u>ni</u> <u>wa</u> <u>ani</u>　　　　<u>to</u> <u>ane</u>　　<u>ga</u> <u>hitori</u>
　　I　　　at　T　elder brother　and　elder sister　S　one

<u>zutsu</u> <u>arimasu.</u>[1]
each　possess

私には兄と姉が一人ずつあります。

(I have one elder brother and one elder sister.)

[1]. *Zutsu* is used when the quantity of more than two separate items is identical, similarly to English *each*. It is placed after the quantifier as shown in this sentence.

Practice

----
small change　N　*komakai okane*　細かいお金
　　　　　　　　(or *komakai no* 細かいの)
record　　　　N　*rekoodo*　　　レコード

Assume that you possess the items 1 through 4. How would you describe that fact? Provide question-answer pairs by asking if your friend possesses these items.

1. siblings
2. small change
3. about 200 records
4. a good dictionary

———— Some Sample Answers ————

1. A: *Anoo, gokyoodai ga arimasu ka.*
   　　あのう、ご兄弟がありますか。
   B: *Ee. San-nin desu.* ええ。三人です。
2. A: *Anoo, komakai okane arimasu?*
   　　あのう、細かいお金あります？
   B: *Ee, arimasu yo.* ええ、ありますよ。
3. 　　*Rekoodo o ni-hyaku-mai gurai motte-imasu.*
   　　レコードを二百枚ぐらい持っています。
4. A: *Ii jisho o motte-masu ka./Ii jisho ga arimasu ka.*
   　　いい辞書を持っていますか。/いい辞書がありますか。
   B: *Ee, motte-masu yo./Ee, arimasu yo.*
   　　ええ、持ってますよ。/ええ、ありますよ。

61. Expressing Gratitude

> *Thank you very much.*
> ### *Doomo arigatoo gozaimasu.*
> どうもありがとうございます。

Strategic Explanation

Expressing gratitude is important in many societies, but some of the regulatory rules of saying thank you in Japanese differ from those in other countries. But first, let us learn the formulaic phrases expressing gratitude.

Arigatoo. ありがとう。'Thanks.' ☺
Arigatoo gozaimasu. ありがとうございます。 'Thank you.' (polite)
Arigatoo gozaimashita. ありがとうございました。 'Thank you for . . .' (often after the favor is done)
Doomo (doomo). どうも(どうも)。 'Thanks.' ☺
Doomo sumimasen. どうもすみません。 'Thank you for your trouble.'
Doomo sumimasen-deshita. どうもすみませんでした。 'Thank you for doing . . .' (after the favor is done)

An expression *osewa ni narimashita* 'lit. thanks for taking care of me' is used when one parts from someone whose care he or she has been under. For example, when parting the host family (for good), this expression is used to mean 'thank you for taking care of me.' It is advisable to bow as these words are uttered. *Sumimasen(-deshita)* is an expression of apology, but is often used as an expression of gratitude. By apologizing for bothering someone on one's behalf, appreciation is indirectly expressed.

When you are thanked, the response should be:

(a) *Iie, doo itashimashite.*
いいえ, どういたしまして。
(You are welcome, it's my pleasure.)

Or, you can simply say *iie* or *iya* (used by males only) to deny that what you did for the other person deserves such an expression of gratitude.

In Japan it is customary for a person who received a favor earlier to express gratitude again the next time they meet. Let's assume that your teacher invited you to his or her home and served dinner a week ago. What follows is a typical interaction when you run into him or her again.

A: *Aa, Suzuki sensei, ohayoo gozaimasu.*
ああ，鈴木先生，おはようございます。
(Ah, Professor Suzuki, good morning.)

B: *Aa, ohayoo.* ☺
ああ，おはよう。
(Good morning.)

A: *Sensei, **kono aida wa doomo arigatoo gozaimashita.***
先生，この間はどうもありがとうございました。
(Thank you very much for [your favor] the other day.)

B: *Iya, iya.* ☺ M
いや，いや。
(You are quite welcome.)
Iie.
いいえ。
(You are quite welcome.)

It is important to follow the ritual of mentioning the favor given by the other at a previous occasion. Among friends, a shortened expression *kono aida wa doomo* 'thanks for the other day' suffices. Repeated thanks expresses the depth of your appreciation.

If a person learned only one or two phrases in Japanese, he or she couldn't do better than *sumimasen* and *doomo*. Both *sumimasen* and *doomo* can express apology, gratitude, leave-taking and other things. See the following interaction.

A: ***Sumimaseeen.*** [At the door, requesting attention]
すみませーん。
(Excuse me!)

B: *A, **doomo doomo.*** [Answering to A casually]
あ，どうもどうも。
(Oh, Hi.)

A: *Kore onegai-shimasu.* [A hands B a community bulletin]
これお願いします。
(Here is [the bulletin] for you.)

B: *Aa, **sumimasen nee.*** [B thanks A for distributing the bulletin]
ああ，すみませんねえ。
(Oh, thanks.)

A: *Iie. Jaa **doomo.*** [A performs informal leave-taking]
いいえ。じゃあどうも。
(Don't mention it. See you.)

B: ***Doomo.*** [B responds to A's leave-taking]
どうも。
(I'll see you.)

Additional Information

At work, the boss sometimes shows gratitude toward the workers by saying *gokuroosan* or *gokuroosama (desu/deshita)*. The word *kuroo* means 'toil' and 'hardship.' The phrase *gokuroosan* and *gokuroosama* are used to express appreciation for the effort put in by a subordinate who is expected to perform certain duties for the direct or indirect benefit of the speaker. A housewife may say *gokuroosama* to a delivery man; a husband, spotting a newspaper delivery man, may say *gokuroosan* to express his acknowledgment and appreciation of his service. This phrase is not to be used when addressing the people you must be polite toward.

Practice

How would you express gratitude when:

1. a stranger tells you how to get to the station
2. your co-worker brings you a cup of coffee
3. you meet your teacher who treated you to a dinner last week
4. you spot a mailperson delivering mail to your door

——— Some Sample Answers ———
1. *Doomo arigatoo (gozaimashita)*.
   どうもありがとう(ございました)。
2. *Doomo (doomo)*.　どうも(どうも)。
3. *Kono aida wa doomo arigatoo gozaimashita*.
   この間はどうもありがとうございました。
4. *Gokuroosama (desu)*.　ごくろうさま(です)。

62. Stating Purpose

> *I'm going (in order) to see Ms. Kato.*
> **Katoo-san ni ai ni ikimasu.**
> 加藤さんに会いにいきます。
> *I'm saving money (in order) to travel.*
> **Ryokoo-suru tame ni (o)kane o tamete-iru.** ♦
> 旅行するために（お）金をためている。
>
> [Vstem + *ni* + *iku/kuru*]
> [Vbasic + *tame ni*]
> [N + *no tame ni*]

Grammatical Explanation

In expressing purpose, two patterns are used. One, for the main verb of *iku* 'to go' and *kuru* 'to come,' and other directional verbs such as *kaeru* 'to return,' *hairu* 'to enter,' combine [Vstem (that is, take off *-masu* from the *-masu* form of the verb) + *ni*]. For example; *tabe ni ikimasu* 'go (in order) to eat.' Second, for all verbs, add *tame ni* after the [Vbasic] form. When [*tame ni*] is preceded by *da*, however, *da* changes to *no*. (*Tame* itself is a noun meaning 'benefit,' 'purpose' and 'cause.') For example, *kuruma o kau tame ni (o)kane o tameru* '(I) save money in order to buy a car.' When the phrase *tame ni* is used for the directional verbs, including *iku* and *kuru*, it carries the effect of a somewhat dramatized narrative style.

When the purpose is described in the noun form, the same restriction applies. *Ni* can be attached immediately after the nouns which refer to activity if the relevant verb is directional; as in *benkyoo ni ikimasu* 'go for studying' or *kaimono ni ikimasu* 'go for shopping.' The expression of purpose takes the [N + *no tame ni*] structure when it co-occurs with verbs other than directional; as in *kazoku no tame ni hataraku* 'to work for (the sake of) the family.'

Examples

jiyuu	自由	N	freedom, liberty
tatakau	戦う	V	to fight

(1) *Sumimasen ga san-ji ni Tanaka-san ni ai ni itte-kudasai-*
     masen ka.
     すみませんが，三時に田中さんに会いに行ってくださいませんか。
     (Could you please go see Mr. Tanaka at three o'clock?)

(2) | *Nihongo* | *o* | *benkyoo-suru* | *tame ni* | *atarashii* |
     |---|---|---|---|---|
     | Japanese | O | study | for | new |

jisho	*o*	*kaimashita.*
dictionary	O	bought

     日本語を勉強するために新しい辞書を買いました。
     (I bought a new dictionary in order to study Japanese.)

(3) A: *Imooto (no tame) ni kore katte-ikoo ka.* ☺
      妹(のため)にこれ買っていこうか。
      (Shall we buy this for our younger sister?)
    B: *Un, soo shiyoo* ☺
      うん，そうしよう。
      (Yeah, let's.)

(4) *Jiyuu no tame ni tatakaoo.*
     自由のために戦おう。
     (Let us fight for the sake of freedom.)

(5) A: | *Nihon* | *e* | *wa* | *nani* | *o* | *shi ni* | | *ikimasu* | *ka.* |
      |---|---|---|---|---|---|---|---|---|
      | Japan | to | T | what | O | do in order to | | go | Q |

      日本へは何をしに行きますか。
      (lit. In order to do what do you go to Japan?] For what purpose
      are you going to Japan?)
    B: *Benkyoo-shi ni ikimasu.*
      勉強しに行きます。
      (I'm going in order to study.)

Practice

----
ticket	N	*kippu*	切符
guest	N	*okyaku-san*	お客さん
to welcome	V	*mukaeru*	迎える
part-time job	N	*paato no shigoto,*	
		arubaito	
		パートの仕事，アルバイト	
to support financially	V	*yashinau*	養う
family	N	*kazoku*	家族

Complete the following by adding purposes of your choice.

1. working so hard?
2. please go to the station
3. going to Narita
4. working part-time at night

——— Some Sample Answers ———

1. *Nan no tame ni isshookenmei hataraite-imasu ka.*
   何のためにいっしょうけんめい働いていますか。
2. *Ryokoo no kippu o kai ni eki e itte-kite-kudasaimasen ka.*
   旅行の切符を買いに駅へ行ってきてくださいませんか。
3. *Amerika kara no okyaku-san o mukae ni Narita e ikimasu.*
   アメリカからのお客さんを迎えに成田へ行きます。
4. *Kazoku o yashinau tame ni yoru paato no shigoto o shite-imasu.* 家族を養うために夜パートの仕事をしています。

Additional Information

The expression of purpose may precede adjectival predicates. In both [Adj-*i*] and [Adj-*na*], *ni* is used. This combination takes either [N + *ni*] or [Vbasic + *no ni*]. This *no* is a nominalizer which will be discussed in Entry 105. Thus, we have *seiyoo ni ii* 'good for a rest,' and *seiyoo-suru no ni ii* 'good for resting.' Additional examples are:

(a) <u>Kono kusuri</u>   <u>wa zutsuu</u>   <u>ni</u>   <u>ii-desu ka.</u>
    this   medicine   T   headache   for   good   Q
    この薬は頭痛にいいですか。
    (Is this medicine good for headaches?)

(b) *Kono heya wa hon o yomu no ni ii-desu nee.*
    この部屋は本を読むのにいいですねえ。
    (This room is good for reading books.)

(c) *Kore wa chiisai mono o miru no ni benri desu yo.*
    これは小さいものを見るのに便利ですよ。
    (This is useful for looking at small items.)

There is a similar expression *yooni* which is equivalent to the English use of 'so that.' This use of *yooni* takes the [Vbasic] form. For example:

(d) <u>Wasurenai</u>   <u>yooni</u>   <u>memo</u>   <u>o</u>   <u>shimasu.</u>
    not forget   so that   memo   O   do
    忘れないようにメモをします。
    (I write it down so that I won't forget.)

(e) <u>*Hayaku*</u> <u>*repooto*</u> <u>*o*</u> <u>*shiageru*</u> <u>*yooni*</u> <u>*ganbarimasu.*</u>
　　soon　　report　　O　finish　　so that　　do my best

早くレポートを仕上げるようにがんばります。

(I'll do my best so that I'll complete the report soon.)

Warning

The structure [*(no) tame ni*] also expresses cause. For example, *jiko no tame ni densha ga okuremashita* 'because of an accident, the train was late.' When [*tame ni*] expresses cause, unlike when it expresses purpose, it is preceded by [V/Adj pre-nominal] forms. [Adj pre-nominal] and [V pre-nominal] forms are introduced in Entries 38 and 74, respectively. To determine the meaning of [*(no) tame ni*]—as to whether it implies purpose or cause—, it is necessary to examine the context in which it appears (this is pointed out again in Entry 77).

63. Physical Condition—1. Hunger and Thirst

Target Expression

> *Boy, am I hungry!*
> > **Onaka ga suita naa.** ☺
> > おなかがすいたなあ。

Grammatical Explanation

When expressing one's physical condition in Japanese, the actual conditions of the parts of one's body are described. For example, *onaka ga suita* 'lit. (my) stomach got empty,' rather than saying as in English 'I am hungry.' When describing that you are hungry now, the past tense of the verb is used as shown in the target sentence. *Onaka ga sukimasu* is possible; but this expression simply describes a universally applicable, neutral statement, as in *hataraku to onaka ga sukimasu* 'when you work, you get hungry.' In male casual speech, *hara ga suita/hetta*, instead of *onaka ga suita*, may be used, although this expression is blunt and is permissible only when used by males among *uchi* members in very casual situations. Another frequently used expression is *nodo ga kawakimashita* '(lit. my throat got dry) I'm thirsty.'

Since the condition of one's stomach being empty continues when expressing 'I am hungry,' the present progressive tense form, that is, *onaka ga suite-imasu* 'lit. I am in the state of being hungry.' is also used to describe the state of being hungry.

Expressions introduced here take predicates of "reactive description"; *onaka* and *nodo* are the elements of primary predicate focus followed by *ga*, unless of course they are topicalized in which case they are marked by *wa* (or possibly by *mo*). The experiencer may also appear in this structure as in *watashi wa onaka ga suita* 'I am hungry.'

Examples

A: *Aa, nodo ga kawaita.* ☺
   ああ、のどがかわいた。
   (Oh, I am thirsty.)
B: *Watashi mo.*
   私も。
   (Me, too.)
A: *Nani-ka tsumetai mono demo nomi ni ikimasen ka.*
   何か冷たいものでも飲みに行きませんか。
   (Won't you go out for some cold drinks or something?)
B: *Ii-desu nee. Soo shimashoo yo.*
   いいですねえ。そうしましょうよ。
   (That's a good idea. Let's do so.)

Practice

not much	Adv	*amari, anmari*
		あまり、あんまり
		(colloquial)
then	Conj	*soredewa, sorejaa*
		それでは、それじゃあ
thank you	Int	*enryo naku* 遠慮なく
		(lit. without hesitation)

1. How would you express your physical condition when:
   a. you are hungry ☺
   b. you are thirsty

2. Create an interaction in which:
   A: you ask whether your friend is hungry
   B: your friend answers not very

A: you suggest something to drink
B: your friend thinks it over and agrees

─────── Some Sample Answers ───────
1a. *Onaka ga suita.* ☺   おなかがすいた。
  b. *Nodo ga kawakimashita.*   のどがかわきました。
2.A: *Onaka suite-imasen ka.*   おなかすいていませんか。
  B: *Iie, anmari.*   いいえ，あんまり。
  A: *Sorejaa nani-ka tsumetai nomimono demo ikaga desu ka.*
     それじゃあ何か冷たい飲みものでもいかがですか。
  B: *Soo desu ne. Jaa, enryo naku.* そうですね。じゃあ，遠慮なく。

Warning

The direct expressions of physical condition introduced in this entry are used only by the person who experiences these conditions. Only the first-person subject can be used for affirmative and negative statements, and only the second-person subject in interrogative sentences. In Japanese a grammatical distinction is required when expressing what one can or cannot directly experience. In describing someone else's physical condition, you must express something like 'it seems, or it appears, that he is hungry,' that is, *kono ko wa onaka ga suite-iru yoo da* 'this child seems to be hungry.' The [*yoona*] expression will be learned later. It is important to remember that expressions such as **ano hito wa onaka ga suita* is not normally used. Of course a writer of a novel, being omniscient, may express the third-person's personal experience and feelings directly.

 Comparative and Superlative Forms

Target Expression

> *This personal computer is newer than that one.*
> **Kono pasokon no hoo ga are yori atarashii-desu yo.**
> このパソコンの方があれより新しいですよ。
>
> > [N + *no hoo ga*   N + *yori*]
> > [V/Adj informal non-past + *hoo ga*
> > V/Adj informal non-past + *yori*]
> > [*(no naka) de ichiban*]

Grammatical Explanation

Comparative and superlative forms in English call for *-er* and *-est* endings in adjectives or for the addition of adverbs *more* and *most*. Japanese adjectives do not change forms when used in comparative and superlative expressions. Instead, for comparative and superlative purposes specific sentence patterns are used.

When comparing two items, the expression [N + *no hoo*], [V informal non-past + *hoo*] or [Adj informal non-past + *hoo*] is used in order to point out one in comparison to the other (the word *hoo* is a noun and it literally means 'direction').

   (a)   ***Nihon no hoo*** *ga chiisai.* ☺
       日本の方が小さい。
       (Japan is smaller.)

   (b)   *Kuruma de **iku hoo** ga kantan da yo.* ☺
       車で**行く方**が簡単だよ。
       (It is easier to go by car.)

   (c)   ***Chikai hoo*** *ga ii-desu.*
       近い方がいいです。
       (Being near is better.)

When making a statement about one item in contrast to the other, *yori* is added to the item with which it is being contrasted.

   (d)   *Nihon wa **Huransu yori** chiisai-desu.* ☺
       日本は**フランスより**小さいです。
       (Japan is smaller than France.)

   (e)   *Densha de iku hoo ga basu de **iku yori** hayai.* ☺
       電車で行く方がバスで**行くより**速い。
       (Going by train is faster than going by bus.)

For the superlatives, *ichiban* '(lit. number one)' or *mottomo* 'most' is added to the adjectives and adverbs. The particle *de* is used to indicate the limit within which the comparison is made. When the limitation is defined in terms of members of a group, [*no nake de*] is used instead of *de*.

   (f)   *Kono tatemono wa Kyooto **de ichiban/mottomo** hurui-desu.*
       この建物は京都で**一番**/**最も**古いです。
       (This building is the oldest in Kyoto.)

   (g)

Petto	***no naka de***	***wa***	*inko*	*ga*	***ichiban***	*kawaii*
pet	among	T	parakeet	S	most	endearing

<u>*yo.*</u> ☺
IP

ペットの中ではインコが一番かわいいよ。
(Among [all] pets, parakeets are the most endearing.)

As an extension of the comparative form, another important use should be mentioned here. The structure [V pre-nominal (excluding negative past form) + *hoo ga ii*] is equivalent to the English pattern *had better*. For example, *hayaku iku/itta hoo ga ii-desu yo* '(lit. going early is better) you had better go early.' *Itta hoo ga ii* is considered slightly more polite than *iku hoo ga ii*. This [*hoo ga ii*] construction is used to express suggestions and advice and we will return to this later under Entry 118.

When the compared items are thought to be equal, [*to onaji yooni/kurai ni*] is used. For example, *Sachiko-san mo Hiroko-san to onaji yooni wakai-desu ne* 'Sachiko is just about as young as Hiroko, isn't she?' When you need to negate the comparative statement, *hodo* '(not) to the degree' is used, as in *Sachiko-san wa Hiroko-san hodo wakakunai-desu yo* 'Sachiko is not so young as Hiroko.'

To form a comparative question, use the pattern [A *to* B *to dochira (no hoo) ga* Adj/(Adv + V)]. A and B must be nouns; when using verbs and adjectives the nominalizer *no* must be inserted before *to*. For example:

(h)　*Kono sakana **to** ano sakana **to dochira (no hoo) ga** oishii-deshoo ka.*
この魚とあの魚とどちら（の方）がおいしいでしょうか。
(Which is more delicious, this fish or that fish?)

(i)　*Densha de iku no **to** basu de iku no **to dochira ga** hayai-deshoo ka.*
電車で行くのとバスで行くのとどちらが速いでしょうか。
(Which is quicker, going by train or going by bus?)

(j)　A:　*Takashi-chan **to** Maki-chan **to dochira ga** hayaku okiru?* ☺
たかしちゃんとまきちゃんとどちらが早く起きる？
(Who gets up earlier, Takashi or Maki?)
　　B:　*Maki-chan da yo.* ☺
まきちゃんだよ。
(Maki.)

For superlative questions, the pattern [question words + grammatical particle + *ichiban*] is used: *kazoku no naka de dare ga ichiban yoku terebi o mimasu ka?* 'among family members, who watches television the most?'

Examples

(1)　　Densha no hoo ga benri da yo. ☺ M
　　　　電車の方が便利だよ。
　　　　(Trains are more convenient.)

(2)　　Ima wa Nyuuyooku no hoo ga Tookyoo yori samui-deshoo.
　　　　今はニューヨークの方が東京より寒いでしょう。
　　　　(Now New York is probably colder than Tokyo.)

(3)　A:　Kono kurasu no gakusei no naka de dare ga ichiban hayaku
　　　　kimashita ka.
　　　　このクラスの学生の中で誰が一番早く来ましたか。
　　　　(Who came the earliest among all the students in this class?)
　　B:　Kyasii-san desu.
　　　　キャシーさんです。
　　　　(Cathy did.)

(4)　　Hayaku <u>neru</u>/<u>neta</u> hoo ga ii yo. ☺
　　　　早く<u>寝る</u>/<u>寝た</u>方がいいよ。
　　　　(You had better go to bed early.)

(5)　　Dare ga ichiban hayaku okimashita ka.
　　　　誰が一番早く起きましたか。
　　　　(Who got up the earliest?)

Practice

----
bright, light　Adj　*akarui*　　明るい
to go out　　　V　　*dekakeru*　出かける
to talk　　　　V　　*hanasu*　　話す

1.　Compare the following items. Provide appropriate answers.
　　a.　delicious: this apple or that apple
　　b.　bright, light: this room or your room (addressed to Kazuko)
　　c.　work harder: Hayashi or Yamada

2.　How would you offer the following advice to your friend
　　informally?
　　a.　to work harder ☺
　　b.　not to go out at night ☺
　　c.　to talk with the teacher ☺

——— Some Sample Answers ———

1a. A: *Kono ringo to ano ringo to dochira no hoo ga oishii-desu ka.*
このりんごとあのりんごとどちらの方がおいしいですか。

B: *Dochira mo oishii desu.* どちらもおいしいです。

b. A: *Kono heya to Kazuko-san no heya to dochira ga akarui-desu ka.*
この部屋と和子さんの部屋とどちらが明るいですか。

B: *Watashi no heya no hoo ga akarui-deshoo.*
私の部屋の方が明るいでしょう。

c. A: *Hayashi-san no hoo ga Yamada-san yori isshookenmei hatarakimasu yo nee.*
林さんの方が山田さんよりいっしょうけんめい働きますよねえ。

B: *Ee, soo desu ne.* ええ，そうですね。

2a. *Motto isshookenmei hataraku hoo ga ii yo.* ☺
もっといっしょうけんめい働く方がいいよ。

b. *Yoru wa dekakenai hoo ga ii yo.* ☺
夜は出かけない方がいいよ。

c. *Sensei to hanashita hoo ga ii yo.* ☺
先生と話した方がいいよ。

65. Expressing Desire

Target Expressions

I want money.

Okane ga hoshii naa. ☺
お金が欲しいなあ。

I want to eat a bit more!

Moo chotto tabetai! ☺
もうちょっと食べたい！

[*hoshii*]
[Vstem + *tai* (*desu*)]
[*hoshigatte-iru*]
[Vstem + *tagatte-iru*]

Grammatical Explanation

Two patterns are used for expressing desire. If what one desires takes a grammatical noun, *hoshii* 'to want,' 'to desire' is used. If what one wants involves action and it is expressed by a verb, [Vstem + *tai*] is used, except when the verb is *da*, in which case *dearu* or *de-iru* are used. The verbs used in this pattern are limited to those expressing controllable action only. *Hoshii* is an [Adj-*i*]; -*tai* is an [AuxAdj] and both conjugate as [Adj-*i*].

Two interesting observations must be noted in regard to the way Japanese express desire. First, since desire is internal, a feeling unobservable to others, [*hoshii*] and [-*tai*] forms are used only for the first person, and in question forms for the second-person. For describing a third-person's desire, -*gatte-iru* (a present progressive form of -*garu*, a marker to indicate expression of emotion) must be added. When followed by -*gatte-iru*, the final *i* of *hoshii* and -*tai* is deleted (that is, [Adj stem]), thus we have *hoshigatte-iru* 'to want' and *tabetagatte-iru* 'to want to eat.' This distinction is required in Japanese grammar because an epistemological distinction is made between what a person directly experiences or feels and information a person has only indirect access to. (When accompanied by other expressions like 'it seems,' 'it appears,' and 'they say,' it is possible to use both *hoshii* and -*tai* for the third-person subject. An expression such as 'it seems . . .' makes the direct statement semantically indirect and therefore, does not violate the rule of "not expressing others' personal experience and feelings directly.")

Second, when expressing desire, Japanese describe the object of desire as a source that causes one to respond to it. Going back to our broader notion of subject, that is, the element of primary predicate focus, the source that causes desire is considered the information of central focus. When *hoshii* is used, the source is marked by the subject marker *ga*, unless it constitutes a topic, in which case it is marked by *wa* (or possibly by *mo*). When the -*tai* expression is used, the source is marked either by *o* or *ga*; or *wa*, in case of a topic. When [*hoshigatte-iru*] and [Vstem + *tagatte-iru*] are used, the source is marked by *o* (not *ga*), or *wa* in case of a topic.

In English translation, the source or the object of one's desire constitutes a grammatical object. In Japanese, desire is expressed somewhat passively—something one desires simply exists there and one responds to it. *Hoshii* and *tai* are predicates of "reactive" description and the experiencer may also appear in the form of [N + *ga*]. For example, *dare ga nomimono ga hoshii?* 'who wants something to drink?' *watashi ga (nomimono ga) hoshii* 'I want something to drink.' If the experiencer becomes the topic, an expression such as *(watashi wa) nomimono ga hoshii* is possible.

Examples

```
hanashi      話    N     talking
```

Watashi wa eigo de hanashi ga shitai. ☺
私は英語で話がしたい。
(I wish to speak in English.)

Dakara, Igirisu-jin ka Amerika-jin no tomodachi ga hoshii. ☺
だから，イギリス人かアメリカ人の友だちが欲しい。
(That's why I want a British or American friend.)

Eigo no hon mo yomitai. ☺
英語の本も読みたい。
(I want to read English books also.)

Dakara, ii jisho mo hoshii. ☺
だから，いい辞書も欲しい。
(So I also want a good dictionary.)

Imooto wa Huransugo no hon o hoshigatte-iru. ☺
妹はフランス語の本を欲しがっている。
(My younger sister wants French books.)

Soshite, benkyoo-suru tame ni Huransu e ikitagatte-iru. ☺
そして，勉強するためにフランスへ行きたがっている。
(And she wants to go to France to study.)

Warning

Although in English the expression *do you want to* and *don't you want to* are informal invitations, as in 'do/don't you want to go out tonight?,' the Japanese question with [-*tai*] expression does not connote this invitational meaning. *Kon'ya dekaketai-desu ka?* is a straightforward question asking if one wants to go out; it is not meant to be an invitation. To express an invitation, as we studied earlier, the non-past negative form is used; *kon'ya dekakemasen ka?* 'won't you go out tonight?'

Note also that the [-*tai*] expression is not normally used when addressing one's superior.

Practice

```
to stay up     V      okite-iru      起きている
till late      Adv    osoku made     遅くまで
```

First, describe your desire for the following items. Second, ask your friend if he or she has those desires. Third, provide a question-comment pair as to whether Ms. Inoue has those desires.

1. to see one's younger sister
2. to buy a new car ☺
3. not to stay up late ☺
4. to watch TV tonight
5. to drink sake tonight ☺ (Try in both male and female styles.)

——— Some Sample Answers[1] ———

1. *Imooto ni aitai-desu.* 妹に会いたいです。
2. *Atarashii kuruma (ga) kaitai?* ☺ 新しい車（が）買いたい？
3. *Yoru osoku made okite-itakunai naa.* ☺
   夜遅くまで起きていたくないなあ。
4. A: *Inoue-san wa kon'ya terebi o mitagatte-imasu ka.*
   井上さんは今夜テレビを見たがっていますか。
   B: *Ee.* ええ。
5. *Kon'ya sake nomitai naa.* ☺M 今夜酒飲みたいなあ。
   Kon'ya osake nomitai wa. ☺F 今夜お酒飲みたいわ。

[1]. In case you are wondering about particles in these answers, the following points may be helpful. For sentence 1, an idiomatic use of the object of the verb *au* 'to see,' 'to meet,' requires *ni*. For 2 and 5, the noun directly associated with the verb takes either *ga* or *o* which need not be mentioned in casual speech. For sentence 4, the noun takes *o*, since the relevant verb has the form of *-tagatte-iru*.

Additional Information

Hoshii is also used in the structure [(N *ni*) V*te* + *hoshii*] to express a desire to have someone (marked by the particle *ni*) do something for him or her. This use normally occurs in the first person declarative and the second person interrogative. For example:

(a) *Kore Yamada-san ni yonde hoshii n desu kedo.*[2]
   これ山田さんに読んでほしいんですけど。
   (I want Yamada to read this.)

(b) *Ja, Akiko-san ni sugu itte hoshii n desu ka.*
   じゃ，あき子さんにすぐ行ってほしいんですか。
   (Then you want Akiko to go right away?)

[2]. The *n* in *n desu* expression is used for the purpose of making a request less blunt. We will study this use of *n(o)* later.

66. Physical Condition—2. Health Problems

> *I have a headache.*
>
> *Atama ga itai.* ☺
> 頭が痛い。

Grammatical Explanation

When describing your physical condition, the actual condition of specific organs and body parts or their symptoms are stated. Many of these expressions take predicates for "reactive" description with the element of primary predicate focus marked with *ga*. Contrast the Japanese sentence structure presented here with the English equivalent of [I have . . .], [I feel . . .] structure.

atama ga itai	頭が痛い	to have a headache
onaka ga itai	おなかが痛い	to have a stomachache
kaze o hiku	かぜをひく	to catch a cold (To express 'I have a cold,' *kaze o hiita* or *kaze o hiite-iru.*)
koshi ga itai	腰が痛い	to have a back pain
seki ga deru	せきが出る	to have a cough
tsukareru	疲れる	to be tired (To express 'I got tired' and 'I am tired,' *tsukareta* or *tsukarete-iru.*)
netsu ga aru	熱がある	to have a fever
nodo ga itai	のどが痛い	to have a sore throat
ha ga itai	歯が痛い	to have a toothache
hukutsuu ga suru	腹痛がする	to have a stomach pain (more formal than *onaka ga itai*)
byooki ni naru	病気になる	to become sick
me ga mawaru	目がまわる	to feel giddy
memai ga suru	めまいがする	to feel dizzy

You should be reminded here again that expressions which can only be personally experienced cannot directly describe a third-person's physical condition. Adding expressions such as *-garu* or *yoona* is necessary.

Additional Information

There is no expression equivalent to "bless you" (said to the person who sneezes) in Japanese. Normally nothing is said. According to Japanese folklore, if you sneeze, someone is gossiping about you.

Practice

1. Describe the following physical conditions as a cause for doing or not doing something.
   a. having a stomach pain
   b. having had a toothache
   c. being tired
   d. having caught a cold

2. Imagine that you have a cold. Describe your symptoms.

3. Describe your current physical condition.

——— Some Sample Answers ———

1a. *Onaka ga itai node hayaku kaeritai n desu ga . . .*
おなかが痛いので早く帰りたいんですが……

  b. *Ha ga itakatta node ichinichijuu nani-mo tabemasen-deshita.* 歯が痛かったので一日中何も食べませんでした。

  c. *Tsukareta node hayaku nemasu.* 疲れたので早く寝ます。

  d. *Kaze o hiita node kyoo wa kaisha e wa ikimasen.*
かぜをひいたので今日は会社へは行きません。

2. *Atama ga itai-desu. Netsu ga arimasu. Nodo mo itai-desu.*
頭が痛いです。熱があります。のども痛いです。

3. *Nihongo no benkyoo o shite tsukaremashita. Atama ga itai-desu.* 日本語の勉強をして疲れました。頭が痛いです。

67. Verbal Predicate—7. Spontaneous Verbs

Target Expression

Music is heard. (I hear music.)
Ongaku ga kikoemasu.
音楽が聞こえます。

[*kikoeru*]
[*mieru*]

Grammatical Explanation

As we discussed earlier regarding transitive and intransitive verbs (Entry 46), when describing an event, Japanese often prefer to express "something spontaneously happened," without focusing on "who made something happen" (refer to characteristic 10: *Non-agent Orientation*). For example, you hear some music in the air. Rather than saying 'I' hear music, the expression preferred is *ongaku ga kikoeru* '(lit. the music is audible) the music is heard.' In order to accommodate the Japanese preference for describing events spontaneously and passively, some verbs have "spontaneous" forms. Spontaneous verb forms are best understood as a special case of intransitive verbs. In English the [*be* + Vpast-participle] or [*be* + Adj] structure is used for this purpose, as in "the music is heard." Verb spontaneous forms (for verbs that have spontaneous forms only) are derived by changing the final *-u* to *-eru* (Exception: *kiku* becomes *kikoeru*). The following are frequently used examples.

Transitive Verbs		Spontaneous Intransitive Verbs		
kiku	聞く	*kikoeru*	聞こえる	to be heard
kiru	切る	*kireru*	切れる	to be cut
miru	見る	*mieru*	見える	to be seen
nuku	ぬく	*nukeru*	ぬける	to come off, to come out
yaku	焼く	*yakeru*	焼ける	to be burned, to be grilled
waru	割る	*wareru*	割れる	to be broken

The expression with structural equivalence to the English "I listen to music" is *ongaku o kikimasu*, which is possible in Japanese. *Ongaku o kiku*, however, means that a person listens to music with an intention to listen.

Examples

---
kaji 火事 N fire
---

(1) *Kyoo wa Hujisan ga miemasu yo.*
今日は富士山が見えますよ。
(Today Mt. Fuji is seen.)

(2) *Kaji de biru no san-gai ga yakemashita.*
火事でビルの三階が焼けました。
(Due to a fire, the third floor of the building was burned.)

Additional Information

Although spontaneous verb forms take intransitive verb forms, there are some differences between them. When using spontaneous verbs, an event is described as spontaneously and naturally taking place. While with intransitive verbs the agent or the actor of the action is identified or assumed, with spontaneous verbs information regarding the agent of the event is kept out of consciousness.

The spontaneous form *mieru* may also be used as a respectful form of *kuru* 'to come.' For example, in describing the teacher coming to visit you, *sensei ga miemashita* 'the teacher came,' instead of *sensei ga kimashita.* We will discuss respectful forms in Entry 86.

* * * * *

"Oto wa kikoeru-deshoo ka?"
「音は聞こえるでしょうか？」
([lit. Would the sound be heard] Do you think we will hear that sound?)
—Matsumoto, 1982, p.175.

The expression *kikoeru* is the spontaneous verb. Note that *wa* is used to mark *oto* 'sound' as a topic; if it is not the topic, the expression *oto ga kikoeru-deshoo ka* is appropriate.

68. Personal Preference

Target Expression

> *Do you like classical music?*
> **Kurashikku ongaku wa suki desu ka.**
> クラシック音楽は好きですか。
>
> [sukina]
> [kiraina]

Grammatical Explanation

Personal preference or dislike are expressed by the *na*-type adjective *sukina* 'favorite' and *kiraina* 'disliked.' Again, what one likes takes *ga*; the source of one's preference is the element of primary predicate focus. The way to understand this structure may be to put the target sentence into a different English expression, that is, 'classical music is preferred.' For expressing dislike for something, an [Adj-*na*] *kiraina* 'disliked' is used, also co-occurring with [N + *ga*]. *Sukina* and *kiraina* follow the conjugation of [Adj-*na*], that is, it follows *da* conjugation. For emphatic purposes, the prefix *dai-* may be added to both *sukina* and *kiraina*. For example, *chokoreeto ga daisuki desu* 'I like chocolate a lot.'

Sukina and *kiraina* are predicates of "reactive" description. In the target sentence, the noun *kurashikku ongaku* is what is preferred, which is the element of primary predicate focus. Recall that any noun phrase can become a topic, and if so chosen, *wa* (or possibly *mo*) replaces *ga* in its process. Since the target sentence is a question about 'classical music,' it is chosen to be the topic; thus it is marked by *wa*.

Also to be noted is that *sukina* and *kiraina* (including *daisukina* and *daikiraina*) can modify nouns, and so can their negative counterparts, *sukide (wa-)nai* and *kiraide (wa-)nai*; for example, *sukina hito* 'my favorite person,' and *sukide (wa-)nai tabemono* '(lit. disliked food) food I do not like.'

Examples

jazu	ジャズ	N	jazz
tabemono	食べもの	N	food
sashimi	さしみ	N	sashimi (sliced raw fish)
ima de mo	今でも	Adv	even now

(1) A: *Ongaku wa donna no o kikimasu ka.*
音楽はどんなのを聞きますか。
(What kind of music do you listen to?)

B: *Watashi wa jazu ga suki.* ☺
私はジャズが好き。
(As for myself, I like jazz.)

(2) A: *Tabemono wa nani ga suki desu ka.*
食べものは何が好きですか。
(As for food, what do you like?)

B: *Sashimi ga suki desu.*
さしみが好きです。
(I like sashimi.)

(3) *Ima de mo ano hito ga suki.* ☺
今でもあの人が好き。
(Even now I like [love] her.)

(4) A: *Amerika no biiru suki?* ☺
アメリカのビール好き？
(Do you like American beer?)

B: *Ee, mochiron.*
ええ，もちろん。
(Yes, of course.)

(5) A: *Anoo, nani-ka kiraina tabemono (ga) arimasu ka.*
あのう，何かきらいな食べもの(が)ありますか。
(Do you have any food that you dislike?)

B: *Iie, nani mo (arimasen).*
いいえ，何も(ありません)。
(No, I don't.)

Additional Information

The expression with structural equivalence to the English "I listen to nominalized clauses. Use [Vbasic + *no* + *ga* + *sukina/kiraina*] structure for this purpose. For example, *kurashikku ongaku o kiku no ga suki* 'I like to listen to classical music.' The use of this *no*, called "nominalizer," will be discussed further in Entry 105.

Practice

sports	N	*supootsu*	スポーツ
baseball	N	*yakyuu*	野球
California	PN	*Kariforunia*	カリフォルニア

1. Describe your preference for the following.
    a. sports
    b. person
    c. fruit ☺
    d. wine

2. Choose items you like and dislike from the list of food items given below and express your culinary preference.

    aisukuriimu (ice cream)   *kaki* (persimmon)
    kudamono (fruit)   *keeki* (cake)
    sakana (fish)   *sukiyaki* (sukiyaki)
    sushi (sushi)   *suteeki* (steak)

chuuka ryoori (Chinese cuisine)   *tenpura* (tempura)
hanbaagaa (hamburger)   *banana* (bananas)
Huransu ryoori (French cuisine)   *mikan* (tangerine oranges)
yooguruto (yogurt)   *ringo* (apples)

—— Some Sample Answers ——

1a. *Supootsu wa yakyuu ga suki-desu.* スポーツは野球が好きです。
  b. *Sasaki-san no imootosan ga suki desu.*
     佐々木さんの妹さんが好きです。
  c. *Kudamono wa meron ga suki.* ☺ 果物はメロンが好き。
  d. *Kariforunia no wain no hoo ga Huransu no wain yori suki desu.*
     カリフォルニアのワインの方がフランスのワインより好きです。
2. *Sakana wa amari suki dewa-arimasen.*
     魚はあまり好きではありません。

---

69. Listener Responses in Conversation

Target Expressions

yeah, uh-huh, I see

hai, un, naruhodo
はい, うん, なるほど

Strategic Explanation

As listeners, Japanese display a great deal of feedback. Frequent head nods and much encouraging chatter are sent from a Japanese conversation partner. The brief utterances such as *un* 'uh-huh,' *huun* 'I see' and other non-verbal signs such as nods called *aizuchi* (listener response or back-channel expressions) occur frequently. This listener activity is thought to be good manners. In general, Japanese speakers send many more frequent listener responses. Japanese speakers may feel uneasy when speaking to an American who just listens quietly, even if he or she listens attentively.

In casual conversation it is important to send *aizuchi* when the speaker

pauses and at the point where the speaker uses particles and tag-like auxiliary verbs. See, for example, the conversation segment taken from a
videotaped Japanese casual conversation in Sample Text 1.

The speaker's request for listener's response is frequently expressed by (1)
final particles such as *ne*, (2) auxiliary tags such as *-desho?*, and (3) brief
questions such as *soo omowanai?* 'don't you think so?' Some listener
responses occur concurrently with speakers' head nods which often indicate
the end of the utterance.

Here are different types of listener responses.

1. *Expressing confirmation:*

Soo desu ka.	そうですか。	I see.
Soo desu ne.	そうですね。	That's right.
Yappari.	やっぱり。	That's what I thought.
Naruhodo.	なるほど。	I see. (used when resolving doubt)

2. *Showing one's attention:*

Un. ☺	うん。	Uh-huh.
Huun. ☺	ふーん。	I see.
Soo. ☺	そう。	Right.
Hai./Ee.	はい。/ええ。	Yeah. Yes. (can be used in formal situations)

3. *Expressing reservation or doubt:*

Saa.	さあ。	Well . . .
(Maa) tabun.	（まあ）たぶん。	Perhaps . . .
Soo desu ka nee . . .	そうですかねえ…	Well, I am not sure . . .
Soo?	そう？	Really?
Soo ka naa . . . ☺	そうかなあ……	I wonder . . .

4. *Showing surprise:*

Ee?	ええ？	What?
Honto? ☺	ほんと？	Really? (in casual conversation only)
Uso! ☺	うそ！	You're kidding. (in casual conversation only)
Masaka! ☺	まさか！	It can't be. Nonsense!

5. *Offering sympathy:*

Komarimashita nee.	困りましたねえ。	It's a problem, isn't it?

Yowatta naa. ☺**M**	弱ったなあ。	Oh, boy, what trouble!
Komatta wa nee.☺**F**	困ったわねえ。	Oh, no, what trouble!
Zannen (desu) nee.	残念(です)ねえ。	Sorry to hear that. That's too bad.
Kawaisooni.	かわいそうに。	Poor thing. That's pitiful.
Kinodokuni.	気の毒に。	I'm sorry to hear that.

Practice

When you are conversing casually with a Japanese, attach the particle *ne* to the end of your phrase and then pause. Notice what happens. Your Japanese friend will most likely send some feedback. When you have access to native Japanese speakers' interaction or videotapes of it, carefully study what goes on during pauses within and between speaking turns. That is where the invisible glue is bonding the two in conversation often with the help of *aizuchi* expressions. Listener responses are key elements in Japanese and therefore it is important to know how to express your interest and considerateness as a listener through *aizuchi* expressions.

Additional Information

As you will see in Sample Texts 1 and 2, non-verbal signs like nodding are frequently used as listener responses. Non-verbal communication is very important in any culture. We will study only limited aspects of non-verbal signs in this book.

One point of importance relating to non-verbal signs should be noted. Japanese do not normally look directly into the eyes of the person they are talking to. Sustained eye-contact (which is normally avoided) is an expression of confrontation or suspicion. Avoid looking constantly into the eyes of your Japanese listener. As a listener, you should also avoid too much eye-contact. Especially if the speaker is your social superior, staring into your superior's eyes consistently is considered rude. Look toward the speaker and cast your eyes in the general area of the speaker's neck and shoulders as you look into your partner's eyes from time to time. Contrast this with American culture where gazing steadfastly into the eyes of one's partner is by and large thought to be positive behavior. In fact averting your eyes in American culture somehow makes you a suspicious person, sometimes to the extent that saying someone is shifty-eyed is to practically say that the person is a crook.

You might be interested in knowing that the Japanese word for social

superior is *meue* (lit. above eye level) while social inferiors are called
meshita (lit. below eye level). The right to gaze freely is granted to social
superiors; continuous gaze is more permissible from higher to lower eye
level, i.e., from superiors to subordinates but not vice versa.

70. Adverbs—3. Sentential Adverbs

> *You won't be in time anyway.*
> ### Doose maniawanai daroo.
> どうせ間に合わないだろう。

Grammatical Explanation

Some Japanese adverbs do not directly modify the verb. Instead they express the speaker's attitude toward what is being talked about. These are
similar to English sentential adverbs, such as *regrettably* as in the sentence
"Regrettably, the concert was canceled due to the illness of the performer."
These adverbs convey an emotional or evaluative attitude toward the
statement.

Another type of adverb functions primarily as a cohesive element in
discourse. For example, *tsumari* 'in other words' signals that what is coming is a paraphrase of what was just said. These two types of adverbs are
called "sentential adverbs," and they include:

ittai	いったい	how, what, why on earth (in the world)
sekkaku	せっかく	with much trouble and effort
doose	どうせ	anyway, after all
yatto	やっと	at last, with difficulty
sunawachi	すなわち	in other words
tatoeba	たとえば	for example
tsugini	次に	next
tonikaku	とにかく	at any rate

As an example, let's concentrate on the use of *sekkaku* and *doose*. *Sekkaku* is frequently attached when you express the feeling that although you've made a special effort, you didn't quite succeed. For example:

(a) **Sekkaku**   *itta*   *noni,*   *rusu*   *deshita.*
    purposefully went   despite absence was
    せっかく行ったのに留守でした。
    (Although I went there for the [explicit] purpose of seeing them, they weren't in.)

As an extension to this basic meaning, *sekkaku* is used to express the feeling a subsequent action ought to follow when it is performed with some degree of purpose or sacrifice. For example:

(b) **Sekkaku** *Amerika made iku no da kara*[*1], *Nyuuyooku e mo ikitai-desu.*
    せっかくアメリカまで行くのだから，ニューヨークへも行きたいです。
    (Since I am going purposefully [all the way] to America, I want to get to New York, too.)

                        *1. The *no* in *no da kara* will be studied later (Entry 105).

The sentential adverb *doose* expresses the speaker's emotional attitude — resignation to an unfavorable yet unavoidable fate or fact. For example:

(c) **Doose**   *maniawanai*   *daroo.*
    anyway   not be in time perhaps
    どうせ間に合わないだろう。
    (I probably won't be in time anyway.)

More specifically, *doose* in (c) is a device to directly express the speaker's attitude, i.e., 'well, I won't be in time anyway, although I wish it were otherwise, but, anyway, I cannot change the fact.'

Sentential adverbs also function to express discourse cohesion. For these phrases, the discourse context in which they occur has a direct bearing on their meaning; special attention should be paid to the context in which they appear. Cohesive devices such as *tatoeba* 'for example' and *tsugini* 'next' are useful when you connect a group of utterances, especially when you take a long speaking turn expressing complex thoughts and opinions.

71. Verbs of Giving and Receiving

Target Expression

> *Mr. Turner gave me this map.*
> **Taanaa-san ga kono chizu o kudasaimashita.**
> ターナーさんがこの地図をくださいました。
>
> > [*kureru*] [*ageru*] [*morau*]

Grammatical Explanation

Japanese verbs of giving and receiving involve elements not necessarily significant in English. First, depending on who receives, two different types of verbs for 'give' are used. If you are the receiver, or someone in your *uchi* group is the receiver, the verb chosen for expressing 'to give' is *kureru*; Someone 'gives' *kureru* something to self or the member of self's group. On the other hand if you or a member of your group is not the receiver, for the expression 'to give' something to someone, *ageru* is used. Simply put, if someone else gives you an object, use *kureru*. When you give something to someone, use *ageru*. For the verb of receiving, *morau* is used regardless of whether you receive, or someone else receives.

Second, depending on the relative social status of the participants and the person who is mentioned in the description of the giving/receiving event, different verb forms are chosen. For each of the *kureru*, *ageru* and *morau*, the following additional expressions are available.

Verbs of Giving and Receiving:

Verbs:		Social status of the giver and the receiver:
kureru (someone gives to self)		
kudasaru	くださる	giver is higher
kureru	くれる	giver is equal
kureru	くれる	giver is lower
ageru (self or other gives to someone)		
sashiageru	さしあげる	giver is lower
ageru	あげる	giver is equal
yaru	やる	giver is higher

morau (self or other receives from someone)

itadaku	いただく	receiver is lower
morau	もらう	receiver is equal
morau	もらう	receiver is higher

To recapitulate, consider that the transferance of an object or service can be described in two ways. First, we can say that A 'gives' it to B. Second, the same incident can be reported from the receiver's point of view in which case the main verb to describe this incident is that B 'receives' something from A. But in Japanese, there is an additional dimension. Recall the tendency of Japanese to identify with *uchi* members. If the object or service is transferred from a *soto* member to an *uchi* member (including self), that incident must be described as 'giving-to-me.' Your empathy as you describe this incident is with the *uchi* member, the receiver. It is not grammatically correct to say someone *ageru* something to me or to the *uchi* member. Instead, the other 'give' *kureru*, must be used. If the transaction occurs between self and other members of the *uchi* group, use *kureru* to describe when someone else gives you something and use *ageru* when you are giving something to another. If the transaction occurs between *uchi* members other than self, *ageru* is chosen for expressing 'to give.'

For describing the giver (G), receiver (R), and the things exchanged (T), the following case markers are used:

[G *ga* R *ni* T *o kudasaru/kureru*]
[G *ga* R *ni* T *o sashiageru/ageru/yaru*]
[R *ga* G *ni/kara* T *o itadaku/morau*]

The particle *ni* is preferred when the receiver has direct personal contact with the giver, whereas the particle *kara* is preferred when the source is somewhat impersonal. Thus, *daigaku kara shoogakukin o morau* 'to receive a scholarship from the university' versus *chichi ni okane o morau* 'to receive money from one's father.'

Examples

hana	花	N	flower
mizu	水	N	water

(1)	*Sensei*	*ga*	*kono*	*hon*	*o*	*kudasaimashita.*
	teacher	S	this	book	O	gave-to-me

先生がこの本をくださいました。

(The teacher gave this book to me.)

(2) | *Imooto* ___ | *wa* | *sensei* | *ni* | *kore* | *o* |
|---|---|---|---|---|---|
| younger sister | T | teacher | from | this | O |

itadakimashita.
received

妹は先生にこれをいただきました。
(My sister received this from the teacher.)

(3) *Hana ni mizu o yatte-kudasai ne.*
花に水をやってくださいね。
(Please give some water to the flowers.)

(4) *Otooto wa imooto ni purezento o moraimashita.*
弟は妹にプレゼントをもらいました。
(My younger brother received a present from my sister)

Practice

---
section chief   N   *kachoo*   課長

Describe the following incidents of someone having received something (1 through 4) and you giving something to someone (5 and 6).

1. you: from your younger sister, birthday present
2. your mother: from her teacher, a book
3. you: from your American friend, a letter
4. you: from your friend, this magazine ☺F
5. you: to no one: money ☺
6. you: to the section chief, souvenir of the trip

——— Some Sample Answers ———

1. *Imooto kara tanjoobi no purezento o moraimashita.*
   妹から誕生日のプレゼントをもらいました。
2. *Haha wa sensei kara hon o itadakimashita.*
   母は先生から本をいただきました。
3. *Amerika-jin no tomodachi kara tegami o moraimashita.*
   アメリカ人の友だちから手紙をもらいました。
4. *Tomodachi ni kono zasshi o moratta no yo.* ☺F
   友だちにこの雑誌をもらったのよ。
5. *Okane wa dare ni mo agenai yo.* ☺
   お金は誰にもあげないよ。
6. *Kachoo-san ni omiyage o sashiagemasu.*
   課長さんにおみやげをさしあげます。

Additional Information

There is another verb, *ataeru* 'to give' in Japanese. *Ataeru* is used only when the giver has a higher social status than the receiver. When a giver is of a significantly higher social status, *sazukeru* 'award, confer' is used. Both *ataeru* and *sazukeru* are primarily used in written Japanese.

(a)

Imooto	*wa*	*mudazukai*		*o*	*suru*	*noni*
sister	T	wasteful spending		O	do	despite

haha	*wa*	*itsumo*	*kane*	*o*	*ataeru.*◆
mother	T	always	money	O	give

妹はむだ使いをするのに母はいつも金を与える。

(Although my younger sister wastes money, my mother always gives her some.)

72. Action-accompanying Expressions—1. When Giving and Receiving Gifts

Target Expression

> *Here's a little something for you, it's not much but . . . .*
> **Tsumaranai mono desu ga . . .**
> つまらないものですが……

Strategic Explanation

Expressions such as "here's something for you" or "I thought you might like this" are spoken when giving a gift in America. In Japan, in formal situations, particularly toward one's superiors, expressions to minimize the value of the gift are often used. For example, in formal gift-giving as one presents the formal gift in both hands (using both hands conveys politeness and sincerity), one might say, *makoto ni tsumaranai mono desu ga . . .* 'lit. this isn't of much value, but . . . .' The potential gift receiver may refuse it initially as a part of a ritual by saying *konna koto o shite-itadaite . . .* 'lit. I don't deserve such a favor . . .' or *Ii n desu yo, sonnani ki o tsukatte-itadakanakute . . .* 'It isn't unnecessary to be so kind and considerate . . .' However, to really refuse a gift is considered an ultimate insult in Japan. The second time around the potential receiver may answer, *jaa sekkaku desukara* 'lit. well since you went through all the trouble of giving me this gift, I will thankfully receive this . . .'

Today, between good friends and in familiar personal relationships, this ritual is frequently ignored especially when what is presented is a personal and small gift. It is useful, nonetheless, to be aware of the ritual of formally giving and receiving a gift in Japan.

It should also be mentioned that when visiting a friend or a family, it is polite to bring some small gift (*(o)miyage*). Perishable items such as sweets, fruits or beverages are recommended. This is not considered a personal gift (*okurimono*); it just expresses consideration and appreciation to the host or hostess.

Examples

honno sukoshi ほんの少し	N	just a little
arigataku choodai itashimasu ありがたく頂載いたします	(idiomatic)	I accept your gift with gratitude

A: *Tsumaranai mono desu ga . . .*
つまらないものですが……
(This is just something for you.)

B: *Sumimasen nee, ki o tsukatte-itadaite . . .*
すみませんねえ，気をつかっていただいて……
(Thank you for your kindness and consideration . . .)

A: *Iie, honno sukoshi desu kara.*
いいえ，ほんの少しですから。
(Oh, it is just a small amount.)

B: *Dewa arigataku choodai-itashimasu. Doomo sumimasen.*
ではありがたく頂載いたします。どうもすみません。
(Well then, I accept your kindness. Thank you very much.)

Additional Information

Twice a year Japanese ritually give formal gifts to people whose care or guidance they are under. For example, students (actually parents of students) give gifts to *juku* 'private cram school' teachers. Service industry agents frequently send gifts to clients and patrons. The summer gift-giving is called *ochuugen*, and the winter gift-giving is called *oseibo*. Every year there is a trend of popular gifts; frequently favored are liquor (imported whiskey and wine), imported dry goods, dried seaweed and mushrooms and specially-ordered gourmet food items unique to certain parts of Japan.

73. Giving and Receiving Favorable Actions

Target Expressions

> *My friend kindly helped me.*
> ***Tomodachi ga tetsudatte-kuremashita.***
> 友だちが手伝ってくれました。
> *I had my teacher write a letter of recommendation.*
> ***Sensei ni suisenjoo o kaite-itadakimashita.***
> 先生に推薦状を書いていただきました。
>
> [V*te* + -*kureru*]
> [V*te* + -*ageru*]
> [V*te* + -*morau*]

Grammatical Explanation

When favorable actions are performed for the benefit of someone (and occasionally for bringing damage to someone), it is customary in Japanese to express the benefit by using the various levels of verbs of giving and receiving we studied earlier. The [V*te*] form precedes the verbs of giving and receiving: thus, we have *kaite-ageru* 'give the favorable action of writing,' that is, 'to write something for someone's benefit.' Among verbs, the *be*-verb *da* must be changed to *de-iru*; for example, *tomodachi de-ite-ageru* 'to be friends with someone for his or her benefit.' If the action is performed for yourself or for *uchi* members, and you express the action from the recipient's point of view, *kaite-morau* 'receive the favorable action of writing' that is, 'have someone write something for me' is useful. If the action is performed for yourself or *uchi* members and if you are describing the action from the point of view of the person who is doing the giving, *kaite-kureru* 'give (to self) the favorable action of writing' that is, '(she kindly) wrote this for me' is appropriate. Describing events in terms of favors given for the benefit of others is obligatory in Japanese. Expressions without the [V*te* + -*kureru*] structure, for example, **tomodachi ga tetsudaimashita* instead of the first target expression given above, are awkward; appropriate verb choice for giving and receiving is obligatory.

The specific verb of giving and receiving chosen for this structure depends on the relative social status of the giver and the receiver. The appropriate verb should be chosen depending on the social status of participants and referents involved from the group we learned earlier. For example, if the action of writing is performed by a superior, and the event is described as 'receiving,' the verb selected is *-itadaku*, which is the case demonstrated in the second of the target expressions. Note also that in sentences using the verb *morau*, the indirect object, that is, the person who performs the action, is marked by *ni*.

Characteristics of the three relationships of giving and receiving, [Vte + -*ageru*], [Vte + -*kureru*], and [Vte + -*morau*] along with extended uses are given below:

urusai	うるさい	Adj	noisy, bothersome
naguru	なぐる	V	to beat, to hit
itsuka	いつか	Adv	someday
kitto	きっと	Adv	surely
konkuuru		N	(from French *con-*
	コンクール		*cours*) contest
ittoo	一等	N	first prize
yurusu	許す	V	to approve, to permit, to forgive

1. [Vte + -*ageru*]:
   Describes self-performed, other-influencing action; conveys doing a favor, occasionally disfavor, strong will, and sometimes as an extended use, a feeling of self-abandonment.

   (1a) *Kono hon o yonde-agemashoo.*
   この本を読んであげましょう。
   (I will read this book [for you].) [favor]

   (1b) *Otooto ga urusai node nagutte-yatta.*
   弟がうるさいのでなぐってやった。
   (I hit my younger brother since he is bothersome.) [disfavor]

   (1c) *Itsuka kitto piano no konkuuru de ittoo o totte yaru.*
   いつかきっとピアノのコンクールで一等をとってやる。
   (Someday I will win the first-prize in the piano contest.) [strong will]

(1d)   *Kekkon o yurushite-kurenai. Shinde-yaru!*
結婚を許してくれない。死んで**やる**！
(They don't approve of my marriage. I'm going to die!) [self-abandonment]

2.   [V*te* + *-kureru*]
Describes other-performed, self-benefiting occasionally disfavorable, damaging action; expresses the feeling of thankfulness or occasionally regrets.

(2a)   *Tomodachi ga hon o kashite-kureta.*
友だちが本を貸して**くれた**。
(My friend [kindly] loaned me a book.) [favor]

3.   [V*te* + *-morau*]:
Describes self initiated, self-benefiting action; expresses that the action was performed by others, but beneficial to self, and such action is often requested by self.

(3a)   *Tomodachi ni kasa o kashite-moratta.*
友だちに傘を貸して**もらった**。
(I had my friend loan me an umbrella.) [favor]

Examples

omocha	おもちゃ	N	toy
yorokobu	喜ぶ	V	to be pleased, to rejoice
shiraseru	知らせる	V	to notify

(1)   A: *Kono suisenjoo wa?*
この推薦状は？
(How about this letter of recommendation?)
  B: *Aa, sore wa Yamashita sensei ga kaite-kudasaimashita.*
ああ，それは山下先生が書いてくださいました。
(Oh, that one . . . Professor Yamashita wrote it for me.)

(2)   A: *Otootosan no tanjoobi no paatii wa doo deshita ka.*
弟さんの誕生日のパーティーはどうでしたか。
(How was your younger brother's birthday party?)
  B: *Otooto wa chichi ni omocha o katte-moratte totemo yorokonde-imashita.*
弟は父におもちゃを買ってもらってとても喜んでいました。
(My younger brother had my father buy him toys, and he was quite pleased.)

(3)　A: *Kore dare ga shite-kureta?* ☺
　　　これ誰がしてくれた？
　　　(Who did this [for me]?)
　　B: *Yooko-chan.* ☺
　　　洋子ちゃん。
　　　(Yoko [did].)

(4)　A: *Tanaka-san ni sono nyuusu shirasete-agemashita ka.*
　　　田中さんにそのニュース知らせてあげましたか。
　　　(Did you [kindly] notify Tanaka of the news?)
　　B: *Ee, totemo yorokonde-imashita.*
　　　ええ，とても喜んでいました。
　　　(Yes, she was very pleased.)

Practice

tonari	となり	N	neighbor
kagi	かぎ	N	key, lock
kagi o akeru かぎを開ける		V	(idiomatic) to unlock
hondana	本棚	N	bookshelf
tsukuru	作る	V	to make, to build
okuru	送る	V	to take someone home

How would you express the following in Japanese? Incorporate verbs of giving and receiving into the verbal predicate in order to express who did what for whom, or, who received what from whom.

1.　I will teach you how to drive the car.
2.　My neighbor (kindly) unlocked the door.
3.　Did you have someone make this bookshelf?
4.　Ms. Goto had her friend take her home.

─────── Answers ───────

1. *Kuruma no unten oshiete-agemasu yo.*
　車の運転教えてあげますよ。
2. *Tonari no hito ga doa no kagi o akete-kuremashita.*
　となりの人がドアのかぎを開けてくれました。
3. *Kono hondana wa dare-ka ni tsukutte-moraimashita ka.*
　この本棚は誰かに作ってもらいましたか。
4. *Gotoo-san wa tomodachi ni uchi made okutte-moraimashita.*
　後藤さんは友だちに家まで送ってもらいました。

Additional Information
When the verbs of giving and receiving accompany verbs, they imply that
the action that took place is in some way involved with the recipient's interest. In asking a question 'who did this?,' if no personal interest is involved, a speaker would ask *kore dare ga shita no?* However, if there is either a
positive or negative influence to personal interest, *kore dare ga shite-kureta
no?* is preferred. Depending on the context this latter expression can imply
gratitude or reprimand.

Because of the implication of personal interest, special care is required
when using [V*te* + *-ageru*] expression. When used in a question like *kore
katte-agemashoo ka?* 'shall I buy this for you?,' the listener may resent it.
This expression gives an impression that since the listener is helpless and is
perhaps incapable of performing the action, he or she must receive charity
from the other. A thoughtful Japanese will use instead *kore kaimashoo ka?*
'shall I buy this?'

The [V*te* + *-morau*] structure is often used as an expression of request.
For example:

(a) *Kore o taipu-shite-moraitai n desu kedo . . .*
これをタイプしてもらいたいんですけど……
(I would like to have this typed . . .)

(b) *Sore wa Yamada-san ka Kinoshita-san ni oshiete-moratte-
kudasai.*
それは山田さんか木下さんに教えてもらってください。
(Please have either Mr. Yamada or Mr. Kinoshita teach that to
you.)

(c) *Suisenjoo o kaite-itadakemasen-deshoo ka.* [*1]
推薦状を書いていただけませんでしょうか。
(Would it be possible for you to write a letter of recommendation?)

[*1.] *Itadakemasu* is the formal version of *itadakeru*, which is a potential
form of *itadaku*.
Note that in the last example, the person who is requested to perform the action is marked by an indirect object marker *ni*. We have
studied similar use of *ni* with another request expression in Entry 65,
namely, [V*te* + *hoshii*].

* * * * *

. . . *Kanojo wa "Jon Wein ni nite-iru" to itte-kureta.*
彼女は「ジョン・ウェインに似ている」と言ってくれた。

(She [kindly] said [for me], "You look like John Wayne.")
— Terayama, 1973, p. 86.

In this example, the writer feels it an honor, or at least a pleasant experience to be pointed out that he resembles John Wayne. The feeling expressed by *itte-kureta* is that it was her kindness that made her say such a thing.

74. Predicate with Explanatory Mode—*No da, N da* and *Wake da*

Target Expression

> *(Where did you go?)*
> *(It's that) I went to the bank.*
> ***Ginkoo e itte-kita n desu.***
> 銀行へ行ってきたんです。
>
> [V/Adj pre-nominal
> + *no/wake* + *da*]

Grammatical Explanation

Predicates with explanatory mode are expressed by two similar forms; (1) placing *no*, or its colloquial version *n*, and (2) placing *wake* 'reason' before the *be*-verb *da*. When adding *no/n* or *wake*, use [Adj pre-nominal] forms, directly preceding *no* and *wake*. (See [Adj pre-nominal] forms given in Entry 38.) When [V] precedes *no* and *wake*, use [V pre-nominal] forms which are given below except when *no* is preceded by [N + *da*] structure. In that case use only [N + *na no*] construction. In using the *wake da* expression, when it is preceded by the [N + *da*] structure, use [N + *no wake da*] or [N + *to yuu wake da*].

Verbs:

informal non-past	*oyogu*
informal past	*oyoida*
negative informal non-past	*oyoganai*
negative informal past	*oyoganakatta*

Existential Verbs:

informal non-past	*iru, aru*
informal past	*ita, atta*
negative informal non-past	*inai, nai*
negative informal past	*inakatta, nakatta*

Be-verb:

informal non-past	*no* (instead of *da*)
informal past	*datta*
negative informal non-past	*dewa-nai*
negative informal past	*dewa-nakatta*

Since there is already a main verb, adding these phrases 'extends' the predicate and therefore the [*no da*] and [*wake da*] structures are called 'extended predicates.' Although the extended predicate may sound redundant when translated into English, i.e., 'it is (the case) that,' or 'it is for the reason that,' this structure is used quite commonly in Japanese and needs to be learned with care.

The basic function of [*n(o) da*] is to appeal to the assumed common understanding or knowledge shared between the speaker and the listener. When such common knowledge does not exist, [*n(o) da*] is used to describe the information as if the knowledge is shared; it encourages emotional rapport since it assumes that they share the same information. More specifically, there are at least three related but distinct functions of extended predicates as listed below.

1. To signal that what precedes *no da* offers the reason or cause related to the issue at hand.
2. To emphasize what precedes *no da*.
3. To present the request in a milder tone.

Wake da is used in the manner similar to the first use of *no da* described above (*Wake* is a noun, meaning 'reason'). When a speaker intends to explain a reason, cause or circumstances which lead to the known result or conclusion, *wake da* is used. *Wake da* is often used to explain something one might have wondered about and may be best described by the English expression 'that means . . .' or 'no wonder . . .'

It should be noted that *no da* and *wake da* are often used even when the reason and cause are not strongly implied and/or when strong emphasis is not evident. This additional use occurs when the speaker or the writer wishes to point out some facts and when he or she wishes the listener to realize the special, important meaning that statement carries.

Examples

----

saikin	最近	Adv	recently
mikakeru	見かける	V	to see in passing
byooki	病気	N	illness
urikire	売り切れ	N	sell-out
koojichuu	工事中	N	under construction
tooreru	通れる	V	(potential form of *tooru*) to be able to pass through

----

1. *Reason for the previous statement:*

   (1a) A: *Saikin Toda-san o amari mikakemasen ga . . .*
   最近戸田さんをあまり見かけませんが……
   (I haven't seen Ms. Toda recently . . .)

   B: *Aa, Toda-san wa byooki datta n desu yo.*
   ああ，戸田さんは病気だったんですよ。
   (Oh, Ms. Toda has been ill.)

2. *Emphasis:*

   (2a) *Doo shita n desu ka.* (idiomatic)
   どうしたんですか。
   (What happened to you?)

   (2b) *Suupaa e itta n desu ga, (o)sashimi wa moo urikire datta n desu yo.*
   スーパーへ行ったんですが，（お）さしみはもう売り切れだったんですよ。
   (I went to the supermarket, but all the sliced raw fish was sold out.)

3. *Milder request:*

   (3a) *Kyoo sukoshi hayaku kaeritai n desu kedo . . .*
   今日少し早く帰りたいんですけど……
   (I would like to leave a little earlier today . . .)

4. *Reason for known result:*

   (4a) *Asoko wa koojichuu desu ka. Sore de kuruma ga toorenai wake desu ne.*
   あそこは工事中ですか。それで車が通れないわけですね。
   (Oh, that place is under construction. That's why it is closed to automobiles.)

Let us examine the dialogue example below to understand how extended predicates are used to express emphasis and reason for the previous statement.

atsumaru	集まる	V	to gather
ooyasuuri	大安売り	N	big sale
onna no hito	女の人	N	woman

A: *Dooshite hito ga takusan atsumatte-iru n desu ka.*
どうして人がたくさん集まっているんですか。
(Why are there so many people gathered?)

B: *Sakana no ooyasuuri ga aru n desu yo.*
魚の大安売りがあるんですよ。
(There is a big fish sale.)

A: *Aa, sore de onna no hito ga takusan iru wake desu ne.*
ああ，それで女の人がたくさんいるわけですね。
(Oh I see, no wonder there are many women here.)

In this dialogue, first Speaker A uses *n desu* to catch attention, B uses *n desu* to provide reason for the question, and A uses *wake desu* to convey a reason for the known result.

Practice

to answer the phone	V	*denwa ni deru* 電話に出る
to inquire	V	*kiku, tazuneru* 聞く，たずねる

How would you express the following? Use extended predicates in expressions 1B, 2 and 3.

1. A: You didn't answer the phone all day yesterday. ☺**M**
   B: (It's that) I was gone all day. ☺**M**
2. Why didn't you come?
3. I would like to inquire about something, but . . .

─────── Answers ───────

1. A: *Kinoo denwa ni zenzen denakatta daro?* ☺**M**
   きのう電話に全然出なかっただろ？
   B: *Ichinichijuu dekakete-ta n da yo.*[*1] ☺**M**
   一日中出かけてたんだよ。

2. *Dooshite konakatta n desu ka.* どうして来なかったんですか。
3. *Chotto kikitai n desu ga . . .* ちょっと聞きたいんですが……

*1. *Dekakete-ta* is a shortened version of *dekakete-ita.*

Additional Information

The extended predicate may be shortened by eliminating *da/desu* and leaving only *no.* This *no,* classified earlier as an interactional particle, is used by female speakers more often than males. With rising intonation placed at *no,* for example, *ashita iku no?* 'are you going tomorrow?,' is a shortened version of *ashita iku no desu ka?* and functions as a question.

75. Expressions of Potential and Ability

Target Expressions

Can you speak French?
> **Huransugo o hanasu koto ga dekimasu ka.**
> フランス語を話すことができますか。
> **Huransugo ga hanasemasu ka.**
> フランス語が話せますか。
> **Huransugo hanaseru?** ☺
> フランス語 話せる？
> **Huransugo dekiru?** ☺
> フランス語できる？

[N + *ga dekiru*]
[Vbasic + *koto ga dekiru*]
potential [V + *-ru*, V + *-rareru*]

Grammatical Explanation

The expression of ability is achieved by two different methods. First, the [*koto ga dekiru*] pattern is attached immediately after the [Vbasic] form. *Koto* 'thing(s)' functions as a nominalizer and *dekiru* literally means 'can do.' Thus, *hanasu koto ga dekiru* '(I) can speak.' For the *be*-verb *da, de-iru* is used when co-occurring with [*koto ga dekiru*]. *Dekiru*, which is a potential form of the irregular verb *suru*, may be directly attached to a noun as in:

(a) <u>Hikooki</u>   <u>no</u> <u>soojuu</u>   <u>ga</u> **<u>dekimasu.</u>**
    airplane   L control   S   can do.
    飛行機の操縦ができます。
    (I can fly [lit. control] an airplane.)

Second, potential and ability are expressed by potential verb endings which are formed as shown below.

U-verbs: replace the final *-u* with *-eru*.
    kaku   *kakeru*
    asobu   *asoberu*

(exception: *yuu* 'to say' changes into *ieru*. Remember to consider *yuu* as *iu* for conjugation purposes.)

RU-verbs: replace the final *-ru* with *-rareru*.
    taberu   *taberareru*
    hairu   *hairareru*

As an alternative to this change, the final *-ru* may be replaced by *-reru.*
    taberu   *tabereru*
    hairu   *haireru*

Irregular verbs:
    kuru   **koreru**
    suru   **dekiru**

Among existential verbs, *iru* meaning 'to stay' has the potential form *irareru* 'can stay.' the verb *da* does not have a potential form; instead *de-iru* is used with its potential form *de-irareru* 'can be.'

When using the potential expression *dekiru*, which is a verb of "reactive" description, *ga*-marked noun, the thing a person can do, is the element of the primary predicate focus. For example, as shown in the target expression, *Huransugo ga hanaseru* means that someone is good at speaking French, and *Huransugo ga dekiru* means that someone has a full capacity to function in the French language.

The person who can speak may be optionally marked by *ni*; when the person is simultaneously a topic *watashi (ni) wa Huransugo ga hanasemasu* is possible. For the [*koto ga dekiru*] structure, the particle *o* marks what a person can do within the clause preceding *koto*. Still, the *koto* clause itself is marked by *ga* as in *nihongo o hanasu koto ga dekiru* 'I can speak Japanese.'

The potential verb forms behave similarly—*ga* marks the item which one can do (but only when the item is the direct object of the verb.) When the potential verb reflects the speaker's volition, what one can do may be optionally marked by *o*. In this case what one can perform is considered a grammatical object rather than the *ga*-marked element of primary predicate focus.

Examples

```
----------------------------------------------------------------
nemuru      眠る     V     to sleep
minna       みんな   N     everything
zutto       ずっと   Adv   for a long time
dokushin    独身     N     bachelor
----------------------------------------------------------------
```

(1) A: *Jimu-san wa kuruma no   unten   ga dekimasu ka.*
        Jim   T   car   L   driving   S   can do   Q
        ジムさんは車の運転ができますか。
        (Jim, can you drive a car?)

    B: Ee.
        ええ。
        (Yes.)

(2) A: *Yuube yoku nemureta?* ☺
        ゆうべよく眠れた？
        (Could you sleep well last night?)

    B: *Un, yoku neta yo.* ☺
        うん，よく寝たよ。
        (Yes, I slept well.)

(3) A: *Otootosan wa goruhu mo tenisu mo dekimasu ne.*
        弟さんはゴルフもテニスもできますね。
        (Your younger brother can play both golf and tennis, can't he?)

    B: *Ee. Supootsu wa minna dekiru n desu yo.*
        ええ。スポーツはみんなできるんですよ。
        (Yes. He does well in all sports.)

(4) A: *Nakagawa-san wa kekkon-shimashita ka.*
        中川さんは結婚しましたか。
        (Did Mr. Nakagawa get married?)

    B: *Iie, mada desu.*
        いいえ，まだです。
        (No, not yet.)

    A: *Demo zutto dokushin de-iru koto wa dekinai-deshoo?*
        でもずっと独身でいることはできないでしょう？

(But he won't be able to remain a bachelor indefinitely, will he?)

B: *Doo deshoo ka nee.*
どうでしょうかねえ。
(I wonder about that.)

Additional Information

Some potential forms are also used for passive and respectful forms as will be explained later, and therefore, it is extremely important to learn their conjugation at this point.

For some verbs potential forms and the spontaneous forms are identical; for example, *kireru* 'to be able to cut,' *mieru* 'to be able to see,' *wareru* 'to be able to break' and so forth. When potential forms are used, normally the persons who are capable of the stated action are specified or at least assumed. When spontaneous verbs are used, the actor is not stated and is not in the consciousness of the speaker. In using potential forms, the speaker's intention to perform the act must be presumed. Therefore as shown in (a) when the matter is beyond the speaker's control, the spontaneous verb form is used. Since (b) indicates intention, the spontaneous form is not appropriate.

(a) *Aite no koe ga chiisakute kikoenai.*
相手の声が小さくて聞こえない。
(My companion's voice is too small and it isn't heard.)

(b) **Aite no koe ga chiisakute kikenai.*

Even when the person who is capable of the stated action is not specified, and the grammatical form may be identical, there is a distinct difference in the meaning between spontaneous and potential verbs. For example:

(c) *Kono yoohuku wa uremasu ka.*
この洋服は売れますか。
(Does this dress sell?)—spontaneous interpretation
(Can you sell this dress?)—potential interpretation

Another difference between spontaneous and potential forms lies in the fact that while spontaneous verbs can occur in the [V*te* + -*iru*] form, i.e., *wareteimasu* 'is in the state of being broken,' the potential form cannot. Since the potential form of the verb describes the state rather than the action, it seems natural that it is less likely to take the [V*te* + -*iru*] form.

Practice

For the following actions, claim that either you can or cannot perform them. Then ask your friend if he or she can or cannot do the same.

244

```
--------------------------------------------------------------
novelist     N     sakka           作家
to recall    V     omoidasu        思い出す
to ski       V     sukii o suru    スキーをする
to run       V     hashiru         走る
--------------------------------------------------------------
```

1. to speak Japanese
2. to sleep in an airplane
3. to recall that novelist's name
4. to sing Japanese songs
5. to ski
6. to drive a car ☺
7. to run fast

——— Some Sample Answers ———

1. *Nihongo ga hanasemasu.* 日本語が話せます。
2. *Hikooki no naka de nemuru koto ga dekimasu.*
   飛行機の中で眠ることができます。
3. *Sono sakka no namae ga omoidasemasen.*
   その作家の名前が思い出せません。
4. *Nihon(go) no uta ga utaemasu ka.* 日本（語）の歌が歌えますか。
5. *Sukii ga dekimasu ka.* スキーができますか。
6. *Kuruma no unten dekiru?* ☺ 車の運転できる？
7. *Hayaku hashiru koto wa dekimasen.*
   速く走ることはできません。

Warning

Although we have translated Japanese potential expressions into English "can" in this entry, you must avoid expressing the English "can" into Japanese potential forms unless you have given it careful scrutiny. This is because the English "can" is used not only for potential expressions but for many other purposes including permission and possibility. The English expression such as "it can happen" cannot be translated into Japanese potential forms studied here. In using Japanese potential expressions, the action described must be supported by the agent's willingness to perform the act.

76.   The Use of the Gerundive Forms

Target Expression

> *I didn't have time and (so) I couldn't read it.*
> **Jikan ga nakute yomemasen-deshita.**
> 時間がなくて読めませんでした。
>
> [V/Adj *te*]

Grammatical Explanation

We have already learned the gerundive [V*te*] form in three contexts; (1) to form an expression of request [V*te* + *-kudasai*], (2) to form the progressive form [V*te* + *-iru*], and (3) to conjoin clauses. In this section we will learn additional uses of the gerundive forms of the verb and the adjectives. We restrict our study here, however, to those cases where [V/Adj *te*] occurs independently without another verbal suffix. For verb and adjective gerundive forms, see the list below.

	basic form	te-form	informal non-past negative	negative te-form
U-verb	*iku*	*itte*	*ikanai*	*ikanaide* *ikanakute*[*1]
U-verb	*nomu*	*nonde*	*nomanai*	*nomanaide* *nomanakute*
RU-verb	*taberu*	*tabete*	*tabenai*	*tabenaide* *tabenakute*
Existential	*aru* *iru*	*atte* *ite*	*nai* *inai*	*nakute* *inakute*
Irregular	*kuru* *suru*	*kite* *shite*	*konai* *shinai*	*konaide/konakute* *shinaide/shinakute*
Be-verb	*da*	*de*	*dewanai*	*dewanakute*
[Adj-*i*]	*takai*	*takakute*	*takakunai*	*takakunakute*
[Adj-*na*]	*benrina*	*benri de*	*benri de (wa) nai*	*benri de (wa) nakute*

As stated earlier, the [V te] forms are created by changing the final -ta and -da of [V informal past] to -te and -da, respectively.

*1. The -nakute ending is optional for the verb negative gerundive form.

What the gerundive form fundamentally conveys is that the said action or the state is realized. This points to the similarity between the Japanese te-form and the English verb -ing (gerundive) form. Since grammatically a gerundive form is frequently combined with another verb and adjective, it gives the impression that something else is to be mentioned. This is why adding the conjunction and in its English translation is useful, particularly when the [V/Adj te] form appears independently at the end of a clause. The semantic relationship between the two clauses connected by the gerundive form depends on the specific context in which the utterance is made. The following examples provide some illustrations.

Examples

hubenna	不便な	Adj	inconvenient
ninki ga aru	人気がある	V	to be popular
kagu	家具	N	furniture
nakanaka	なかなか	Adv	not easily
minasama	皆様	N	everyone
(o)genkina	（お）元気な	Adj	healthy, well

1. *Enumeration 'and':*

   (1a) *Kesa hayaku okite jogingu o shimashita.*
   今朝早く起きてジョギングをしました。
   (I got up early and jogged.)

   (1b) *Kasa o motanaide kaisha e ikimashita.*
   傘を持たないで会社へ行きました。
   (Not bringing an umbrella, he went to the office.)

   (1c) *Kono sakana yasukute oishii-desu ne.*
   この魚安くておいしいですね。
   (This fish is inexpensive and delicious, isn't it?)

2. *Specifying cause and reason, 'as, since':*

   (2a) *Jikan ga nakute yomemasen-deshita.*
   時間がなくて読めませんでした。
   (There wasn't time and that's why I couldn't read it.)

(2b) *Koko wa totemo huben de amari ninki ga arimasen.*
ここはとても不便であまり人気がありません。

(This place is very inconvenient and (so) it's not too popular.)

(2c) *Konna kagu wa takakute nakanaka kaemasen.*
こんな家具は高くてなかなか買えません。

(Such furniture is expensive and so I cannot buy it easily [too expensive to buy].)

3. *Ending statements to soften the impact:*

(3a) *Osoku narimashite . . .*
遅くなりまして……

([lit. It has become late] Sorry, I'm late . . .)

(3b) *Yoku minasama ogenki de . . .*
よく皆様お元気で……

([idiomatic] It's nice to know that everyone is well . . .)

Practice

By connecting clauses using the [V/Adj *te*] form, express the following.

1. A: What time did you get up and where did you go?
   B: I got up at six and went to Kyoto.
2. I was busy, and so I couldn't come yesterday.
3. I had a headache, and so I was absent.
4. It's so hot tonight, and (so) I cannot sleep.

――――― Answers ―――――

1. A: *Nan-ji ni okite, doko e ikimashita ka.*
   何時に起きて，どこへ行きましたか。

   B: *Roku-ji ni okite, Kyooto e ikimashita.*
   六時に起きて，京都へ行きました。

2. *Isogashikute kinoo wa koraremasen-deshita.*
   忙しくてきのうは来られませんでした。

3. *Atama ga itakute yasumimashita.* 頭が痛くて休みました。

4. *Kon'ya wa atsukute nemuremasen.*今夜は暑くて眠れません。

Additional Information

The difference between two gerundive negative forms, i.e., *-naide* and *-nakute*, is that the [*-naide*] clause is more closely connected to the main clause than the [*-nakute*] clause. The [*-nakute*] clause tends to be separate from the main clause. This affects the use of these gerundive negative forms as explained below.

(a) *Benkyoo-shinaide/*-shinakute tesuto o ukemasu.*
勉強<u>しないで</u>/*<u>しなくて</u>テストを受けます。
(I take exams without studying.)

(b) *Benkyoo-shinaide/-shinakute komarimasu.*
勉強<u>しないで</u>/<u>しなくて</u>困ります。
(He doesn't study, which is troublesome.)

(c) *Ano hito wa Amerika-jin ja -nakute/*-naide Igirisu-jin deshoo.*
あの人はアメリカ人じゃ<u>なくて</u>/*<u>ないで</u> イギリス人でしょう。
(He is probably not an American, but British.)

Benkyoo-shinaide in (a) serves as an adverbial clause associated with the main clause. In this context *-nakute* is not acceptable. In (b), however, either *benkyoo-shinakute* or *benkyoo-shinaide* is acceptable since the two clauses are semantically connected (the first clause offers the reason for the second) and the first clause is not considered to be an adverbial phrase. In (c), since two clauses are independent, only *-nakute* negation is acceptable.

The verb and adjective gerundive forms may be followed by the particle *mo*, which is similar to English 'even though, even when' (See Entry 97 for details).

(d) *Isshookenmei benkyoo-shite mo yoku wakarimasen.*
いっしょうけんめい勉強してもよくわかりません。
(Even though I study hard, I don't understand well.)

(e) *Takakute mo kaimashoo.*
高くても買いましょう。
(Even though it is expensive, let's buy [it].)

(f) *Shizuka de mo eki kara tookute huben nee.* ☺ F
静かでも駅から遠くて不便ねえ。
(Even though it is quiet, it is far from the station and is inconvenient, isn't it?)

77. Conjunctions—3. Cause-effect Conjunctions

> *Because I got up late, I took a taxi.*
> **Osoku okita kara takushii de ikimashita.**
> 遅く起きたからタクシーで行きました。
>
> [*kara*] [*node*]

Grammatical Explanation

Conjunctions [*kara*] and [*node*] are frequently used to express cause or reason and its resulting effect as shown in the target expression. Be warned that the order of the conjunction and the clause within a sentence is the reverse of what it is in English. Just like particles, these conjunctions are attached to the clause-final position whose clause is conjoined with another. It may be helpful to think of *kara* as 'that's why' and *node* as 'and so' in English; this way the correct order is easily understood. *Kara* and *node* are attached to both formal and informal forms of the verb. There is one exception: when *node* is preceded by *da*, it changes into *na*, producing [*na node*] structure.

Normally the formality markers in Japanese appear at the utterance- and sentence-final position. Therefore in *kara* and *node* clauses informal endings are used more frequently. When formal endings are used preceding *kara* and *node*, the main verb ending must also be formal; As a result the degree of formality increases. When *kara* is used in [*kara da*] pattern, what precedes *kara* must be in the informal form.

While the [*kara*] conjunction focuses more readily on the reason/cause, the [*node*] conjunction focuses more strongly on the resulting effect. This is why the [*kara*] clause is used independently, while [*node*] is less likely to be so used. An independent [*kara*] clause can also be used as an answer to a question as shown below. Semantically the [*kara*] clause provides a personally interpreted cause or reason for the personal opinions expressed in the main clause. For this reason, sentences expressing personal judgment such as speculation, opinion, intention, command, suggestion, question, request, and so forth must take the [*kara*] conjunction. The [*node*] conjunction, on the other hand, presents the cause more objectively without projecting the speaker's personal opinion.

Examples

```
-----------------------------------------------------------------
kyuuni      急に          Adv   suddenly
yooji ga dekiru          V     a chore (appoint-
用事ができる                      ment, errand, etc,)
                               comes up
mezamashidokei           N     alarm clock
目覚まし時計
naru        鳴る          V     to ring
                               (this verb has low-
                               mid tone and is
                               different from
                               naru 'to become'
                               which has
                               high/low tone.)
kaigi       会議          N     meeting
tenki       天気          N     weather
-----------------------------------------------------------------
```

(1) A: *Dooshite/Naze konakatta n desu ka.*
どうして/なぜ来なかったんですか。
(Why didn't you come?)

B: *Kyuuni yooji ga dekita kara desu.*
急に用事ができたからです。
(It's because suddenly an errand came up.)

(2) A: *Dooshite okureta no?* ☺
どうして遅れたの？
(Why were you late?)

B: *Mezamashidokei ga naranakatta kara.* ☺
目覚まし時計が鳴らなかったから。
(Because the alarm clock didn't go off.)

(3) *Ashita haha ga roku-ji goro kimasu kara, sore made ni kaette-kite-kudasai.*
あした母が六時頃来ますから、それまでに帰ってきてください。
(Since my mother is coming tomorrow about six o'clock, please be back by then.)

(4) *Kesa kaigi ga arimasu kara, Yamada-san wa hayaku kuru-deshoo.*
今朝会議がありますから、山田さんは早く来るでしょう。
(There is a meeting this morning and so [I think] Mr. Yamada will come early.)

(5)   *Asa kara zutto shigoto o shita node, onaka ga sukimashita.*
朝からずっと仕事をしたので，おなかがすきました。
(Since I worked straight through the morning, I got hungry.)

(6)   *Tenki ga yokatta node Hujisan ga miemashita.*
天気がよかったので富士山が見えました。
(Since the weather was good, we could see Mt. Fuji.)

Practice
Connect the following pairs of statements by using either *kara* or *node*.

1.   I studied Japanese for three months. I can speak it a little.
2. A: (Why did you help him?)
   B: Because he is my younger sister's friend.
3.   I bought a lot of beer. My friends are coming over.

———— Some Sample Answers ————
1. *San-kagetsu nihongo o benkyoo-shita node/kara sukoshi hanasemasu.* 三か月日本語を勉強したので/から少し話せます。
2. *Imooto no tomodachi da kara (tetsudaimashita).* 妹の友だちだから（手伝いました）。
3. *Tomodachi ga kuru kara/node, biiru o takusan kaimashita.* 友だちが来るから/ので，ビールをたくさん買いました。

Additional Information
Recall here another strategy for expressing cause or reason, namely, the phrase [*tame ni*]. For this use, the form preceding [*tame ni*] is the [V/Adj pre-nominal]. Some additional examples are given below.

kootsuujiko	交通事故	N	traffic accident
juutai	渋滞	N	traffic jam
tsuzuku	続く	V	to continue

(a)   *Ame ga hutta tame ni haikingu ni ikemasen-deshita.*
雨が降ったためにハイキングに行けませんでした。
(Because it rained, we couldn't go hiking.)

(b)   *Kootsuujiko no tame ni juutai ga tsuzuite-imasu.*
交通事故のために渋滞が続いています。
(Due to the traffic accident, there is an extensive traffic jam.)

(c) *Kono doogu wa benrina tame ni yoku uremasu.*
この道具は便利なためによく売れます。
(This tool sells well because it is useful.)

78. Requesting—3. More about Requests and Special Requests

Please, please, come right away!
　　　Tanomu kara sugu kite. ☺
　　　たのむからすぐ来て。
　　　Onegai da kara sugu kite! ☺
　　　お願いだからすぐ来て！

Strategic Explanation

We have studied several ways to make requests in Japanese. Here we review those expressions. The following strategies are listed in the order of the request made most directly followed by those that are less direct.

Denwa-shinasai. (Entry 79)
電話しなさい。
Sumimasen ga, denwa-shite-kudasai. (Entry 40)
すみませんが，電話してください。
Denwa-shite hoshii n desu kedo. (Entry 65)
電話してほしいんですけど。
Denwa-shite-moraitai n desu ga . . . (Entry 73)
電話してもらいたいんですが……
Odenwa-shite-itadakemasen-deshoo ka. (Entry 73)
お電話していただけませんでしょうか。
Sumimasen ga, odenwa-shite-itadakemasen-deshoo ka.
すみませんが，お電話していただけませんでしょうか。
　　(Entries 58, 73 and 80)

When one needs to make an urgent and desperate plea, some phrases may be added before the [V*te (kudasai)*] pattern already introduced. These are; toward social equals or subordinates only, *onegai da kara* 'I'm pleading with you' and *tanomu kara* 'please, I beg of you.' Toward your social superior, *murina onegai da to wa omoimasu ga* '(lit. although I think it is an unreasonable request to grant . . .)' is attached to appeal to the addressee by expressing your respect and sympathy toward him or her.

In responding to requests, the following expressions are representative.

Granting request:

(a) *Hai, shoochi-shimashita.*
はい，承知しました。
(Yes, certainly.)

(b) *Hai, wakarimashita.*
はい，わかりました。
(Yes, I'll take care of it.)

(c) *Hai.*
はい。
(Yes, I will.)

(d) *Ookee.* ☺
オーケー。
(OK.)

Refusing request:

(a) *Soo iwaremashite mo nee . . .*
そう言われましてもねえ……
(Well, my apologies, but I cannot . . .)

(b) *Sore ga, chotto nee . . .*
それが，ちょっとねえ……
(Well it's a bit of a problem . . .)

(c) *Gomen. Chotto muzukashii naa, sore wa . . .* ☺
ごめん。ちょっとむずかしいなあ，それは……
(Sorry. It's a bit too difficult, I'm afraid . . .)

Examples

kyoojuu	今日中	Adv	within the day
shiageru	仕上げる	V	to finish, to complete

murina	無理な	Adj	unreasonable
to omou	と思う	V	to think that (with *to* being a quotative marker)

----

(1) A: *Onegai da kara, kuruma kashite-kurenai?* ☺
お願いだから，車貸してくれない？
(Please, [I beseech you] please kindly lend me [allow me to use] your car.)

B: *Ii yo.* ☺M
いいよ。
(Sure.)

(2) A: *Tanomu kara kyoojuu ni shiagete-kudasai yo.* ☺M
たのむから今日中に仕上げてくださいよ。
(Please, [I beg of you] please finish it by the end of the day.)

B: *Sore ga nee . . . chotto muzukashii naa.* ☺M
それがねえ……ちょっとむずかしいなあ。
(Well, that might be a problem.)

(3) A: *Murina onegai da to wa omoimasu ga, yoroshiku onegai-shimasu.*
無理なお願いだとは思いますが，よろしくお願いします。
(Although this request is unreasonable, please give favorable consideration to it.)

B: *Hai, shoochi shimashita.*
はい，承知しました。
(Yes, certainly.)

Additional Information

Sometimes even when an explicit request is not made, if you share the problem, your friend may come to your rescue. See, for example, the following exchange:

A: <u>*Kyoo*</u>　<u>*saihu*</u>　<u>*o*</u>　<u>*wasurete-kichatta.*</u>[1]　*Doo shiyoo.* ☺
today　wallet　O　forgot　what should I do
今日さいふを忘れてきちゃった。どうしよう。
(I forgot my wallet today. What should I do?)

B: *Okane kashite-ageyoo ka.* ☺
お金貸してあげようか。
(Shall I loan you some money?)

[1]. Recall that *kitchatta* is a colloquial version of *kite-shimatta* (as explained in Entry 54).

Practice

```
------------------------------------------------------------
office (of a professor)   N   kenkyuushitsu
                              研究室
------------------------------------------------------------
```

Provide an interaction in which a request is made and is then either granted or not granted.

1. teacher to student: to study hard
2. you to your teacher: to write a letter of recommendation
3. you to your friend: to call you tonight ☺
4. you to your colleague: for Mr. Hoshi to come to Professor Yamada's office

────── Some Sample Answers ──────

1. A: *Isshookenmei benkyoo shite-kudasai ne.*
   いっしょうけんめい勉強してくださいね。
   B: *Hai.* はい。

2. A: *Suisenjoo o kaite-itadakemasen-deshoo ka.*
   推薦状を書いていただけませんでしょうか。
   B: *Ee.* ええ。

3. A: *Kon'ya denwa-shite.* ☺   今夜電話して。
   Kon'ya denwa-shite-kurenai? ☺   今夜電話してくれない？
   B: *Ii yo.* ☺   いいよ。

4. A: *Hoshi-san ni Yamada sensei no kenkyuushitsu e kite-moraitai n desu ga . . .*
   星さんに山田先生の研究室へ来てもらいたいんですが……
   B: *Hai, wakarimashita.*   はい，わかりました。

79.   Orders and Commands

Study!

Benkyoo-shinasai!
勉強しなさい！

[Vstem + *nasai*]

Grammatical Explanation

Order-giving expressions, [Vstem + *nasai*], and the abrupt command form of the verb introduced here are used strictly by one who is socially superior to the addressee. The reverse, a command from one who is socially inferior, is considered extremely rude. One may give two levels of commands to social inferiors. [Vstem + *nasai*] form is used both by males and females, and the abrupt command form predominantly by males. Since the abrupt command form is restricted in use and is considered rude unless the situation is absolutely appropriate, it is perhaps best not to use it, at least in the early stage of your Japanese training. [Vstem + *nasai*] form may be used toward children or subordinates. In general, however, even when a social superior gives a command, if addressed to an adult, the [V*te* + *-kudasai*] pattern is recommended. It shows consideration for others and is more pleasantly accepted.

Both types of order-giving expressions co-occur only with verbs that refer to controllable action. If the person receiving a command is unable to control the outcome, giving a command does not make sense. For the [N + *da*] structure, use [N + *de-iru*]; *shoojiki de-inasai* 'be honest,' for example. For existential verbs, only *iro* (command form of *iru*) is used.

For your reference, the abrupt command is formed by:

U-verbs: replace last *-u* with *-e*

kaku	*kake*
kau	*kae*
iku	*ike*

RU-verbs: replace last *-ru* with *-ro*

taberu	*tabero*
okiru	*okiro*

Be-verb:

da	**de-iro**
dearu	**deare**

Irregular verbs:

kuru	**koi**
suru	**shiro**

The negative abrupt command forms are formed by adding *-na* to the [Vbasic] form.

kaku	*kakuna* (don't write)

okiru   okiru**na** (don't get up)

kuru   kuru**na** (don't come)

Additional Information

An abbreviated form of [Vstem + nasai], that is, [Vstem + na] may also be used for expressing demand. Thus instead of saying tabenasai 'eat!,' tabena may be used, the latter of which is colloquial, more informal and even more abrupt than [Vstem + nasai].

The negative abrupt command forms are frequently used as a warning sign, such as koko wataruna 'don't cross here.'

Examples

----

rasshu-awaa		N	rush hour
ラッシュアワー			
kiotsukeru	気をつける	V	to be careful
tooru	通る	V	to pass through

----

(1)   Hayaku okite benkyoo-shinasai.

早く起きて勉強しなさい。

(Get up early and study.)

(2) A: Rasshu-awaa da kara kiotsukenasai yo.

ラッシュアワーだから気をつけなさいよ。

(Be careful because it's rush-hour.)

     B: Hai.

はい。

(Yes, I will.)

(3)   Koko tooruna. (as used on a sign post)

ここ通るな。

(Don't trespass here.)

80. Managing Conversation—1. Openers and Fillers

Target Expression

> *Well* . . .
>
> *Maa, ano* . . .
> まあ，あの……

Strategic Explanation

Conversational utterances are filled with fragments that do not carry meaning in a strict sense. When assuming the speaking turn, speakers often start with openers, that is, brief expressions claiming the turn and alerting others that the speaker is about to say something. This happens in English also; the conjunction *so* in *so, what's up?*, for example. Speaker's turns are also interposed by fillers, which are equivalent to *uhh* and *like* in English Conversation, as in "*uhh*, you know, he's *like*, he is really crazy." Conversational fillers may just simply fill in the pause or they may signal the speaker's hesitation or trouble spots. These openers and fillers are useful because they allow the speaker to hold on to the speaking turn. Here are some frequently used examples of openers and fillers.

Openers:

1. *Marking a new topic:*
   (Sore) de （それ）で   (So)
   De kyoo wa . . . で今日は……   (So, today . . .)

2. *Signaling that what you are going to say is off the topic:*
   Tokorode ところで   (By the way)
   Hanashi chigau kedo 話ちがうけど   ☺   ([Not] to change the subject)

3. *Adding to the current topic:*
   Soo ieba nee . . . そう言えばねえ……   (Speaking of . . .)
   Iikaereba/Iikaeruto 言いかえれば/言いかえると   (In other words)
   Tatoeba たとえば   (For example)
   Gutaiteki ni yuu to 具体的に言うと   (More concretely)

4. *Introducing the main important topic:*
   Jitsu wa . . . 実は……   (To discuss the serious matter . . . /Seriously, though)

Openers and Fillers:

1. *Hesitation sounds that can be used as openers and fillers:*
    Anoo . . . あのう……   (Well . . .) [this expression is very common]

    Maa, soo desu ne . . . まあ, そうですね……   (Oh, I guess [so] . . .)

    Eeto . . . ええと……   (Well, let's see . . .)

    Ee . . . ええ……   (Uhh . . .)

    Maa . . . まあ……   (Well, say . . .)

    Maa, sorede . . . まあ, それで……   (So, then . . .)

    Nan-ka . . . なんか……   (Uhh . . .)

2. *Expressions used to fill otherwise awkward pauses:*
    Nan to iimashoo ka . . . 何と言いましょうか……   (What should I say . . .)

    Muzukashii shitsumon desu ne . . . むずかしい質問ですね……
    (It's a difficult question to answer . . .)

When using openers and fillers, avoid overusing any one expression. It is acceptable to combine several short fillers to fill the time, for example, *anoo . . . maa . . . eeto . . .* You will find native speakers using these "fillers" quite frequently.

Japanese male adult speech (especially when formal) is characterized by an inhaling hissing sound. The inhaling hissing sound functions as an opener and a filler. Observe male speech when you have access to native speakers. There is no need to imitate it, however, unless you are a male and you want to.

Practice

In Sample Texts 1 and 2, you will find a transcript of casual conversations. Examine how and where openers and fillers are inserted into the conversation. When you have access to native speakers' interaction, pay attention to how each utterance starts and ends. How often are openers used? Do they use different kinds of openers? What do speakers do during the pause between speaker turns?

81. Conjunctions—4. Enumerative Actions or States

I went to London, Paris and Amsterdam.

Rondon to, Pari to, Amusuterudamu e itta.

ロンドンと，パリと，アムステルダムへ行った。

I went to London and also went to Paris; this summer was really fun.

Rondon e (mo) ittashi, Pari e (mo) ittashi, kotoshi no natsu wa tanoshikatta.

ロンドンへ（も）行ったし，パリへ（も）行ったし，
今年の夏は楽しかった。

[V/Adj + *shi*]

[. . . *tari,* . . . *tari* . . . *suru/da*]

Grammatical Explanation

There are several ways in which enumeration of actions and states are described. Naturally one can express enumeration by connecting nouns with the particle *to* as shown in the first example of the target expression. Here, instead of connecting nouns our focus is placed on three ways to connect verbs or clauses.

1. [V/Adj *te*]

   One can enumerate simply by changing verbs into [V/Adj *te*] forms. In the [V*te*] pattern if the verb is not stative, the actions occur in the order of the statement.

   (1a) *Rondon e itte, Pari e ikimashita.*
       ロンドンへ行って，パリへ行きました。
       (I went to London and [then] Paris.)

   (1b) *Kono biru wa atarashikute, kirei de, benri da nee.* ☺**M**
       このビルは新しくて，きれいで，便利だねえ。
       (This building is new, pretty, and convenient.)

2. [V/Adj + *shi*] (Adjectives must be in predicate forms.)

   This pattern is used when enumerative actions or states combined together lead to certain results or expectations. For example, you express that you had a real good summer this year partly because you went on a European tour. If you want to list the cities you visited, you might say:

(2a) *Rondon e (mo) ittashi, Pari e (mo) ittashi, kotoshi no natsu wa tanoshikatta.*

ロンドンへ（も）行ったし，パリへ（も）行ったし，今年の夏は楽しかった。

(I went to London and also went to Paris; this summer was really fun.)

In this enumeration strategy actions and states occur in random alternatives. They are not necessarily chronologically ordered. Other examples include:

(2b)

Yuki	*ga*	*hutte-irushi*	*taihen*	*samui*	*node*	*kyoo*	*no*
snow	S	is falling and	very	cold	since	today	L

kooen	*wa*	*chuushi*	*desu.*
lecture	T	cancellation	is

雪が降っているし大変寒いので今日の講演は中止です。
(Since it is snowing and it is very cold, today's public lecture is canceled.)

(2c) *Kono hen wa samuishi, kuraishi, kiken dashi, amari ii tokoro dewa-arimasen ne.*

この辺は寒いし，暗いし，危険だし，あまりいい所ではありませんね。

(This area is cold, dark and dangerous, and it's not really a nice place, is it?)

(2d) *Shigoto mo shinaishi, benkyoo mo shinaishi, dooshita n desu ka.*[*1]

仕事もしないし，勉強もしないし，どうしたんですか。

(You don't work, and you don't study; what happened to you?)

    [*1.] *Dooshita n desu ka?* is an idiomatic expression meaning 'what happened (to you)?, what's wrong with you?'

3. [. . . *tari*, . . . *tari* . . . *suru/da*]; *tari* is produced by [V/Adj informal past + *ri*].

This pattern is used normally with two *tari*'s (although more than two is possible) with the second one normally followed by *suru* or *da*. As in the case of the [*shi*] enumeration, the actions and states expressed in this enumeration are not necessarily chronologically ordered.

(3a) *Rondon e ittari, Pari e ittari shimashita.*
ロンドンへ行ったり，パリへ行ったりしました。
(I went to London, and I also went to Paris.)

(3b) *Nichiyoobi wa dekaketari dekakenakattari desu.*
日曜日は出かけたり出かけなかったりです。
(On Sundays, I sometimes go out, sometimes not.)

(3c) *Gakusei wa nihon-jin dattari, Amerika-jin dattari desu.*
学生は日本人だったり，アメリカ人だったりです。
(Students are Japanese and also Americans.)

(3d)
Koko	*ni*	*aru*	*booshi*	*wa*	*watashi*	*ni*	*wa*
here	at	there is	hat	T	me	for	T

chiisakattari	*ookikattari*	*shite,*	*ii*	*no*	*ga*
small	large	do	good	one	S

mitsukarimasen.
cannot be found

ここにある帽子は私には小さかったり大きかったりして，いいの
がみつかりません。

(These hats [that are] here are [too] small or [too] large and
I can't find an appropriate one.)

(3e)
Shinbun	*o*	*yondari*	*shite,*	*yukkuri-shite-ita.*
newspaper	O	read	do	relax

新聞を読んだりして，ゆっくりしていた。
(I read the newspaper [among other things], and I relaxed.)

Practice

to drink (sake)	V	*sake o nomu*	酒を飲む
to smoke	V	*tabako o suu*	タバコをすう
to stop (raining)	V	*yamu*	やむ
sightseeing bus	N	*kankoo basu*	観光バス
to ride	V	*noru*	乗る
		(Recall that *noru* takes *ni* to	
		indicate the item one rides.)	

Describe the following actions by using enumerative patterns introduced
here.

1. He drinks and smokes; it's not good for his health.
2. My husband comes home sometimes early and sometimes late.

3. All day long, the rain is starting and stopping.
4. In Hawaii, we spent a week swimming, shopping and sightseeing.

─────── Answers ───────

1. *Sake mo nomushi, tabako mo suushi, karada ni yokunai-
   desu.* 酒も飲むし，たばこもすうし，体によくないです。
2. *Shujin wa hayakattari osokattari desu./Shujin wa hayaku
   kaettari osoku kaettari shimasu.*
   主人は早かったり遅かったりです。/主人は早く帰ったり遅く帰った
   りします。
3. *Ichinichijuu ame ga huttari yandari shite-imasu.*
   一日中雨が降ったりやんだりしています。
4. *Hawai de wa isshuukan oyoidari, kaimono o shitari, kankoo
   basu ni nottari shimashita.*
   ハワイでは一週間泳いだり，買いものをしたり，観光バスに乗ったり
   しました。

Warning

The enumerative particles [*to*] [*ya*]and [*mo*] we learned in Entries 17 and 29
are used to connect nouns and noun phrases only. When combining clauses
one of the above strategies must be chosen. It is also useful to remember
that there is a similarity in the way enumeration is presented between
[*to*] and [V/Adj *te*]; between [*ya*] and [. . .*tari*]; between [*mo*] and
[V/Adj + *shi*].

Additional Information

The enumerative endings [V/Adj *te*] and [V/Adj + *shi*] are used for weak-
ening the statement or to obscure the cause or reason in conversation. They
often appear at the utterance-final position, leaving the impression that the
statement is incomplete, and therefore, implying a less imposing attitude of
the speaker.

(a) *Konshuu wa chotto isogashii n desu yo. Shutchoo ga arushi .. ..*
    今週はちょっと忙しいんですよ。出張があるし……
    (This week I'm a bit busy. There is a business trip and . . .)

82. Managing Conversation—2. Repair for Trouble Spots

Target Expressions

> *Uh?*
>
> *Ee? Haa?*
> ええ？ はあ？

Strategic Explanation

A repair in conversation is especially useful for language learners. You may need, at least in the beginning, to ask for clarification. *Ee?* or *haa?*, with rising intonation indicate that you did not hear what was just said. These expressions give the impression that the enunciation on the part of the speaker was not clear, and therefore the speaker is to blame. Unless it is obvious that the problem is of physical sound quality, these short expressions are to be avoided.

Politer strategies are (1) to repeat the part you understand and trail off, with a facial expression of confusion, and (2) to ask the meaning of a specific word if you can repeat it. Imagine that you cannot understand the word *jinjika* 'personnel division' in the following utterance.

> A: *Dewa ashita hachi-ji ni jinjika ni kite-kudasai.*
> ではあした八時に人事課に来てください。

Possible repair strategies:

> B: (a) *Ashita hachi-ji ni . . .?*
> あした八時に……？
> (Tomorrow at eight o'clock . . .?)
>
> (b) *Jinjika tte yuu no wa?*
> 人事課っていうのは？
> ([What is] *jinjika?*)
>
> (c) *Jinjika tte?*
> 人事課って？
> (*Jinjika?*)
>
> (d) *Sumimasen, jinjika tte yuu kotoba no imi ga wakarimasen ga . . .*
> すみません，人事課っていう言葉の意味がわかりませんが……
> (Sorry, but I don't understand the meaning of the word *jinjika.*)

As a last resort, if one can't tell what one doesn't understand, request the partner to speak slowly, or to repeat it one more time. For example:

> (e) *Sumimasen, moo sukoshi yukkuri onegai-shimasu.*
> すみません，もう少しゆっくりお願いします。
> (Sorry, but could you speak a little more slowly?)

> (f) *Sumimasen, moo ichido onegai-shimasu.*
> すみません，もう一度お願いします。
> (Sorry, but could you repeat it one more time?)

These repair strategies are not often used by native speakers; as a result they often mark the speaker as a "foreigner." These repair remedies are good to know; the worst course of action is to ignore the problem and to be left in the dark.

When you have difficulty producing Japanese, use fillers discussed in Entry 80. Here are some more examples.

> (g) *Nan deshita ka.*
> 何でしたか。
> (What was that?)

> (h) *Tsumari, anooo . . .*
> つまり，あのう……
> (In other words, uh . . .)

> (i) *Ee, maa . . .*
> ええ，まあ……
> (Well, uhh, so . . .)

When you make a wrong statement and wish to correct it, you should use a negation *dewa-nakute*; for example:

> (j) *Kinoo . . . dewa-nakute, ototoi aimashita yo.*
> きのう……ではなくて，おととい会いましたよ。
> (Yesterday, no . . . rather, the day before yesterday I saw him.)

83. Modifying—3. Clausal Modifiers

The book my father wrote is selling well.
Chichi ga kaita hon wa yoku urete-imasu.
父が書いた本はよく売れています。

I forgot my promise to see my friend.
Tomodachi ni au yakusoku o wasurete-shimaimashita.
友だちに会う約束を忘れてしまいました。

[clausal modifier + N]

Grammatical Explanation

Characteristic 6, the modifier precedes the modified, applies when modification is achieved by a modifying subordinate clause. The clausal modification is widely used in English (in fact more common in English than in Japanese) in expressions such as *the book (that) my father wrote,* in which *my father wrote* modifies the noun *the book.* Unlike English, the Japanese clausal modification reverses the order of elements; the clausal modifier precedes the noun modified, and the modifying clause takes [V/Adj pre-nominal] forms. When the predicate of the modifying clause ends with [N + da], it takes the pre-nominal form *no* preceding nouns, for example, *hurusato ga Yamanashi no tomodachi* 'a friend whose hometown is Yamanashi.' The [N + da] structure may also take [N + dearu] 'to be' preceding the noun. If the sentence requires a formal style, it is expressed by the verb of the main clause. There are no relative pronouns in Japanese—such as the English ''who,'' ''which,'' and ''that'' (in for example, *the book [that] my father wrote*).

Since the modifying clause is a subordinate clause and since topic identifies the topic of the whole sentence, topic marker *wa* must be avoided unless *wa* conveys strong contrast; instead of *wa*, whatever appropriate case marker is used within the modifying subordinate clause. The subject marker *ga* in the modifying clause is optionally changed into *no*. For example; *Katoo-san no kaita hon* 'the book Mrs. Kato wrote' and *nihongo no hanaseru hito* 'a person who can speak Japanese.' This applies to the particle *ga* in reactive predicate as well; for example, *umi no mieru machi ni sunde-iru* 'he lives in the town from where one can see the ocean.'

There are two types of clausal modifiers. The first, the basic type, is the kind where the modified noun constitutes a part of the propositional content of the modifying clause. For example, in the first target sentence, the relationship between *asoko ni tatte-iru* and *hito* is such that they constitute a proposition [*asoko ni hito ga tatte-iru*]. The second, the extended type, is the case in which the modified noun is semantically associated with the modifying clause, but the noun itself does not constitute an item within the relevant propositional content. See, for example, in the second target expression the relevant proposition is *watashi ga tomodachi ni au*; *yakusoku* is not an essential element within the proposition.

Out of these two types, only the first type functions similarly to so-called English clausal modifiers with relative pronouns. In order to understand the clausal modification of the second type, it is necessary to adopt an extended meaning of clausal modification, and sometimes in order to make sense in English it is necessary to add appropriate phrases. Here we focus on the first basic type; the second type is discussed in Entry 114.

Verb Tense in Subordinate Clauses

Before proceeding too far, we must pay attention to the verb tense within the modifying clause in relation to the tense of the main verb. For the active verb, [Vnon-past] in the subordinate clause refers to the action not yet completed. When the verb in the modifying clause is [Vpast], it refers to action completed before the time of speech as in (c) or the tense defined by the main verb as in (d). The past tense in the subordinate clause used here is best characterized as "perfective" or "previous" tense. Thus:

(a) *Kon'ya **taberu** mono o **kaimashoo**.*
今夜**食べる**ものを**買いましょう**。
(Let's buy things that we will eat tonight.)

(b) *Kon'ya **taberu** mono o **kaimashita**.*
今夜**食べる**ものを**買いました**。
(We bought things that we would eat tonight.)

(c) *Kon'ya **tabeta** mono wa moo nidoto **kawanai-deshoo**.*
 tonight ate thing T never will not buy
今夜**食べた**ものはもう二度と**買わないでしょう**。
(I will never buy the [kind of] food I ate tonight.)

(d) *Kaimono o **shita** hito wa hayaku **modotte-kimashita**.*
 shopping O did person T early return
買物を**した**人は早くも**もどって来ました**。
(Those who had shopped returned early.)

Note that if the semantic focus is placed on the perfective nature of the past tense, [Vpast] may be used even when the action referred to is not yet completed as shown in (e).

(e) *Kaimono o **shita** hito wa hayaku basu ni **modotte-kudasai**.*
買物をした人は早くバスにもどってください。
(Those who shopped [already], please return to the bus.)

When the verb within the modifying clause is stative, existential, *be*-verb, adjectival or [V*te* + *-iru*], the [V/Adj non-past] form is interpreted as the same tense as the main verb, and the [V/Adj past] form is interpreted only as occurring in the past.

(f) *Kodomo-tachi wa ki ga takusan **aru** kooen de **asobu**.*
子供たちは木がたくさんある公園で遊ぶ。
(Children *play* in the park where there *are* many trees.)

(g) *Kodomo-tachi wa ki ga takusan **aru** kooen de **asonda**.*
子供たちは木がたくさんある公園で遊んだ。
(Children *played* in the park where there *were* [*and are*] many trees.)

(h) *Kodomo-tachi wa ki ga takusan **atta** kooen de **asobu**.*
子供たちは木がたくさんあった公園で遊ぶ。
(Children *play* in the park where there *were* [*but are not now*] many trees.)

(i) *Kodomo-tachi wa ki ga takusan **atta** kooen de **asonda**.*
子供たちは木がたくさんあった公園で遊んだ。
(Children *played* in the park where there *were* [*but are not now*] many trees.)

(j) *Ano megane o **kakete-iru** hito wa doko e **ikimasu** ka.*
あのめがねをかけている人はどこへ行きますか。
(Where is the person wearing glasses going?)

(k) *Ano megane o **kakete-iru** hito wa doko e **ikimashita** ka.*
あのめがねをかけている人はどこへ行きましたか。
(Where did the person wearing glasses go?)

Examples

otto	夫	N	husband
josei	女性	N	woman
tomaru	泊まる	V	to stay over-night

(1) *Senshuu yonda hon omoshirokatta yo.* ☺
先週読んだ本おもしろかったよ。
(The book I read last week was interesting.)

(2)　　*Chiisakatta ki ga ookiku narimashita.*
　　　小さかった木が大きくなりました。
　　　(The tree that was small became large.)

(3) A:　*Nee, mainichi tsukau mono desu kara kaimashoo yo.*
　　　ねえ，毎日使うものですから買いましょうよ。
　　　(Because it is something that we use every day, let's buy it.)

　　B:　*Soo shimashoo.*
　　　そうしましょう。
　　　(Sure, why not?)

(4)　　*Otto ga Amerika-jin* <u>*dearu*</u>/<u>*no*</u> *nihon-jin josei ga atsumatta.*
　　　夫がアメリカ人<u>である</u>/<u>の</u>日本人女性が集まった。
　　　(Japanese women whose husbands are American gathered.)

(5)　　*Hawai de wa umi* <u>*no*</u>/<u>*ga*</u> *mieru hoteru ni tomarimashita.*
　　　ハワイでは海<u>の</u>/<u>が</u>見えるホテルに泊まりました。
　　　(In Hawaii we stayed at a hotel with an ocean view.)

Practice

to send	V	*okuru* [1]	送る
place	N	*tokoro*	ところ
to make up 　questions for 　an exam	V	*shiken mondai o dasu* 試験問題を出す	

[1]　The verb *okuru* means either 'to send some items (to someone)' or 'to see someone off,' the latter of which was introduced in Entries 49 and 73.

1.　Provide question/answer pairs for the following situations:
　　a.　You notice someone watching TV in the next room, but you don't know who it is. Ask your friend the name of that person.
　　b.　You run into your colleague to whom you sent a letter the other day. Ask if the letter has arrived.
　　c.　Your friend asks you whether you visited many places while in Hawaii. You answer there are many places you didn't go.

2.　By using clausal modifiers, create phrases that explain the characteristics of the following.
　　a.　teacher: always gives difficult exams
　　b.　company president: comes to the company in an old car
　　c.　friend: went to Europe during the summer vacation

---- Some Sample Answers ----

1a. A: *Tonari no heya de terebi mite-iru hito dare?* ☺
      となりの部屋でテレビ見ている人だれ？
   B: *Saa, watashi mo shiranai hito da kedo . . .* ☺
      さあ，私も知らない人だけど……

 b. A: *Konnichiwa. Aa, kono aida okutta tegami tsukimashita ka.* こんにちは。ああ，この間送った手紙着きましたか。
   B: *Ee. Kinoo.*
      ええ。きのう。

 c. A: *Iroirona tokoro e itta-deshoo?*
      いろいろなところへ行ったでしょう？
   B: *Iyaa, ikanakatta tokoro ga takusan aru kedo . . .*
      いやあ，行かなかったところがたくさんあるけど……

2a. *itsumo muzukashii shiken mondai o dasu sensei*
    いつもむずかしい試験問題を出す先生
 b. *hurui kuruma ni notte kaisha ni kuru shachoo/hurui kuruma de kaisha ni kuru shachoo*
    古い車に乗って会社に来る社長／古い車で会社に来る社長
 c. *natsuyasumi ni Yooroppa e itta tomodachi*
    夏休みにヨーロッパへ行った友だち

84. Conjunctions—5. Temporal Conjunctions

Target Expressions

When I was a child, I played around here often.
   Kodomo no koro yoku koko de asonda n desu yo.
   子供の頃よくここで遊んだんですよ。

After I clean my room, I'll play tennis.
   Heya no sooji o shite kara, tenisu o shimasu.
   部屋のそうじをしてから，テニスをします。

While drinking beer, wouldn't you like to have a talk?
   Biiru demo nominagara, hanashi o shimasen ka.
   ビールでも飲みながら，話をしませんか。

[*toki*] [*koro*]
[V*te + kara*]
[Vstem + *nagara*]

Grammatical Explanation

When connecting clauses with temporal phrases, nouns such as *toki* 'time,' *koro* 'approximate time' are used. What precedes *toki* and *koro* is a modifying clause ending with the [V/Adj pre-nominal] forms. (Refer to Entry 83 for tense relations between the modifying and main clause. They operate the same way.)

If the tense of the verb in the [*toki*] clause is non-past, the actions described are interpreted as happening simultaneously with the tense of the main clause verb as in (a) and (c). If the tense of the verb in the [*toki*] clause is past, the action referred to is already completed as in (b) and (d). If the verb in the subordinate clause involves duration, [Vpast] can mean simultaneous with the main clause verb as in (e).

(a) *Kaimono o **suru** toki, chuui-shimashoo.*
買い物を**する**時，注意しましょう。
(Let's be careful when [before] you shop.)

(b) *Kaimono o **shita** toki, chuui-shimashoo.*
買い物を**した**時，注意しましょう。
(After we've bought [something], let's be careful.)

(c) *Nihon e **iku** toki, atarashii kamera o kaimasu.*
日本へ**行く**時，新しいカメラを買います。
(When I go to Japan [i.e., before I go], I will buy a new camera.)

(d) *Nihon e **itta** toki, atarashii kamera o kaimasu.*
日本へ**行った**時，新しいカメラを買います。
(When I get to Japan, [i.e., after arriving Japan], I will buy a camera [in Japan].)

(e) *Nihon ni **sunde-ita** toki, atarashii kamera o **kaimashita**.*
日本に**住んでいた**時，新しいカメラを**買いました**。
(When [i.e., while] I was living in Japan, I bought a new camera.)

Additionally, as strategies for connecting sequential events, the following connecting devices are available.

1. [V*te* + *kara*] 'after doing . . .'
The verb must indicate action or change in state. The *be*-verb and adjectival predicates as they are cannot co-occur.

(1a) *Shokuji o **shite kara** ikimashoo.*
食事を**してから**行きましょう。
(Let's go after eating supper.)

2. [Vinformal past (affirmative only) + *ato de*] 'after doing. . .'
   This expression is used primarily with active verbs.

   (2a) *Bangohan o **tabeta ato de** sanpo-shimashoo.*
   晩ごはんを**食べたあとで**散歩しましょう。
   (Let's go for a walk after eating supper.)

3. [Vbasic + *mae ni*] 'before [doing] . . .'
   This expression is used primarily with active verbs.

   (3a) *Kuraku **naru mae ni** kaette-kinasai.*
   暗く**なる前に**帰ってきなさい。
   (Come back before it gets dark.)

For connecting concurrent events, the following strategies are used.

4. [V/Adj pre-nominal + *aida ni*]
   This expression normally requires verbs that describe continuing action or state.

   (4a) *Ano hito o **matte-iru aida ni** shinbun o yomimasu.*
   あの人を**待っている間に**新聞を読みます。
   (While waiting for him, I read a newspaper.)

   (4b) ***Suzushii aida ni** benkyoo-shiyoo.*
   涼しい間に勉強しよう。
   (While it's cool, I will study.)

   (4c) *Kodomo ga **nete-iru aida ni** hon o yomoo.*
   子供が**寝ている間に**本を読もう。
   (I'll read a book while the child is sleeping.)

5. [Vstem + *nagara*]

   (5a) *Ano hito o **machinagara** shinbun o yomimasu.*
   あの人を**待ちながら**新聞を読みます。
   (While waiting for him, I read a newspaper.)

   (5b) *Terebi **minagara** benkyoo dekiru?* ☺
   テレビ**見ながら**勉強できる？
   (Can you study while watching TV?)

The *nagara* expression is used when the same agent performs two actions simultaneously. For this reason the verb in the [*nagara*] clause must designate an action which lasts over a period of time. Non-durative verbs cannot be used within a [*nagara*] clause.

Examples

kankookyaku	観光客	N	tourist
matsuri	祭り	N	festival
asobu	遊ぶ	V	to play
aruku	歩く	V	to walk

(1) *Asoko wa chichi ga genki datta koro yoku issho ni ikimashita.*
あそこは父が元気だった頃よくいっしょに行きました。
(When my father was well, we went there together often.)

(2) *Sanhuranshisuko ni sunde-ita toki, nihon-jin no kankookyaku o yoku <u>mikakemashita ga</u> . . .*
サンフランシスコに住んでいた時，日本人の観光客をよく見かけましたが……
(When I lived in San Francisco, I saw many Japanese tourists.)

(3) *Matsuri no koro hurusato e kaerimasu.*
祭りの頃ふるさとへ帰ります。
(About the time of the festival, I will return to my hometown.)

(4) *Benkyoo-shite kara asobinasai!*
勉強してから遊びなさい！
(Play after you study.)

(5) *Mono o tabenagara arukanaide-kudasai.*
ものを食べながら歩かないでください。
(Please do not walk while eating.)

Practice

grade school student	N	shoogakusei 小学生
high school student	N	kookoosei 高校生
to clean	V	sooji o suru そうじをする

Express the following in Japanese by adding main clauses of your choice.

1. When I came back home, . . .
2. When I went to Europe, . . .
3. When I was a grade school student, . . .
4. When I was a high school student, . . .
5. When you study, . . .

6. After arriving at the airport, . . .
7. While drinking sake, . . .
8. Before the guest arrives, . . .
9. While my son is studying, . . .
10. Before you go, . . .

———— Some Sample Answers ————

1. *Uchi ni kaette-kita toki, imooto wa terebi o mite-imashita.*
   家に帰ってきた時，妹はテレビを見ていました。
2. *Yooroppa e itta toki, tomodachi ni aimashita.*
   ヨーロッパへ行った時，友だちに会いました。
3. *Shoogakusei no koro wa mainichi tomodachi to asobimashita.* 小学生の頃は毎日友だちと遊びました。
4. *Kookoosei no toki yoku benkyoo-shimashita.*
   高校生の時よく勉強しました。
5. *Benkyoo-suru toki yoku jisho o tsukaimasu ka.*
   勉強する時よく辞書を使いますか。
6. *Kuukoo ni tsuite kara denwa o shimasu kara.*
   空港についてから電話をしますから。
7. *Sake o nominagara tomodachi to hanashi o shimashita.*
   酒を飲みながら友だちと話をしました。
8. *Saa, okyaku-san ga tsuku mae ni sooji o shimashoo.*
   さあ，お客さんがつく前にそうじをしましょう。
9. *Musuko ga benkyoo-shite-iru aida ni shigoto o shimasu.*
   息子が勉強している間に仕事をします。
10. *Iku mae ni denwa-shimashoo.* 行く前に電話しましょう。

Additional Information

Conjunctions *ato de* and *mae ni* may also be preceded by [N + *no*]. Thus:

(a) *Hiruyasumi* **no** **ato de** *aimashoo.*
    lunch break L later let's meet
    昼休み**の**あとで会いましょう。
    (Let's meet after the lunch break.)

(b) *Hiruyasumi* **no mae ni** *kono shigoto o shimashoo.*
    昼休み**の前に**この仕事をしましょう。
    (Let's get to this work before the lunch break.)

The [*nagara*] expression can also be used to mean 'despite,' especially when the verb is stative. Note also that *da* changes to *dearu* when it precedes *nagara*, resulting in the expression, *dearinagara*. For example:

(c) *Ano hito wa daigakusei **dearinagara** yoku kanji o shiranai.*
あの人は大学生でありながらよく漢字を知らない。
(Despite the fact that he is a university student, he doesn't know kanji well.)

In some cases two readings are possible; the correct interpretation is based on the discourse context in which it is placed.

(d) | *Nando mo* | ***shippai-shinagara*** | *soredemo* | *saigo* | *made* | *shiageta.* |
| --- | --- | --- | --- | --- | --- |
| many times | fail | | even then | end | till | finished |

何度も失敗しながらそれでも最後まで仕上げた。

Reading 1: 'In spite of the fact that I made mistakes many times, still, I finished it (stuck with it) to the end.'

Reading 2: 'While I was making many mistakes, I finished it (stuck with it) to the end.'

85. Leave-taking and Parting

Target Expression

> *Goodbye.*
>
> ***Jaa, mata. Sayoonara.***
> じゃあ，また。さようなら。

Strategic Explanation

Although *sayo(o)nara* is best known as a greeting for farewell, it is important to know that among *uchi* members, one says *sayo(o)nara* only when the separation is long; saying *sayo(o)nara* implies that they may never see each other again. It would be quite upsetting for Japanese parents to hear their son or daughter leave the house saying *sayo(o)nara* in the morning. The parents would think their child is running away from home or even ready to commit suicide! If you stay with a Japanese family, for example, the only time you should use *sayo(o)nara* to family members is when leaving them for good.

The *uchi* group applies to company employees as well. When leaving one's office, *jaa osakini (shitsurei-shimasu)* 'excuse me for leaving before you' is normally used for leave-taking. Schoolchildren do use *sayo(o)nara* to teachers at the end of the day, however, even when they will meet the teacher the next day. It is useful to know a variety of Japanese parting phrases to be used in different social situations.

1. When leaving the house:
   Itte-mairimasu. 行ってまいります。 (lit. I will go and return. [formal])
   Itte-kimasu. 行ってきます。 (lit. I will go and return. [less formal])

2. When saying goodbye to someone you meet every day or frequently:
   Ja(a),mata. じゃ(あ)、また。 (See you again.)
   Ja(a),ato de. じゃ(あ)、あとで。 (Well then, see you later.)
   Ja(a), ashita. じゃ(あ)、あした。 (See you tomorrow.)
   Soredewa mata. それではまた。 (Well then, see you again.)
   Dewa nochi hodo. では後ほど。 (Well then, see you later. [polite form])

3. When leaving the office before others:
   Osakini (shitsurei [-shimasu]). お先に(失礼[します])。 (lit. Excuse me for leaving early.)

4. When someone is leaving for a long time:
   Sayo(o)nara. さよ(う)なら。 (Goodbye.)
   Ogenki de. お元気で。 (Take care of yourself.)

5. Schoolchildren and teachers greeting at the end of the day:
   Sensei sayo(o)nara. 先生さよ(う)なら。 (Goodbye, [teacher].)
   Sayo(o)nara. さよ(う)なら。 (Goodbye.)

6. When asking to send one's regards:
   Okusan ni yoroshiku. 奥さんによろしく。 (Please give my regards to your wife.)

Additional Information

When visiting a Japanese family, it is common that the family encourages the guest to stay longer. A typical phrase is *mada ii ja-nai-desu ka* 'it's still early, (please stay longer).' Leave-taking is a ritual in which the guest indicates that he or she is leaving while the host often attempts to discourage the guest's parting. One should not take the host's kind words at face value, however. It is important not to overextend your stay. Particularly when your visit extends into mealtime, the host or the hostess may feel obliged to serve you a meal. Mealtime visits should be avoided in general, unless invited beforehand. Regardless of how hard (it seems) the host tries to encourage you to stay, you should take various facts into consideration and express your interest in leaving. *Jaa sorosoro shitsurei shimasu node. . .* 'Well I should be leaving soon . . .' is useful when expressing your intention to leave.

When a co-worker leaves the office by saying *osakini (shitsurei [-shimasu])*, the remaining co-workers will respond with *otsukare sama (deshita)* 'lit. Thank you for your effort.' If your superior leaves by saying *osakini*, you should respond *aa doomo* and not with *otsukare sama*, unless the superior is considered a member of your immediate work group. When a family leaves home saying *itte kimasu* (or *itte mairimasu*), the remaining members respond with *itte (i)rasshai* 'lit. Go and return.'

Warning

A non-verbal sign for parting is waving sideways with one's palm facing the partner. The hand gesture of flapping your fingers with the palm facing the partner—a gesture accompanying greetings of farewell in America—is a sign asking someone to come toward you in Japan.

86. Speech Style—3. Honorifics: Respectful and Humble Forms

Target Expression

> *The company president has come.*
> **Shachoo-san ga irasshaimashita.**
> 社長さんがいらっしゃいました。
>
> [o + Vstem + *ninaru*]
> [o + Vstem + *suru*]
> respectful [V + -*reru*, V + -*rareru*]

Strategic Explanation

Earlier we learned the styles of formal and informal speech. Formalness indicated by the *desu* and *masu* style, as we have been using, is basically an expression of politeness. Honorifics as stated in characteristic 5 is another aspect of Japanese speech style which generates politeness. Honorifics describe two different strategies. Beyond being formal or informal, the verb can be expressed in its respectful and humble forms. Respectful forms are used when addressing, or talking about someone whose social status is relatively higher than yours. In the same situation of relative social status, humble forms of the verb may be used in reference to one's own action and state; by humbling the speaker's action, social differentiation is achieved. The use of respectful and humble forms is not optional; appropriate forms must be chosen in each social situation, except when social equals interact, or when the *uchi* relationship is firmly established.

There are two distinct respectful forms, (1) by using the verb respectful form, and (2) by using the pattern [*o* + Vstem + *ninaru*], with the latter considered to be slightly more formal. The prefix *o* is normally attached to Japanese words, while *go* is attached to vocabulary of Chinese origin.

The verb respectful forms are formed as shown below.

U-verbs: replace *-u* by *-areru*

> *kaku*　　　　　　　*kakareru*
> *omou*　　　　　　　*omowareru*

Note that *-u* + *-areru* produces *-wareru*. When the verb ends with a mora consisting of *u* as in *kau* and *utau*, the respectful form takes *kawareru* and *utawareru*, respectively.

RU-verbs: replace *-ru* by *-rareru*

> *taberu*　　　　　　*taberareru*
> *hairu*　　　　　　　*hairareru*

In fact in both *U*- and *RU*-verbs, the change is identical; the final *-u* becomes *-areru*. For *RU*-verbs, the respectful forms introduced here are identical to potential forms introduced in Entry 75. Among verb potential forms, the alternative potential forms (for example, *kaereru* 'to return' instead of *kaerareru*) are not used as respectful forms.

Humble forms are generated by the pattern [*o* + Vstem + *suru*]. If you are telling your boss that you will 'deliver' *todokeru* the file later, you should say *otodokeshimasu*. All humble and respectful forms introduced here can be used either in informal or formal style, depending on the situation, although it is often the case that formal style is used in the polite *masu* forms.

(a) *Sensei wa moo **okaerininarimashita** ga . . .*　　(respectful form of
　　先生はもうお帰りになりましたが……　　　　　　*kaeru*)
　　(The professor has already [gone home] left . . .)

(b)   *Sensei wa moo* **kaeraremashita** *ga* . . .   (respectful verb form of
先生はもう**帰られました**が……   *kaeru*)
(The professor has already left . . .)

(c)   *Sugu odenwa* **okakeshimasu** *node* . . . (humble form of *kakeru*)
すぐお電話**おかけ**しますので……
(I will call right away.)

Verbs listed below have special respectful and humble forms. As shown, some do not go through [*o* + Vstem + *suru*] nor [*o* + Vstem + *ninaru*] structures; these forms must be learned one by one.

Special Verb Honorific Forms

	respectful	humble
au	*oaininaru*	*omenikakaru*
会う	お会いになる	お目にかかる
iru	*irassharu/oideninaru*	*oru*
いる	いらっしゃる/おいでになる	おる
iku/kuru	*irassharu/oideninaru*	*mairu/ukagau*
行く/来る	いらっしゃる/おいでになる	参る/うかがう
omou	*oomoininaru*	*zonjiru*
思う	お思いになる	存じる
kariru	*okarininaru*	*haishakusuru*
借りる	お借りになる	拝借する
suru	*nasaru*	*itasu*
する	なさる	いたす
taberu/nomu	*meshiagaru*	*itadaku*
食べる/飲む	めしあがる	いただく
da	*de-irassharu*	—
だ	でいらっしゃる	
miru	*goranninaru*	*haikensuru*
見る	ごらんになる	拝見する
yuu	*ossharu*	*moosu/mooshiageru*
言う	おっしゃる	申す/申し上げる

Additionally, a special form *de-gozaru* (normally used as *de-gozaimasu*) represents a neutrally polite style. *De-gozaimasu* usage is chosen more because of style rather than social status.

It is also possible to change *suru* into its humble form, *itasu*; creating an even more humble form *otodokeitashimasu*, for example. When the progressive form [V*te* + *-iru*] is used, it is possible to use respectful and humble forms of [V*te* + *-iru*]; [V*te* + *-irassharu*] and [V*te* + *-oru*], *sensei wa ima (o)tegami o yonde-irasshaimasu*, for example.

As a special class of verbs among verbs listed above, the following special verbs, which are *-aru* ending verbs, conjugate as shown below.

Vbasic	formal non-past	informal past	formal past
irassharu	*irasshaimasu*	*irasshatta*	*irasshaimashita*
ossharu	*osshaimasu*	*osshatta*	*osshaimashita*
kudasaru	*kudasaimasu*	*kudasatta*	*kudasaimashita*
gozaru	*gozaimasu*	*gozatta*	*gozaimashita*

Another strategy for respectful expressions takes [*o* + Vstem + *da*]. For example, *kaeru* can take *okaeri desu*. This strategy carries a slightly lesser degree of respect than the [*o* + Vstem + *ninaru*] strategy.

Examples

----
buchoo　部長　　　N　　manager
----

(1)　*Sensei irasshaimasu ka.*
　　先生いらっしゃいますか。
　　(Is the professor in? [respectful/formal])

(2)　*Kaigi de Koide buchoo ni oaininarimashita ka.*
　　会議で小出部長にお会いになりましたか。
　　(Did you see manager Koide at the meeting? [respectful/formal])

(3)　*Otegami haiken-itashimashita.*
　　お手紙拝見いたしました。
　　(I read your letter. [super humble/formal])

(4)　*Soredewa sukoshi okikishimasu ga . . .*
　　それでは少しお聞きしますが……
　　(Now I would like to ask you something . . . [humble/formal])

(5)　*Ashita irassharu?* ☺F
　　あしたいらっしゃる？
　　(Are you going tomorrow? [respectful/informal])

Practice

```
---------------------------------------------------------
to leave,        V   (go)shuppatsu-suru
  to depart          (ご)出発する
advertisement    N   kookoku  広告
to attend        V   (go)shusseki-suru
                     (ご)出席する
---------------------------------------------------------
```

1. How will you ask the following questions or make statements as listed below addressed to your superior?
   a. when your teacher leaves for Europe
   b. if your boss saw the new ad
   c. if he went to yesterday's meeting
   d. if you can see her at three o'clock
   e. that you will visit your teacher's office tomorrow about ten o'clock

2. The following statement is made about your brother. Make the same statement about Professor Kato as you make necessary changes in honorific expressions.
   a. *Ani wa senshuu Yooroppa kara kaette-kimashita.*
   b. *Rondon de tomodachi ni atte, kaimono o shimashita.*
   c. *Pari e mo ikimashita.*
   d. *Pari de wa kaigi ni shusseki-shimashita.*

3. The politeness strategy in general is more frequently used by female speakers. It is particularly useful for female students to learn to use respectful and humble forms in the informal style. The following practice is for female speakers only. How would you address the following to your superior's wife in a casual and very friendly situation?
   a. What time are you going? ☺F
   b. Please (help yourself) and drink the juice. ☺F

——— Some Sample Answers ———

1a. *Itsu Yooroppa e irasshaimasu ka.*
　　いつヨーロッパへいらっしゃいますか。
　　Itsu Yooroppa e goshuppatsu-nasaimasu ka.
　　いつヨーロッパへご出発なさいますか。
　b. *Atarashii kookoku goranninarimashita ka.*
　　新しい広告ご覧になりましたか。
　c. *Kinoo no kaigi irasshaimashita ka.*
　　きのうの会議いらっしゃいましたか。
　　Kinoo no kaigi goshusseki-nasaimashita ka.
　　きのうの会議ご出席なさいましたか。

    d. *San-ji ni omenikakaritai no desu ga . . .*
　三時にお目にかかりたいのですが……

    e. *Dewa ashita juu-ji ni oukagaiitashimasu node . . .*
　ではあした十時におうかがいいたしますので……

2a. *Sensei wa senshuu Yooroppa kara okaerininarimashita.*
　先生は先週ヨーロッパからお帰りになりました。

  b. *Rondon de goyuujin ni oaininatte, kaimono o nasaimashita.*
　ロンドンでご友人にお会いになって，買物をなさいました。

  c. *Pari e mo irasshaimashita.* パリへもいらっしゃいました。

  d. *Pari de wa kaigi ni goshusseki-nasaimashita.*
　パリでは会議にご出席なさいました。

3a. *Nan-ji ni irassharu?* ☺F　何時にいらっしゃる？

  b. *Meshiagatte.* ☺F　めしあがって。

Additional Information

The term "politeness" is a general term that encompasses various aspects of interaction. The humble and respectful forms of the honorific system which are our focus here are only a part of the overall "politeness" phenomenon. To be polite in human interaction involves social etiquette, euphemism, and conversational strategies—including things such as what to talk about, how and how not to ask questions, and how non-verbal and paralinguistic (intonation, for example) features are incorporated in your interaction.

87. Eye-witness Conjecture—*Soona*

Target Expressions

That cake looks delicious.

    Sono keeki oishisoo da naa. ☺M
　そのケーキおいしそうだなあ。

    Sono keeki oishisoo nee. ☺F
　そのケーキおいしそうねえ。

[V/Adj stem + *soona*]

Grammatical Explanation

The auxiliary adjective [*soona*] is attached to [Vstem] and [Adj stem] and functions to add the meaning of 'looks (as if) . . .,' and 'appears as if.' (The [Adj stem] is obtained by: for [Adj-*i*], delete the final -*i*, for [Adj-*na*], delete the final -*na*.) *Soona* cannot co-occur with [N + *da*] structure except when it is negative; *gakusei ja nasasoo da* 'he doesn't seem to be a student.' When using [*soona*], the speaker conjectures the likelihood of a future event, or the current condition of something, based on what the speaker personally perceives. When using [*soona*], the speaker conveys that as far as he or she is concerned, the information typically accompanying what one conjectures is immediately available and is directly observed. For example, you are looking at a beautifully rich-looking cake at a pastry shop. You conjecture based on that directly perceived information that it looks good, *oishisoo .desu nee!*

There are two exceptions to be noted when using the [*soona*] form; for the adjective *yoi* (or *ii*), *yosasoona* is used and similarly for the adjective *nai*, *nasasoona* is used. For example:

(a) *Kono hon wa **yosasoo** yo.* ☺F
この本は**よさそう**よ。
(This book looks [as if it is] good.)

(b) *Taberu mono amari **nasasoo** desu ne.*
食べる物あまり**なさそう**ですね。
(It appears [as if] there is not much food.)

The [Vstem + *soona*] pattern is often used for conjecturing future events. For example:

(c) *Ame ga **hurisoo** da yo.* ☺M
雨が**降りそう**だよ。
(It looks as if it is going to [it is likely] rain.)

You might imagine the following situation where the expression above is appropriately used. You just stepped out of your house and realize that the sky is covered with dark rain clouds. You notice the wind kicking up, and the anticipation of summer rain is felt in the air. You call out to your brother with whom you are about to go out to play catch with, warning that the weather isn't cooperating. "Hey, it looks like rain is coming!" Again, this expression is used to mean "I am personally under the impression that something is likely to be the case or to happen," and that conclusion is based on the speaker's own sense perception (usually sight, occasionally smell).

Regarding the negation of [*soona*] the following is to be noted. [*Soona*] itself can be negated to mean 'doesn't look as if'; *oishisoo dewa-arimasen*. It is also possible to negate the adjective; *oishikunasasoo desu*, to mean 'looks as if it is not delicious.' When [*soona*] is preceded by a verb, however, only [*sooni nai*] or [*soomo nai*] negative forms are possible, with the latter conveying slightly stronger negation; *ame wa hurisoomo arimasen yo* 'it doesn't look (as if) it will rain at all.'

Since the [*soona*] expression itself conjugates as an [Adj-*na*], this structure can modify a noun directly. For example:

(d) **Oishisoona** *keeki desu ne.*
おいしそうなケーキですね。
(It is a delicious-looking cake, isn't it?)

(e) **Muzukashisoona** *hon desu ne.*
むずかしそうな本ですね。
(This is a difficult-looking book, isn't it?)

Practice

You have direct access to information that allows you to conjecture the following. How will you express your impression?

1. to snow
2. for the meeting to begin soon (*sorosoro*)
3. the speaker's luggage (*nimotsu*) being heavy ☺M
4. the new department store not being good ☺F
5. the store being expensive
6. for the manager's speech not to be over

──── Some Sample Answers ────

1. *Yuki ga hurisoo desu.*　雪が降りそうです。
2. *Kaigi wa sorosoro hajimarisoo desu.*
会議はそろそろ始まりそうです。
3. *Sono nimotsu wa omosoo da naa.* ☺M
その荷物は重そうだなあ。
4. *Atarashii depaato wa amari yokunasasoo yo.* ☺F
新しいデパートはあまりよくなさそうよ。
5. *Takasoona mise desu ne.*　高そうな店ですね。
(or *Kono mise wa takasoo desu ne.*　この店は高そうですね。)
6. *Buchoo no supiichi owarisoomo arimasen nee.*
部長のスピーチ終わりそうもありませんねえ。

88. Connecting Clauses with *To*

> *When April comes, cherry blossoms bloom.*
> **Shigatsu ni naru to sakura ga sakimasu.**
> 四月になると桜が咲きます。
>
> conjunction [*to*]

Grammatical Explanation

The conjunction [*to*] 'when' or 'whenever' (a different word from the particle [*to*] for joint action and enumerative expression) connects clauses in the following situations. The form preceding this [to] is [Vbasic].

1. When an action occurs, something else always or habitually occurs:

   (1a) | *Ano* | *hito* | *wa* | *sake* | *o* | *sukoshi* | *nomu* | **to** |
        |-------|--------|------|--------|-----|----------|--------|--------|
        | that | person | T | sake | O | little | drink | when |

yookini	*narimasu.*
cheerfully	become

   あの人は酒を少し飲むと陽気になります。
   (When [whenever] she drinks a little, she becomes cheerful.)

2. When an action is followed by something else which occurs as a natural and obvious consequence:

   (2a) | *San* | *to* | *go* | *o* | *tasu* | **to** | *hachi* | *ni* | *naru.*[*1] ♦ |
        |-------|------|------|-----|--------|--------|---------|------|---------------|
        | three | and | five | O | add | when | eight | to | become |

   3と5を足すと8になる。
   (When you add three and five, it becomes eight.)

3. When an action follows immediately after another action:
   (This expression is normally followed by *sugu* 'immediately.')

   (3a) | *To* | *ga* | *aku* | **to** | *sugu* | *koinu* | *ga* |
        |------|------|-------|--------|--------|---------|------|
        | door | S | open | when | right away | puppy | S |

tobidashite-kimashita.
jumped out

   戸が開くとすぐ小犬が飛び出してきました。
   (When the door opened, a puppy jumped out right away.)

*1. The verb *naru* 'to become' takes [N + *ni*] to indicate the result of becoming. *Sensei ni naru* 'to become a teacher,' and *otona ni naru* 'to become an adult.' When *naru* co-occurs with adjectives, both [Adj-*i*] and [Adj-*na*] take adverbial forms; *Akaruku naru* 'to become light' and *benrini naru* 'to become convenient.'

Warning

As shown in sentence (3a) above, in Japanese there is no grammatical "tense agreement" as observed in English. In English when the tense of the main verb is past, the tense of the subordinate clause must agree with this past tense. In Japanese the tense of the *to* clause, which cannot take the past tense, is interpreted on the basis of the tense of the main verb. In (3a), although the verb *aku* is in the non-past form, since the main verb is in past tense form, *tobidashite-kimashita* 'jumped out,' the time that the door opened is interpreted as past tense as reflected in the English translation.

Practice

By using the *to* clause, complete the following sentence.

1. When December comes, . . .
2. When the movie started, . . .
3. When I work till late at night, . . .

———— Some Sample Answers ————

1. *Juuni-gatsu ni naru to sukii ni ikitaku narimasu.*
十二月になるとスキーに行きたくなります。

2. *Eiga ga hajimaru to sugu minna shizukani narimashita.*
映画が始まるとすぐみんな静かになりました。

3. *Yoru osoku made shigoto o suru to tsugi no hi wa asaneboo o shite-shimaimasu.*
夜遅くまで仕事をすると次の日は朝寝坊をしてしまいます。
(When I work till late at night, I end up getting up late the next day.)

---

*   *   *   *   *

Kokkyoo no nagai tonneru o nukeru to yukiguni deatta.
国境の長いトンネルを抜けると雪国であった。
—Kawabata, 1966, p.7.
The train came out of the long tunnel into the snow country.
—Seidensticker, 1956, p.11.

kokkyoo	国境	N	country border
tonneru	トンネル	N	tunnel
nukeru	抜ける	V	to pass through
yukiguni	雪国	N	snow country

This is the first sentence appearing in the novel *Snow Country*. In the original Japanese [*to*] connects two clauses although the meaning of 'when' is not directly reflected in the translation. A careful reader will find that in the Japanese version, there is no subject. Seidensticker's English translation shows a good contrast between agent-less orientation in Japanese and the subject-predicate frame in English.

89. Pointing Out Resemblance and Likelihood—*Yoona*

Target Expressions

> *He speaks like a Japanese.*
> **Ano hito wa nihon-jin no yooni shaberu ne.** ☺
> あの人は日本人のようにしゃべるね。
> *It seems (to me) that it began to rain.*
> **Ame ga hutte-kita yoo desu ne.**
> 雨が降ってきたようですね。
>
> [*yoona*]

Grammatical Explanation

When pointing out resemblance and expressing the likelihood, the [Adj-*na*] *yoona*, is used. (The word *yoo* means 'manner' and 'appearance.') [*Yoona*] may be used as an adjective in the form of [*yoona*] and an adverb in the form of [*yooni*]. [*Yoona*] cannot be used independently; it must be preceded by modifiers such as demonstratives, [N + *no*] structure, adjectives, and clausal modifiers. The verb and adjective forms immediately preceding [*yoona*] is [V/Adj pre-nominal].

The [*yoona*] pattern is used in two distinctive ways. First, it is used to mean in English 'it resembles' to express that something is approximately X although it is not quite X. We will call this use the "resemblance" [*yoona*].

Second, it is used to mean in English 'it appears (to me)' or 'it seems (to me)' when the speaker expresses a personal judgment as to the likelihood of a state or event. We will call this use of [*yoona*] the "likelihood" *yoona*. The "resemblance" *yoona* co-occurs only with the noun; *ano ko wa otoko no ko no yoo da*, 'that child resembles a boy,' for example, is used when describing a tomboy.

For negation of the [*yoona*] expression, in the case of "resemblance" use, it is possible to negate both the noun-statement and *yoona* itself. In case of "likelihood" *yoona*, however, negation of *yoona* itself is not normally used. For example:

(a)	*Otoko no ko **dewa nai** yoo da.*	男の子では**ない**ようだ。
(b)	*Otoko no ko no yoo **dewa-nai.***	男の子のよう**ではない**。
(c)	*Ame wa **hutte-inai** yoo da.*	雨は**降っていない**ようだ。
(d)	**Ame wa huru yoo **dewa-nai**.*	

By now you might be wondering about the difference between the "likelihood" [*yoona*] and [*soona*] which we learned two entries earlier. The difference between these two can be found by contrasting use of these forms in the following situation. You see a fork sticking partly off the table, in a precarious position. Here you must use *ochisoo da* 'looks (as if) it's going to fall' in order to describe the fork. You have direct visual evidence to make this statement. Imagine another situation. You are in your dorm room with poor soundproofing. You aren't quite sure if your next-door resident left his room or not. You do hear some noise, however, which seems to come from his room, although you are not sure. Considering the fact that he is sometimes in his room at nine in the morning, you say, *mada iru yoo da* 'it is likely that he is still there.' When using *yoona*, the evidence consists of a combination of various facts (including some that are gained through sense perception), and the speaker does not have access to decisive direct evidence to conjecture as in the case of [*soona*]. What is involved in using [*yoona*] is that the speaker uses information available to reach a conclusion after going through a certain reasoning process.

Unlike [*soona*], "likelihood" *yoona* can be used to point out the likelihood of a past event or state. While it is not possible to conjecture a past event when using [*soona*], it is possible with the [*yoona*] expression as shown in example (3) to follow. The [*yoona*] pattern is different from the [*soona*] structure in that the [*yoona*] expression describes approximately the way things are. [*Soona*] on the other hand is used primarily for predicting something in the future or for describing states relevant to the future.

The adverbial form of [*yoona*], that is [*yooni*], has many useful functions. First, [N + *no yooni*] and [clause + *yooni*] are equivalent to the English conjunction 'as.' For example:

(e) *Gozonji* **no yooni** . . .
ご存知のように……
(As you know . . .)

(f) **Sensei ga osshata yooni** *kono hon wa totemo muzukashikatta-desu.*
先生がおっしゃったようにこの本はとてもむずかしかったです。
(As you told me, professor, this book was quite difficult.)

Additionally, [*yooni*] expresses purpose, as in:

(g) **Hayaku owaru yooni** *isoide shigoto o shimashoo.*
早く終わるように急いで仕事をしましょう。
(Let's do the work in a hurry so that it will be over soon.)

Other idiomatic uses include, *yooni yuu* 'to tell to,' and *yooni naru* 'to become,' which we will come back to again later.

The [*yoona*] expression is favored by Japanese even when the meaning of 'it appears' and 'it seems' is only weakly traced. For example, it is customary to say *kono yoona baai* 'in this case,' not *kono baai.* Instead of saying *sonna koto,* using *sono yoona koto* makes the statement more formal and somewhat softer, indirect and less impactful.

Examples

hukusoo o suru 服装をする	V	to wear clothes
shaberu しゃべる	V	to speak, to chatter
mawari まわり	N	surrounding
yume 夢	N	dream
huukei 風景	N	scenery, scene
hushigina ふしぎな	Adj	strange

(1) *Koko wa doko?*
ここはどこ？
(Where am I?)

Minna kaishain no yoona hukusoo o shite-iru.
みんな会社員のような服装をしている。
(Everybody is dressed like a businessman.)

Shikashi kodomo no yoona nihongo de shabette-iru.
しかし子供のような日本語でしゃべっている。
(But they are all speaking childish Japanese.)

Mawari ma shizuka de, amari mise mo nai yoo da.
まわりは静かで，あまり店もないようだ。
(The surroundings are quiet and there seem to be no stores.)

Eki dake atte hito ga oozei iru.
駅だけあって人が大勢いる。
(There is only a station where there are a lot of people.)

Minna densha o matte-iru yoo da.
みんな電車を待っているようだ。
(They all seem to be waiting for a train.)

Kore wa yume no naka ni dete-kita huukei.
これは夢の中に出てきた風景。
(This is a scene which appeared in a dream.)

Hushigina huukei da.
ふしぎな風景だ。
(It's a strange scene.)

(2) *Maa Yamanaka-sensei no yoona sensei wa amari imasen yo ne.*
まあ山中先生のような先生はあまりいませんよね。
(Well, there aren't too many teachers like Ms. Yamanaka.)

(3) *Kaigi wa moo owatta yoo da ne.* ☺ M
会議はもう終ったようだね。
(The meeting seems like it ended.)

Practice

Create Japanese sentences by using the [*yoona*] expression for describing the following situation.

1. After processing some relevant information you conclude that your friend looks tired, and you want to comment on it.
2. You are interested in finding out whether or not your friend can speak French just like a native French person.
3. You sense that people are walking out of the banquet room. There is some commotion and voices are coming from that direction. You conjecture that the party is likely to have concluded.
4. Your boss asks you to send the mail by overnight express. You answer by saying 'I will do that (lit. I will do like that).'

—— Some Sample Answers ——
1. *Tsukareta yoo desu ne.*　疲れたようですね。
2. *Huransu-jin no yooni Huransu-go ga hanasemasu ka.*
   フランス人のようにフランス語が話せますか。
3. *Paatii wa owatta yoo desu.*　パーティーは終わったようです。
4. *Sono yooni shimasu.*　そのようにします。

Additional Information

A colloquial expression [*mitaina*] is also used similarly to "likelihood" [*yoona*]. [*Mitaina*] is preceded by a noun or [V/Adj pre-Aux] forms.

---
baka	ばか	N	fool
isoge	急げ	V	command form of
			isogu 'to hurry'

(a)　*Nee, ano hito hontoni baka mitai.* ☺F
　　ねえ，あの人ほんとにばかみたい。
　　(He's really like a fool.)

(b)　*Hora, isoge yo, eiga wa moo owatta mitai da kara.*[1] ☺M
　　ほら，急げよ，映画はもう終わったみたいだから。
　　(Come on, hurry, the movie seems to have ended.)

[1].　You may not recognize *isoge*. *Isoge* is an abrupt command form briefly discussed in Entry 79.

90.　Language of Emotion—1.　Pleasure, Loneliness and Sadness

Target Expressions

> *Wow, am I glad!*
> 　　　　**Yaa, ureshii yo, hontoni!** ☺M
> 　　　　やあ，うれしいよ，ほんとに！
> 　　　　**Waa, ureshii!** ☺F
> 　　　　わあ，うれしい！

Grammatical Explanation

Although there may be an impression held by Westerners that Japanese do not show emotion, among familiar *uchi* members in informal and intimate situations, Japanese show their emotions quite readily. When expressing one's own emotions, descriptive terms of [Adj-*i*] and [Adj-*na*] are used as shown below. Since emotion is frequently expressed straightforwardly without regard to the speech style, informal expressions are widely used.

(a) *Ureshii naa!* ☺M
うれしいなあ！
(Great!)

(b) *Shiawase!* ☺
幸せ！
(I am happy!)

(c) *Zannen desu nee.* ☺
残念ですねえ。
(I'm sorry to hear that.)

(d) *Sabishii wa.* ☺F
寂しいわ。
(I'm lonely.)

(e) *Kanashii naa.* ☺
悲しいなあ。
(I'm sad.)

When emotion is expressed in written style, it is often accompanied by the phrase *omou* 'to think,' as in *kanashiku omou* '(lit. to think) to feel sad.'

When describing someone else's emotion, a different strategy must be used. This is because these personal emotions are only indirectly describable. The only way to have access to someone's internal feelings is to observe an outward sign that someone is actually feeling the emotion. When such a sign is evident, the [*soona*] expression or the [Adj stem + *gatte-iru*] structure is used.

(f) *Rarii-san wa okusan o nakushite sabishisoo da.*
Larry   T   wife   O lose   seems lonely
ラリーさんは奥さんをなくして寂しそうだ。
(Larry seems lonely since his wife passed away.)

(g) *Rarii-san wa totemo sabishigatte-imasu yo.*
ラリーさんはとても寂しがっていますよ。
([lit. Larry shows that he is very lonely] Larry is very lonely.)

Additional Information

Direct expressions of psychological state and emotion may be used when describing someone else's emotion in a narrative. For example, when a writer chooses an expression *Saeko wa sabishikatta* 'Saeko was lonely,' the writer assumes an omniscient viewpoint; the writer has access to Saeko's internal feelings.

It should also be mentioned that there is a group of verbs to express active emotional experience. For example, *kanashimu* 'to grieve' as in *gakusei wa tomo no shi o kanashinda* 'the student grieved over his or her friend's death.'

91. Non-self-committing Speculation—*Rashii*

Target Expression

> *The person who newly joined the company seems to be from Kyoto.*
> **Kondo nyuusha-shita hito wa Kyooto no shusshin rashii.**
> 今度入社した人は京都の出身らしい。
>
> [*rashii*]

Grammatical Explanation

A structure using the *i*-type auxiliary adjective *rashii* 'it seems' expresses speculation based on information primarily obtained from sources other than self. *Rashii* follows [V/Adj pre-Aux] forms. The [*rashii*] pattern is used when there is speculation based on a definite source or reason, but most likely to have come from someone else as hearsay. [*Rashii*] is not used when your speculation is merely based on a purely personal impression or interpretation. When using *rashii*, the speaker conveys a likeliness of it being so, but little commitment is made as to whether the speaker himself or herself believes the certainty of it. This is partly because speculation is based on secondhand information. In other words, when using *rashii*, unlike *yoona*, the speaker distances himself or herself from the statement made; the speaker conveys that he or she is not totally committed to nor is totally responsible for the statement made. This speaker's attitude may be best described in English as 'it seems . . . and it apparently is the case, according to what I hear, although I'm not going to bet on it.'

The negation of this expression is achieved by negating the verb preceding *rashii*, and not by negating *rashii* itself.

Another use of *rashii* should not be forgotten, although it does not express speculation nor estimation. This *rashii* expresses an appropriate quality of action and state when it appears as [N + *rashii*]. For example, a teacher who behaves as a teacher should, is *sensei rashii* 'teacher-like.' When using *rashii* in this sense, the speaker has made an evaluative judgment that X exhibits the kind of standard quality and characteristics necessary to be X. For this use of *rashii*, a negative *rashikunai* 'of inappropriate quality' is used.

Examples

```
----------------------------------------------------------
himitsu        秘密      N      secret
sukoshimo . . . nai      Adv    not at all
  少しも……ない
onna no ko   女の子     N      girl
kichinto     きちんと    Adv    appropriately
koodoo-suru  行動する   V      to behave
----------------------------------------------------------
```

(1) A: *Himitsu de, Sasaki-san kekkon-shita rashii wa yo.* ☺F
秘密で，佐々木さん結婚したらしいわよ。
([lit. Being a secret] Secretly Ms. Sasaki seems to have gotten married.)

B: *Eh, hontoo?*
えっ，本当？
(Oh my, really?)

(2) A: *Tomu-san wa sengetsu Amerika e kaetta rashii-desu yo.*
トムさんは先月アメリカへ帰ったらしいですよ。
(It seems that Tom went back to the States last month.)

B: *Soo desu ka. Shirimasen-deshita.*
そうですか。知りませんでした。
(Is that right? I didn't know that.)

(3) A: *Tonari no Kimura-san wa kinoo kara rusu rashii ne.* ☺
となりの木村さんはきのうから留守らしいね。
(Ms. Kimura, the next door neighbor, seems to have been gone since yesterday.)

B: *Ee, soo rashii wa.* ☺F
ええ，そうらしいわ。
(Yes, so it seems.)

(4)   *Kono ko wa asa kara nani-mo tabete-nai rashii.* ☺
        この子は朝から何も食べてないらしい。
        (It seems that this child hasn't eaten anything since morning.)

(5)   *Tsukareta rashiku, kodomo wa nete-shimaimashita.*
        疲れたらしく，子供は寝てしまいました。
        (Seeming to be tired, the child has gone to sleep.)

(6)   *Ano hito wa sukoshimo sensei rashikunai ne.* ☺
        あの人は少しも先生らしくないね。
        (That person is not teacher-like at all, is he?)

(7)   *Yuuka-chan wa hontooni onna no ko rashii-desu nee.*
        ゆうかちゃんは本当に女の子らしいですねえ。
        (Yuka is really girl-like, isn't she?)

(8)   *Gakusei rashiku kichinto koodoo-shite-kudasai.*
        学生らしくきちんと行動してください。
        (Please behave appropriately by doing what students are expected to do.)

Additional Information

Here is a summary of differences among the three expressions [*soona*] (Entry 87), [*yoona*] (Entry 89) and [*rashii*], all of which share similar meanings represented by English 'seem' or 'appear to.'

[*soona*]: [Adj-*na*]   'it looks (as if)' 'it appears as if'
                        Expresses the speaker's conjecture regarding the present state and the future event based on the speaker's own perceptual evidence.

[*yoona*]: [Adj-*na*]   'resemble' 'looks like (to me)'
                        Expresses "resemblance" and "likelihood" of facts including past events, based on indirectly obtained evidence. The speculation is reached after reasoning. [*mitaina*] is similar to [*yoona*] except that it is more colloquial.

[*rashii*]: [Adj-*i*]   'it seems, (it apparently is the case)'
                        Expresses speculation based on evidence often witnessed or obtained by others; the deductive and speculative thought process is conducted based on secondhand information. Weak or no personal commitment to the statement.

Good sentences to memorize for these expressions are:

(a) *Ame ga hurisoo desu.*
雨が降り**そう**です。
(It appears to rain.)

(b) *Oishisoona keeki desu ne.*
おいし**そうな**ケーキですね。
(It's a delicious-looking cake.)

(c) *Merii wa otoko no ko no yoo desu.*
メリーは男の子の**よう**です。
(Mary resembles [behaves like] a boy.)

(d) *Kaigi wa moo owatta yoo desu yo.*
会議はもう終わった**よう**ですよ。
(The meeting seems to have ended.)

(e) *Sasaki-san wa gaikoku de kekkon-shita rashii yo.* ☺
佐々木さんは外国で結婚した**らしい**よ。
(Miss Sasaki seems to have gotten married abroad.)

(f) *Otoko rashii otoko wa Jon Wein ka na.* ☺
男**らしい**男はジョン・ウェインかな。
(A manly man may be John Wayne?)

Practice

to fall down	V	korobu	ころぶ
lecture	N	kooen	講演

1. You observe a drunk staggering along the street. Now he stumbles; now he sways. You point out that it appears as if he will fall down.

2. You hear hands clapping and you think it's coming from the conference room. It's about the time the guest's lecture was scheduled to be over. The lecture seems to have finally ended.

3. You hear hands clapping in the distance and you think it's coming from the conference room. Your friend speculates that the guest's lecture is over. You don't want to take full responsibility for your opinion but you also feel that the guest's lecture is over and so you comment on it.

4. Under the same circumstance as described in 2 above, but you whisper this casually to your friend.

5. Your girlfriend comes back with a lot of toiletry items. How do you state: because it was inexpensive it appears that she bought a lot.

─────── Answers ───────

1. *Korobisoo desu.* ころびそうです。
2. *Kooen wa owatta yoo desu.* 講演は終わったようです。
3. *Kooen wa owatta rashii-desu ne.* 講演は終わったらしいですね。
4. *Kooen owatta mitai yo.* ☺F 講演終わったみたいよ。
   Kooen owatta mitai da yo. ☺M 講演終わったみたいだよ。
5. *Yasukatta kara takusan katta yoo desu.*
   安かったからたくさん買ったようです。

*　　*　　*　　*　　*

"II hito ne." 「いい人ね」
"Sore wa soo, ii hito rashii." 「それはそう，いい人らしい」
"Hontoni ii hito ne. Ii hito wa ii ne."
　「ほんとにいい人ね。いい人はいいね」

—Kawabata, 1950, p.33.

"He's nice, isn't he," the girl's voice came again.

"He seems to be very nice."

"He really is nice. I like having someone so nice."

—Seidensticker, 1965, p.25.

92. Conditional—1. *Ba*-form

Target Expressions

> *If it rains tomorrow, I won't go.*
> **Ashita ame ga hureba ikimasen.**
> あした雨が降れば行きません。
>
> *If it's fresh fish, it will be delicious.*
> **Shinsenna sakana nara(ba) oishii-deshoo.**
> 新鮮な魚なら（ば）おいしいでしょう。
>
> conditional [-*ba*]
> [V/Adj pre-Aux + *nara(ba)*]

Grammatical Explanation

The conditional *ba*-form is used to express condition, that is, something is required in order for the event or state of something else to occur. In other words, in the [-ba] pattern, the condition specified in the [-ba] clause must be satisfied first; then on that condition, the event described in the main clause is expected to occur. First, let's study the conditional [-ba] form.

U-, RU-, Existential and Irregular Verbs: Replace the final *-u* with *-eba*.

*ik**u***	*ik**eba***
*ir**u***	*ir**eba***
*kur**u***	*kur**eba***
*taber**u***	*taber**eba***
*hair**u***	*hair**eba***

[Adj-*i*]: Replace the final *-i* with *-kereba*.

*taka**i***	*taka**kereba***
*suzushi**i***	*suzushi**kereba***

Note that the negation of verbs takes *-nai* form, which conjugates like [Adj-*i*]; *ikanai*, for example, takes *ikanakereba*.

[Adj-*na*]:   Replace *da* with *nara(ba)*. The *ba* of *nara(ba)* is frequently deleted.

*benri **da***	*benri **nara(ba)***

[*Be*-verb]:   Replace the verb with *nara(ba)*. The *ba* of *nara(ba)* is frequently deleted.

*nihon-jin **da***	*nihon-jin **nara(ba)***
*go-sen-en **da***	*go-sen-en **nara(ba)***

The negative conditional also has the meaning of 'unless' in situations as shown below:

(a)   *Hayaku* *oki**nakereba*** *go-ji*   *no* *densha ni* *maniaimasen*
   early   do not get up   five o'clock   L   train   be in time

yo.
IP

早く起き**なければ**五時の電車に間に合いませんよ。
(Unless you get up early, you will be late for the five-o'clock train.)

The [-ba] conditional is the most general straightforward conditional expression in Japanese. Beyond the *ba*-form, condition is expressed by [V/Adj pre-Aux + *nara(ba)*]. The [*nara(ba)*] condition preceded by [V/Adj] is used when the information given as condition originates not in the speaker, but is suggested by someone else, often by the addressee. For example, when the addressee says or shows signs to indicate that he or she is going to pay for the drinks, the appropriate conditional expression is something like 'if (you say that) you are going to pay for it, I will go with you,' *kimi ga harau nara isshoni iku yo.* In these situations, the addressee has expressed or at least has hinted the idea of presenting a condition. While the *ba*-form condition originates in the speaker, the [*nara(ba)*] condition is preferred when the condition is suggested by the addressee. When *nara(ba)* is preceded by [N], it has both straightforward and condition-originating-in-the-addressee readings. For example:

(b) *(O)kanemochi **nara(ba)** nan de mo kaeru ne.* ☺
   (お)金持ち**なら**(ば)何でも買えるね。
   (If you are rich, you can buy anything.)

(c) *(O)kanemochi **nara(ba)** sukoshi (o)kane kashite.* ☺
   (お)金持ち**なら**(ば)少し(お)金貸して。
   (If [you say that] you are rich, loan me some.)

Examples

tadashii	正しい	Adj	correct
to omou	と思う	V	to think that

(1) *Kore o yomeba wakarimasu yo.*
   これを読めばわかりますよ。
   (If you read this you will understand.)

(2) *Oosaka o hachi-ji ni dereba Tookyoo ni juu ichi-ji ni wa tsukimasu.*
   大阪を八時に出れば東京に十一時には着きます。
   (If you leave Osaka at eight o'clock, you will arrive at Tokyo by eleven.)

(3) *Anata ga ikanakereba Kawai-san mo ikanai wa yo.* ☺F
   あなたが行かなければ河井さんも行かないわよ。
   (If you don't go, Mr. Kawai won't go either.)

(4) *Gakusei nara gakusei rashiku koodoo-shinasai.*
   学生なら学生らしく行動しなさい。
   (If you are a student, behave like a student should.)

(5) *Soo desu nee, go-sen-en nara kaimasu kedo . . .*
   そうですねえ、五千円なら買いますけど……
   (Well . . ., if it is five thousand yen, I will buy it.)

(6) *Soo shitai nara soo shimashoo.*
そうしたいならそうしましょう。
(If you want to do so, let's do so.)

(7) *Yamada-san ga soo yuu nara sore ga tadashii n ja-nai-deshoo ka.*
山田さんがそう言うならそれが正しいんじゃないでしょうか。
(If Yamada-san says so, wouldn't that be correct?)

(8) *Kimi ga tadashii to omou nara, soo suru yo.*☺M
君が正しいと思うなら、そうするよ。
(If you think it right, I will do it.)

Practice

question, inquiry	N	*shitsumon*	質問
answer	N	*kotae*	答え
to be solved	V	*wakaru*	わかる

Complete the following with the conditions given below.

1. If you come this far, . . .
2. If you ask this question to an American teacher, . . .
3. If it is not expensive, . . .

――― Some Sample Answers ―――
1. *Koko made kureba Hujisan ga yoku miemasu yo.*
ここまで来れば富士山がよく見えますよ。
2. *Amerika-jin no sensei ni tazunereba kono shitsumon no kotae ga wakarimasu yo.*
アメリカ人の先生にたずねればこの質問の答えがわかりますよ。
3. *Takakunakereba katte-ikimashoo ne.*
高くなければ買っていきましょうね。

Additional Information

The conditional phrase *nara(ba)* may also be used to introduce topics as shown in the following examples. Unlike the topic marker *wa* which introduces the topic originating from the speaker, *nara(ba)* introduces topics which have often been suggested by the addressee. The speaker picks up the topic suggested by the addressee and continues by offering his or her personal opinions on the topic.

(a) A: *Kyooto daigaku ni ikoo to omotte-imasu.*
京都大学に行こうと思っています。
(I'm thinking about going to Kyoto University.)

B: *Ano daigaku **nara(ba)** ii benkyoo ga dekimasu yo.*
あの大学**なら**（ば）いい勉強ができますよ。
([lit. if that university] As for that university, you can study well.)

(b) A: *Tashiro-san doo shite-ru-deshoo nee . . .*
田代さんどうしてるでしょうねえ……
(How is Ms. Tashiro doing, I wonder . . .)

B: *Tashiro-san **nara** genki desu yo.*
田代さん**なら**元気ですよ。
(Oh, Ms. Tashiro, she's fine.)

The [-*ba*] conditional is also used in the structure [V + -*ba yokatta*]—with *yokatta* being informal past tense of the [Adj-*i*] *yoi* (or *ii*) 'good'—meaning 'I wish I had done so . . .' For example:

(c) *Paatii ni ike**ba yokatta**.*
パーティーに行け**ばよかった**。
(I wish I went to the party.)

(d) *Denwa-shinakere**ba yokatta**.*
電話しなけれ**ばよかった**。
(I wish I had not called.)

93. Conditional—2. *Tara*

Target Expression

> *If and when you have read this letter, please call right away.*
> ***Kono tegami o yondara sugu denwa-shite-kudasai.***
> この手紙を読んだらすぐ電話してください。
>
> [-*tara*]

Grammatical Explanation

The conditional [-*tara*] has both a temporal and conditional function. [-*Tara*] is formed by [V/Adj informal past + -*ra*] structure. For negation, use *tabenakattara* 'if you don't eat,' which is the product of the same process by changing *nai* to past informal *nakatta*. The [-*tara*] conditional offers several interpretations depending on the types and the tense of the verbs.

1. When the situation expressed in the [-*tara*] clause is certain to happen, temporal interpretation 'when . . .' is appropriate. For example:

   (1a) *Rokuji ni **nattara** kaerimashoo.*
   六時に**なったら**帰りましょう。
   (When it becomes six o'clock, let's go back.)

2. When the situation expressed in the [-*tara*] clause is uncertain, use a conditional interpretation. Thus:

   (2a) *Jikan ga **attara** nomi ni ikimashoo.*
   時間が**あったら**飲みに行きましょう。
   (If there's time, let's go out drinking.)

3. When the main clause is in past tense, temporal reading is appropriate.

   (3a) *Eki ni **tsuitara** sugu Yamamoto sensei ga irasshaimashita.*
   駅に**ついたら**すぐ山本先生がいらっしゃいました。
   (When I arrived at the station, soon Professor Yamamoto came.)

4. When the verb in the [-*tara*] clause is stative, or [-*tara*] occurs with an adjective, only the conditional reading is appropriate.

   (4a) *Kaitai hon ga **attara**, kaimashoo.*
   買いたい本が**あったら**，買いましょう。
   (If there are books you'd like to buy, let's buy some.)

   (4b) ***Takakattara** kawanaide-kudasai.*
   高かったら買わないでください。
   (If it is expensive, please do not buy it.)

When the stative verb is used in the [-*tara*] clause, the main verb is normally non-past.

5. When the action referred to in the main clause is in the past tense, that action must be uncontrollable by the speaker. Thus:

   (5a) **Uchi e kaettara benkyoo-shita.*

   (5b) *Uchi e **kaettara** sugu tomodachi ga kita.*
   家へ**帰ったら**すぐ友だちが来た。
   (When I returned home a friend came right away.)

When using the [-*tara*] clause, two events are always interpreted in the chronological order in which they appear; the [-*tara*] clause event occurs prior to the main clause event, as shown in (5b). However, if the stative verb is involved, the two events may occur simultaneously as in (5c).

(5c) *Uchi e **kaettara** haha ga ita.*
家へ帰ったら母がいた。
(When I returned home, my mother was there.)

Additionally, the [-*tara*] clause can be used independently to express desire. For exmple, *okane ga attara naa/nee* 'I wish I had money . . .' It describes a situation contrary to facts. We will discuss the subjunctive expressions later under a separate entry.

The difference between the [-*tara*] conditional and the [-*ba*] conditional is found in the degree which the speaker assumes that the condition will be realized. Compare the following sentences.

(a) *Haruko-san   ga   **kaette-kitara** kore   o   watashite-kudasai.*
Ms. Haruko   S   return   this   O   please hand
春子さんが帰ってきたらこれをわたしてください。
(If and when Haruko returns, please hand this to her.)

(b) *Haruko-san ga **kaette-kureba** kono mondai no kotae wa wakaru n desu ga . . .*
春子さんが帰ってくればこの問題の答えはわかるんですが……
(If Haruko should return, this problem would be solved.)

In (a) the speaker feels that the condition (of Haruko returning) is likely to be met. In (b), the speaker is less committed as to the possibility of the condition to be met, and communicates that 'if Haruko returns at all,' expressing a greater sense of doubt.

Examples

----
yoroshiku yuu   V   to give regards
　よろしく言う
tamaru　たまる   V   to accumulate, to be saved
kokoa　ココア   N   cocoa
zehi　ぜひ   Adv   by all means
yoru　寄る   V   to stop by, to visit
----

(1) *Jakuson-san ni attara yoroshiku itte-kudasai.*
ジャクソンさんに会ったらよろしく言ってください。
(If and when you see Mr. Jackson, please give my regards.)

(2)   *Uchi ni kaettara sugu denwa ga kimashita.*
家に帰ったらすぐ電話が来ました。
(When I came home, the phone call came immediately.)

(3) A: *Okane ga tamattara Ahurika ryokoo o shitai naa.* ☺
お金がたまったらアフリカ旅行をしたいなあ。
(If and when I save [enough] money, I want to make a trip to
Africa.)

  B: *Soo nee, watashi mo Ahurika e ikitai wa.* ☺F
そうねえ，私もアフリカへ行きたいわ。
(Yeah, I want to go to Africa, too.)

(4)   *Sumimasen ga, kokoa ga nakattara koohii o onegaishimasu.*
すみませんが，ココアがなかったらコーヒーをお願いします。
(If there is no cocoa, I will take coffee, please.)

(5) A: *Shikago ni irasshattara zehi oyori-kudasai.*
シカゴにいらっしゃったらぜひお寄りください。
(If and when you come to Chicago, please stop by.)

  B: *Haa, arigatoo gozaimasu.*
はあ，ありがとうございます。
(Yes, thank you.)

Practice

----
more   Adv   *motto*   もっと
younger   Adj   *motto wakai*   もっと若い
----

1. How would you express the following in Japanese?
    a. If and when you have a lot of money, what do you want to do?
    b. If and when you arrive in New York, please give us a call.
    c. If you have time, please call me.

2. How will you express your unrealizable desires?
    a. to have more money
    b. to be younger
    c. to be living in Colorado

————— Answers —————
1a. *Okane ga takusan attara nani ga shitai-desu ka.*
お金がたくさんあったら何がしたいですか。
b. *Nyuuyooku ni tsuitara denwa-shite-kudasai.*
ニューヨークに着いたら電話してください。

    c. *Jikan ga attara denwa-shite-kudasai.*
    時間があったら電話してください。

2a. *Motto okane ga attara naa . . .*
    もっとお金があったらなあ……

    b. *Motto wakakattara nee . . .*   もっと若かったらねえ……

    c. *Kororado ni sunde-itara naa.*   コロラドに住んでいたらなあ。

Additional Information

The [-*tara*] conditional has an idiomatic use as shown below.

(a) *Atama ga itai nara kaettara doo desu ka.*
    頭が痛いなら帰ったらどうですか。
    (If you have a headache, [lit. how about returning home] why don't
    you go home?)

(b) *Kon'ya wa hayaku netara doo?* ☺
    今夜は早く寝たらどう？
    (How about going to bed early tonight?)

As shown here, -*tara doo (desu ka)?* is an expression of mild invitation and
suggestion. In its colloquial version, the main clause may be totally deleted,
as in *hayaku netara doo?*, which can be shortened further to *hayaku
netara?*

94. Greetings—2. Formulaic Expressions for Special Occasions

Target Expression

> *Take care of yourself.*
>
>   **Odaiji ni.**
>   お大事に。

Strategic Explanation

A number of formulaic phrases are used for greetings at special occasions in
Japan. Greeting with appropriate phrases is important for smooth social interaction. The following expressions are useful.

1. *New Year's celebration:*
   At the end of the year, the latter half of December to those who you will not meet before New Year's Day:

   (1a) *Soredewa yoi otoshi o (omukae kudasai).*
   それではよいお年を（お迎えください）。
   (I wish you'll have a good new year.)

   During New Year's days (Jan. 1 to 3), up through the middle of January, when you meet someone for the first time in the New Year:

   (1b) A: *Akemashite omedetoo gozaimasu. Kotoshi mo yoroshiku onegai-shimasu.*
   明けましておめでとうございます。今年もよろしくお願いします。
   (Happy New Year. [lit. Please treat me kindly.])
   B: *Omedetoo gozaimasu. Kochira koso yoroshiku onegai-shimasu.*
   おめでとうございます。こちらこそよろしくお願いします。
   (Happy New Year. Same here.)

2. *Celebration:*

   (2a) A: *Omedetoo (gozaimasu).*
   おめでとう（ございます）。
   (Congratulations.)
   B: *Arigatoo gozaimasu.*
   ありがとうございます。
   (Thank you.)

   (2b) *(Go)kekkon omedetoo gozaimasu.*
   （ご）結婚おめでとうございます。
   (Congratulations on your wedding.)

   (2c) *Tanjoobi omedetoo.*
   誕生日おめでとう。
   (Happy birthday.)

3. *Seeing someone after a long absence:*

   (3a) A: *Gobusata-shite-orimasu.*
   ごぶさたしております。
   (lit. I haven't <u>seen</u>/<u>written</u> you for a long time.)
   B: *Kochira koso.*
   こちらこそ。
   (Same here.)

(3b)   *Ohisashiburi desu.*
お久しぶりです。
(Long time no see.)

(3c)   A: *Yoo, hisashiburi!* ☺M
よう，久しぶり！
(Hey, how have you been?)

       B: *Hisashiburi nee.* ☺F
久しぶりねえ。
(Long time no see.)

4. *Showing sympathy:*

(4a) A: *Taihen desu nee.*
大変ですねえ。
([lit. It's terrible, isn't it?] It's tough; I sympathize with you.)

      B: *Ee . . .*
ええ……
(Yes . . .)

(4b)   *Sore wa ikemasen nee.*
それはいけませんねえ。
(That's too bad.)

(4c)   *Sore wa zannen desu nee.*
それは残念ですねえ。
([lit. It is regrettable.] I'm sorry to hear that.)

5. *To a sick person:*

(5a)   *Okaze wa ikaga desu ka.*
おかぜはいかがですか。
(How's your cold?)

(5b) A: *Kaze wa doo?* ☺
かぜはどう？
(How is your cold?)

      B: *Okagesama de yoku narimashita.*
おかげさまでよくなりました。
(Thanks to your help, I've gotten well.)

(5c)   *Guai wa doo desu ka.*
具合はどうですか。
([lit. How is your condition?] How are you feeling?)

(5d) A: *Odai ji ni.*
お大事に。
(Please take care.)

B: *Arigatoo gozaimasu.*
ありがとうございます。
(Thanks.)

6. *At a store:*
When a store attendant welcomes a customer or a guest:

(6a)   *Irasshaimase.*
いらっしゃいませ。
(Welcome [to our place].)
—Or *(i)rasshaai!* often spoken by male mom-and-pop storekeepers.

When the customer leaves:

(6b)   Store clerk: *Doomo   arigatoo   gozaimashita.   Mata doozo.*
どうもありがとうございました。またどうぞ。
(Thank you very much. Please come again.)

Customer: *Doomo.*
どうも。
(Bye.)

7. *General greetings in very familiar situations among uchi members:*
(not to be used when addressing your superior)

(7a) A: *Yoo!* ☺M
よう！
(Hi!)

B: *Aa, ohayoo!* ☺
ああ、おはよう！
(Oh, Good morning!)

(7b) A: *Doo? Saikin wa.* ☺
どう？ 最近は。
(How are you doing these days?)

B: *Un, maa maa da ne.* ☺M
うん、まあまあだね。
(So-so.)

(7c) A: *Genki?* ☺
元気？
(How have you been?)

B: *Un, nantoka . . .* ☺
うん，なんとか……
(Oh, I've been fine . . .)

95. Describing State—4. Current State in Reference to Past and Future

The window is open.
Mado ga akete-arimasu.
窓が開けてあります。
I bought drinks (in preparation) for the party.
Paatii no tame no nomimono, katte-okimashita yo.
パーティーのための飲みもの，買っておきましたよ。

[V*te* + -*aru*]
[V*te* + -*oku*]

Grammatical Explanation

The [V*te* + -*aru*] structure

In Japanese there are preferred methods for describing states in relation to the relevant past and present events. Here we concern ourselves with two such expressions. The first is the use of [V*te* + -*aru*] with transitive verbs, especially those that describe volitional action. The pattern [V*te* + -*aru*] indicates a state created as a result of someone's specific action described by the active verb. For example, when describing the window being open, if you wish to convey that someone opened it, *mado ga akete-aru* 'the window (was opened by someone and as a result it) is open' should be used. In other words, this pattern is used when the speaker is conscious of someone having caused the particular state being described. More specifically, there are two situations where [V*te* + -*aru*] is ideally used; first, to focus on the existing result of an action implying that someone performed the action, and second, to focus on the fact that the preparation and/or efforts are made and the resulting state exists. Stative verbs and the *be*-verb are not used in this structure. This pattern cannot be used with the verb that the result of action is not observable or the result is not accumulative. For example, *shinjite-aru* (*shinjiru* 'to believe in') and *utatte-aru* (*utau* 'to sing') are not normally used.

Recall that we learned the [V*te* + -*iru*] structure earlier. Here we contrast the usage of [V*te* + -*aru*] and [V*te* + -*iru*].

	Transitive	*Intransitive*
V*te-iru*	state/action in progress	state/action in progress or, state resulting from an action
	(a) *Mado o akete-iru.* 窓を開けている。	(b) *Mado ga aite-iru.* 窓が開いている。
V*te-aru*	state resulting from an action	not used
	(c) *Mado ga akete-aru.* 窓が開けてある。	

Each of the three sentences appearing above is best used in the following circumstances.

1. When describing the very action of someone opening the window:

    (a) *Mado o akete-iru.*
    窓を開けている。
    ([Someone] is opening the window.)

2. When describing the fact that the window is open, without concern as to who opened it or how it became open:

    (b) *Mado ga aite-iru.*
    窓が開いている。
    (The window is open.)

3. When describing a cause/effect relationship where someone or something opened the window, and as a result the window is open:

    (c) *Mado ga akete-aru.*
    窓が開けてある。
    (The window is opened.)

The [V*te* + -*oku*] structure

Let us examine another useful structure shown in the second target expression using the [V*te* + -*oku*] structure. [V*te* + -*oku*] structure describes a state achieved intentionally for some future purpose. The verbs used in this pattern are only those that describe volitional action. What you cannot control cannot be done intentionally in preparation for future use. As a colloquial version [V*te* + -*oku*] changes to [V + -*toku*], dropping *e* of *te* and combining *t* and the initial *o* of *oku*, for example, *tabetoku* and *asondoku* in casual, fast speech.

Examples

kesu	消す	V	to turn off
kieru	消える	V	to be turned off
keeki	ケーキ	N	cake
hanbun	半分	N	half
nyuugakushiken 入学試験		N	entrance exam
kaigairyokoo	海外旅行	N	travel abroad
renshuu	練習	N	practice
happyoo-suru	発表する	V	to make a presentation
hookoku	報告	N	report

[V*te* + -*aru/iru*]

(1) A: *Terebi keshite!*
テレビ消して！
(Turn off the TV.)

B: *Terebi wa keshite-arimasu yo.*
テレビは消してありますよ。
(The TV *is* off.)

A: *Hontoo?*
本当？
(Really?)

B: *Ee, sakki keshimashita kara.*
ええ，さっき消しましたから。
(Yes, I turned it off a while ago.)

A: *Aa, honto! Kiete-iru wa!*
ああ，ほんと！ 消えているわ！
(Ah, really. It is off.)

(2) A: *Akiko-chan wa?*
あき子ちゃんは？
(Where's Akiko?)

B: *Sakki terebi o mi-nagara nani-ka tabete-ita wa yo.*
さっきテレビを見ながら何か食べていたわよ。
(She was eating something while watching TV a while ago.)

A: *Ara, honto, keeki hanbun tabete-aru wa.*
あら，ほんと，ケーキ半分食べてあるわ。
(Sure enough, the cake is half eaten.)

[V*te* + *-oku*]

(3) *Ashita wa nyuugakushiken no hi da kara, yoku nemutte-okinasai.*
あしたは入学試験の日だから，よく眠っておきなさい。
(Tomorrow is the day for the entrance exam, so sleep well [for that].)

(4) *Shiken ga aru (no) nara yoku benkyoo shite-okinasai yo.*
試験がある(の)ならよく勉強しておきなさいよ。
(If there's an exam, study well [in preparation for it].)

(5) *Kaigairyokoo o suru mae ni yoku eigo no renshuu o shite-okimashita.*
海外旅行をする前によく英語の練習をしておきました。
(Before we traveled abroad, we practiced English [in preparation for it].)

(6) A: *Ashita no kaigi de happyoo-suru hookoku wa moo kaite-arimasu ka.*
あしたの会議で発表する報告はもう書いてありますか。
(Is the report to be presented at tomorrow's meeting written already?)

B: *Ee, moo senshuu kaite-okimashita kara daijoobu desu.*
ええ，もう先週書いておきましたから大丈夫です。
(Yes, I wrote it last week, so it should be fine.)

Practice

air-conditioning	N	*reiboo*	冷房
to break down	V	*koshoo-suru*	故障する
airplane ticket	N	*kookuuken*	航空券
body	N	*karada*	体
to train	V	*kitaeru*	きたえる

How would you express the following in Japanese?

1. Since the air-conditioning broke down, (someone opened the window of the train and now) the windows are open.
2. (Someone prepared dinner so) dinner is prepared.
3. (Did you already purchase the airplane ticket and) is it purchased?
4. When you are young, train your body (for future).
5. Please read this by tomorrow (implying in preparation for tomorrow's meeting—addressing your senior).

--- Answers ---

1. *Reiboo ga koshoo-shita node densha no mado ga akete-arimasu.* 冷房が故障したので電車の窓が開けてあります。
2. *Bangohan no junbi ga shite-arimasu.*
   晩ごはんの準備がしてあります。
3. *Kookuuken wa katte-arimasu ka.* 航空券は買ってありますか。
4. *Wakai toki karada o kitaete-okinasai.*
   若い時体をきたえておきなさい。
5. *Ashita made ni kore o yonde-oite-itadakemasen-deshoo ka.*
   あしたまでにこれを読んでおいていただけませんでしょうか。

96. Compliments and Compliment Responses

Target Expressions

> *Your Japanese is very good.*
> > **Nihongo (o)joozu desu ne.**
> > 日本語（お）上手ですね。
> *Oh, no, I still have a lot to learn.*
> > **Iie, mada mada desu.**
> > いいえ，まだまだです。

Strategic Explanation

Often in American culture people comment on your clothing or other visual signs (such as hairstyle) and offer compliments like ''I like your sweater.'' These compliments express friendliness and are used to ''break the ice'' in conversation. In Japan, however, it is rare to call attention to another person's wardrobe or hairstyle in order to ''break the ice'' or to start a conversation. Among close friends compliments on clothing are made, but usually only when it is somehow relevant to the topic of the talk. More often than not a person's skill or intelligence becomes the object of compliments in Japanese conversation. Japanese people love to comment on foreigners' ability to speak Japanese. (Remember these *are* compliments; so one should take them with a grain of salt.) But even so, how should one respond to these well-meaning compliments?

The typical response to a compliment in Japanese is to deny it. Instead of saying "Thank you" which is common in American English, something in the order of '*iie, soo de mo nai n desu, maa maa desu* (lit. no, not so [nice], but I guess it's fine)' is commonly voiced. The word *maa* means 'a little,' or 'more or less.' It often appears in a pair as *maa maa (desu)* 'it's OK, more or less.' An English equivalent to the straight interpretation of *maa maa* is the American gesture of holding out a hand in front of you with palm facing down and flapping it several times. I have seen this in answer to a question like 'how do you like the new project?' Of course in Japanese *maa maa* can be used even when everything is going very well if you want to humbly minimize your glorious success.

In response to compliments, usually something negative about the item being complimented is added in one's response. At first you may think this strategy "spoils" the good feeling, but compliment response in Japanese is part of the public humility face that a Japanese person likes to wear, and so it should be learned with care since the incorrect "thank you" response actually "spoils" the compliment-giving sentiment.

As you may guess, Japanese do readily accept compliments from family members or close friends. Simple responses such as *ee, maa* 'yeah, I guess' may suffice in such cases. Some people even boast a little! But in the company of those people with whom you have to show modesty and reserve, it is best not to accept a compliment unconditionally. As shown in the target expressions, it is recommended that you show modesty by expressing in some way that you still have a lot to achieve. Saying something like *ee, sensei no okage desu* 'with the help from the teacher . . .' is also favorably accepted.

Examples

(o)ryoori	（お）料理	N	cooking
mada	まだ	Adv	not yet
semai	せまい	Adj	small (in space)
minasan	みなさん	N	you all

(1)　A: *Oryoori ga joozu desu nee.*
　　　お料理が上手ですねぇ。
　　　(You are an excellent cook.)

B: *Iie, mada mada.*
いいえ，まだまだ。
(No, not yet, at all.)

(2) A: *Shizuka de ii-desu nee.*
静かでいいですねえ。
(It's quiet and nice, isn't it?)

B: *Ee, maa. Demo semai n desu yo.*
ええ，まあ。でもせまいんですよ。
(I guess. But it's so small.)

(3) A: *Nihongo ojoozu desu nee.*
日本語お上手ですねえ。
(Your Japanese is very good.)

B: *Soo desu ka, minasan no okage desu.*
そうですか，みなさんのおかげです。
(Really? Well, thanks to you all . . .)

Practice

---

handwriting, character	N	*ji* 字
place of residence	N	*(o)sumai*
		（お）住まい

How would you compliment?
1. excellent (or wonderful) handwriting
2. a nice residence

How would you respond to the following compliments?
3. *Kanji o takusan shitte-imasu nee.*
4. *Tenisu (o)joozu desu nee.*

——— Some Sample Answers ———
1. *Subarashii ji desu nee.*   すばらしい字ですねえ。
2. *Rippana osumai desu nee.*   立派なお住まいですねえ。
3. *Iie, mada mada desu kedo . . .* いいえ，まだまだですけど……
4. *Iya, iya, mada korekara desu yo.*
いや，いや，まだこれからですよ。

97. Particles—4. *Mo* Revisited

Target Expressions

> *It took FIVE hours (surprisingly).*
> **Go-jikan mo kakatta n da yo.** ☺ **M**
> 五時間もかかったんだよ。
> **Go-jikan mo kakatta no yo.** ☺ **F**
> 五時間もかかったのよ。

Grammatical Explanation

We studied the topic marking particle *mo* earlier. *Mo* also appeared in combination with interrogative words such as *dare-mo*, meaning 'no one' in negative statements. *Mo* has additional functions; we will study and review here how *mo* is used for a variety of purposes.

(o)shoogatsu お正月		N	New Year's days (Jan. 1 to 3)
banshuu	晩秋	N	late fall
sugiru	過ぎる	V	to pass
iyoiyo	いよいよ	Adv	all the more, increasingly
shotoo	初冬	N	early winter
kehai	気配	N	sign, indication
saru	猿	N	monkey
ochiru	落ちる	V	to fall down
kakaru	かかる	V	to take (time)
ippai da	一杯だ	V	to be filled

1. A general meaning of 'additionalness' or 'also' and for the purpose of enumeration:
   (*Mo* connects nominals; for connecting clauses, use the nominalizers *no* or *koto*, which will be studied in Entry 105.)

   (1a) *Watashi **mo** ikitai naa.* ☺
   私も行きたいなあ。
   (I want to go, too.)

   (1b) *(O)shoogatsu ni wa ani **mo** imooto **mo** hurusato ni kaette-kimasu.*

お正月には兄も妹もふるさとに帰ってきます。
(For New Year's, both my elder brother and younger sister will return to our home town.)

(1c) *Benkyoo **mo** shigoto **mo** taisetsu desu.*
勉強も仕事も大切です。
(Study and work are both important.)

2. Pointing out the coming and passing of seasons or things in general:

(2a) *Banshuu **mo** sugi, iyoiyo shotoo no kehai desu ga . . .* ◆
晩秋も過ぎ，いよいよ初冬の気配ですが……
(Late fall is over and it is already the beginning of winter . . .)

3. Equivalent to 'even':

(3a) *Saru **mo** ki kara ochiru.* (Proverb)
猿も木から落ちる。
(Even monkeys fall from trees.)

(3b) *Sono ko wa muzukashii hon **mo** yomemasu.*
その子はむずかしい本も読めます。
(That child can read even difficult books.)

4. With quantity, meaning 'about':

(4a) *Go-juu-nin **mo** atsumareba ii n desu ga . . .*
五十人も集まればいいんですが……
(If fifty people gather, that would be fine . . .)

5. With quantity, implying surprise over the unexpected quantity (unlike the case of 4 above, this use receives phonological prominence on quantifiers when pronounced):

(5a) *Go-jikan **mo** kakaru n desu yo.*
五時間もかかるんですよ。
(It takes *five* hours.)

6. *Mo* used after interrogative words (see Appendix 6):

With affirmative: 'every'

(6a) *Doko-**mo** ippai desu.*
どこも一杯です。
(Every place is filled [with people].)

With negative: 'not anything,' 'nothing'

(6b) *Nani-**mo** arimasen.*
何もありません。
(There isn't anything.)

Additional Information

Mo can also be added to [V/Adj *te*] to convey the meaning of 'even though.' For example:

(a) *Benkyoo-shite **mo** wakaranai.*
勉強してもわからない。
(Even though I study, I don't understand.)

(b) *Kore wa muzukashikute sensei de **mo** wakaranai.*
これはむずかしくて先生でもわからない。
(This is difficult and even the teacher cannot understand.)

A strictly colloquial version of the gerundive form plus *mo* is the *-tatte* *(-datte)* form. The *-tatte* form is obtained as follows:

All verbs: [Vpast informal + *-tte*]
Adj-*i*: change the final *-i* to *-kutatte*
Adj-*na*: [Adj-*na* informal past + *-tte*]

(c) *Benkyoo-shi**tatte**, wakaranai sa.* ☺
勉強したって，わからないさ。
(Even when you study, you won't understand.)

(d) *Takaku**tatte** kaoo yo.* ☺
高くたって買おうよ。
(Even when it is expensive, let's buy [it anyway].)

(e) *Benri **datte** tooi daroo?* ☺
便利だって遠いだろう？
(Although it is convenient, it is far away, isn't it?)

The [V/Adj *te* + *mo*] can also appear in expressions such as:

(f) *Ame ga hutte **mo** huranakute **mo** ikimasu kara . . .*
雨が降っても降らなくても行きますから……
([Regardless of] whether it rains or not, I will go.)

[V/Adj *te* + *mo*] also appears in expressions of permission, which will be discussed in Entry 110.

98. Word Order—2. Postposing

Target Expression

> *Did you see, Mariko's new car?*
> **Mita? Mariko-san no atarashii kuruma.** ☺
> 見た？まり子さんの新しい車。

Grammatical Explanation

Although we studied that Japanese is a verb-final language (as described in characteristic 1), in spoken discourse there are cases where verbs precede some postposed elements. Postposed sentences may be used as the result of (1) adding something afterward, perhaps realizing there is a need to provide additional information in the postposed phrase, and (2) focusing on the postposed element, when the postposed phrase is pronounced with phonological prominence. Note that sentence-final intonation occurs at the point where a normally ordered sentence ends. In (2) for example, *no* is marked with slightly rising intonation, but *okaasan* is not.

Examples

(1) *Sorede Shinjuku itta n da yo, Suzuki to.* ☺ **M**
それで新宿行ったんだよ，鈴木と。
(So I went to Shinjuku, with Suzuki.[1])

(2) A: *Irasshatta no? Okaasan.* ☺**F**
いらっしゃったの？ お母さん。
(Did she come, your mom?)

B: *Ee, soo na no.* ☺**F**
ええ，そうなの。
(Yeah, she did.)

[1]. Among male friends last names without *-san* are used in very informal situations.

Practice

hikidashi	引き出し	N	drawer
otsuri	おつり	N	change
moo	もう	Adv	already

Create postposed utterances for the following.

1. [*hikidashi no naka, ni, okane, aru*]
2. [*Andaason-san, irassharu, kaisha e*]
3. [*otsuri, morau, moo*]

────── Some Sample Answers ──────

1. *Okane aru yo, hikidashi no naka ni.* ☺
   お金あるよ，引き出しの中に。
2. *Kaisha e irasshaimashita? Andaason-san.*
   会社へいらっしゃいました？ アンダーソンさん。
3. *Moratta? Otsuri, moo.* ☺ もらった？ おつり，もう。

*　　*　　*　　*　　*

"Sono hito no haka desu ka, Zooshigaya ni aru no wa."
「その人の墓ですか，雑司ケ谷にあるのは」

—Natsume, 1951, p.52.

"Is the grave in Zoshigaya that friend's?"

—Kondo, 1941, p.47.

In this expression, the topic of the utterance, *Zooshigaya ni aru no wa* is postposed, although it is not reflected in the English translation.

99. ⁹⁻¹⁻⁹⁸ Guessing with Doubt—*Daroo* and *Kamoshirenai*

Target Expressions

It will probably rain tomorrow.
> ***Ashita wa ame ga huru-daroo.***
> あしたは雨が降るだろう。
> ***Ashita wa ame deshoo.***
> あしたは雨でしょう。

He may be a Japanese.
> ***Nihon-jin kamoshiremasen.***
> 日本人かもしれません。

[V/Adj pre-Aux + *kamoshirenai*]
[V/Adj pre-Aux + *kashira*]

Grammatical Explanation

As we have learned earlier, when conveying doubt, the [-*daroo*] expression along with its formal counterpart [-*deshoo*] is used, sometimes together with the adverb *tabun* 'perhaps.' Although we learned -*daroo* only in the context of future uncertainty, it should be noted that the speaker's uncertainty and imprecision regarding present and past events and states is also expressed by adding -*daroo*. [-*Daroo*] is also used to soften the statement when one wishes to avoid making a definite statement. If your sense of doubt is stronger [-*daroo ka*] is used. [-*Daroo*] follows [V/Adj pre-Aux] form. Since -*daroo* is the tentative equivalent of *da*, when the *be*-verb appears, *daroo* is used in the place of *da*.

For females only, an expression using [*kashira*] is optional. [*Kashira*] is preceded by [V/Adj pre-Aux] forms. A similar expression used by both genders is [V/Adj pre-Aux form + *ka na*]. This pattern is close to the English phrase 'I wonder. . .'

Another structure using an [Aux Adj], *kamoshirenai*, is often used to indicate that the speaker is guessing. [*Kamoshirenai*] is preceded by [V/Adj pre-Aux] forms, meaning X may be true, or, maybe X. It is used when one doesn't know all the facts, yet may conclude a reasonable likelihood that it is so. *Kamoshirenai* and its formal version *kamoshiremasen* express speculation similar to the English expression of 'might (may) be.' The phrases *moshika suruto* 'if it is,' or *moshika shitara* 'if it should be' may be added to express even greater uncertainty, although one feels that there is some possibility of it. In very casual speech, a shortened version of *kamoshirenai*, *kamo*, may be used.

Examples

| *komu* | 混む | V | to be crowded |
---

(1) A: *Ano hito wa Amerika-jin deshoo ka.*
　　　あの人はアメリカ人でしょうか。
　　　(Is he or she possibly an American?)

　　B: *Soo deshoo.*
　　　そうでしょう。
　　　(Perhaps.)

(2) A: *Kore ikura kashira.*☺F
　　　これいくらかしら。
　　　(I wonder how much this is.)

　　B: *Takasoo nee.* ☺F
　　　高そうねえ。
　　　(It looks expensive.)

(3) A: *Maikeru-san wa itsugoro nihon e kita no kashira nee.* ☺F
   マイケルさんはいつごろ日本へ来たのかしらねえ。
   (I wonder when Michael came to Japan.

   B: *Saa, itsu goro kashira.* ☺F
   さあ，いつごろかしら。
   (I wonder when . . .)

(4) A: *Ashita no paatii, moshika suruto korarenai kamoshirenai.* ☺
   あしたのパーティー，もしかすると来られないかもしれない。
   (I may not be able to come.)

   B: *Watashi mo.* ☺F
   私も。
   (Me, either.)

(5) *Saihu wa densha no naka de otoshita no kamoshiremasen.*[1]
   さいふは電車の中で落としたのかもしれません。
   (I may have dropped my wallet in the train.)

(6) *Ima ninki no aru eiga da kara konde-iru kamoshiremasen yo.*[2]
   今人気のある映画だから混んでいるかもしれませんよ。
   (Since it's a popular movie, it may be crowded.)

[1]. The particle *no* in *no kamoshiremasen* is an example of extended predicate. In this case instead of *no da*, *no kamoshirenai* is used.

[2]. If you are wondering about the *no* in this phrase, recall that the subject marker *ga* is optionally interchanged with *no* within the modifying clause.

Practice

how old	N	*ikutsu, nan-sai*	いくつ，何歳
price	N	*bukka*	物価
to rise	V	*agaru*	上がる

Express your uncertain guess about the following.

1. tomorrow's weather
2. Nancy's age (Try in both male and female styles.) ☺
3. prices rising again
4. (if it doesn't snow tomorrow), not being able to ski
5. her being an American ☺

——— Some Sample Answers ———

1. *Ashita wa tabun yuki ga huru-deshoo.*
あしたはたぶん雪が降るでしょう。
2. *Nanshii-san wa ikutsu kashira.* ☺F
ナンシーさんはいくつかしら。
Nanshii-san wa ikutsu daroo. ☺M
ナンシーさんはいくつだろう。
3. *Bukka wa mata agaru kamoshiremasen yo.*
物価はまた上がるかもしれませんよ。
4. *Ashita yuki ga huranakereba sukii wa dekinai kamoshiremasen.*
あした雪が降らなければスキーはできないかもしれません。
5. *Amerika-jin kamo ne.* ☺ アメリカ人かもね。

Additional Information

-Deshoo is frequently used in questions as in *itsu deshoo (ka)* 'when is it?' instead of *itsu desu ka. Itsu deshoo (ka)* is considered a slightly more friendly expression, as discussed earlier in Entry 23.

100. Language of Emotion—2. Interjections and Exclamations

Target Expression

What! No kidding!

Eh, nani! Masaka!
えっ，なに！ まさか！

Strategic Explanation

Exclaiming in a foreign language requires a solid understanding of the target culture and often is achieved only after considerable experience. After all, without thinking, in situations where we are most vulnerable and excited, our native language seems to appear from nowhere. And of course, if the appropriate expression does not come to your mind instantly, what you will say will sound as if you are reading a memorized statement, a far cry from what exclamatory expressions are meant to convey. Always using the same interjection also reveals a poor command of the language, something one should try hard to avoid. Interjections and exclamations appear, being what they are, almost always in direct informal style. When you have the opportunity to hear Japanese people exclaiming in films or in real situations, observe them closely. Listen to how they say it, and note their facial expressions. You'll want to imitate their manner as well as their tone. Unless delivered just so, these interjections can make people feel uncomfortable.

Interjections and exclamations are used sparingly, if at all, in formal situations. Until you are comfortable, it is best to keep these phrases to a minimum. Here is a list of interjections frequently used for your reference.

1. *Surprise:*

   (1a) *A; Aa* あ；ああ (Oh)
   (1b) *Aree; Oya; Maa* あれえ；おや；まあ   (Oh my!, Why!, Gee whiz!) [female only]
   (1c) *Kyaa!* きゃー！ (*screaming*) [female only]

2. *Surprised at the content of the statement:*

   (2a) *E?* え？ (What?)
   (2b) *Masaka!* まさか！ (No kidding!)
   (2c) *Hee!* へえ！ (Really!)

3. *Doubt:*

   (3a) *Hate na?* はてな？ (I wonder . . .)
   (3b) *Uso!* うそ！ ([lit. lie] I don't believe it!)

4. *Resolving doubt:*

   (4a) *Hee.* へえ。 (Is that right!)
   (4b) *Naruhodo.* なるほど。 (I see.)

5. *Distress:*

   (5a) *Aaa.* あーあ。 (Whew!)
   (5b) *Yare yare.* やれやれ。 (Oh, boy!)

If you are interested in these and other exclamatory expressions, take a look at Japanese comic books. They contain many exclamatory phrases and onomatopoeic words that might interest you.

Examples

boonasu	ボーナス	N	bonus
huroshiki	ふろしき	N	huroshiki (a wrapping cloth)

nante koto da (idiomatic) what a disaster!
何てことだ

----

(1) A: *Kyoo boonasu ga deta n da!*
今日ボーナスが出たんだ！
(I got my bonus today.)

B: *Hee, sore wa yokatta ne.*
へえ，それはよかったね。
(Wow, that's great.)

(2) A: *Kore nani?*
これ何？
(What's this?)

B: *Huroshiki desu yo. Koo tsukau n desu yo.*
ふろしきですよ。こう使うんですよ。
(It's huroshiki. You use it this way.)

A: *Aa, naruhodo ne. Benrina n desu ne.*
ああ，なるほどね。便利なんですね。
(Ah, I see. It's convenient, isn't it?)

B: *Ee, totemo.*
ええ，とても。
(Yes, very much so.)

(3) *Ame ga hurushi, kuruma wa koshoo-surushi . . . aa yare yare, nante koto da!*
雨が降るし，車は故障するし……ああやれやれ，何てことだ！
(It's raining, and the car breaks down on me . . . oh boy, what a disaster!)

Additional Information

Two additional expressions associated with expressions of emotion should be mentioned. First are the so-called exclamatory sentences. Exclamatory sentences in Japanese are not frequently uttered in isolation, but are followed by verbs such as *omou* 'to think,' and are used generally in written language to express the extremity of emotion. It takes the phrase *nante* or *nanto* followed by [Adj prenominal (+ N + na) + n(o) daroo/deshoo] or, *nante/nanto* followed by [Adv + Vinformal + koto ka]. See for example:

(a) *Nante **ii hito na n daroo** to omotta!*
何ていい人なんだろうと思った！
(I thought what a nice person he is!)

(b) *Ano ko wa nanto **utsukushiku natta koto ka**!*
あの子は何と美しくなったことか！
(How beautiful that child has become!)

Another expression is equivalent to the English 'I cannot help. . . ,' or 'I am dying to . . .' It takes [Vstem + *takute* + *tamaranai/tamarimasen*]. *-Takute* is a gerund of *-tai*, an expression of desire that we learned earlier. *Tamaranai* which is always in negative form means 'cannot bear' or 'cannot stand.' For example, *uchi ni kaeritakute tamarimasen* 'I am dying to return home.' Its colloquial version is *uchi ni kaeritakute tamannai.*

101. Responding to Questions—3. Avoiding "No"— Expressions of Doubt and Opposition

Target Expression

> *That is so, but . . .*
>
> > **Sore wa soo desu ga . . .**
> > それはそうですが……

Strategic Explanation

Japanese are known to go to great lengths in their avoidance of saying "no." Although this characterization is not entirely accurate, there is no question that Japanese have a marked preference for avoiding direct confrontation. Naturally if you are an American and are asked whether you are British, a straightforward "no" is appropriate. When the question involves suggestion or request, however, or if the speaker's statement seeks recognition and agreement, even when an American might say "no" straightforwardly, a Japanese may only mildly suggest it. Not saying "no" directly to a person's face is motivated by the feeling that such a direct act of denial lacks consideration and courtesy. Saying "no" in the face of those to whom you are supposed to show respect, therefore, is not a recommendable strategy. Among family members where the *amae* relationship is established, however, the direct "no" is often heard. In this warm and forgiving relationship, self-assertion and selfishness are perhaps unconditionally accepted. In such an environment saying "no" with no accommodation to others' feelings, which sometimes is taken as a sign of immaturity and selfishness, is allowed.

In casual conversation, expressions of doubt such as *soo ka naa* 'I wonder about it' are frequently used to express disagreement as a buffer to any real confrontation. In formal meetings, particularly if one is speaking in Japanese, a flat "no" is almost never the best strategy to express disagreement (especially toward your social superiors). Of course the rationale that straightforward disagreement hurts the other's feelings is not received as readily in America where frankness is considered a virtue. Naturally disagreeing with one's superior in any culture requires tact, but it is fair to say that for Americans, being able to say "no" and being able to express oneself clearly is important. It is precisely this quality that Americans consider trustworthy and reliable. Ironically, this quality of frankness may establish you as "persona non grata" in Japanese circles.

The statement above does not mean that you should never say "no" in Japanese. I am sure there will be times you have to say "no"; the important thing is to remember that disagreeing and refusing take different levels of expressions and different kinds of strategies in Japanese. To respond to requests and suggestions, Japanese use the following strategies.

1. *Expressions implying negative answers:*

   (1a) *Maa, kangaete-okimasu.*
       まあ，考えておきます。
       (I will think about it.)

   (1b) *Maa, mata yoosu o mite to yuu koto de.*
       まあ，また様子を見てということで。
       (Well, we will see what happens . . .)

   When using these expressions, the speaker does not really intend to literally think about the request at a later date.

2. *Using fillers:*
   Use fillers to agree with the speaker first, and then to suggest disagreement, to agree with certain points the speaker has made and disagree with others, or to lessen the impact of the straightforward disagreement.

   (2a) <u>*Gensokuteki ni*</u> <u>*wa*</u> <u>*sansei desu*</u> <u>*kedo*</u> . .
       in principle   T   agreement   but

       <u>*san-ban*</u> <u>*ni tsuite*</u> <u>*oukagaishimasu.*</u>
       number 3   about   inquire

       原則的には賛成ですけど……三番についておうかがいします。
       (I agree with you in principle, but concerning number 3, I would like to ask some questions.)

(2b) *Maa sore wa chotto . . ., watashi wa soo wa omoimasen ga . . .*
まあそれはちょっと……, 私はそうは思いませんが……
(Well, that's a bit [difficult] . . ., I [personally] don't think so.)

(2c) *Soo ka naa, sonna koto nai n ja-nai?* ☺
そうかなあ, そんなことないんじゃない?
(I wonder about that, isn't it the case that it isn't so?)

(2d) *Soo kamoshirenai kedo, watashi wa soo wa omowanai no yo ne.* ☺F
そうかもしれないけど, 私はそうは思わないのよね。
(It may be so, but I [personally] do not think so . . .)

These expressions of doubt are preceded by clausal fillers. This strategy is useful in warning the listener that what follows may be against the listener's opinion. This further warns that the disagreeing opinion to follow is a personal preference and is not necessarily an opinion against the listener's position. Also in the first example, the first-person pronoun which is normally deleted is used to express 'I personally.'

3. *Disagreement equivalent to English "I doubt it":*

(3a) *Soo deshoo ka./Soo desu ka nee./Soo kashira.* (female only)
そうでしょうか。/そうですかねえ。/そうかしら。
(lit. I wonder if that is so.)

Some of the strategies introduced above must certainly be familiar to the reader; these are not uniquely Japanese. In fact there are many indirect, suggestive ways to say "no" in English. I have heard people say things like "I don't feel too warm toward that idea, you know" or "It's interesting. But frankly I don't feel quite so enthusiastic about it." Even still, Japanese avoidance of confrontation and opposition in all aspects of life is overall much stronger than it is for Americans, especially in formal situations.

Another general strategy useful for disagreement in Japanese is to increase the frequency of response-seeking interactional particles. *Nee*, for example, serves to bond the participants of conversation and helps create empathy and rapport even while expressing disagreement.

Practice

irasuto	イラスト	N	illustration (art work)
namakemono	なまけもの	N	a lazy person
purojekuto	プロジェクト	N	project

How will you express doubt or your disagreement about the following?

1. *Kono irasuto raishuu made ni dekimasu ka.*
   このイラスト来週までにできますか。

2. *Sumimasen ga zehi onegai-shimasu.*
   すみませんがぜひお願いします。

3. *Yamada-san wa hontoo wa namakemono desu yo.*
   山田さんは本当はなまけものですよ。

4. *Kono purojekuto wa sugu hajimeta hoo ga ii desu nee.*
   このプロジェクトはすぐ始めた方がいいですねえ。

——— Some Sample Answers ———

1. *Raishuu desu ka. Maa sore wa chotto . . .*
   来週ですか。まあそれはちょっと……

2. *Soo desu nee, maa, kangaete-okimasu.*
   そうですねえ，まあ，考えておきます。

3. *Soo deshoo ka nee.* そうでしょうかねえ。

4. *Ee, maa . . . demo doo deshoo ka. Sukoshi matta hoo ga ii n janai-deshoo ka.*
   ええ，まあ……でもどうでしょうか。少し待った方がいいんじゃ
   ないでしょうか。

102. Particles—5. *Ka* Revisited

Target Expression

I don't know whether she is a student, but . . .
Gakusei ka doo ka shiranai kedo . . . ☺
学生かどうか知らないけど……

Grammatical Explanation

The question marker *ka* is used in various structures and needs special summing-up. *Ka* is used for signaling questions and in combination with negation it functions as an expression of invitation. Beyond these two basic functions there are roughly four different places you will find *ka*.

---
shiraberu	調べる	V	to examine
kimeru	決める	V	to decide
ikiru	生きる	V	to live
---

1. *After interrogative words:*
   Adds the meaning of 'any' or 'some.' (See Appendix 6 for the list.)

   (1a) **Dare-ka** *imasu ka.*
   誰かいますか。
   (Is anyone there?)

   (1b) A: **Nani-ka** *tsumetai nomimono demo ikaga desu ka.*
   何か冷たい飲みものでもいかがですか。
   (How about something cold to drink?)
   B: *Sumimasen.*
   すみません。
   (Thank you.)
   A: *Juusu ka* **nani-ka.**
   ジュースか何か。
   (Juice or something?)
   B: *Dewa, orenji juusu onegaishimasu.*
   では、オレンジジュースお願いします。
   (Then, I would like some orange juice.)

2. *In subordinate questions:*
   When questions with question words become subordinate clauses, they are followed by *ka*. For yes/no questions, *ka* and *ka doo ka* 'whether or not' are used. It is also possible to form alternate questions by using negation as in (2b). When *da* appears immediately preceding *ka*, delete it; there is no combination *da ka*.

   (2a) A: *Sore ga hontoo* **ka doo ka** *moo ichido oshirabe-itashi-mashoo.*
   それが本当かどうかもう一度お調べいたしましょう。
   (I will examine whether [or not] that is true.)
   B: *Soo desu ka. Jaa sumimasen ga onegai shimasu.*
   そうですか。じゃあ、すみませんがお願いします。
   (Oh, thanks. I'd appreciate it.)

(2b)　A:　*Raishuu no ryokoo ni irasshaimasu ka.*
　　　　　来週の旅行にいらっしゃいますか。
　　　　　(Are you going on a trip next week?)

　　　B:　*Mada iku **ka** ikanai **ka** kimete-nai n desu . . .*
　　　　　まだ行く**か**行かない**か**決めてないんです……
　　　　　(I haven't decided yet whether we go or not.)

3.　*For expressing uncertainty and doubt:*

(3a)　　*Soo deshoo **ka**.*
　　　　そうでしょう**か**。
　　　　(I wonder if it is so.)

(3b)　A:　*Junbi-nasatte-oita hoo ga yoroshii n ja-nai deshoo **ka**.*
　　　　　準備なさっておいた方がよろしいんじゃないでしょう**か**。
　　　　　(Wouldn't it be better to prepare [for the future] beforehand?)

　　　B:　*Soo kamoshiremasen nee.*
　　　　　そうかもしれませんねえ。
　　　　　(I guess so.)

(3c)　A:　*Junbi-shite-oita hoo ga ii n ja-nai **ka** to omoimasu ga . . .*
　　　　　準備しておいた方がいいんじゃない**か**と思いますが……
　　　　　(I think it would be better to prepare [for the future] beforehand.)

　　　B:　*Soo deshoo **ka** . . .*
　　　　　そうでしょう**か**……
　　　　　(I wonder about that . .)

4.　*Presenting alternatives:*

(4a)　A:　*Kaigi ga aru n desu yo.*
　　　　　会議があるんですよ。
　　　　　(There's a meeting.)

　　　B:　*Doko de?*
　　　　　どこで？
　　　　　(Where?)

　　　A:　*Tookyoo **ka** Yokohama de.*
　　　　　東京**か**横浜で。
　　　　　(Either in Tokyo or Yokohama.)

　　　B:　*Soo desu ka. Itsu?*
　　　　　そうですか。いつ？
　　　　　(Is that so? When?)

A: *Raishuu no kayoobi **ka** suiyoobi.*
来週の火曜日**か**水曜日。
(Either next Tuesday or Wednesday.)

(4b) A: *Ueda-san **ka** Hayashi-san ni kite-moratte.*
上田さん**か**林さんに来てもらって。
(Have either Ms. Ueda or Ms. Hayashi come [here].)

B: *Ueda-san mo Hayashi-san mo doko-ka itte rusu desu ga*
. . .
上田さんも林さんもどこか行って留守ですが……
(Both Ms. Ueda and Ms. Hayashi are out somewhere
. . .)

(4c) *Ikiru **ka** shinu **ka**, sore ga mondai da.* ♦
生きる**か**死ぬ**か**，それが問題だ。
(To live or to die, that is the question.)

103. Expressing One's Intentions—*Tsumori*

Target Expression

> *I intend to finish this job by tomorrow.*
> ***Asu made ni kono shigoto o shiageru tsumori desu kara.***
> あすまでにこの仕事を仕上げるつもりですから。
>
> [Vinformal non-past + *tsumori*]

Grammatical Explanation

Since the word *tsumori* 'intention' is a pseudo-noun, it might be best to
think of this structure as a clausal explanation of the noun. There are two
distinct [*tsumori*] structures. The first type appears following [Vinformal
non-past] and it expresses intentions or personal expectations. For this type
of [*tsumori*], only verbs referring to controllable action can be used. You
cannot intend to do things that you cannot possibly control. [*Tsumori*] cannot be used alone; it has to be modified either by a demonstrative or a
clause. It is usually followed by the copula *da*, but occasionally it occurs in

the [*tsumori ga aru*] or [*tsumori wa nai*] structure. For negation use [*tsumori dewa-nai*]. Or, use the negative form of the [Vinformal non-past] preceding [*tsumori*], as shown in example (3).

The second use of [*tsumori*] occurs when it appears following [V/Adj pre-nominal] forms, excluding [Vnon-past]. In this use, *da* is possible and takes the [pre-nominal] form including non-past tense. This *tsumori* is associated with "impression" or "to think" or "to mean to be/to pretend to be." For negating purposes, normally negation of the verb preceding *tsumori* is used.

Examples

(1) A: *Rainen nihon e iku tsumori desu ka.*
来年日本へ行くつもりですか。
(Do you intend to go to Japan next year?)
B: *Ee, sono tsumori desu ga . . .*
ええ，そのつもりですが……
(Yes, I intend to.)

(2) *Kondo no nichiyoobi kaisha e kuru tsumori.* ☺
今度の日曜日会社へ来るつもり。
(I intend to come to the office this coming Sunday.)

(3) A: *Moo ano hito to wa ryokoo-shinai tsumori.* ☺
もうあの人とは旅行しないつもり。
(I intend not to travel with him.)
B: *Dooshite?* ☺
どうして？
(Why not?)

(4) A: *Ashita kaeru tsumori de orimasu ga . . .*
あした帰るつもりでおりますが……
(I intend to return tomorrow.)
B: *Aa, soo desu ka. Jaa minasan ni yoroshiku.*
ああ，そうですか。じゃあみなさんによろしく。
(Oh I see. Please give my regards to everyone.)

(5) *Isshookenmei benkyooshita tsumori desu ga . . .*
いっしょうけんめい勉強したつもりですが……
(I think I studied hard, but . . .)

(6) *Ano hito piano ga joozuna tsumori na n da yo.* ☺M
あの人ピアノが上手なつもりなんだよ。
(She/he thinks she/he is good at playing the piano.)

Additional Information

Similar expressions of personal intentions are available by using nouns *yotei* and *keikaku*, both meaning 'plan.' The [Vinformal non-past + *yotei/keikaku* + *da/ga aru*] structure expresses 'plan to do . . .' For example, *ashita wa hayaku kaeru yotei desu* 'I plan to return early,' or *Oosaka e iku keikaku wa arimasen yo* 'there isn't a plan to go to Osaka.' Grammatically, when using these patterns, think of them as extended [clausal modifier + N] structures.

Practice

all night	Adv	*hitobanjuu*	一晩中
winter vacation	N	*huyuyasumi*	冬休み

Express your intentions to do the following.
1. to return at seven in the evening
2. to study all night
3. not to clean the room today

Ask about your friend's intentions or plans to do the following. How would your friend respond?
4. what to do during the winter vacation
5. when to return to Boston ☺
6. to take the kids along ☺

―――― Some Sample Answers ――――

1. *Yuugata shichi-ji ni kaette-kuru tsumori desu.*
   夕方七時に帰ってくるつもりです。

2. *Hitobanjuu benkyoo-suru tsumori na n desu.*
   一晩中勉強するつもりなんです。

3. *Kyoo wa heya no sooji wa shinai tsumori desu.*
   今日は部屋のそうじはしないつもりです。

4. A: *Huyuyasumi wa nani o suru tsumori desu ka.*
   冬休みは何をするつもりですか。

   B: *Huyuyasumi nee, mada kimete-nai kedo . . .*
   冬休みねえ，まだ決めてないけど……

5. *Nee, itsu Bosuton e kaeru keikaku/yotei?* ☺
   ねえ，いつボストンへ帰る計画/予定？

6. A: *Kodomosan o tsurete-iku tsumori?* ☺
   子供さんを連れていくつもり？

   B: *Ee, soo suru tsumori.* ☺ ええ，そうするつもり。

104. Pointing Out Facts as a Natural Course of Events
—*Hazu*

(Is Professor Yamada coming to his office today?)
Yes, he is supposed to come today.
Ee, irassharu hazu desu ga . . .
ええ，いらっしゃるはずですが……

[V/Adj pre-nominal + *hazu*]

Grammatical Explanation

As in the pattern of *tsumori* and *yotei/keikaku*, [*hazu*] is also a noun normally modified by demonstratives or clauses. It is preceded by [V/Adj prenominal] forms. When using [*hazu*], the speaker expects and anticipates events and facts as a natural outcome, based on the objective conditions and situation that the speaker has direct access to. The speaker has every reason to believe that things will turn out just as expected—equivalent to the English expression of "what ought naturally be true," or "what one would normally expect." It is often translated into the English 'is expected to,' 'is supposed to,' or 'should' for convenience. For negation, *Aoki-san wa konai hazu da* 'it is expected that Mr. Aoki will not come.' and its formal version, *konai hazu desu* are used. Negation of *hazu* itself is also used, as in *Aoki-san wa kuru hazu ga nai* 'there is no likelihood that Mr. Aoki will come.'

Kuru hazu ga nai is a strong negative assertion indicating no possibility of Aoki coming in, whereas the [*konai hazu da*] negation implies some possibility that Aoki might come.

The [*hazu*] structure is different from the pattern using *beki* which is also translated into the English 'should.' In the case of *beki*, 'should' is used in a sense of obligation, literally 'ought to.' We will study *beki* in Entry 106. As in the case of 'can,' the English 'should' has many distinctive meanings and therefore we must avoid equating *hazu* merely with 'should.'

Examples

nesage	値下げ	N	price reduction
shuppi	出費	N	expense

gookei	合計	N	total, sum
roopu	ロープ	N	rope
joobuna	丈夫な	Adj	strong, durable

----

(1)　　*Haha wa yo-ji han made ni modotte-kuru hazu desu.*
母は四時半までにもどってくるはずです。
(My mother is supposed to be back by 4:30.)

(2)　A: *Anoo, kono aida onegai-shita kozutsumi desu ga . . .*
あのう，この間お願いした小包みですが……
(Excuse me, about the package I requested the other day . . .)

　　B: *Sono kozutsumi wa moo tsuite-iru hazu desu ga . . .*
その小包みはもう着いているはずですが……
(That package should have arrived by now . . .)

　　A: *Iya, sore ga mada tsuite-inai n desu yo.*
いや，それがまだ着いていないんですよ。
(Not really, it has not arrived yet.)

　　B: *Sonna hazu wa arimasen ga nee . . .*
そんなはずはありませんがねえ……
(It shouldn't be so . . .)

(3)　A: *Takai-desu nee.*
高いですねえ。
(It's expensive, isn't it?)

　　B: *Saikin nesage ga atta hazu desu ga . . .*
最近値下げがあったはずですが……
(There should have been a price reduction recently.)

(4)　　*Shuppi no gookei wa yaku go-man-en no hazu desu ga . . .*
出費の合計は約五万円のはずですが……
(The total of the expense is expected to be approximately fifty
thousand yen.)

(5)　　*Joobuna hazu da kedo nee, kono roopu wa.* ☺M
丈夫なはずだけどねえ，このロープは。
(This rope, you know, it is expected to be durable.)

Practice

You have access to information that the following are to happen. How will
you express that "is-supposed-to" feeling?

1. Professor Yamamoto to come with her husband
2. the train to arrive at 5:00
3. this restaurant's food to be delicious

——————— Answers ———————

1. *Yamamoto sensei wa goshujin to irassharu hazu desu ga.*
   山本先生はご主人といらっしゃるはずですが。

2. *Ressha wa go-ji ni tsuku hazu desu ga . . .*
   列車は五時に着くはずですが……

3. *Kono resutoran no ryoori wa oishii hazu desu.*
   このレストランの料理はおいしいはずです。

Additional Information

Hazu is also used to mean 'no wonder,' or 'it makes sense.' See the example below paying attention to the semantic context.

(a) <u>*Kore*</u>   *wa*   <u>*jookyuu*</u>   <u>*no*</u>   *mondai*   *desu*   *kara*
    this   T   upper class   L   question   is   since

    <u>*muzukashii hazu desu.*</u>
    difficult

これは上級の問題ですからむずかしいはずです。

(Since this is a question for the advanced level, no wonder it is difficult.)

105.   Nominalization of a Clause—*Koto* and *No*

Target Expression

> *It is difficult to keep promises.*
> **Yakusoku o mamoru koto wa muzukashii-desu.**
> 約束を守ることはむずかしいです。
>
>   [*koto*] [*no*]

Grammatical Explanation

The two devices, *koto* 'fact(s), intangible things' and *no* 'thing(s), one(s),' are nominalizers which make clauses into noun phrases. In English there are ways to make a clause into a grammatical noun: by using *that* in forming a that-clause (that I keep promises), by attaching *to* (to keep promises) and by making a verb into a gerundive form (keeping promises). [*No*] is used for nominalizing concrete actions or events, whereas [*koto*] nominalizes the clause which refers to actions or events in more abstract, indirect or general ways. The [*no*] clause is used to express facts directly and immediately as perceived, while the [*koto*] clause is used to express a formal and more distant feeling, pointing out facts reached after giving the matter some thought. Simply put, *utau koto* refers to the general meaning of 'singing' while *utau no* refers to a specific case of someone 'singing.' If the main verb requires concrete immediate action such as *mieru* 'to be seen,' or *kikoeru* 'to be heard,' the nominalizer *no* is required. *Koto* is often used with verbs connoting a deductive or abstract thinking process.

Koto and *no* are preceded by [V/Adj pre-nominal] forms, except when the verb immediately preceding is [N + *da*]. In such a case instead of taking the pre-nominal form *no*, it takes [N *da to yuu*] before *koto* and it takes [N *na*] before *no*. By making clauses into grammatical nouns, you can insert a clause in place of a noun. Mastering the nominalizers *koto* and *no* opens various possibilities. For example, you can expand the use of *sukina* as shown below.

(a) *Terebi de yakyuu o miru **no** ga suki da.*
テレビで野球を見る**の**が好きだ。
(I like to watch baseball on television.)

Recall the expression of potential, [*koto ga dekiru*]. In that structure *koto* is in fact a nominalizer. So is *no* in the extended predicate [*no da*] expression.

Examples

te	手	N	hand
huru	振る	V	to wave
yameru	やめる	V	to stop

(1) *Yasuda-san ga te o hutte-iru no ga miemasu.*
安田さんが手を振っているのが見えます。
(I can see Yasuda waving.)

(2) *Yoru osokatta node Sumisu-san ni denwa-suru no wa yamemashita.*
夜遅かったのでスミスさんに電話するのはやめました。
(I did not call Mr. Smith because it was late at night.)

(3) *Yuu koto wa kantan desu ga, suru koto wa muzukashii-desu nee.*
言うことは簡単ですが，することはむずかしいですねえ。
(It is easy to say but is difficult to do.)

(4) *Koronbusu ga Amerika o hakken-shita koto wa dare de mo shitte-imasu yo.*
コロンブスがアメリカを発見したことはだれでも知っていますよ。
(Everyone knows that Columbus discovered America.)

(5) *Benkyoo-suru no mo shinai no mo kimi no jiyuu sa.*
勉強するのもしないのも君の自由さ。
(Whether you study or not is up to you.)

Practice

```
-------------------------------------------------------------
truth            N      shinjitsu    真実
quit smoking     V      tabako o yameru
                        たばこをやめる
-------------------------------------------------------------
```

How will you express the following in Japanese? Use either *koto* or *no* for nominalizing the underlined clauses.

1. It is difficult to know the truth.
2. From here I can see trains go by.
3. Is it difficult to quit smoking?

———— Answers ————

1. *Shinjitsu o shiru koto wa muzukashii.*
真実を知ることはむずかしい。
2. *Koko kara densha ga tooru no ga miemasu.*
ここから電車が通るのが見えます。
3. *Tabako o yameru koto wa muzukashii-desu ka.*
たばこをやめることはむずかしいですか。

Additional Information

Koto may be used as a regular noun, meaning '(intangible) thing(s)' or 'fact(s).' For example:

(a) *Sensei ga osshatta koto wa ima demo oboete-orimasu.*
先生がおっしゃったことは今でも覚えております。
(I still remember what the teacher said.)

(b) *Iyana koto wa wasuremashoo.*
いやなことは忘れましょう。
(Let's forget unpleasant things.)

Adding *koto* to nouns can make the noun more abstract, making the statement less blatant. For example, instead of saying *Taroo-san ga suki* 'I like Taro,' *Taroo-san no koto ga suki* 'I like (things about) Taro' is preferred because it points out facts in a more abstract way.

106. Social Responsibility—*Beki*

When young, you ought to work hard.
Wakai toki wa isshookenmei hataraku beki da. ♦
若い時はいっしょうけんめい働くべきだ。

[Vbasic + *beki*]

Grammatical Explanation

Beki is used in the pattern [Vbasic + *beki* + *da*] and expresses social responsibility. When *beki* is preceded by [Adj-*na*] and the *be*-verb, instead of *da*, *dearu* is used. If it is preceded by [Adj-*i*], it takes the adverbial form of the adjective—*wakaku* instead of *wakai*—followed by *aru*. [*Beki*] is a prenominal form of literary *beshi*. It points out that such action is an obligation that should be followed as a rule and as an action naturally expected of a person. [*Beki*] can modify nouns directly; for example, *kaku beki tegami* 'the letter that ought to (or, should) be written.' *Beki* sentences may be translated into English 'ought to,' 'be supposed to,' or 'should.'

It is possible to form the past tense by [Vbasic + *beki* + *datta*], meaning 'ought to have' and 'should have.' For negation of *beki* sentences, negate [*beki*] to [*beki dewa-nai*] or [*beki dewa-nakatta*]. The phrase [*dewa*] as elsewhere may be shortened to [*ja*], as in [*beki ja-nai*].

Examples

```
----------------------------------------------------------
soodan-suru   相談する   V     to consult
----------------------------------------------------------
```

(1)   *Isogashii hi wa asa hayaku okiru beki da.* ◆
忙しい日は朝早く起きるべきだ。
(On busy days, you ought to get up early.)

(2) A: *Muzukashii mondai wa dare-ka ni soodan-suru beki deshoo?*
むずかしい問題は誰かに相談するべきでしょう？
(Shouldn't we consult someone about the difficult problems?)

    B: *Demo dare ni?*
でも誰に？
(But whom?)

    A: *Mazu sensei ni soodan-suru beki deshoo ne.*
まず先生に相談するべきでしょうね。
(First you should consult your teacher.)

(3) A: *Yomu beki hon wa takusan aru kedo, isogashikute zenzen yomenai n desu.*
読むべき本はたくさんあるけど，忙しくて全然読めないんです。
(There are so many books I should read, but I can't read them because I'm too busy.)

    B: *Soo desu ka. Demo, gakusei nara mainichi sukoshi demo yomu beki desu yo.*
そうですか。でも，学生なら毎日少しでも読むべきですよ。
(Is that so? But since you're a student, you should read a little bit every day.)

(4)   *Motto benkyoo-shite-oku beki datta.* ☺
もっと勉強しておくべきだった。
(I ought to have studied more thoroughly.)

(5)   *Sonna koto suru beki ja-nai yo.* ☺
そんなことするべきじゃないよ。
(You shouldn't do such a thing.)

(6)   *Ningen wa itsumo tadashiku aru beki desu.*
人間はいつも正しくあるべきです。
(A person should always be righteous.)

Practice

others	N	*hoka no hito*	他の人

Express that you feel the following ought to be done as a social responsibility and as an action naturally expected of a decent person.

1.   to prepare before the guest arrives

342

2. to assist others when one can
3. to have called before visiting

──────── Some Sample Answers ────────

1. *Okyaku-san ga irassharu mae ni junbi-shite-oku beki desu.*
   お客さんがいらっしゃる前に準備しておくべきです。
2. *Dekiru toki ni wa hoka no hito no shigoto o tetsudau beki desu.* できる時には他の人の仕事を手伝うべきです。
3. *Iku mae ni denwa-suru beki deshita.*
   行く前に電話するべきでした。

107. Social and Personal Obligation

Target Expression

> *I must get to Tokyo station by eight o'clock.*
> **Hachi-ji made ni Tookyoo-eki e ikanakereba narimasen.**
> 八時までに東京駅へ行かなければなりません。
>
> [*-nakereba naranai*]
> [*-nakereba ikenai*]

Grammatical Explanation

Duty and obligation in Japanese are expressed indirectly by using the negative conditional *-ba*, that is, the [*-nakereba*] form, and negation of [V/Adj *te*], that is, the [*-nakute wa*] form. Literally these expressions mean 'if you do not do this, it is not good, or it bothers me,' and is normally translated into the English auxiliary verb 'must.' The expression *-nakereba naranai* describes absolute obligation as described in a law; *kono tatemono ni hairu ni wa kyoka o enakereba naranai* 'you must obtain permission to enter this building.' It also describes logical truth; *wareware wa kanarazu shinanakereba naranai* 'without doubt we must die.' Obligation and duty patterns include:

-*nakereba naranai*
-*nakute wa naranai*
-*nakereba ikenai*
-*nakute wa ikenai*

Among expressions, the [-*nakereba ikenai*] structure is often used to offer advice, give orders, or to make an emphatic request from one's social subordinates. It is addressed directly to the listener. On the other hand, the [-*nakereba naranai*] pattern is frequently used with the first-person subject; it has an explanatory function in that it often implies that one must do certain things due to legal or personal obligations.

The difference between [*beki*] and [-*nakereba naranai*] is that while [*beki*] points out one's social responsibility as an action expected from a person, [-*nakereba naranai*] provides a straightforward command with the purpose of controlling and restricting human behavior. For example, when conveying that the cars ought to (must) be driven on the left side in Japan, we must use -*nakereba naranai*.

Examples

shokuba	職場	N	job, employment
kaban	かばん	N	bag
ookisa	大きさ	N	size
taisetsuna	大切な	Adj	precious

(1) *Atarashii shokuba desu kara, isshookenmei hatarakanakereba narimasen.*
新しい職場ですから，いっしょうけんめい働かなければなりません。
(Because it is a new job, I must work hard.)

(2) *Moo ikanakereba (narimasen) . . .*
もう行かなければ(なりません)……
(I must be going now . . .)

(3) A: *Kaban wa chiisakunakute wa ikemasen yo.* ☺
かばんは小さくなくてはいけませんよ。
(As for the bag, it must be small.)

B: *Jaa, dono kurai no ookisa ga ii n desu ka.*
じゃあ，どのくらいの大きさがいいんですか。
(Then how large should it be?)

(4) A: *Taisetsuna tegami da kara ji o kichinto kakanakereba ikemasen yo.*
大切な手紙だから字をきちんと書かなければいけませんよ。
(Since this is an important letter, you must write the characters neatly.)

B: *Hai, wakarimashita.*
はい，わかりました。
(Yes, I will.)

(5) A: *Kon'ya wa hayaku nenakute wa ikemasen yo.*
今夜は早く寝なくてはいけませんよ。
(You must go to bed early tonight.)

B: *Doo shite?* ☺
どうして？
(Why?)

A: *Ashita asa hayaku dekakenakereba narimasen kara.*
あした朝早く出かけなければなりませんから。
(Tomorrow morning we must leave early.)

Additional Information

Instead of *ikemasen* in the structure introduced in this entry, [*dame da*] and [*komaru*] may be used.

(a) *Hayaku okinakereba **dame** yo.*
早く起きなければ**だめ**よ。
(You must get up early.)

(b) *Oogoe o dashite wa **komarimasu** yo.*
大声を出しては**困ります**よ。
(You must not shout in a loud voice.)

[-*Nakereba*] and [-*nakute wa*] can be shortened to -*nakerya/nakya* and -*nakucha* respectively in casual fast speech.

(c) *Benkyoo-shi**nakya dame** yo.* ☺
勉強し**なきゃだめ**よ。
(You must study!)

Practice

dentist	N	*haisha (-san)*	歯医者(さん)
departure	N	*shuppatsu*	出発
soon	Adv	*sorosoro*	そろそろ
laundry	N	*sentaku*	洗たく

Give advice to your student or child regarding the following obligations.

1. finish the work by tomorrow morning

2. go to the dentist next week
3. tell the truth

Describe your own obligation regarding the following.
4. the need to go to the airport two hours before departure
5. the need to return soon
6. the need to do shopping and laundry

--------- Some Sample Answers ---------

1. *Ashita no asa made ni kono shigoto shiagenakute wa ikemasen yo.*
   あしたの朝までにこの仕事仕上げなくてはいけませんよ。

2. *Raishuu haisha e ikanakereba ikemasen.*
   来週歯医者へ行かなければいけません。

3. *Hontoo no koto o iwanakereba dame desu yo.*
   本当のことを言わなければだめですよ。

4. *Shuppatsu no ni-jikan mae ni hikoojoo e itte-inakereba narimasen.*
   出発の二時間前に飛行場へ行っていなければなりません。

5. *Moo sorosoro kaeranakute wa narimasen.*
   もうそろそろ帰らなくてはなりません。

6. *Kaimono to sentaku o shinakereba naranai n da.* ☺
   買い物と洗たくをしなければならないんだ。

108. Guessing with Confidence—*Ni Chigainai*

Target Expression

> *He must be a Japanese.*
> **Nihon-jin ni chigainai.** ♦
> 日本人にちがいない。
>
> [V/Adj pre-Aux + *ni chigainai*]

Grammatical Explanation

When you are quite certain of your assumptions, [*ni chigainai*] is used. The [*ni chigainai*] expression is preceded by [V/Adj pre-Aux] forms. Here is a list of forms for your reconfirmation. (See Entry 41 for negative forms.)

predicate types	pre-Aux	[V/Adj pre-Aux + *ni chigainai*]
Verb	*iku*	*iku ni chigainai*
	itta	*itta ni chigainai*
***Be*-verb**	(deletion)	*nihon-jin ni chigainai*
	datta	*nihon-jin datta ni chigainai*
Adj-*i*	*tanoshii*	*tanoshii ni chigainai*
	tanoshikatta	*tanoshikatta ni chigainai*
Adj-*na*	*benri*	*benri ni chigainai*
	benridatta	*benridatta ni chigainai*

The [*ni chigainai*] pattern shows strong confidence in your assumption more strongly than those guessing expressions we have learned earlier, that is, [*-daroo*] and [*kamoshirenai*]. As reflected in the literal meaning of the phrase *chigainai* 'there is no mistake,' this expression is used when the speaker guesses about some facts based on his or her assumption and holds it strongly with confidence. It conveys the sense of the English 'must' supported by the speaker's strong commitment to his or her conjecture.

When you use [*ni chigainai*], it is as if you are speaking in monologue and convincing yourself that what you are thinking or assuming must be true. For example, the target sentence, *nihon-jin ni chigainai* is used almost self-convincingly. If you are describing your confident guesses directly addressed to others, you are more likely to use, *ano hito kitto nihon-jin da yo* 'he is certainly a Japanese' or *ano hito zettai nihon-jin da to omou* 'I think for sure that he is a Japanese.' (*Kitto* and *zettai* are both adverbs meaning 'certainly' and 'for sure.') The [*ni chigainai*] expression, however, may appear independently in written Japanese.

For negation, negate the preceding verbs, as in *nihonjin dewa-nai ni chigainai* 'It must be the case that he is not a Japanese.'

Examples

(1) *Moo hachi-ji da kara Sumisu-san wa dekaketa ni chigainai.* ◆
もう八時だからスミスさんは出かけたにちがいない。
(Since it is already eight o'clock, Mr. Smith must have left the house.)

(2) *Imooto wa kitto hurusato ni kaette-kuru ni chigainai.* ◆
妹はきっとふるさとに帰ってくるにちがいない。
(My sister will certainly return to our hometown.)

(3) *Ano hito wa ii hito da kara watashi no kimochi wakatte-kureru ni chigaiarimasen.* ◆

あの人はいい人だから私の気持ちわかってくれるにちがいありません。

(Since she is a good person, I am sure that she understands my feelings.)

Practice

---
income tax   N   *shotokuzei*   所得税

Express your confident opinion concerning the following. Use written style.

1. that person being Sasaki's elder brother
2. that the income tax will rise next year
3. that Mr. Anderson's house is (this one) here

—————— Answers ——————
1. *Ano hito wa Sasaki-san no oniisan ni chigainai.* ◆
   あの人は佐々木さんのお兄さんにちがいない。
2. *Shotokuzei wa rainen agaru ni chigainai.* ◆
   所得税は来年上がるにちがいない。
3. *Andaason-san no uchi wa koko ni chigainai.* ◆
   アンダーソンさんの家はhere にちがいない。

109. Passive Expressions—Direct and Indirect Passive

Target Expressions

I was chased by a strange man.
Henna otoko ni oikakerareta. ◆
へんな男に追いかけられた。

I got caught in the rain.
Ame ni hurarete nee . . . ☺
雨に降られてねえ……

passive [V + *-reru*, V + *-rareru*]

Grammatical Explanation

Passive in Japanese is grammatically formed by the verb ending changes. The passive forms of *U-* and *RU*-verbs are identical to the respectful [V + -*reru*] and [V + -*rareru*] forms we studied in Entry 86. For existential verbs use *irareru* for the passive of *iru*. The *be*-verb *da* does not have a passive form. For irregular verbs, *suru* and *kuru* take *sareru* and *korareru*, respectively.

Functions of the Passive Structure

There are two primary motivations for using passive verb endings in Japanese. First, passives are used when the need for referring to the agent of the action is weak or nonexistent. This is similar to how English passives are used. In English, passives are used with or without the agent indicated by the "by" phrase, as in "America was discovered by Columbus," and "this house was built in the 1930s." The Japanese equivalent for this expression would be: *Amerika wa Koronbusu niyotte hakken-sareta* and *kono tatemono wa sen kyuu-hyaku san-juu nendai ni taterareta.* (*hakken-suru* means 'to discover' and *tateru*, 'to build.')

The second and more important function of the passive structure in Japanese is to indicate that the speaker is suffering from someone else's action or is experiencing something unpleasant. For this pattern, the subject noun of the passive sentence is always animate. Although in English only transitive verbs are used to form the passive, in Japanese both transitive and intransitive verbs may be used to form this passive. For example, the intransitive verb *shinu* 'die' may be used in the passive form *shinareru* when you wish to express that you are suffering from and experiencing the negative results of someone's death. This feeling of negative consequences is often expressed in English by passive sentences with *on*, as in "I got rained *on*" or an expression as "my pet died *on* me."

When there is a transitive/intransitive pair of verbs, only the transitive verb can be changed into the passive form. For example, for a pair such as *kowasu* 'to break something,' and *kowareru* 'something breaks,' only *kowasareru* is possible.

Direct and Indirect Passives

In terms of the grammatical structure of the passive sentences there are two types; direct and indirect. In direct passives the object of the related active sentence is the subject of the passive sentence. In indirect passives such correlation between the active and its passive counterpart does not exist. The passive sentence structure takes [N *ga/wa* + (N *ni*) + Vpassive].

The illustration below contrasts direct and indirect passive structures with the sentence structure we have learned so far. The term 'agent' refers to the actual performer of the action.

1. *Direct Passive:*

Active: Sasaki-san wa Yamada-san o damashita.
佐々木さんは山田さんをだました。
(Ms. Sasaki deceived Ms. Yamada.)

Passive: <u>Yamada-san **wa**</u>   <u>Sasaki-san **ni**</u>   <u>**damasareta**</u>.
　　　　　Subject　　　　　　Agent　　　　　Vpassive
山田さんは佐々木さんにだまされた。
(Ms. Yamada was deceived by Ms. Sasaki.)

2. *Indirect Passive:*

Active: Imooto ga okashi o tabeta.
妹がお菓子を食べた。
(My younger sister ate sweets.)

Passive: <u>Watashi **wa**</u>　　　<u>imooto **ni**</u>　<u>okashi **o**</u>　<u>**taberareta**</u>.
　　　　　Person influenced　　Agent　　　Object　　Vpassive
わたしは妹にお菓子を食べられた。
(I got my sweets eaten up by my younger sister.)

Active: Ame ga hutta.
雨が降った。
(It rained.)

Passive: <u>Watashi **wa**</u>　　　　<u>ame **ni**</u>　<u>**hurareta**</u>.
　　　　　Person influenced　　Agent　　Vpassive
わたしは雨に降られた。
(I was rained on.)

Note that in indirect passives, the person who becomes the subject/topic of the passive sentence is the person who is influenced by the event and that person does not constitute a part of the related active sentence. In this sense the relation between the event described by the active sentence and the ensuing influence are only indirectly related; thus the term ''indirect'' passive is appropriate.

It should be noted parenthetically that it is possible to have a positive influence when indirect passives are used, but overwhelmingly the implication is negative. In fact when a positive indirectness is stressed, normally the verbs of giving and receiving are used. For example:

(a) Sensei ni tegami o **kaite-itadaita**.
先生に手紙を書いていただいた。
(I had the teacher write me a letter.)

In order to indicate the source of the action in passive sentences, most frequently [N + *ni*] is used. However, there are cases where [N + *kara*] and [N + *niyotte*] are preferred. When emphasizing the source from which something is made, *kara* is normally used. For example:

(b) <u>*Sake*</u> <u>*wa*</u> <u>*kome*</u> <u>**kara**</u> <u>*tsukurareru.*</u>
    sake   T   rice   from is made
    酒は米**から**作られる。
    (Sake is made from rice.)

In written Japanese *niyotte* is often preferred, as in the sentence given earlier, *Amerika wa Koronbusu niyotte hakken-sareta.*

Examples

aru	ある	Dem	one
Kinkakuji	金閣寺	PN	the Golden Pavilion
kigi	木々	N	trees
midori	みどり	N	green
kakomareru 囲まれる		V	to be surrounded by
zubunure	ずぶぬれ	N	being soaked, drenched
jirojiro mirareru ジロジロ見られる		V	to be stared at

Rokugatsu no aru nichiyoobi Kyooto e itta.
六月のある日曜日京都へ行った。
(On one Sunday in June I went to Kyoto.)

Eki kara basu ni notte Kinkakuji e itta.
駅からバスに乗って金閣寺へ行った。
(I got on the bus at the station and went to the Golden Pavilion.)

Kigi no midori ni kakomareta Kinkakuji wa utsukushikatta.
木々のみどりに囲まれた金閣寺は美しかった。
(The Golden Pavilion was beautiful surrounded by green trees.)

Gaikoku kara kita kankookyaku ni hanashikakerareta ga, nan to itte-iru no ka wakaranakatta.
外国から来た観光客に話しかけられたが,何と言っているのかわからなかった。
(I was spoken to by a foreign tourist, but I didn't understand what he was saying.)

Itariago ka Supeingo datta to omou.
イタリア語かスペイン語だったと思う。
(I think it was either Italian or Spanish.)

Kaeri wa ame ni furareta.
帰りは雨に降られた。
(While returning I got caught in the rain.)

Zubunure ni natta node, hito ni jirojiro mirarete komatta.
ずぶぬれになったので，人にジロジロ見られて困った。
(As I got drenched, I was stared at by people and that was uncomfortable.)

Practice

to go through hardships	V	*kuroo-suru*	苦労する
to use, to utilize	V	*riyoo-suru*	利用する
(Catholic) father	N	*shinpu*	神父
to respect	V	*sonkei-suru*	尊敬する
everyone	N	*minna*	みんな

How will you describe the facts in the following situations?

1. Your father read a personal letter you received. You are not happy with this invasion of privacy.
2. Your father passed away when your mother was still young. How do you express the fact that your mother suffered from this and she had to suffer great hardships?
3. You are to write about the very library you are currently studying in—that is, that this library serves (lit. is used) by many people.
4. You want to state positively that Father Thompson is respected by everyone.

──────── Some Sample Answers ────────

1. *Chichi ni tegami o yomaremashita.* 父に手紙を読まれました。
2. *Wakai toki chichi ni shinareta node, haha wa taihen kuroo-shita yoo desu.*
   若い時父に死なれたので，母は大変苦労したようです。
3. *Kono toshokan wa takusan no hito ni riyoo-sarete-iru.* ♦
   この図書館はたくさんの人に利用されている。
4. *Tonpuson shinpu wa minna ni sonkei-sarete-iru n desu yo . . .* トンプソン神父はみんなに尊敬されているんですよ……

110. Requesting and Granting Permission

Target Expressions

> *May I enter the room?*
>
> **Heya ni haitte mo ii-desu ka.**
> 部屋に入ってもいいですか。
>
> *Yes, please.*
>
> **Ee, doozo.**
> ええ, どうぞ。
>
> [V/Adj *te + mo + ii*]

Grammatical Explanation

The pattern [V/Adj *te + mo + ii/yoroshii (desu ka)*] is used for requesting permission to do something as shown in Target Expressions. These requests can also be made with the [V/Adj negative gerundive] forms. However, in these expressions *-nakute* endings are more frequently used. The verb negative gerundive forms ending with *-naide* may be used in spoken language.

(a) *Kyoo kaisha e **ikanakute mo ii**-desu ka.*
今日会社へ**行かなくても**いいですか。
(Is it all right not to go to the company today?)

Other forms similar to this pattern are:

[V/Adj *te + mo + daijoobu (desu ka)*]
(Is it all right if . . .?)

[V/Adj *te + mo + kamaimasen ka*]
(It isn't bothersome if . . ., is it?)

In colloquial style, *mo* may be deleted. For example:

(b) *Heya ni **haitte ii**?* ☺
部屋に**入ってい**い？
(Can I go into the room?)

The affirmative answers granting permission are:

Ee/Hai, ii/yoroshii-desu. ええ/はい, いい/よろしいです。 (Yes, it is fine.)

Ee/Hai, kekkoo desu. ええ/はい，けっこうです。 (Yes, it is all right.)

Ee/Hai, kamaimasen. ええ/はい，かまいません。 (Yes, that's no trouble at all.)

Ee/Hai, doozo. ええ/はい，どうぞ。 (Yes, please.)

The negative answer to these questions are:

1. *Prohibition:*
   [V/Adj *te* + *wa* + *ikenai/komaru/dame da*]

   (1a) A: *Tabete mo ii-desu ka.*
   食べてもいいですか。

   B: *(Mada **tabete wa**) **dame desu** yo.*
   (まだ**食べては**)だめですよ。

These negative answers are translated into English 'you must not . . .' which convey prohibition. These expressions are discussed again in Entry 111.

2. *Softer denial of permission:*
   The prohibition expressed above is a strong refusal to grant permission. Softer strategies are to be used particularly to those socially equal to or superior to you. Here are some examples.

   (2a) A: *Karite mo ii-desu ka.*
   借りてもいいですか。
   (May I borrow this?)

   B: ***Iyaa, chotto* . . .**
   いやあ，ちょっと……
   (Well . . . I'm afraid not.)

   (2b) A: *Tabete mo ii-desu ka.*
   食べてもいいですか。
   (May I eat?)

   B: *Sumimasen nee, **moo sukoshi matte-kudasai.***
   すみませんねえ，**もう少し待ってください。**
   (I'm afraid not, please wait a little longer.)

Examples

(1) A: *Anoo, kaette mo ii desu ka.*
あのう，帰ってもいいですか。
(May I leave?)

B: *Aa, sore ga . . . sumimasen ga, moo sukoshi matte-kudasaimasen ka.*

ああ、それが……すみませんが、もう少し待ってくださいませんか。
(Sorry, but could you wait a bit longer?)

(2) A: *Sumimasen ga, ikanakute mo yoroshii-deshoo ka.*
すみませんが、行かなくてもよろしいでしょうか。
(Is it all right if I don't go?)

B: *Ee, kamaimasen yo.*
ええ、かまいませんよ。
(Yes, that's all right.)

(3) *Takakute mo daijoobu?* ☺
高くても大丈夫？
([lit. Is it all right to be expensive?] Is the expensive one all right?)

(4) A: *Kono uisukii de ii-deshoo ka.*
このウイスキーでいいでしょうか。
(Would this whiskey be all right?)

B: *Soo desu nee . . . Motto ii no wa airmasen ka.*
そうですねえ……もっといいのはありませんか。
(Let's see . . . do you have anything better?)

(5) A: *Kore katte ii?*
これ買っていい？
(Can I buy this?)

B: *Dame desu yo.*
だめですよ。
(No, you may not.)

Practice

Create an interaction in which one person seeks permission and the other grants it for each of the following. Create another pair in which permission is not granted.

1. to borrow this pen
2. to eat
3. to watch TV
4. (to do it) the day after tomorrow

——— Some Sample Answers ———

1. A: *Kono pen karite mo ii-desu ka.*
このペン借りてもいいですか。
   B: *Ee, doozo (doozo).* ええ、どうぞ（どうぞ）。
2. A: *Tabete mo ii?* ☺ 食べてもいい？
   B: *Ii yo.* ☺ いいよ。

3. A: *Nee, terebi mite mo ii?* ☺ ねえ，テレビ見てもいい？
   B: *Ikemasen yo.* ☺   いけませんよ。
4. A: *Asatte de yoroshii kashira?* ☺F
   あさってでよろしいかしら。
   B: *Sore ga. . . . Ashita made ni dekimasen-deshoo ka nee*
   ・・・それが……あしたまでにできませんでしょうかねえ……

Additional Information

The expressions using [*de (mo) ii*] and [*de (mo) yoroshii*] imply that contrary to an ideal state, the best available is being offered. Therefore, these expressions should be avoided when you answer an invitation. See for example, in the following interaction, it is impolite to answer *ee, koocha de iidesu* 'yes, tea will do.'

(a) A: *Koocha de (mo) ii* kashira? ☺ F
   紅茶で(も)いいかしら？
   (Would tea be fine?)
   B: *Ee, mochiron. Sumimasen.*
   ええ，もちろん。すみません。
   (Of course. Thanks.)

Warning

Note the difference between *mo ii* and *de mo ii* when they co-occur with *dochira*. *Dochira mo ii*, meaning 'both are good,' while *dochira de mo ii* means 'either one is good' (refer to Appendix 6 for related forms).

111. Prohibition—*Te Wa Ikenai*

Target Expression

> *You must not say such a thing.*
> ***Sonna koto o itte wa ikemasen yo.***
> そんなことを言ってはいけませんよ。
>
> [V*te*/Adj *te* + *wa* + *ikenai*]

Grammatical Explanation

To express prohibition, or strong negative command, [Vte/Adj *te + wa + ikenai/komaru/dame da* (and their formal counterparts *ikemasen/komarimasu/dame desu*] are used with slight connotative differences as listed below. All these are translated into the English 'must not' or 'should not.'

ikenai	it is wrong
komaru	it is problematic
dame da	it is bad

When addressing your superiors, the command forms introduced here should be avoided. Instead, the negative request form *. . . naidekudasaimasen ka*, or, a form with *itadaku* 'to receive,' *itadakemasendeshoo ka* are recommended.

Examples

chuui	注意	N	warning
chooshuu	聴衆	N	audience
kao	顔	N	face
oogoe o ageru 大声をあげる		V	to shout
inshuunten	飲酒運転	N	drunken driving

(1) *Supiichi o suru toki no chuui:*
   スピーチをする時の注意：
   (Points to be careful of when giving a speech:)

   • *Amari nagaku hanashite wa ikenai.*
   あまり長く話してはいけない。
   (You should not speak too long.)
   • *Yoku junbi-suru beki.*
   よく準備するべき。
   (You should be well prepared.)
   • *Chooshuu no kao o minagara hanasanakute wa dame.*
   聴衆の顔を見ながら話さなくてはだめ。
   (You should look at the faces of your audience when you speak.)

(2) *Koko wa byooin desu kara, oogoe o agete wa komarimasu.*
   ここは病院ですから，大声をあげては困ります。
   (Since this is a hospital, you must not speak loudy [lit. speaking in a loud voice is problematic].)

(3) *Inshuunten o shite wa ikemasen.*
飲酒運転をしてはいけません。
(You must not drive while intoxicated.)

Practice

Imagine you are a teacher in a grade school. Express the following prohibitions to your students.

1. not to drink this water
2. characters not to be badly written (*kitanai*)
3. not to stay up late at night

—— Some Sample Answers ——
1. *Kono mizu wa nonde wa ikemasen.*
この水は飲んではいけません。
2. *Ji ga kitanakute wa dame desu.* 字がきたなくてはだめです。
3. *Yoru osoku made okite-ite wa ikemasen yo.* [*1]
夜遅くまで起きていてはいけませんよ。

*1. *Okite-ite* is a [V*te*] form of *okite-iru* 'to stay up,' the progressive form of the verb *okiru* 'to get up,' indicating the continuing result of an action.

Additional Information

Te wa and *de wa* are contracted to *cha* and *ja* respectively in casual speech. For example, *inshuunten o shicha ikemasen yo* 'you must not drive while intoxicated' will be used in a familiar colloquial environment.

112. Reporting—1. Direct and Indirect Quotations

Target Expression

> *Mr. Suzuki said, "I forgot that completely."*
> **Suzuki-san wa "Sukkari wasurete-imashita" to iimashita.**
> 鈴木さんは「すっかり忘れていました」と言いました。
>
> [*to yuu*]

Grammatical Explanation

The quoted portion of direct quotations in Japanese is normally either graphologically marked with quotation marks 「　」 (in written Japanese) or marked by intonation and voice quality. (There are cases where direct quotations are not marked by graphological marks in written Japanese, however.) Direct quotation reflects styles of the quoted person and carries features similar to spoken Japanese. After the quoted portion the quotative particle *to* is attached followed by the verb *yuu* 'say.' In the colloquial style *to* changes to *tte*, except when it is preceded by the syllabic *n* in which case *to* changes to *te*. Recall that the verb *yuu* conjugates by replacing *yu* with *i*: *yuu* conjugates *iimasu, itta, itte,* and so forth.

In indirect quotations the quoted portion often takes [V/Adj informal] endings and the [*to yuu*] expression follows. There is no verb tense agreement such as observed in English, however. The non-past tense in the quoted clause refers to actions not yet complete, whereas the past tense indicates that the action has or had occurred.

(a) *Takahashi-san mo **iku** tte iimashita yo.*
高橋さんも**行く**って言いましたよ。
(Takahashi also said that he *will go*.)

(b) *Takahashi-san mo **itta** tte iimashita yo.*
高橋さんも**行った**って言いましたよ。
(Takahashi also said that he *went*.)

When the quoted speech is in command form, *yooni yuu* is also used for indirect quotation. For example, *yoku chuui-suru yooni iimashita* 'they said to be on alert' for the indirect quote of *"yoku chuui-shinasai."*

A quotative expression may be particularly useful when one is interested in finding out the equivalents of foreign words. For example, if you want to know how to say 'manager' in Japanese, you can simply ask:

(c) A: | *"Manager"* | *wa* | *nihongo* | *de* | *nan* | *to* | *iimasu* | *ka.* |
|---|---|---|---|---|---|---|---|
| manager | T | Japanese | in | what | QT | say | Q |

「manager」は日本語で何と言いますか。
(How do you say "manager" in Japanese?)

B: *Nihongo de wa "buchoo" desu.*
日本語では「部長」です。
(In Japanese, it is *"buchoo."*)

Some extended uses of [*to yuu*] should also be pointed out.

1. The quotative expression [*to yuu*] may be used to connect clauses and nominalizers, *koto* and *no*, when it is preceded by *da*. The phrase [*to yuu*] must also precede other modified nouns if the rela-

tionship between the modifying clause and the modified noun is appositional and is related to the action of "saying" or "reporting" (this point will be discussed again in Entry 114). See the following examples.

(1a) *Daigakusei da **to yuu** koto o wasurenaide kudasai.*
大学生だ**ということ**を忘れないでください。
(Don't forget the fact that you are college students.)

(1b) *Sasaya **to yuu** ryooriya e ikimashita.*
笹や**という**料理屋へ行きました。
(We went to a [Japanese] restaurant called Sasaya.)

(1c)

Sono	*otoko*	*wa*	*mujitsu*	*da*	*to*	*yuu*	*setsu*	*mo*
that	man	T	innocent	be	QT	say	opinion	also

aru. ♦
is

その男は無実だ**という**説もある。
(There is an opinion that [states that] the man is innocent.)

(1d) *Kawai-san wa moo Amerika e itte-shimatta **to yuu** hanashi deshita ga . . .*
川井さんはもうアメリカへ行ってしまった**という**話でしたが……
(The story was that Mr. Kawai had left for America already.)

2. The expression [*to yuu*] can also end an utterance to indicate hearsay.

(2a)

Yamaoku	*no*	*sono*	*mura*	*ni*	*wa*	*ima*
deep in the mountains	L	that	village	in	T	now

demo	*kuma*	*ga*	*deru*	*to*	*yuu.*
even	bear	S	appear	QT	say

山奥のその村には今でも熊が出る**という**。
(They say that in that village deep in the mountains, bears appear even now.)

3. An idiomatic use of [*to yuu*] should also be mentioned. As seen in the example below, when [N *to yuu* N] is used it has a meaning of 'every N.'

(3a)

*Ningen **to yuu** ningen*	*wa*	*subete*	*shiawase*	*o*
every man	T	all	happiness	O

motomete-iru.
is seeking

人間**という**人間はすべて幸せを求めている。

(Every human being seeks happiness.)

Examples

---
shiai	試合	N	match (of sports)
makeru	負ける	V	to lose
zannenna	残念な	Adj	sorry, regrettable
oshaberi	おしゃべり	N	chatter
---

(1) *"Itte kimaasu" to itte, imooto wa dekakete-ikimashita.*
「行ってきまーす」と言って，妹は出かけていきました。
(Saying "bye," my sister left the house.)

(2) *Sensei wa "Yoku benkyoo-shite-okinasai" to osshaimashita.*
先生は「よく勉強しておきなさい」とおっしゃいました。
(The teacher said, "Study hard.")

(3) *Yamamoto-san wa tenisu no shiai ni makete zannen da to itte-imashita.*
山本さんはテニスの試合に負けて残念だと言っていました。
(Mr. Yamamoto lost the tennis match and said he was sorry for the loss.)

(4) A: *Arupusu to yuu kissaten o shitte-imasu ka.*
アルプスという喫茶店を知っていますか。
(Do you know the coffee shop called Alps?)
B: *Ee, shitte-imasu yo. Eki no chikaku desu ne.*
ええ，知っていますよ。駅の近くですね。
(Yes, I do. It's near the station, isn't it?)
A: *Ee. soko de aimashoo yo.*
ええ。そこで会いましょうよ。
(Yes. Let's meet there.)

(5) *Chichi mo eki made iku to mooshite-orimashita.*
父も駅まで行くと申しておりました。
(My father said that he too would go as far as the station.)

(6) A: *Ano hito ga tsutomete-ita no wa nan te yuu kaisha deshita ka.*
あの人が勤めていたのは何ていう会社でしたか。
(What was the name of the company that he worked at?)

B: *Saa . . ., aa, Kawai Toreedingu to ka yuu kaisha ja arimasen ka.*
さあ……, ああ, 川井トレーディングとかいう会社じゃありませんか。
(Hmm . . ., oh, isn't it a company called "Kawai Trading" or something?)

(7)   *Sensei wa itsumo "Jugyoochuu oshaberi o shite wa ikemasen" to osshaimasu.*
先生はいつも「授業中おしゃべりをしてはいけません」とおっしゃいます。
(The teacher always says, "Don't chatter during the class.")

Additional Information

The phrase *to yuu to, to iimasu to* and *to ieba* 'speaking of . . .' function to present a topic into conversation. See, for example:

(a)   *Yooko-san **te yuuto**, moo Amerika kara kaette kita no ka na.* ☺
洋子さん**ていうと**, もうアメリカから帰ってきたのかな。
(Speaking of Yoko, I wonder if she returned from the United States.)

The quotative [*to*] may also appear with verbs of thought and reporting as indirect quotation. In these cases the form preceding the quotative particle is [V/Adj informal], and [*to*] marks the content of the thought and reporting. For example:

(b)

Hayaku	*nihon*	*e*	*kaeroo*	***to***	*kesshin-shita.*
soon	Japan	to	will return	QT	decided

早く日本へ帰ろう**と**決心した。
(I decided to return to Japan soon.)

(c)   *Rainen wa Hokkaidoo ryokoo o shiyoo **to** omotte-imasu.*
来年は北海道旅行をしよう**と**思っています。
(I'm thinking that I will make a trip to Hokkaido next year.)[*1]

> [*1.] See volitional forms introduced in Entry 44 if you are not sure of the expression *shiyoo.*

There are a number of verbs that involve reporting and thought process that may take the quotative [*to*] as listed below.

to kaku と書く (to write)
*Sono tegami ni wa raigetsu ryooshin ga Amerika e kuru **to kaite-arimashita**.*
その手紙には来月両親がアメリカへ来る**と書いてありました**。
(In that letter it was written that my parents would come to the United States next month.)

to oshieru　と教える　(to teach)

to kokuhaku-suru　と告白する　(to confess)
> Hannin wa sono musume o koroshita **to kokuhaku-shita**. ♦
> 犯人はその娘を殺した**と告白した**。
> (The criminal confessed to killing the young woman.)

to kangaeru　と考える　(to think, to consider)
> Atarashii mado o tsukereba yoku naru **to kangaeta**. ♦
> 新しい窓をつければよくなる**と考えた**。
> (I thought if I install the new window, it will be better.)

to omou　と思う　(to think)

to noberu　と述べる　(to state)

to kiku　と聞く　(to hear about)
> Koyama-sensei wa moo Yooroppa e irasshatta **to kikimashita** ga . . .
> 小山先生はもうヨーロッパへいらっしゃった**と聞きました**が……
> (I heard that Professor Koyama had already left for Europe . . .)

These verbs can also take *to yuu koto o* instead of *to*, when the content of the report and thought is presented not verbatim but in the abstract. Compare the following:

(d)　Genki de ganbaru yooni **to yuu koto o** kaite-yatta.
　　元気でがんばるように**ということを**書いてやった。
　　(I wrote that [in gist] she should be well and do her best.)

(e)　Genki de ganbaru yooni **to** kaite-yatta.
　　元気でがんばるように**と**書いてやった。
　　(I wrote to her to keep well and to do her best.)

When verbs of reporting and thought are preceded by *to* as above, the speaker is only weekly committed to presupposing that what is reported is a fact. If the verb expressing thought requires that the speaker believes it to be fact, *to* cannot be used. For example, one can only forget *(wasureru)* or recall *(omoidasu)* what one believes to be fact; thus *to omoidasu* and *to wasureru* are not acceptable. Instead use *koto* as in (f).

(f)　Koyama sensei ga Yooroppa e irasshatta **(to yuu)** koto o wasurete-imashita.
　　小山先生がヨーロッパへいらっしゃった（**という**）ことを忘れていました。
　　(I forgot that Professor Koyama went to Europe.)

```
------------------------------------------------------------
rikon      離婚      N         divorce
------------------------------------------------------------
```

*Tomodachi no Tagawa-san kara no tegami ni wa kayoobi ni watashi
ni ai ni kuru to kaite-atta.*
友だちの田川さんからの手紙には火曜日に私に会いに来ると書いてあった。
(In my friend Mr. Tagawa's letter, it was written that he would come
to see me on Tuesday.)

*Watashi wa kitto shigoto no koto de hanashi ni kuru n daroo to
omotta.*
私はきっと仕事のことで話しに来るんだろうと思った。
(I thought that surely he was coming to talk to me about his job.)

Kayoobi no gogo Tagawa-san ni atta.
火曜日の午後田川さんに会った。
(On Tuesday afternoon I met Mr. Tagawa.)

Kare wa narubeku hayaku rikon-suru tsumori da to kokuhaku-shita.
彼はなるべく早く離婚するつもりだと告白した。
(He confessed that he was going to get divorced as soon as possible.)

*Hoka no yuujin kara Tagawa-san no okusan ga uchi o dete-itta rashii
to kiite-ita ga watashi wa shinjinakatta.*
他の友人から田川さんの奥さんが家を出て行ったらしいと聞いていたが私は
信じなかった。
(I heard from other friends that Mr. Tagawa's wife seems to have left
home, but I didn't believe it.)

Shikashi Tagawa-san wa sore mo hontoo da to itta.
しかし田川さんはそれも本当だと言った。
(But Mr. Tagawa said that it was true.)

Saikin nihon de mo rikon ga huete-iru to kiku.
最近日本でも離婚がふえていると聞く。
(I hear that recently even in Japan divorce is increasing.)

Nihon-jin no kangae-kata mo kawatte-kita no da to omou.
日本人の考え方も変わってきたのだと思う。
(I think the way Japanese people think is changing.)

Practice

Report 1, 2 and 3 in either direct or indirect quotation. How do you express
4?

1. My mother said, "Be well and work hard," and waved goodbye.
2. Ms. Kanai said, "I'll return by eight o'clock."
3. The manager told me to come back before eleven.

4. Do you know a person by the name of Kazuhiko Hayashi? (addressed to your superior.)

―――― Some Sample Answers ――――

1. *Haha wa "Genki de isshookenmei hatarakinasai yo," to itte te o hurimashita.*
   母は「元気でいっしょうけんめい働きなさいよ」と言って手をふりました。
2. *Kanai-san wa hachi-ji made ni kaeru to iimashita.*
   金井さんは八時までに帰ると言いました。
3. *Buchoo wa juu ichi-ji mae ni kaette-kuru yooni to osshaimashita.*
   部長は十一時前に帰って来るようにとおっしゃいました。
4. *Hayashi Kazuhiko-san to yuu hito o gozonji desu ka.*
   林一彦さんという人をご存知ですか。

*   *   *   *   *

"Hirayama to yuu gakusei o oboete-imasu ka."
「平山という学生を覚えていますか」
"Donna hito kashira."
「どんな人かしら」
("Do you remember a student by the name of Hirayama?" "What kind of person, I wonder . . .")

―Yuki, 1977, p.31.

Here is an example of [*to yuu*] used to mean 'by the name of,' or 'called.' Note also the use of *kashira* (by a female speaker) as explained in Entry 99.

113. Action-accompanying Expressions―2. When Visiting Someone's Place

Target Expression

> *Please (come in).*
>
> **Saa, doozo, doozo.**
> さあ，どうぞ，どうぞ。

Strategic Explanation

Japanese seems to be filled with a great number of formulaic phrases that accompany specific actions. It becomes so much of a ritual to say, for example, 'I am leaving' when you are going out the door, or 'I am about to eat' before you pick up your chopsticks, that if you fail to say these words, you may well be thought to be rude. These ritualistic expressions may strike you as being obvious and even redundant. Nevertheless, one is expected to say them. The following expressions are some of the more common phrases you are likely to use when visiting a Japanese family. If you forget the use of these Japanese favorites, use *sumimasen* and *doomo* which have a wide range of application.

1. *At the door:*

    (1a)   Guest: *Gomenkudasai.* ごめんください。
               ([lit. Excuse me.] Hello.)
           Host: *Irasshai.* いらっしゃい。 (Welcome.)

2. *As you enter the room:*

    (2a)   Host: *Kochira e doozo.* こちらへどうぞ。
               (This way, please.)
           Guest: *Ojama-shimasu.* おじゃまします。
               (Excuse me. [said with a slight bow])
               Shitsurei-shimasu. 失礼します。
               (Excuse me. [said with a slight bow])

3. *When your host begins to prepare drinks and food:*

    (3a)   *Doozo okamainaku.*
           (lit. Please don't go to any trouble.)
           どうぞおかまいなく。

4. *When you present some gift:*

    (4a)   *Tsumaranai mono desu ga . . .*
           (Here's something for you.)
           つまらないものですが……

5. *When drinking or eating:*

    (5a)   Host: *Doozo meshiagatte-kudasai.*
               どうぞめしあがってください。
               (Please help yourself.)

Guest: *(Dewa) itadakimasu.* （では）いただきます。
(lit. Thank you, I'll help myself.)

Itadakimasu may be said either when the guest accepts the offer or immediately before the guest eats or drinks.

(5b) Host: *Okawari wa?* おかわりは？
(How about another serving?)

Guest: *Sumimasen. Jaa sukoshi onegai-shimasu.*
すみません。じゃあ少しお願いします。
(Thanks, a little, then.)

(5c) Host: *Moo sukoshi ikaga desu ka.* もう少しいかがですか。
(How about some more?)

Guest: *Ee, moo takusan itadakimashita kara.*
ええ，もうたくさんいただきましたから。
(Thank you, but no thank you . . . I already had plenty.)

(5d) Guest (when finished drinking or eating):
(Doomo) gochisoosama deshita.
（どうも）ごちそうさまでした。
(Thank you for the delicious food/drink.)

6. *When thinking about leaving:*

(6a) *Sorosoro shitsurei-shimasu node* . . .
そろそろ失礼しますので……
(It's about time, I should be leaving.)

7. *When you leave the host's home:*

(7a) *Ojama-shimashita.* おじゃましました。 (Excuse me . . .)
Dewa gomenkudasai. では，ごめんください。
(Well then, goodbye.)

(7b) Female Host: *Okiotsukete.* お気をつけて。
([lit. please return safely.] Goodbye.)

114. Modifying—4. Clausal Explanation

Target Expressions

> *The room was filled with the smell of meat being grilled.*
> **Heya wa niku o yaku nioi de ippai datta.**
> 部屋は肉を焼くにおいでいっぱいだった。
> *Did you hear the rumor that Ms. Kato got married?*
> **Katoo-san ga kekkon-shita tte yuu uwasa kiita?** ☺
> 加藤さんが結婚したっていううわさ聞いた？

Grammatical Explanation

We have studied clausal modifiers earlier in Entry 83. In this entry we concentrate on the second extended type. In this type the modification clause provides general explanation about the noun which does not constitute an element necessary for the proposition. As seen in the first target expression, *niku o yaku nioi* 'lit. smell of grilling meat' is structurally different from *chichi ga kaita hon* 'the book my father wrote.' In the latter, *hon* constitutes the grammatical object, an essential element of the proposition, [*chichi ga hon o kaita*]. In the grilling-meat example, the smell is something that is closely associated with the process of grilling, but it is not a part of the propostion, *niku o yaku.* Since these modifiers are quite common in Japanese, it becomes necessary to interpret the meaning in an extended way. Recall the similar example in Entry 83; *tomodachi ni au yakusoku o wasurete-shimaimashita* 'I forgot the appointment to see my friend.'

Although clausal explanation takes [V/Adj pre-nominal] forms, among extended types, there are some that obligatorily take the quotation phrase [*to yuu*], some that optionally take it, and some that normally do not. The clausal explanation that is semantically associated with reporting or that represents the reporter's view is followed by [*to yuu*]. For the clause that directly explains sensory information [*to yuu*] cannot be used. When [*to yuu*] is optional, and when it is used, the speaker creates a somewhat abstract or distant position when presenting the explanation.

Examples

----

kenkyuushitsu	N		(professor's) office
研究室			
waru	割る	V	to break

oto	音	N	sound
bin	ビン	N	bottle

----

(1) A: *Yamada sensei kara ashita juu ichi-ji ni kenkyuushitsu ni kuru yooni to yuu odenwa o itadakimashita yo.*

山田先生からあした十一時に研究室に来るようにというお電話をいただきましたよ。

(I received a phone call from Professor Yamada telling you to go to his office at eleven o'clock tomorrow.)

B: *Soo, komatta naa. Ashita wa juu ichi-ji ni Kawaguchi to au yakusoku ga aru n da yo.*

そう，困ったなあ。あしたは十一時に川口と会う約束があるんだよ。

(Well, that's a problem. I have an appointment to see Kawaguchi at eleven tomorrow.)

(2) A: *Are, doko-ka de garasu o waru oto ga suru yo.*

あれ，どこかでガラスを割る音がするよ。

(Listen! I hear someone breaking glass.)

B: *Are wa dare-ka ga bin o hako ni irete-iru oto deshoo.*

あれは誰かがビンを箱に入れている音でしょう。

(That sound comes from someone putting glass bottles into a box.)

A: *Soo ka naa.*

そうかなあ。

(I wonder.)

(3) A: *Hon o katta otsuri wa koko ni okimasu yo.*

本を買ったおつりはここに置きますよ。

(I'm leaving the change from the book I bought right here.)

B: *Aa, arigatoo.*

ああ，ありがとう。

(Oh, thanks.)

A: *Hon'ya-san de Chieko-san ga kekkon-shita tte yuu uwasa o kiita kedo . . .*

本屋さんでちえ子さんが結婚したっていううわさを聞いたけど……

(I heard a rumor at the bookstore that Chieko got married.)

B: *Sonna no tada no uwasa deshoo?*

そんなのただのうわさでしょう？

(That's just a rumor, isn't it?)

A: *Soo kashira.*

そうかしら。

(I doubt it.)

Additional Information

Here is a note regarding the tense of the explanatory clause in relation to the main clause. If the noun semantically calls for a future event, [Vnon-past] co-occurs as in example (a) below; if the noun semantically calls for the past event, [Vpast] is used as in (b); if the noun involves relative tense, either [Vpast] or [Vnon-past] is chosen depending on the noun as in (c) and (d).

(a) *Tomodachi to au/*atta yakusoku o shimashita*
友だちと会う/*会った約束をしました。
(I promised to see my friend.)

(b) *Tanoshii   ryokoo o shita/*suru   omoide   wa*
enjoyable   trip   O did/do   memories   T

taisetsuni shitai. ☺
want to treasure

楽しい旅行をした/*する思い出は大切にしたい。
(I want to treasure the memories of having made enjoyable trips.)

(c) *Kaimono o shita kaeri ni ojisan no uchi ni yotte-kimasu.*
買い物をした帰りにおじさんの家に寄ってきます。
(On the way back from shopping, I will visit my uncle's place.)

(d) *Kaimono o suru mae ni ojisan no uchi ni yotte-ikimasu.*
買い物をする前におじさんの家に寄っていきます。
(Before [on the way to] going shopping, I will visit my uncle's place.)

Practice

----
to come down	V	*orite-kuru*	降りてくる
stairs	N	*kaidan*	階段
incident	N	*jiken*	事件
to murder	V	*korosu*	殺す
photo	N	*shashin*	写真
to laugh	V	*warau*	笑う

Create phrases using clausal explanatory modification for the following.

1. the sound that is associated with someone coming down the stairs
2. the incident that a Japanese person is murdered
3. the picture in which a child is smiling

――――― Answers ―――――

1. *dareka ga kaidan o orite-kuru oto*
   誰かが階段を降りてくる音
2. *nihon-jin ga korosareru (to yuu) jiken*
   日本人が殺される(という)事件
3. *kodomo ga waratte-iru shashin*　子供が笑っている写真

＊　　＊　　＊　　＊　　＊

Igarashi Kyooko ga kane ni komatte-iru to yuu uwasa mo, tannaru uwasa de naku jijitsu kamoshirenai.

五十嵐京子が金に困っているという噂も，単なる噂でなく事実かも知れない。
(The rumor that Kyoko Igarashi is having financial trouble may not be just a rumor but a fact.)

—Nishimura, 1986, p. 140.

In this example, the explanatory clause and the noun *uwasa* are appositional, the former adding explanation to the latter.

115. Reporting—2. Hearsay—*Soo da*

Target Expression

> *They say Mr. Baker quit his job.*
> ***Beikaa-san wa shigoto o yameta soo desu yo.***
> ベイカーさんは仕事をやめたそうですよ。
>
> [V/Adj informal + *soo da*]

Grammatical Explanation

The pattern [V/Adj informal + *soo da*] is used to report hearsay. This expression is used when the speaker makes a general report regarding what he or she heard or obtained indirectly. Compare this with the reporting devices we have learned earlier, *to yuu* or *to kiku*, which report information where the speaker had direct access to the source. When using [*soo da*], the speaker's intention is merely to give a report which is often based on secondhand information. When using this expression of hearsay, you are not making any personal commitment as to the truth of the content of the sentence preceding *soo da.*

Examples

Amerika taishikan   N   American Embassy
アメリカ大使館
kikai 機械   N   machine

---

(1) A: *Sumisu-san te ieba kinoo nihon e itta soo desu yo.*
スミスさんて言えば，きのう日本へ行ったそうですよ。
(I hear that Mr. Kawasaki left for Japan yesterday.)

   B: *Soo desu ka. Kare shigoto de nihon e iku to itte-imashita ga.*
そうですか。彼仕事で日本へ行くと言っていましたが。
(Is that so? He said he was going to Japan because of his job.)

   A: *Ee, Amerika taishikan no shigoto da soo desu yo.*
ええ，アメリカ大使館の仕事だそうですよ。
(Yes, I hear it's a job at the American Embassy.)

(2) A: *Atarashii kikai wa subarashii soo desu nee.*
新しい機械はすばらしいそうですねえ。
(They say that the new machine is just wonderful.)

   B: *Ee, soo na n desu yo. Goran ni narimasu ka.*
ええ，そうなんですよ。ご覧になりますか。
(Yes, it is. Would you like to see it?)

Practice

---

winter   N   *huyu*   冬
mild   Adj   *odayakana*   おだやかな

Report the following which you heard from someone else.

1. The new movie isn't too good.
2. This year's winter is not so cold, but mild.
3. It snowed yesterday in Tokyo. ☺

--------- Answers ---------

1. *Atarashii eiga wa amari yokunai soo desu.*
新しい映画はあまりよくないそうです。

2. *Kotoshi no huyu wa amari samukunakute odayaka da soo desu.* 今年の冬はあまり寒くなくておだやかそうです。

3. *Tookyoo de wa kinoo yuki ga hutta soo da yo.* ☺
東京ではきのう雪が降ったそうだよ。

Warning

The use of [*soo da*] for reporting is preceded by the [V/Adj informal] forms. Contrast this with the [*soona*] used to express conjecture which takes [V/Adj stem] (as given in Entry 87). Contrast the meaning of the following two sentences.

Used when you hear from some source about the likelihood of rain:

(a) *Ame ga **huru soo desu.***
雨が**降る**そうです。
(They say it will rain.)

Used when you see a rain cloud hanging low and you conjecture that it is likely to rain:

(b) *Ame ga **hurisoo da.***
雨が**降り**そうだ。
(It looks [as if] it is going to rain.)

116. Causative and Permissive Expressions

Target Expression

> *I made my brother go to the bookstore.*
> ***Otooto o hon'ya e ikasemashita.***
> 弟を本屋へ行かせました。
>
> [V + -*seru*/-*saseru*]

Grammatical Explanation

Causatives express the idea that someone or something causes, influences, or allows a third party to do something. Causative expressions normally do not co-occur with stative verbs, existential verbs and the *be*-verb. Certain restrictions apply among some verbs; when there are transitive verbs that correspond with intransitive counterparts, transitive verbs are used instead of the causative forms. Causative forms are used as permissives when the causee performs an action willingly. As in the case of respectful and passive forms, causatives and permissives are expressed by verb endings which are changed by the following rules.

U-verbs: change the final *-u* to *-aseru* (when the final *-u* is not preceded by a consonant, change *-u* to *-waseru*)

kaku   *kakaseru*
kau   *kawaseru*

RU-verbs: change *-ru* to *-saseru*

taberu   *tabesaseru*

Irregular verbs:

kuru   **kosaseru**
suru   **saseru**

As for existential verbs, use only *isaseru* (causative of *iru*) when it means 'to stay.' Causatives and permissives have shortened forms which are obtained by changing the final *-seru* to *-su*; for example, *kakaseru* to *kakasu*, *tabesaseru* to *tabesasu*, and *saseru* to *sasu*. The shortened causative forms tend to express more direct and forceful causation than the standard causative forms.

Particles in Causatives and Permissives
Particles used for the causative/permissive structure are: the causer takes *ga* (or *wa* if it is a topic), the causee is marked by *o* or *ni*. For the selection of either *o* or *ni*, the following rules apply.

1.   When the verb is transitive and the direct object marker *o* appears, in order to avoid two *o*'s, the causee must be marked with *ni*.

    (1a)   *Otooto **ni** (not *o) heya o sooji-saseta.*
           弟に部屋をそうじさせた。
           (I made my younger brother clean his room.)

2.   When the verb expresses instant change and response, the causee takes *o*.

    (2a)   *Okyakusan **o** (not *ni) okorasete-shimatta.*
           お客さんを怒らせてしまった。
           (I made the customer get angry.)

3. When the causative expression conveys the meaning that one is responsible for the event to happen or to have happened, only *o* is used.

(3a) *Haha o byooki de shinaseta n desu.*
母を病気で死なせたんです。
([I am to blame that] I caused my mother's death due to sickness.)

When these restrictions do not apply, use either *o* or *ni* to mark the causee. The choice of either particle is based on the following guidelines. As a general rule use *o* for either causative or permissive expressions, use only *ni* for permissives. When *ni* is used, the causer acknowledges the causee's desire or will to perform the action, and the causee must be able to perform it. Thus, the verb used in this pattern must refer to a controllable action. Although *o* can be used to express permissives similarly to *ni*, when the causee is marked by *o*, coercive causative meaning is emphasized; the causee performs the act against his or her own wish or will. The verb used for this pattern must also refer to controllable action. *Imooto o ikaseta* 'I made (or, forced) my sister (to) go' is ambiguous between ' I forced my sister to go' and 'I let (permitted) my sister (to) go; *Imooto ni ikaseta* has only a permissive interpretation. The choice of meanings depends on the semantic context in which the utterance appears.

The causative expression may be combined with the passive to form causative passive expressions. The causative ending *-seru* goes through a passive ending change following *RU*-verbs; thus *kakaseru* takes *kakaserareru* 'to be forced to write,' *tabesaseru* takes *tabesaserareru* 'to be forced to eat.' Irregular verbs *kuru* and *suru* take *kosaserareru* and *saserareru*, respectively. For *U*-verbs only, shortened causative passive endings are available; *kakasu* changes according to the *U*-verb conjugation resulting in *kakasareru*.

(a) *Kodomo-tachi wa kiraina tabemono o **tabesaserareta**.*
子供たちはきらいな食べものを**食べさせられた**。
(Children were forced to eat the food they disliked.)

Examples

hitsuyoona	必要な	Adj	necessary
kyuuyoo	急用	N	emergency

(1) *Kodomo-tachi ni wa san-ji made sukina koto o sasemashoo.*
子供たちには三時まで好きなことをさせましょう。
(Let's let the children do whatever they like until three o'clock.)

(2) *Kitte ga hitsuyoo nara Masao o kai ni ikasemashoo.*
切手が必要なら正男を買いに行かせましょう。
(If you need stamps, I will make Masao go buy them.)

(3) *Sonna koto sasenai de.* ☺ F
そんなことさせないで。
Sonna koto saseru na yo. ☺ M
そんなことさせるなよ。
(Don't make me do such a thing.)

(4) A: *Kinoo ginkoo e itta n desu ga, nagai aida matasaremashite nee.*
きのう銀行へ行ったんですが，長い間待たされましてねえ。
(I went to the bank yesterday, but I was made to wait for a long time.)
B: *Sore wa taihen deshita nee. Konde-ita n desu ka.*
それは大変でしたねえ。混んでいたんですか。
(That's too bad. Was it crowded?)
A: *Iie, au yakusoku o shite-oita hito ga rusu de ne, kyuuyoo de. Chotto hoka no shigoto o saserareta rashii n desu.*
いいえ，会う約束をしておいた人が留守でね，急用で。
ちょっと他の仕事をさせられたらしいんです。
(No, the person I was going to see was out due to an emergency. It seems that he was forced to tend to other matters.)

Practice

---
to copy down   V   *utsusu*   うつす

How do you express the following in Japanese?

1. A: What did you make her do?
    B: I made her copy down the entire report.
2. I made my younger sister make a phone call.
3. Because the bus broke down the teacher made the children walk for an hour (emphasizing *one* hour).

─────── Answers ───────

1. A: *Nani o saseta n desu ka.* 何をさせたんですか。
   B: *Hookokusho o zenbu utsusasemashita.*
   報告書を全部うつさせました。
2. *Imooto ni denwa-sasemashita.* 妹に電話させました。
3. *Basu ga koshoo-shita node sensei wa kodomo-tachi o ichi-jikan mo arukaseta n desu yo.*
   バスが故障したので先生は子供たちを一時間も歩かせたんですよ。

117. Subjunctive Expressions

Target Expressions

If it were cheaper, I would have bought it.

Motto yasukereba katta noni.
もっと安ければ買ったのに。

Motto yasukattara katta n desu kedo.
もっと安かったら買ったんですけど。

Grammatical Explanation

When describing one's feelings contradicting realities, the so-called subjunctive mood is used. In Japanese, conditional sentences with [-ba] and [-tara] are frequently used for this purpose. The main clause ends with disjunctive conjunctions such as *kedo* or *noni*. (For forming the *ba*-form see Entry 92, for *tara*-form, see Entry 93.) The verbs and adjectival predicates in the main clause normally take [V/Adj past] forms.

Examples

```
pikunikku      ピクニック    N    picnic
nagaiki o suru  長生きをする   V    to live long
```

(1) *Tenki ga yokereba pikunikku ni iketa noni.*
    天気がよければピクニックに行けたのに。
    (If it was good weather, we could have gone for a picnic.)

(2) *Moo sukoshi nagaiki o shite-tara kaigairyokoo mo dekita noni.*
     もう少し長生きをしてたら海外旅行もできたのに。
     (If they lived a little longer, they would have been able to travel abroad.)

(3) *Okane ga attara yasumi ni wa Yooroppa e ike ta n da kedo nee.*
     お金があったら休みにはヨーロッパへ行けたんだけどねえ。
     (If I had money, I could have gone to Europe for vacation.)

(4) *Motto ganbareba yokatta noni.*
     もっとがんばればよかったのに。
     (If I tried harder, it would have been better.)

Additional Information

A shortened version of subjunctives takes either the *ba*-form or *tara*-form followed by the final particle *nee* or *naa*. These expressions are normally used in casual situations and carry the impression of being a monologue. For example:

(a) *Motto okane ga **attara nee**.*
     もっとお金が**あったらねえ**。
     (I wish I had more money . . .)

(b) *Ano hito ga ato san-pun hayaku **kite-itara naa**.*
     あの人があと三分早く**来ていたらなあ**。
     (I wish he came three minutes earlier . . .)

Practice

Assume that you are put in the situation described in 1 through 3. Express in Japanese your desires that are impossible to realize under such circumstances.

1. You don't have money to buy a new car.
2. Your friend doesn't live nearby.
3. You are no longer young.

——— Some Sample Answers ———

1. *Okane ga attara/areba, atarashii kuruma kaeta n da kedo . . .* お金があったら/あれば新しい車買えたんだけど……

2. *Tomodachi ga chikaku ni sunde-itara naa . . .* 友だちが近くに住んでいたらなあ……

3. *Motto wakakattara naa . . .* もっと若かったらなあ……
    Motto wakakattara yokatta n da kedo . . . もっと若かったらよかったんだけど……

118. Advising

> *Wouldn't it be better for you to go by an earlier Bullet Train?*
> **Motto hayai Shinkansen de itta hoo ga ii-deshoo.**
> もっと早い新幹線で行った方がいいでしょう。
> **Motto hayai Shinkansen de itta hoo ga ii n ja-nai?** ☺
> もっと早い新幹線で行った方がいいんじゃない？
> *Since it is time already, wouldn't it be better to start?*
> **Moo jikan da kara hajimetara doo deshoo ka.**
> もう時間だから始めたらどうでしょうか。
>
> [Vpre-nominal + *hoo ga ii*]

Strategic Explanation

Although we've learned structures introduced here earlier under the heading Comparative and Superlative forms (Entry 64), we will review the strategies for giving suggestions and advice in Japanese.

The first is the [*hoo ga ii*] pattern studied under comparative forms. The [*hoo ga ii*] expression takes [Vpre-nominal], with the [Vinformal past] form considered slightly more indirect. For the *be*-verb *da*, use *de-iru*. For making a negative suggestion, use only the negative [informal non-past form + *hoo ga ii*]. When advising or making suggestions, use only the verbs that refer to controllable action.

The second is the [*-tara*] conditional, followed by the deletable formulaic clause of [*doo da* / *daroo*] followed by the question marker *ka*. It is important to remember in both cases that suggestions and advice given in these expressions are limited to those given to social subordinates or close friends.

When suggesting and advising one's social superiors or those with whom one is expected to be polite, a different expression must be used. For example, *motto hayai Shinkansen de irasshatta hoo ga yoroshii ka to omoimasu ga . . .* 'I think it might be better if you took an earlier Bullet Train.' This use of the verb *omou* 'think' will be discussed shortly.

Let us review a group of strategies used for giving advice and suggestions. The following are listed starting with the most direct to the most indirect. As you can see, in general, the more elaborate the expression is, the more polite it becomes, which is also true in English.

1. *Ike.* 行け。 (Entry 79)

2. *Ikinasai.* 行きなさい。 (Entry 79)
3. *Iku hoo ga ii (desu).* 行く方がいい(です)。 (Entry 118)
4. *Itta hoo ga ii (desu).* 行った方がいい(です)。 (Entry 118)
5. *Itta hoo ga ii-deshoo.* 行った方がいいでしょう。 (Entry 118)
6. *Ittara doo desu ka.* 行ったらどうですか。(Entry 93)
7. *Itta hoo ga yoroshii ka to omoimasu ga . . .*
   行った方がよろしいかと思いますが…… (Entry 122)
8. *Irasshattara?* ☺F いらっしゃったら？ (Entry 93)
9. *Irasshatta hoo ga yoroshii n ja-nai ka to omoimasu ga . . .*
   いらっしゃった方がよろしいんじゃないかと思いますが……
   (Entry 122)

Practice

| *huraito* | フライト | N | flight |
| *(go)shootai* | ご招待 | N | invitation |

How will you make the following suggestions to your colleague or friend?
1. not to leave so early
2. to write a letter
3. to call the hotel (for future convenience)

How would you make the following suggestions to your social superiors?
4. to take an earlier flight
5. to hold a meeting at nine
6. to invite Kato also

—— Some Sample Answers ——

1. *Sonna ni hayaku kaeranai hoo ga ii-deshoo.*
   そんなに早く帰らない方がいいでしょう。
2. *Tegami o kaitara (doo desu ka)?* 手紙を書いたら(どうですか)？
3. *Hoteru ni denwa-shite-oita hoo ga ii n ja-nai-desu ka.*
   ホテルに電話しておいた方がいいんじゃないですか。
4. *Hayai huraito de irasshatta hoo ga yoroshii ka to zonjimasu ga . . .*
   早いフライトでいらっしゃった方がよろしいかと存じますが……
5. *Kaigi wa kuji ni hajimeru hoo ga yoroshii ka to zonjimasu ga . . .* 会議は九時に始める方がよろしいかと存じますが……
6. *Katoo-san mo goshootai nasatta hoo ga yoroshii n ja nai ka to zonjimasu ga . . .*
   加藤さんもご招待なさった方がよろしいんじゃないかと存じますが……

119. Not Only But . . . Special Uses of *Dake*, *Bakari*, and *Hodo*

> *As for kanji, it is important to be able not only to read it but to write it as well.*
>
> **Kanji wa yomeru dake/bakari de naku kakeru koto mo taisetsu desu.**
>
> 漢字は読める<u>だけ</u>/<u>ばかり</u>でなく書けることも大切です。
>
> *I just arrived.*
>
> **Ima kita bakari desu.**
>
> 今来たばかりです。

Grammatical Explanation

Adverbial quantifiers listed here have basic usage as well as useful idiomatic expression, which we will study one by one.

A. **Dake:**

The form preceding *dake* is [V/Adj pre-nominal], except when [N + *da*] precedes *dake* use [N + *dake*].

1. *dake:* 'only' 'just'

   (1a) *Chotto koe ga kikitakatta* **dake** *desu.*
   ちょっと声が聞きたかった**だけ**です。
   (I just wanted to hear your voice.)

2. *dake de naku . . . mo:* 'not only but also . . .'

   (2a) *Nihon-jin* **dake de naku** *Amerika-jin* **mo** *takusan imashita.*
   日本人**だけでなく**アメリカ人**も**たくさんいました。
   (Not only Japanese but many Americans were there.)

B: **Bakari:**

1. *bakari:* 'only'
   The form preceding this is [N], [Adj pre-nominal non-past] and [V*te*]. When [V*te*] precedes *bakari* to mean 'only [V],' it takes the [V*te bakari iru*] structure.

(1a) Musume   wa   amaimono   **bakari**
     daughter   T   sweets   only

     tabete-iru n desu   yo.
     eat   IP

     娘は甘いもの**ばかり**食べているんですよ。
     (My daughter eats just sweets, you know.)

(1b) Musume wa **asonde bakari** imasu.
     娘は**遊んで**ばかりいます。
     ([lit. My daughter only plays.] All my daughter does is to play.)

2. *bakari de naku . . . mo*: 'not only but also . . .'
The form preceding this use is [N], [Vpre-Aux] and [Adj pre-nominal].

(2a) Nihon-jin **bakari de naku** Amerika-jin **mo** takusan kite-imashita.
     日本人**だけでなく**アメリカ人**も**たくさんいました。
     (Not only Japanese but many Americans came.)

3. [Vinformal past (affirmative only) + *bakari da*]: 'just did . . .'

(3a) Ima **hajimatta bakari** desu yo.
     今始まった**ばかり**ですよ。
     (It just started.)

4. [quantifier + *bakari*]: 'about'

(4a) Rondon ni wa **ni-shuukan bakari** imashita.
     ロンドンには**二週間**ばかりいました。
     (I was in London for about two weeks.)

5. [Vbasic + *bakari da*]: '. . . ready to'

(5a) Sate, junbi wa dekimashita yo, moo **taberu bakari** desu.
     さて，準備はできましたよ，もう**食べる**ばかりです。
     (Well, the preparation is complete, we are ready to eat.)

C. *Hodo:*
The form preceding *hodo* is [Vpre-nominal]. When the [N + *da*] precedes *hodo*, use [N + *to yuu hodo*].

1. *hodo*: 'to the degree'

(1a) Kesa   wa   atatakakute   sukoshi   asebamu
     this morning   T   warm   a little   sweat

<u>**hodo**</u>　　<u>deshita.</u>
degree　　was

今朝は暖かくて少し汗ばむ**ほど**でした。

(It was warm this morning to the degree that I sweated a little.)

2.　*hodo dewa nai*: 'not so'

(2a)　<u>*Kono mondai*</u>　<u>*wa*</u>　<u>*muzukashii*</u>　<u>*ga,*</u>　<u>*muzukashikute*</u>
　　　　this question　　T　　difficult　　but　　difficult

　　　<u>*zenzen*</u>　<u>*wakaranai*</u>　<u>**hodo**</u>　<u>**dewa nai.**</u> ♦
　　　at all　　do not understand　　degree　　is not

この問題はむずかしいが，むずかしくて全然わからない
ほどではない。

(This question is difficult, but not so difficult as to not being able to understand it at all)

(2b)　*Ano hito wa namakemono to yuu* **hodo dewa nai** *kedo*
. . .

あの人はなまけものという**ほどではない**けど……

(He is not [lit. to the degree of being a lazy person] exactly a lazy person, but . . .)

3.　[quantifier + *hodo*]: 'about'

(3a)　*Sumimasen ga* **ni-sen-yen hodo** *kashite-kudasaimasen ka.*

すみませんが**二千円ほど**貸してくださいませんか。

(Could you please loan me two thousand yen or so?)

Recall that phrases expressing approximation of quantity such as *hodo*, *kurai/gurai* and *bakari* are closely associated with politeness, particularly when used with small numbers and when used in requests. By presenting the quantity in approximation, the speaker allows more leeway for the interactant to respond.

120. Special Uses of *Mono* and *Koto*

I used to play around here a long time ago.
Mukashi wa koko de yoku asonda mono desu.
昔はここでよく遊んだものです。
We are moving soon, so . . .
Kondo hikkosu koto ni narimashita node . . .
今度引っ越すことになりましたので……

Grammatical Explanation

Here we focus on idiomatic uses of the noun *mono* and *koto*. *Mono* and *koto* are both nouns and mean 'thing(s)' and 'fact(s)' respectively. While *mono* refers to tangible things, *koto* is used to refer to intangible and abstract things or facts. The idiomatic uses of these nouns are frequent and warrant our special attention.

A. **Mono**:
   1. [V/Adj informal past + *mono da*]
      Reflecting on past experience with a sentimental, nostalgic feeling:

   (1a) <u>Kodomo</u> <u>no</u> <u>koro</u> <u>wa</u> <u>koko</u> <u>de</u> <u>yoku</u>
          child   L   time   T   here   at   often

          <u>asonda mono desu</u>.
          played

          子供の頃はここでよく遊んだものです。
          (In my childhood, [I remember] I used to play around here.)

   2. [Adj + *mono*] (Adj must be in predicate forms.), [*da* + *mono*], [V/Adj prenominal + *n* + *da* + *mono*] (If *da* precedes *n*, *da* changes to *na*.)
      Pointing out reason in colloquial speech:

   (2a) A: *Dooshite tabenai no?* ☺
             どうして食べないの？
             (Why don't you eat?)

B: *Oishikunai **mono**.* ☺
　　おいしくないもの。
　　(Because it doesn't taste good.)

(2b) A: *Dooshite katta no?* ☺
　　どうして買ったの？
　　(Why did you buy?)

      B: *Benri **da mono**.* ☺
　　便利だもの。
　　(Because it is useful.)

(2c) A: *Dooshite sonna koto shita no?*
　　どうしてそんなことしたの？
　　(Why did you do such a thing?)

      B: *Oniisan ga suru yooni itta **n da mono**.*
　　お兄さんがするように言った**んだもの**。
　　(Because my brother told me to.)

(2d) A: *Hiroshi-kun no ojisan tte okanemochi na n datte?*
　　ひろしくんのおじさんってお金もちなんだって？
　　(Is it true that Hiroshi's uncle is rich?)

      B: *Soo. Kaisha no shachoo **na n da mono**.*
　　そう。会社の社長**なんだもの**。
　　(Yes. Because he is a company president.)

3. [V/Adj pre-nominal + *mono da*] (Note that the [N + *da*] structure does not normally co-occur with this usage.)
Expressing surprise, empathy with a deep feeling:

(3a) *Kono go-nenkan iroirona koto ga **atta mono da** naa to omou.*
この五年間いろいろなことが**あったものだ**なあと思う。
(I feel overwhelmed when I think that so many things have happened in the past five years.)

(3b) *Amerika wa hontooni **hiroi mono da** naa to omotta.*
アメリカは本当に**広いものだ**なあと思った。
(I was overwhelmed by the vastness of the United States.)

4. [Vinformal + *mono*] (Note that the [N + *da*] structure does not normally co-occur with this usage.)
To add explanation in written style:

(4a)

<u>Kono</u>	<u>tatemono</u>	<u>wa</u>	<u>koko</u>	<u>san-nen</u>	<u>shimin</u>
this	building	T	here	three years	citizen

> | *no* | *doryoku* | *niyotte* | ***taterareta mono.***♦ |
> |------|-----------|-----------|---------------------------|
> | L | effort | by | was built |
>
> この建物はここ三年市民の努力によって**建てられたもの**。
>
> (This building is the one built by the citizens' effort over the last three years.)

5. [Vbasic + *mono da*] (Only controllable verbs are used for this structure.)

   To convey mild, indirect command:

   (5a)   *Yoso no uchi e iku toki wa nani-ka omiyage o **motte-iku mono desu** yo.*

   よその家へ行く時は何かおみやげを**持っていくものです**よ。

   (When you visit someone else's house, you should bring some gift.)

B.   *Koto*:

1. [Vinformal non-past + *koto ni suru*]: (Only controllable verbs are used for this structure.)

   Expression of decision, 'to decide to do,' 'I will do':

   (1a)   *Shinjuku de takushii ni noru **koto ni shimasu**.*

   新宿でタクシーに乗る**ことにします**。

   (I will take a taxi at Shinjuku Station.)

2. [V/Adj informal past + *koto ga aru*]:

   To point out past experience, 'I have experienced it in the past':

   (2a)   *Yooroppa e wa nankai mo itta **koto ga arimasu** yo.*

   ヨーロッパへは何回も行った**ことがあります**よ。

   (I've been to Europe many times.)

   (2b)   *Waapuro wa ichiji taihen takakatta **koto mo arimasu**.*

   ワープロは一時たいへん高かった**こともあります**。

   (There was a time when word processors were quite expensive.)

3. [V/Adj prenominal non-past + *koto ga aru*]:

   To point out that an event or a state occurs sometimes or occasionally:

   (3a) | *Hutsukayoi-suru* | *made* | *nomu **koto ga arimasu** ka.* |
   |-------------------|--------|-------------------------------|
   | have hangover | till | drink |

   二日酔いするまで飲む**ことがあります**か。

   (Do you sometimes drink to the extent that you have a hangover?)

(3b) *Ano suupaa no hoo ga yasui **koto mo arimasu** yo.*
あのスーパーの方が安い**こともあります**よ。
(There are some occasions when that supermarket is less expensive.)

4. [Vinformal non-past + *koto ni naru*]: (For the [N + *da*] structure, use [N + *deiru koto ni naru*].)
To mean 'it has been decided to':

(4a) *Kondo Kyuushuu e iku **koto ni narimashita** node.*
今度九州へ行く**ことになりました**ので。
(It has been decided that we will be going to Kyushu soon, so . . .)

5. [Vbasic + *koto wa nai*]: (For the [N + *da*] structure, use [N + *deiru koto wa nai*].)
To mean 'there is no need to . . .':

(5a) *Isogashii no nara iku **koto wa arimasen** yo.* [*1]
忙しいのなら行く**ことはありません**よ。
(If you are busy, there is no need to go.)

[*1.] *No* in this expression is a nominalizer used for the extended predicate *no da. Da* is then deleted before *nara(ba).*

Practice

Germany   N   *Doitsu*   ドイツ

How would you express the following in Japanese?

1. You played there when you were a child, and you are sentimentally reflecting on that memory:
2. You have experienced living in Germany:
3. You are reporting to your boss that you will be moving to Osaka:

─────── Some Sample Answers ───────
1. *Kodomo no koro asoko de yoku asonda mono desu.*
子供の頃あそこでよく遊んだものです。
2. *Doitsu ni sunda koto ga arimasu.*
ドイツに住んだことがあります。
3. *Oosaka ni hikkosu koto ni narimashita.*
大阪に引っ越すことになりました。

121. Useful Compounds—1. Verb Compounds

Grammatical Explanation

We've studied several verb compounds already. Verb compounds consist of two verbs or a verb and [AuxV]. Compound verbs conjugate according to the category of the latter [V] or [AuxV]. In this section, we add to our repertoire additional useful verb compounds in Japanese.

1. [Vte + -shimau] (See Entry 54.)

2. [Vte + -oku] (See Entry 95.)

3. [Vte + -miru] 'try and see by doing something'
   This expression is used when you attempt to perform an action as a trial for some other purpose.

(3a)   A: *Kore **tsukutte-mimashita** ga.*
　　　　　これ**作ってみました**が。
　　　　　(I tried making this . . .)

　　　B: *Aa, oishisoo desu nee.*
　　　　　ああ，おいしそうですねえ。
　　　　　(Oh, that looks delicious.)

　　　A: *Doozo **meshiagatte-mite**-kudasai.*
　　　　　どうぞ**めしあがってみて**ください。
　　　　　(Please try some.)

　　　B: *Sumimasen. Itadakimasu.*
　　　　　すみません。いただきます。
　　　　　(Thank you.)

(3b)   A: *Kono hon omoshirosoona node **yonde-mite** kudasai.*
　　　　　この本おもしろそうなので**読んでみて**ください。
　　　　　(Please read this book since it looks interesting.)

　　　B: *Aa, sore wa moo yomimashita.*
　　　　　ああ，それはもう読みました。
　　　　　(Oh, I've already read that one.)

　　　A: *Doo deshita?*
　　　　　どうでした？
　　　　　(How was it?)

　　　B: *Totemo ii hon desu ne. Onaji chosha no hon o motto **yonde-mitaku** narimashita.*
　　　　　とてもいい本ですね。同じ著者の本をもっと**読んでみたく**なりました。
　　　　　(It's a very good book. I've come to want to read other books by the same author.)

4. [Vstem + -*kakeru*] 'start doing something'

    (4a)   *Shinbun o **yomi-kaketa** toki denwa ga narimashita.*
          新聞を**読みかけた**時電話が鳴りました。
          (When I began reading the newspaper, the phone rang.)

5. [Vstem + -*hajimeru*], [Vstem + -*dasu*] 'something begins to occur'
Dasu is preferred with verbs which indicate sudden and unexpected changes.

    (5a)   *Shigatsu na noni yuki ga **huri-dashita** n desu yo.*
          四月なのに雪が**降りだした**んですよ。
          (Although it was April, the snow began to fall.)

    (5b) A: *Moo **tabe-hajimete** mo ii-desu ka.*
             もう**食べはじめて**もいいですか。
             (Is it all right to start eating now?)
        B: *Ee, doozo.*
             ええ，どうぞ。
             (Of course.)

6. [Vstem + -*naosu*], [Vstem + -*kaesu*] 'repeating something, especially to amend an earlier error'

    (6a)   *Konna ji de wa komarimasu nee. **Kaki-naoshite** kudasai.*
          こんな字では困りますねえ。**書き直して**ください。
          (Such handwriting will not do. Please rewrite it.)

    (6b)   *Yoku wakaranakatta node **kiki-kaeshita** n desu ga, mada wakarimasen.*
          よくわからなかったので**聞きかえした**んですが，まだわかりません。
          (Since I didn't understand well I asked again, but I still don't understand it.)

7. [V/Adj stem + -*sugiru*] 'do or be in excess'

    (7a)   *Yuube **nomi-sugite** kesa wa atama ga itai n desu.*
          ゆうべ**飲みすぎて**今朝は頭が痛いんです。
          (I drank too much last night, and I have a headache this morning.)

Note that in all structures listed above, in number 4 through 7, the *be*-verb *da* is excluded from the category [V].

Practice

Make short sentences using the following verb compounds:

1. *tabe-sugiru*
2. *tsukuri-naosu*
3. *itte-miru*
4. *kaeri-hajimeru*
5. *chiisa-sugiru*

———— Some Sample Answers ————

1. *Yuube oishii mono o takusan dasarete tabe-sugite-shimatta.*
    ゆうべおいしいものをたくさん出されて食べすぎてしまった。
    (Last night I was served many delicious kinds of food and I ended up eating too much.)
2. *Kono hako wa kowarete-shimatta node tsukuri-naoshite-kudasai ne.*
    この箱はこわれてしまったので作り直してくださいね。
    (This box got broken so please re-make it.)
3. *Shinkansen no kippu ga mada aru ka nai ka, eki made itte-minakereba wakarimasen yo.*
    新幹線の切符がまだあるかないか，駅まで行ってみなければわかりませんよ。
    (Whether or not there still are tickets for the Bullet Train, unless you go there, you won't find out.)
4. *Juu ichi-ji ni naru to minna kaeri-hajimeta.*
    十一時になるとみんな帰りはじめた。
    (When it became eleven o'clock, everyone began to leave [the place].)
5. *Sono kaban wa kaigairyokoo ni wa chiisa-sugiru wa yo.* ☺F
    そのかばんは海外旅行には小さすぎるわよ。
    (That bag is too small for overseas travel.)

*　　*　　*　　*　　*

Watashi wa Nakao no apaato e yotte-miru koto ni shita.
私は中尾のアパートへ寄ってみることにした。
(I decided to stop by at Nakao's apartment and see.)

—Yuki, 1977, p.36.

Note the use of [V*te* + *-miru*]. Review *koto ni suru* which was discussed in Entry 120 if you are uncertain of its use.

122. Expressing Your Thoughts

> *I think it's really wonderful.*
> **Hontooni subarashii to omoimasu.**
> 本当にすばらしいと思います。
> *I'm afraid that the deadline is next week.*
> **Shimekiri wa raishuu ja-nai ka to omoimasu ga . . .**
> 締め切りは来週じゃないかと思いますが……
>
> [*to omou*]

Grammatical Explanation

When expressing one's thoughts, the quotative *to* plus the verb *omou* or *omotte-iru* 'think' are frequently used. Although it is possible to express your feelings without [*to omou*], the [*to omou*] expression in Japanese makes the communication less domineering. So it is used commonly to avoid making blunt assertions. What is quoted ends with the informal volitional form if the content of the quoted clause represents one's intention or one's speculation about a future event or state; for example, *ikoo to omotte-imasu* 'I'm thinking that I will go.' In expressing a thought other than one's volition or one's opinion toward the future, [V/Adj informal] forms are used preceding [*to omou*]; for example, *yuubinkyoku wa ano tatemono da to omoimasu ga* 'I think the post office is that building.' When the speaker is quite uncertain or when the speaker wishes to express hesitation, *ka* may be placed before the quotative *to*. The form preceding *ka* is [V/Adj pre-Aux].

When it is necessary to negate and mean 'I don't think . . . ,' unlike English, the negation is normally placed within the quoted clause. 'I don't think the post office is that building' is most usually expressed as *yuubinkyoku wa ano tatemono dewa-nai to omoimasu ga . . . .* It is possible to negate the verb *omou*, as in *yuubinkyoku wa ano tatemono da to (wa) omoimasen ga . . .*; when this expression is used, it is closer to the English "I doubt that . . ." and expresses stronger doubt on the part of the speaker.

As we have studied when we discussed the expression of advice (Entry 118), [*to omou*] is used to express one's opinion in a socially humble way. It is a frequently used strategy in Japanese conversation.

Examples

| *unga* | 運河 | N | canal |
| *hukin* | 付近 | N | vicinity |

Kesa Amusuterudamu ni tsukimashita.
今朝アムステルダムに着きました。
(I arrived in Amsterdam this morning.)

Kyoo wa sukoshi hoteru de yasumu koto ni shimashita.
今日は少しホテルで休むことにしました。
(I decided to rest at the hotel a bit today.)

Iroiro shinakereba naranai koto ya shitai koto ga arimasu.
いろいろしなければならないことやしたいことがあります。
(There are many things I must do and things I want to do.)

Mazu Amusuterudamu ni sunde-iru tomodachi ni denwa o shiyoo to omotte-imasu.
まずアムステルダムに住んでいる友だちに電話をしようと思っています。
(First, I am thinking about calling a friend who lives in Amsterdam.)

Soshite dekireba isshoni bijutsukan ni itte-mitai to omoimasu.
そしてできればいっしょに美術館に行ってみたいと思います。
(And if it's possible, I'd like to go together to the art museum.)

Sorekara omiyage o kattari, unga no hukin o aruite-mitai to omoimasu.
それからおみやげを買ったり，運河の付近を歩いてみたいと思います。
(And I want to buy some souvenirs and walk along the canal.)

Practice

----
to collect	V	*atsumeru*	集める
data	N	*deeta*	データ
research	N	*kenkyuu*	研究
----

1. Express your opinion on the following topics. How might someone else respond to your opinion?
   a. tomorrow's weather being fine
   b. the price of the book being about eight thousand yen
   c. the movie starting at seven o'clock ☺

2. How do you express the following in Japanese?
   a. A: What do you think?

B: I think it's fine.
   b.　Do you think he is a Japanese? ☺
   c.　Don't you think this is expensive? ☺
   d.　I'm thinking that I will collect data for research in
       Japan.

3.　Express your thoughts and opinion regarding the following. Try
   to use the 'I think' expression.
   a.　your Japanese teacher
   b.　driving a car
   c.　this summer's weather ☺
   d.　air travel

──────── Some Sample Answers ────────

1a. A: *Ashita wa hareru to omoimasu yo.*
        あしたは晴れると思いますよ。
    B: *Watashi mo soo omoimasu.* 私もそう思います。

  b. A: *Soo desu nee, sono hon wa has-sen-en da to omoimasu
        ga . . .* そうですねえ，その本は八千円だと思いますが……
     B: *Takai n desu nee . . .* 高いんですねえ……

  c. A: *Sono eiga wa shichi-ji ni hajimaru to omou kedo . . .* ☺
        その映画は七時に始まると思うけど……
     B: *Hontoo? Jaa isoganakya!* 本当？じゃあ急がなきゃ。

2a. A: *Doo omoimasu ka.* どう思いますか。
    B: *Ii to omoimasu yo.* いいと思いますよ。

  b.　*Ano hito nihon-jin da to omou?* ☺
      あの人日本人だと思う？

  c.　*Kore takai to omowanai?* ☺ これ高いと思わない？

  d.　*Nihon de kenkyuu no deeta o atsumeyoo to omotte-
      imasu.* 日本で研究のデータを集めようと思っています。

3a.　*Oda sensei wa ii sensei da to omoimasu.*
     小田先生はいい先生だと思います。
     (I think Professor Oda is a good teacher.)

  b.　*Rasshu awaa ni kuruma o unten suru no wa tsukareru to
      omoimasen ka.*
      ラッシュアワーに車を運転するのは疲れると思いませんか。
      (Don't you think driving a car in rush hour is tiring?)

  c.　*Kotoshi no natsu wa atsuku naru to omou yo.* ☺
      今年の夏は暑くなると思うよ。
      (I think this year's summer is going to be a hot one.)

  d.　*Hikooki ni noru to nodo ga kawaku to omoimasen ka.*
      飛行機に乗るとのどがかわくと思いませんか。
      (Don't you think you'll get thirsty when you are aboard
      the airplane?)

Additional Information

When you oppose someone else's opinion, it is generally more polite in Japanese to mark the statement with [*to omou*]. Further, by turning the content of the quoted clause into the negative, you will achieve a greater degree of hesitation and softness. The same opinion can be expressed in at least three different ways depending on how indirect you wish to be. As you see, in general the more auxiliary phrases added to an utterance, the politer it becomes. This applies to English as well, as shown in the translations.

1. Straightforward:
   Kore wa chigaimasu yo.
   これは違いますよ。
   (This is wrong.)

2. Polite:
   Soo desu nee . . . kore wa chigau (ka) to omoimasu ga . . .
   そうですねえ……これは違う(か)と思いますが……
   (Well, let's see . . . I think this is wrong, but . . .)

3. More polite and more indirect:
   Maa soo de-gozaimasu nee . . . kore wa sukoshi chigau n ja-nai ka to zonjimasu ga . . .
   まあそうでございますねえ……これはすこし違うんじゃないかと存じますが……
   (Well, let's see . . . I [somehow] think that this isn't the case. . .)

Additionally, there are other expressions you can use when you state your opinion including *chigau n ja-nai ka na*, or feminine style, *chigau n ja-nai kashira.*

When speaking in English with Japanese people, you might notice that Japanese insert 'I think' quite frequently. This 'I think' mirrors the style in their native Japanese; it should not be literally interpreted. As shown above, Japanese tend to end personal opinions with *to omoimasu* just to make the expression less imposing. In fact, even when the Japanese speaker is quite certain of the fact, *to omou* is still added. For example, *ano hito wa kitto kuru to omoimasu yo* '(I think) that he will come for sure'—a style considered to be more pleasant to the ears.

123. Useful Compounds—2. Compounds with Adjectives and Nouns

Grammatical Explanation

Compound words in Japanese are created by combinations between verbs, adjectives, and nouns. The grammatical category of the compound word is based on the last word. We will learn only a few examples of compounds in this book. It is a good idea to look for evidence for compounds when you face Japanese words. Knowing the rules for compounds can help increase your Japanese vocabulary.

A. *Verb-Adjective Compounds*

1. [Vstem + *yasui*] 'easy to do'

   (1a) *Kono kuruma wa **unten-shi yasui** desu ka.*
   この車は運転しやすいですか。
   (Is this car easy to drive?)

2. [Vstem + *nikui*] 'difficult to do'

   (2a) *Kore wa **tsukai nikukute** dame desu yo.*
   これは使いにくくてだめですよ。
   (This is difficult to use and it is not good [at all].)

B. *Nominal Compounds*

Many Japanese noun phrases are generated by adding verbs, adjectives and, of course, nouns. Here are some useful noun compounds. The process specified below for these compounds is not generative in all cases. In short, these rules are applicable to select nouns; one should not create new ones. When you find compounds however, it is helpful to know how they are constructed.

1. Repetition of nouns for indicating plurality:

hitobito	人々	people
hibi	日々	days

2. [Vstem + *mono*] 'thing':

kaimono	買い物	shopping
tabemono	食べ物	food
yomimono	読み物	things to read

3. [N + *dai*] 'fare':

basudai	バス代	bus fare
hondai	本代	book expense

4. [N + *ryoo (kin)*] 'fare':

takushiiryookin	タクシー料金	taxi fare
suidooryookin	水道料金	water fee
nyuujooryoo	入場料	admission fee

5. [Adj stem + *sa*]:
Sa nominalizes the [Adj]. This process creates nouns presenting the degree of the quality identified by the adjective.

hukasa	深さ	depth
hirosa	広さ	size
takasa	高さ	height
atatakasa	暖かさ	warmth
benrisa	便利さ	convenience
suzushisa	涼しさ	coolness
utsukushisa	美しさ	beauty

6. [Adj stem + *mi*]:
Mi also nominalizes the [Adj-*i*]. This pattern tends to express more emotive feeling than -*sa* nominalization.

tanoshimi	楽しみ	fun, pleasure
hukami	深み	depth

7. [Vstem + *kata*] 'the way of doing':

tabekata	食べ方	way (or manner) of eating
oyogikata	泳ぎ方	way (or style) of swimming

8. [N + *yoo*] 'for the use by':

kodomoyoo	子供用	for use by children
renshuuyoo	練習用	used for practice purposes
gakkooyoo	学校用	for consumption at school

9. [N + *muke*] 'bound for,' 'catered toward':

Chuugokumuke	中国向け	bound for, or catered to China
wakamonomuke	若者向け	catered to young people

Examples

```
------------------------------------------------------------
hakaru    計る    V    to measure
------------------------------------------------------------
```

(1)   *Nani-ka yomimono o katte-kimasu.*
何か読み物を買ってきます。
(I'm going to buy something to read.)

(2) A: *Suidooryookin ga mata agarimashita yo.*
水道料金がまた上がりましたよ。
(The water bill went up again.)

    B: *Hontoo desu ka? Ikura gurai agarimashita ka.*
本当ですか？いくらぐらい上がりましたか。
(Really? How much did it go up?)

(3) A: *Saa, kono ki no takasa o hakarimashoo.*
さあ，この木の高さを計りましょう。
(Let's measure the height of this tree.)

    B: *Totemo ookiku natta node chotto hakari nikui n desu ga. . .*
とても大きくなったのでちょっと計りにくいんですが……
(It has grown a lot and it's difficult to measure.)

(4)   *Kono e ni wa hukami ga arimasu nee, hontooni.*
この絵には深みがありますねえ，本当に。
(There is depth in this painting, indeed.)

(5) A: *Kono kasa, kodomoyoo yo.* ☺F
この傘，子供用よ。
(This umbrella is for children.)

    B: *Aa, dakara chiisai wake ne.* ☺F
ああ，だから小さいわけね。
(Oh I see, that's why it's small!)

Practice

```
------------------------------------------------------------
kutsu    くつ    N    shoes
haku     はく    V    to put on, to wear
kani     かに    N    crab, crab meat
------------------------------------------------------------
```

1.   Comment on whether the following items are easy or difficult to do.
    a. *kutsu*   *haku*
    b. *kani*   *taberu*
    c. *hito*   *hanasu*
    d. *pen*   *kaku*

2. Comment on whether the following items are expensive or inexpensive.
   a. bus fare
   b. taxi fare
   c. an entrance (admission) fee

   ——— Some Sample Answers ———

   1a. *Kono atarashii kutsu wa haki yasui desu yo.*
   この新しいくつははきやすいですよ。
   (These new shoes are easy to wear.)

   b. *Kani wa oishii kedo chotto <u>tabe nikui nee</u>.* ☺
   かにはおいしいけどちょっと食べにくいねえ。
   (Crab is delicious but it's a bit difficult to eat.)

   c. *Ano hito wa totemo atatakai hito na node, hanashi yasui desu.* あの人はとても暖かい人なので，話しやすいです。
   (Since he is a very warm person, he is easy to talk to.)

   d. *Kaki yasui pen o katte, chichi ni purezento-shimashita.*
   書きやすいペンを買って，父にプレゼントしました。
   (I bought a pen that's easy to write with and gave it [as a present] to my father.)

   2a. *Basudai wa amari takaku-arimasen.*
   バス代はあまり高くありません。
   (The bus fare isn't too expensive.)

   b. *Tookyoo no takushiiryookin wa taka-sugimasu.*
   東京のタクシー料金は高すぎます。
   (Taxi fare in Tokyo is too expensive.)

   c. *Ongakukai no nyuujooryoo mo takaku narimashita nee.*
   音楽会の入場料も高くなりましたねえ。
   (The concert's admission fee has gotten expensive, hasn't it?)

   ＊ ＊ ＊ ＊ ＊

Sono mizuumi wa kita no kuni ni atta. Hirosa wa sore hodo de mo nai ga, taihen hukakatta. Shikashi, ima wa huyu de atsuku koori ga hatte-ita. ◆
その湖は北の国にあった。広さはそれほどでもないが，たいへん深かった。しかし，いまは冬で厚く氷がはっていた。
(That lake was in the northern country. The size was not so large, but it was very deep. But now it was winter and thick ice covered the lake.)
—Hoshi, 1972, p.20.

Here we see an example of the adjective-changed-into-noun, *hirosa*. The use of topic marker *wa* is interesting in that these topicalized phrases function to set up the spacious framework of the story to follow.

124. The Meaning of Silence

Strategic Explanation

As we have seen throughout this book, values of human interaction are culturally and socially bound. The meaning of words cannot be defined without understanding the context of the society in which they are spoken. What it means when there is an absence of words also differs from culture to culture. We focus here on the silence in Japanese communication.

There is a Japanese tradition that views words as being unnecessary to reach a mutual understanding. In fact, it is widely held that words can destroy the creation of a deep mutual trust. Proverbs abound in Japanese to point out the uselessness of words as shown below. Japanese in general have a higher tolerance and appreciation for silence.

(a) *Mono* *ieba*　*kuchibiru* *samushi* *aki*　　*no* *kaze.*
　　thing　if say　lip　　　cold　　autumn　L　wind.
　　物言えば唇寒し秋の風。
　　([lit. If you utter words, your lips will feel cold] It is safer not to speak.)

(b) *Hugen*　　　*jikkoo.*
　　not-saying　　doing.
　　不言実行。
　　(Don't say it in words, show it by your deeds; or, Action before words.)

Often Japanese negatively judge people (especially males) who (sometimes excessively) express their feelings in words. People who mumble and cannot effectively communicate with words are often considered honest, and trustworthy. In short, being a glib speaker is not as positive a social value as it is in the United States.

Silence may function in two ways. First toward your social superior, it means subordination in that you are refraining from expressing your own view and that you are paying attention to your superior's view. On the other hand, silence can also express strong defiance; absence of response is taken as a sign of disagreement or defiance. Second, toward social subordinates, silence can express dominance. By offering no answer, for example, to your subordinates' request, you convey dominance and power. Comprehending the meaning of silence involves cultural and social interpretation. It is useful to know that the absence of speech is not a mere void to be filled, but it has these conflicting and yet socially significant meanings.

Just as in English you say "the silence was deafening" or "his silence spoke volumes," the concept of "silence" is shaded by paradoxical subtleties that suggest silence is a powerful tool in communication. Knowing when to keep quiet and when to speak up is an art in any language. Your instincts will probably serve you well when you converse in Japanese. But do keep in mind that quite literally, especially if you are a man—Japanese people have a lot of heart for the "strong, silent" type. With "internationalization," the traditional view that values "strong, silent" men is changing. Still, this tradition is very much a part of the establishment and it is useful to know that Japanese society places a positive value on silence. See Lebra (1987) for a more detailed discussion of the cultural significance of silence.

125. Managing Conversation—3. Taking Turns and Designing Utterances

Target Expression

> *And so, I went to see them at the station, you know.*
> **De, eki e mukae ni itta n da yo.** ☺M
> で，駅へ迎えに行ったんだよ。

Strategic Explanation

Throughout this book I have explained many facts about the Japanese grammar and communication strategies. But as I have suggested in several entries, participating in face-to-face human interaction involves much more than being able to create utterances. One must know, to begin with, when to start talking. In other words, how do you find the correct timing to take speaking turns? Once you take a turn you must be able to design each utterance so that it fits comfortably within the on-going conversation. It is fair to assume that in our conversations we would want to express ourselves in ways in which our listeners feel positive about us. It is important to design our utterances to maximize such effect. These and other conversational skills—both in English and Japanese—are skills we will be learning throughout our lives. Being sensitive and curious and keeping the humble attitude of learning anew is the key. Here are some useful clues for you to manage your Japanese conversations.

A. *Turn-taking rules:*

1. You should not take turns (or attempt to take turns) while the other person is speaking, unless there is an emergency. Although in some social and regional dialects of American English, overlapping of speaker turns may be considered a sign of enthusiasm, getting a word in edgewise is not a good idea in Japanese. Overtaking your superior's turns is especially rude.

2. If two speakers simultaneously start to take speaking turns, the socially subordinate partner should yield the turn by (1) stopping speech immediately, and/or (2) saying *doozo*.

3. When your partner stops apparently due to some speech production trouble, give sufficient time (four to five seconds is sufficient), but assist in some way to avoid potential embarrassment.

4. When your speaker turn is overtly assigned, as when you are asked a direct question, it is desirable to take the turn. You have various ways to avoid answering straightforwardly if you don't want to answer. Total silence is not considered polite under this circumstance, especially toward your superiors.

5. When your partner stops at a grammatically complete point such as the end of a sentence structure—ideally with interactional particles—and looks at you, the floor is open to you; you may take the turn.

B. *How to start your turn:*

1. Before starting your turn, it is a good idea to send listener backchannel responses to the partner's previous utterance if such responses are appropriate. Or, you can use echo questions; *raishuu desu ka* 'next week?' in response to a statement as *raishuu Maiami e iku yotei desu ga* 'I plan to go to Miami next week,' for example.

2. Start your turn with openers and fillers as we have studied. This creates a buffer zone where two people meet interactionally. You can also use this moment to prepare your utterance.

C. *How to send turn-yielding signs:*

1. You can overtly yield your turn by asking a question.

2. Pause after you finish an utterance with listener-appealing devices such as tag-like [AuxV] or interactional particles.

3. Overtly solicit your partner's opinion.

4. Make conclusive remarks if your turn is long and extensive.

5. Make eye-contact with the listener at the end of your turn.

In conversation, the actual words used are designed to cater toward the specific needs of the communicators. In face-to-face communication, all aspects of modality play important roles. Often these interpersonal feelings provide the basis for which the propositional meanings are interpreted and for that reason it is important to design one's utterance to maximize empathy. In Japanese, as you have seen throughout this book, the beginning and the end of utterances are accompanied by openers, fillers, hedges and final particles which appeal to interpersonal emotions.

Let us summarize the various strategies for making Japanese utterance more appealing to the listener.

1. *At the beginning of the utterance:*
   Openers (Entry 80)—to inform the listener that you are taking a speaking turn
   Conjunctions (Entry 56)—to signal connections and cohesion

2. *In between the utterance:*
   Interactional particles (Entry 35)—to check the listener's reaction
   Fillers (Entry 80)—to fill in between the utterances, to signal your intention to continue the turn, and to show hesitation for creating rapport

3. *At the end of the utterance:*
   Predicate with explanatory mode (Entry 74)—to connect what is said to the previous statements, to emphasize and to appeal to the listener's empathy
   Ending the statement with [V te] and other premature endings (Entry 81)—to soften the impact of statements
   Adding [*to omou*] (Entry 122)—to convey your opinion with considerateness to the listener
   Tagged [AuxV] (Entry 41)—to appeal to the listener's empathy
   Conjunctions (Entry 57)—to end the statement with after effect
   Interactional Particles (Entry 35)—to solicit the listener's involvement

A careful examination of utterances made during conversation will reveal that almost all utterances are designed with the devices listed above.

Beyond the utterance design strategies mentioned above, in general the following devices are useful to bring about similar effects.

1. Frequent use of apology for sympathy-seeking.

2. Frequent use of degree words, such as *chotto* 'a bit,' *daitai* 'more or less,' and *hotondo* 'almost.'
3. Increased level of listener back-channel responses.
4. adding softening phrases, such as *to ieru to omoimasu* 'can be said . . .,' or *tabun . . . ja-nai deshoo ka* 'perhaps isn't that the case that . . .?'

Examples

(1) A: *De, sono ato doo shita no?*
　　で，そのあとどうしたの？
　　(So what did you do after that?)

　　B: *Dakara, sorekara tomodachi no tokoro e itta n da yo.*
　　だから，それから友だちのところへ行ったんだよ。
　　(So, after that I went to my friend's place.)

(2) *Anoo, sumimasen ga, jikan ga attara kore o yonde-oite-ita-dakemasen ka.*
あのう，すみませんが，時間があったらこれを読んでおいていただけませんか。
(Uhh, excuse me, but if you have time, could you read this [for future purpose]?)

Practice

Examine Sample Texts 1 and 2 paying special attention to how utterances in casual conversation are designed. Can you point out some of the devices used?

126. On the Verb *Naru*

Target Expressions

> *(It has been decided that) I will go to the United States soon.*
> **Kondo Amerika e iku koto ni narimashita.**
> 今度アメリカへ行くことになりました。
>
> *It's a nice warm day, isn't it? (lit. It's gotten warm, hasn't it?)*
> **Atatakaku narimashita nee.**
> 暖かくなりましたねえ。

Grammatical Explanation

As we noted earlier in reference to characteristic 10, Japanese tend to de-emphasize the agent of the action, thereby avoiding the construction of a sentence that reads "subject-does-something-to-something (one)."

Instead, expressing something as 'becoming' is a frequently used strategy. The verb *naru* 'to become' is used in [N + *ni naru*] and [Vbasic + *yooni naru*]. When accompanied by adjectives, they must take adverbial forms; thus *ookiku naru* 'to become large' and *kireini naru* 'to become pretty.' Verb and adjective forms may precede *naru*; *benkyoo-shinaku naru* 'lit. to become not to study' and *kireidenaku naru* 'lit. to become not pretty.' The idiomatic use of *naru* is also frequent. For example, in the target sentence, instead of simply saying 'I will go to the United States soon,' *koto ni narimashita* '(lit. it has become) it has been decided' is added. The agent, or decision maker is not specified in this structure. It only implies that the decision was made by someone else or was reached by some inevitable circumstances. This is how Japanese sometimes prefer to express themselves.

The spontaneous verb is another good example of the agent-less tendency. Instead of saying 'I can see Mt. Fuji,' *Fuji-san ga mieru* is preferred. A group of predicates used for "reactive" description as explained throughout this book also represent this agent-less tendency. As evidenced in the proverb *naseba naru* 'lit. if you do, it will become,' the ultimate force of making things happen is not based on 'doing,' but simply the event 'becomes.' It emphasizes the view that the event is achieved independently of the agent involved in that event; what human beings can control is only to reach that mature point or time at which the action "becomes."

Naturally Japanese is equipped with grammatical structures that clearly express agents of the action. The verb *suru* 'to do' (to be discussed in Entry 128), for example, co-occurs with [Adj] and creates *takaku suru* 'to make (it) expensive,' which complements the structure *takaku naru* 'to become expensive.' What is emphasized here is that in Japanese, language is skewed to favor the *naru* expressions in comparison to what is observed in English.

Nature's seasonal change, getting warm and spring arriving, for example, are best described with *naru* in Japanese. For example, *haru ni narimashita* 'lit. it has become spring.' Compare this with the English expression of 'spring has come.' When learning a language, it is helpful to see how like events are expressed in different languages. The preference for agent-less sentence structure in Japanese is one of the key insights into learning to think in Japanese.

Here is a list of frequently used functions of the verb *naru.*

1. *'To become':*

    (1a)   *Ano hito ga byooki ni **natta**.* ♦
        あの人が病気に**なった**。
        (He got sick.)

    (1b) A: *Yamada-san no ojoosan wa enjinia ni **narimashita** nee.*
             山田さんのお嬢さんはエンジニアに**なりました**ねえ。
             (Mr. Yamada's daughter became an engineer, you know.)
         B: *Soo desu ka. Isha ni **naru** n daroo to omotte-imashita ga.*
             そうですか。医者に**なる**んだろうと思っていましたが。
             (Is that so? I thought she was going to be a doctor.)

    (1c) A: *Samuku **narimashita** nee.*
             寒く**なりました**ねえ。
             (Sure has gotten cold, hasn't it?)
         B: *Ee, hontooni.*
              ええ，本当に。
             (Yes, indeed.)

    (1d)   *Toshokan no hon o kariru no mo kantan dewa-naku **narimashita** nee.*
        図書館の本を借りるのも簡単ではなく**なりました**ねえ。
        (Borrowing books from the library has gotten to be complex [lit. not simple], hasn't it?)

    (1e)   *Saikin Tookyoo e wa ikanaku **narimashita**.*
        最近東京へは行かなく**なりました**。
        (Recently [lit. it has become that] I don't go to Tokyo.)

    (1f)   *Ano hito no kimochi ga wakaranaku **narimashita**.*
        あの人の気持ちがわからなく**なりました**。
        ([lit. it has become that] I don't understand his feelings [anymore].)

2. *'To begin, to develop into':*

This use is often accompanied by *yooni*. While *koto ni naru* is often used when someone's decision is involved, *yooni naru* describes the shift or the change, focusing on the result itself, and meaning 'reach the point where.' This is similar to English "come to" as in "come to realize."

    (2a)   *Nihon ga suki ni **narimashita**.*
        日本が好きに**なりました**。
        (I've come to like Japan.)

(2b) *Nihongo ga sukoshi hanaseru yooni **narimashita**.*
日本語が少し話せるように**なりました**。
(I've reached the point where I am able to speak Japanese a little.)

(2c) *Ano hito no kimochi ga wakaru yooni **narimashita**.*
あの人の気持ちがわかるように**なりました**。
(I've come to understand his feelings.)

3. *'To result in':*

(3a) *Kekkyoku kyoo no tenki wa hare ni **narimashita** nee.*
結局今日の天気は晴れに**なりました**ねえ。
(After all, today's weather turned out to be fine.)

4. *'To have been decided':*

(4a) *Sano-san ni wa ashita juu ichi-ji ni au koto ni **natte-imasu** ga . . .*
佐野さんには，あした十一時に会うことに**なっています**が……
(It is decided that I am to see Ms. Sano at eleven o'clock tomorrow.)

127. Connecting Sentences

Target Expressions

> *I ran to the station in a hurry. But I missed the train.*
> **Isoide eki ni hashitte-itta. Keredomo densha ni okurete-shimatta.** ♦
> 急いで駅に走っていった。けれども電車に遅れてしまった。
> *Azaleas bloomed in the garden. Daffodils also bloomed.*
> **Niwa ni tsutsuji ga sakimashita. Suisen mo sakimashita.** ♦
> 庭につつじが咲きました。水仙も咲きました。

Grammatical Explanation

In this entry we examine how Japanese sentences are connected to each other. First we focus on connecting strategies in Japanese. These include five different types of linguistic devices; (1) conjunctions, (2) demonstratives and pronouns, (3) particles, (4) repetition and lexical cohesion, and (5) response induced by the previous utterance. Second, we examine semantic relationships between two consecutive sentences which are categorized into seven types.

Obviously in order to communicate, we must be able to create not an isolated sentence but also, if not more importantly, multiple sentences connected to each other. A group of sentences and utterances must be organized to make sense. We are not going into discourse organizational principles that characterize different genres of writing or speaking. Our limited discussion on sentence connection is meant to serve only as the beginning for your further study in Japanese.

Sentence-connecting devices:

1. *Conjunctions:* (Entry 56)
   Conjunctions signal the relationship between statements whether, for example, it is a simple addition or a contradiction.

2. *Demonstratives and pronouns:* (Entries 8 and 12)
   Demonstratives and pronouns are "anaphoric" devices—referring to something that has been identified earlier or that is acknowledged among participants. By connecting to previously-mentioned information, these devices signal the direct relationship between what is currently happening to what had happened already.

3. *Particles for topic identification:* (Entries 15 and 16)
   Especially topic-marking particles *wa* and *mo* are useful in this regard. By establishing and maintaining the topic across individual sentences, the group of sentences can become topically connected. (Obviously, the mere existence of common topics cannot create a connected discourse; co-occurring comments must be meaningfully associated with the topic to form a topical coherence.)

4. *Repetition and lexical cohesion:*
   Repeating what was mentioned already is a strong device to immediately connect what precedes the consequent information. Sometimes, the word that is associated with the one previously mentioned (like daffodils to azaleas) or the one that is a part of the one previously mentioned (like window is a part of a room—a cultural knowledge shared by social members) is used to connect statements.

5. *Response induced by a previous utterance:*
   Answering a question, for example, shows a direct connection defined within the question-answer adjacency pair.

With these devices in mind, let us study the following groups of sentences.

Examples

tokai	都会	N	metropolitan, city
koosoo	高層	N	high-rise
isshitsu	一室	N	one room
mukoo	向こう	N	beyond
hirogaru	広がる	V	to expand
umi	海	N	ocean
apaato	アパート	N	apartment
kyuujitsu	休日	N	holiday, off-duty day
nozoku	除く	V	to exclude
shukkin-suru	出勤する	V	to go to work
tokidoki	ときどき	Adv	sometimes
kaeri	帰り	N	returning
dooryoo	同僚	N	colleague
tsutomeru	勤める	V	to be employed
kotaeru	答える	V	to answer

(1) (a) *Koko wa tokai no koosoo hoteru no isshitsu dearu.*
ここは都会の高層ホテルの一室である。

(b) *Sono mado kara wa biru to, sono mukoo ni hirogaru umi ga mieta.*
その窓からはビルと，その向こうに広がる海が見えた。

(This is a room in a high-rise hotel in the city. From the window, one could see [tall] buildings and the ocean expanding beyond them.)

(2) (a) *Aru otoko ga apaato o karite sunde-ita.*
ある男がアパートを借りて住んでいた。

(b) *Kyuujitsu o nozoite kichinto shukkin-shite-ita.*
休日を除いてきちんと出勤していた。

(c) *Otoko wa mada dokushin.*
男はまだ独身。

(d) *Tokidoki kaisha no kaeri ni dooryoo to sake o nomu.*
ときどき会社の帰りに同僚と酒を飲む。

(e) *Shikashi hutsukayoi ni naru hodo nonda koto wa nakatta.*
しかし二日酔いになるほど飲んだことはなかった。

(A man rented and lived in an apartment. He went to work diligently except on his days off. The man was still single.

Sometimes on his way home he goes out drinking sake with his colleagues. However, he never drank to the extent that he would have a hangover.)

(3) (a) *Otooto wa hon'ya ni tsutomete-iru.*
弟は本屋に勤めている。

(b) *Kono hukin de ichiban ookina hon'ya da.*
この付近で一番大きな本屋だ。

(c) *Kinoo otooto no tokoro e itte, watashi wa tazuneta.*
きのう弟のところへ行って，私はたずねた。

(d) *"Saikin denwa ga nai kedo genki?"*
「最近電話がないけど元気？」

(e) *"Mochiron da yo" to otooto wa kotaeta.*
「もちろんだよ」と弟は答えた。

(My younger brother works at a bookstore. [It is] the largest bookstore around here. Yesterday I went to my younger brother's place and I asked him. "There haven't been any phone calls from you recently; are you OK?" "Of course," answered my brother.)

In (1b) we find two demonstratives appearing in *sono mado* and *sono mukoo*. Both of these demonstratives assist in cohesiveness; *sono mado* 'that window' is the window of *hoteru no isshitsu* 'a hotel room' given in (1a), and *sono mukoo* 'beyond those' is beyond the *biru* 'buildings.'

In (2), we see how the particle *wa* assists in establishing *otoko* 'young man' as a topic in (2c). Non-specification of *otoko* in (2b), (2d) and (2e) also signals the topical connection. The conjunction *shikashi* in (2e) is an example of how this statement is related to (2d).

In (3b) we find a case of lexical cohesion achieved by the repetition of the word *hon'ya*. We also find in (3c) *otooto no tokoro* 'my brother's (working) place,' a rephrasing of the very *hon'ya* under discussion. In (3e) we find an answer to the question given in (3d), a case of question-response connection.

Each device examined here assists in comprehending how sentences are put together. It is true that comprehension involves much more than appreciation of these devices. Knowing these as clue words, however, can be a great help when you are trying to comprehend texts in a foreign language.

Additional Information

Another aspect of connecting sentences is how these sentences are semantically connected. Here is a list of possible relationships between sentences taken from Nagano, 1986.

1. *Expansion:*

   The second sentence is an expansion, for example a more detailed description of the first. (Clue words include conjunctions such as *sorede* 'then,' *dakara* 'therefore.')

2. *Opposition:*

   The second sentence expresses an opposing view toward the first. (Clue words include conjunctions *ga*, *shikashi*, and *tokoroga*.)

3. *Addition:*

   A related statement is added to the first sentence. (This is achieved by the [V*te*] form, and other conjunctions such as *de*, *soshite* and *sonoue*.)

4. *Apposition:*

   The first and the second sentence both describe the identical item. (This is marked by conjunctions such as *tsumari* 'in other words,' and *tatoeba* 'for example.')

5. *Supplement:*

   The second sentence is a supplement to the first. (Recall how the predicate with explanatory mode adds relevant cause and reason for the statement made earlier.)

6. *Contrast:*

   The second sentence represents a view or meaning contrasting with the first. (The contrastive use of *wa* and particles expressing alternation such as *ka*, *mata wa* are useful for this purpose.)

7. *Diversion:*

   The second sentence diverts from the first. (For this purpose sentential adverbs and conjunctions including *tsugini* 'next,' and *tokorode* 'by the way' are used.)

In the discussion above we focused on the semantic connections between consecutive sentences only and ignored the overall global structure in discourse. It is important to look for the global organization when reading a group of connected sentences, but that is beyond the scope of this book.

128. The Extended Use of the Verb *Suru* and *Da*

Grammatical Explanation

The verbs *suru* 'to do' and *da* 'to be' have many extended uses that occur quite frequently. These conventional uses should be learned with care.

A. *Idiomatic use of the verb suru*:

1. [adverbial form of Adj-*i* + *suru*] 'to make':
   Change [Adj-*i*] to adverb form by replacing the final -*i* with -*ku*, for example, *ookii* → *ookiku*; *ookiku suru* (to enlarge).

   (1a) *Rajio no oto o moo sukoshi **ookiku shite**-kudasai.*
   ラジオの音をもう少し**大きくして**ください。
   (Please turn up the volume of the radio a little.)

2. [adverbial form of Adj-*na* + *suru*] 'to make':
   Change [Adj-*na*] to adverb form by replacing the final -*na* with -*ni*, for example, *kireina* → *kireini*; *kireini suru* (to clean up).

   (2a) *Kooen o **kireini shimashoo**.*
   公園を**きれいにしましょう**。
   (Let's clean up the park.)

3. [N + *ni suru*] 'to decide':
   This pattern should be used when you are choosing from several available alternatives.

   (3a) ***Biiru ni shimasu**.* (as in a restaurant)
   ビールにします。
   ([lit. I decided on beer] I'll take beer.)

   (3b) *Shiken wa **raishuu ni shimashoo**.*
   試験は**来週にしましょう**。
   (Let's decide that the exam will be next week.)

   Recall the structure [Vinformal non-past + *koto ni suru*] which is similar to this pattern also meaning 'to decide to do.'

4. [loan word + *suru*] (changes the word into a verb):

   (4a) ***Nokku-shite**-kudasai.*
   ノックしてください。
   (Please knock.)

5. [Adv + *suru*] (changes the adverb into verbs associated with them):

yukkuri 'slow, leisurely' + *suru* = stay leisurely, stay long.

(5a) **Yukkuri shite**-*itte-kudasai*.
ゆっくりしていってください。
(Please stay for a long time.)

burabura 'rambling' + *suru* = to walk aimlessly,
to walk around

(5b) *Machi o* **burabura shite**-*ita n desu*.
町をぶらぶらしていたんです。
(I was just walking around the town.)

6. Idiomatically, when accompanied by phrases indicating prices, it means 'to cost':

(6a) *Kono kooto wa* **ni-man-en shimashita**.
このコートは二万円しました。
(This coat cost twenty thousand yen.)

7. Idiomatically, when accompanied by phrases associated with appearance, it means 'to appear':

(7a) <u>*Sono*</u>　<u>*otoko*</u>　<u>*wa*</u>　<u>*aoi*</u>　<u>*kao*</u>　<u>*o*</u>　<u>*shite-ita*</u>.
　　that　　man　　T　　pale　face　O　appeared
その男は青い顔をしていた。
(The man's face was pale.)

B. *Extended use of the* be-*verb,* da:

The *be*-verb is frequently used as an auxiliary verb to replace verbs and adjectives. This is in some sense similar to the English auxiliary verb *do* when used as an answer "yes, I do," to the question, "do you watch television?" In order to use *da* for this purpose, there must be a context suitable for it, where what is not mentioned is understood between the communicators. Examine how the *be*-verb is used in the second pair-part of the following pairs of interaction.

yahari	やはり	Adv	after all, as expected
washoku	和食	N	Japanese-style meal

gohan	ごはん	N	cooked rice
misoshiru	みそしる	N	*miso* soup
nihonshu	日本酒	N	Japanese *sake*

----

(1) **A:** *Watashi wa asa wa toosuto o tabemasu ga, Yamazaki-san wa?*
　　 私は朝はトーストを食べますが，山崎さんは？
　　 (I have toast for breakfast; how about you, Yamazaki-san?)

　　 B: *Yahari washoku de gohan to misoshiru **desu**.*
　　 やはり和食でごはんとみそしるです。
　　 (I have a Japanese-style breakfast [after all], rice and miso soup.)

(2) **A:** *Kon'ya wa doko de shokuji-shimasu ka.*
　　 今夜はどこで食事しますか。
　　 (Where will you eat tonight?)

　　 B: *Eki no chikaku no resutoran **desu**.*
　　 駅の近くのレストランです。
　　 (At the restaurant near the station.)

(3) **A:** *Nomimono de wa nani ga ichiban suki desu ka.*
　　 飲み物では何が一番好きですか。
　　 (Among drinks, what do you like most?)

　　 B: *Biiru **desu**.*
　　 ビールです。
　　 (I like beer most of all.)

(4) **A:** *Wakai koro wa nani o yoku nomimashita ka.*
　　 若い頃は何をよく飲みましたか。
　　 (When you were young, what did you usually drink?)

　　 B: *Nihonshu **desu**.*
　　 日本酒です。
　　 (I used to drink [Japanese] *sake*.)

(5) **A:** *Tsukimashita yo.*
　　 着きましたよ。
　　 (It arrived.)

　　 B: *Nani ga **desu** ka.*
　　 何がですか。
　　 (What [arrived]?)

　　 A: *Tegami ga.*
　　 手紙が。
　　 (The letter!)

(6) A: *Itsu made Tookyoo ni irasshaimasu ka.*
いつまで東京にいらっしゃいますか。
(Until when will you be in Tokyo?)
   B: *Asatte made **desu.***
あさってまで**です**。
(Until the day after tomorrow.)

In all of B's utterances, the *be*-verbs do not logically equate the subject/topic with its complement. Obviously in (1) B, the sentence does not make sense if we translate literally—'I am Japanese-style breakfast, and I am rice and miso soup.' Yet by interpreting the *be*-verb in its extended meaning, it makes sense.

More specifically, the *be*-verb can replace verbs and adjectives (as in (3)) when what precedes *da* is in focus. Note that in each of these pairs, the answers are in focus; they constitute information specifically sought by the question. *Da* also replaces tense as shown in (4), where *nihonshu desu* corresponds to the past tense of the question and is interpreted as 'I used to drink *sake*.' Note that in (6)B, *da* is preceded immediately by a particle. The particles *made* and *kara* are primary examples of particles used in this structure.

Even when there is no obvious context in which the *da* expression replaces a verb, when such an expression is used it is assumed that a predictable relationship exists between the *da* predicate and the noun. For example, if someone says *Tanaka-sensei wa Tookyoo desu*, a literal translation 'Professor Tanaka is Tokyo' does not make sense; appropriate interpretation is 'Professor Tanaka is in Tokyo' or 'Professor Tanaka is from Tokyo' or whatever semantically appropriate interpretation applies within the general context.

Warning

Recall that *da* cannot replace an adjectival predicate when used with *soo.*

(a) A: *Ookii-desu ka.*
大きいですか。
(Is it large?)
   B: **Hai, soo desu.*
Hai (,ookii desu).
はい(、大きいです)。
(Yes, it is large.)

(b) A: *Benri desu ka.*
便利ですか。
(Is it useful?)

B: *Iie soo dewa-arimasen.
  Iie (,benri dewa-arimasen).
  いいえ(,便利ではありません)。
  (No, it isn't useful.)

Practice

| *nan-nin* | 何人 | N | how many people |
| *gengo* | 言語 | N | language |

Answer the following by using extended meanings of the *be*-verb. Then based on your answers, create new questions suitable to induce such answers.

1. *Nan-nin de ryokoo-shimasu ka.*
 何人で旅行しますか。
2. *Donna gengo ga ichiban muzukashii-desu ka.*
 どんな言語が一番むずかしいですか。
3. *Pari ni itte kara wa doko e ikimasu ka.*
 パリに行ってからはどこへ行きますか。
4. *Dono kotoba ga wakaranai n desu ka.*
 どの言葉がわからないんですか。
5. *Doko de shokuji-shimasu ka.*
 どこで食事しますか。

——— Some Sample Answers ———
Answers:
1. *Go-nin desu.* 五人です。
2. *Nihongo desu.* 日本語です。
3. *Amusuterudamu desu.* アムステルダムです。
4. *Kono kotoba desu.* この言葉です。
5. *Depaato no naka no resutoran desu.*
 デパートの中のレストランです。

Questions:
1. *Kazoku wa nan-nin desu ka.* 家族は何人ですか。
2. *Donna gengo ga benkyoo-shitai-desu ka.*
 どんな言語が勉強したいですか。
3. *Rainen no natsu wa dochira e ikimasu ka.*
 来年の夏はどちらへ行きますか。
4. *Ichiban muzukashii kotoba wa dore?* ☺
 一番むずかしい言葉はどれ？
5. *Imooto-san wa doko de arubaito o shite-imasu ka.*
 妹さんはどこでアルバイトをしていますか。

129. Various Uses of the Word *Tokoro*

Target Expression

> *I was just about to leave.*
> **Ima choodo dekakeyoo to shite-ita tokoro desu.**
> 今ちょうど出かけようとしていたところです。

Grammatical Explanation

The noun *tokoro* 'place' is often used in various idiomatic expressions. Fundamentally, *tokoro* means 'place.' In more abstract terms, however, *tokoro* refers to 'the central issue of focus,' or 'the most important point or aspect' as exemplified below:

(a) <u>Ii-tai</u>   <u>**tokoro**</u> <u>wa</u> <u>sooyuu</u> <u>koto</u> <u>datta</u> <u>no</u> <u>ne.</u>
    want to say point T such   fact was IP IP
    言いたいところはそういうことだったのね。
    (What [the important point] you want to say was that, right?)

(b) *Kyoo wa sonna **tokoro** de . . .*
    今日はそんなところで……
    (Well today let's leave it at that point . . .)

Tokoro appears in many idiomatic constructs. In casual rapid speech, *toko* may replace *tokoro*.

1. [Adj + *tokoro*] 'although . . .' (with only limited number of adjectives)

   (1a) **Oisogashii tokoro** o sumimasen nee.
        お忙しいところをすみませんねえ。
        (Although you are busy, thanks for coming.)

2. [Vbasic + *tokoro* + *da*] 'be about to . . .'

   (2a) *Kore kara **dekakeru tokoro** desu.*
        これから出かけるところです。
        (I am about to leave now.)

3. [Vvolitional + *to shite-ita tokoro* + *da*] 'was about to do . . .'

   (3a) *Ima denwa o shiyoo to **shite-ita tokoro** desu.*
        今電話をしようとしていたところです。
        (I was about to give you a call.)

4. [Vinformal past + *tokoro da*] 'just did . . .'

(4a) *Ima okita tokoro desu.*
今起きたところです。
(I just got up now.)

5. [V*te* + *-iru* + *tokoro da*] 'is in the middle of doing . . .'

(5a) *Ima tegami o kaite-iru tokoro desu.*
今手紙を書いているところです。
(I am in the middle of writing a letter.)

In patterns 2 through 5, verbs must be active (non-stative).

Practice

How would you express the following in Japanese?

1. I am watching television right now.
2. We just finished eating our supper now.
3. I was about to call you.
4. My husband just left the house.
5. Saeko is jogging outside right now. ☺

──────── Answers ────────

1. *Ima terebi o mite-ru tokoro desu.*
今テレビを見ているところです。
2. *Ima bangohan o tabe-owatta tokoro desu.*
今晩ごはんを食べ終わったところです。
3. *Denwa-shiyoo to shite-ita tokoro desu.*
電話しようとしていたところです。
4. *Shujin wa ima dekaketa tokoro desu ga . . .*
主人は今出かけたところですが……
5. *Saeko-san wa ima jogingu-shite-ru toko yo.* ☺
さえ子さんは今ジョギングしているとこよ。

Additional Information

The difference between [Vinformal past + *tokoro da*] 'just did' and [Vinformal past + *bakari da*] 'just did . . .' (in Entry 119) is that while *tokoro* implies ensuing action already in progress, *bakari* implies the action just completed and any following action has not yet begun.

130. Order of Sentence-final Elements

Grammatical Explanation

As our final entry, we review how the sentence-final elements themselves are organized. These include verbs, various types of verb endings, auxiliary verbs, verb compounds and final particles. The general principle is that the more personal and emotional the element expresses, the more likely it is to appear toward the very end. Thus starting with the verb, which carries the referential meaning, other elements such as causative, passive and negative follow and so on until the final particle. Here is a chart that shows the order of sentence-final elements. Under each member the expressions, if used, must be chosen in the order listed. *Soo da* (1) is the predicate of the conjecture [*soona*], while *soo da* (2) represents 'hearsay.' *Yoo* (1) is the volitional form of the verb, and *yoo da* (2) is the predicate of [*yoona*] for expressing resemblance and likelihood. (Note: Obviously not all elements are required. The chart specifies the order of elements if they appear.)

The Reference Order of Sentence-final Elements

1	2	3	4	5	6
Verb →	*seru* →	*reru* →	[Adj] →	*soo da* (1) →	Past-*ta* →
	saseru	*rareru*	*nai*	*nai*	
				rashii	

7	8
yoo (1) →	IP
-daroo	
soo da (2)	
rashii	
yoo da (2)	

Now study the following combination of verb-final elements paying special attention to the order of sentence-final elements. Knowing the general order of these items will be helpful when you are uncertain of how to combine sentence-final elements. The best way to remember the order is to memorize a few examples as the one listed here.

(a) **tabesaseraresoo da**

taberu	saseru	rareru	soo	da
eat	causative	passive	soona	be

食べさせられそうだ

(to seem to be forced to eat)

(b) **ikitakunai rashii-desu**

iku	tai	nai	rashii	-desu
go	want	NEG	rashii	formal-marker

行きたくないらしいです

(to seem not to want to go)

(c) **nagurareta yoo da ne**

naguru	reru	ta	yoo	da	ne
beat	passive	past	yoona	be	IP

なぐられたようだね

(seems to have been beaten, doesn't he or she)

(d) **muzukashi soo datta soo desu yo**

muzukashii	soo	da	ta	soo	da	yo
difficult	soona	be	past	soo	be	IP

むずかしそうだったそうですよ

(I hear that it seemed to be difficult)

And as a final note to the final entry, how about:

(e) *Nihongo, hontoo wa sorehodo muzukashiku wa nai yoo desu ne.*
日本語，本当はそれほどむずかしくはないようですね。
(In truth Japanese looks like it is not so difficult.)

You have come a long way covering 130 entries. Although there is always more to learn, these entries offer a basic knowledge of Japanese grammar and communication strategies. Let me close this entry with that ubiquitous Japanese phrase: *Ganbatte-kudasai.*

Part Three:

Sample Texts

420

The three sample texts presented here are taken from two different sources. Two different genres are: (1) casual conversation among college students and (2) short story.

For each sample text a vocabulary list is provided, along with helpful notes which point out all relevant information discussed in this book, and an English translation. (The number given for underlined portions of the text corresponds to the one listed in the section of information useful for interpretation. The letter "E" in the information section stands for "Entry" relevant to the point raised.) The reader is encouraged to try his or her own interpretation. Explanation and translation are provided only for the purpose of facilitating the reader's attempt to tackle the Japanese on his or her own.

Sample Text 1:   ☺ Casual Conversation

(Transcript of casual conversation between two female college students, videotaped in Tokyo, in May, 1985)

Two students are discussing what they will do during the summer vacation. Speaker B, whose home is in Kyushu Island, is currently a college student in Tokyo. She usually flies back home to spend the summer vacation with her folks. The conversation transcribed here discusses accommodation and expenses of air travel. ([H] stand for head nod.)

Vocabulary List:

kyandee	キャンデー	N	candy
deru	出る	V	to be served
ocha	お茶	N	green tea
okashi	お菓子	N	sweets
saitei	最低	N	worst
gaman-suru がまんする		V	to supress, to control oneself from
Honkon	香港	PN	Hong Kong
nakanaka	なかなか	Adv	(not) easily, (not) readily

uku	浮く	V	idiomatic: *(o)kane ga uku*, money is saved, money is left over
kakaru	かかる	V	to cost
yappari	やっぱり	Adv	after all, as expected

Text:

(1) A: *Ii nee,₁ nan ka,₂ kyandee toka₃ deru n desho?₄*

(1) いいねえ，なんか，キャンデーとか出るんでしょ？

(2) B: *Kyandee? (laugh)*

(2) キャンデー？

(3) A: *Denai no?₅ Watashi nee,₆*

(3) 出ないの？　私ねえ，

(4) B: *Aa, ocha to nee,₇*

(4) ああ，お茶とねえ，

(5) (A: *Un₈.*)

(5) （うん。）

(6) B: *okashi ga₉ deru.*

(6) お菓子が出る。

(7) A: *Watashi ne, ichi-do₁₀ mo nee, are ni notta koto ga nai₁₁ no, hikooki.₁₂*

(7) 私ね，一度もねえ，あれに乗ったことがないの，飛行機。

(8) (B: *Hontoo?*)

(8) （本当？）

(9) A: *Saitee₁₃ . . . (laugh)*

(9) 最低……

(B: *(laugh)*)

(10) B: *Demo saa,₁₄ Kyuushuu kaeru no₁₅ ni-kai₁₆ gurai₁₇ ne,*

(10) でもさあ，九州帰るの二回ぐらいね，

(11) (A: [H] *Un.₁₈*)

(11) うん。

(12) B: *gaman-sureba₁₉ kaigairyokoo toka,₂₀*

(12) がまんすれば海外旅行とか，

(13) (A: *Un, ikeru₂₁ ne.*)

(13) （うん，行けるね。）

(14) (B: [H] *Nee.₂₂*)

(14) （ねえ。）

(15) A: *Honkon nara₂₃ ikeru ne.*

(15) 香港なら行けるね。

(16) B: *Demo nakanaka₂₄ ne,*

(16) でもなかなかね，

(17) (A: *Huun [H][H].₂₅*)

(17) （ふうん。）

(18) B: *ikanai to₂₆ ikanaide uita to ka omotte,₂₇*

(18) 行かないと行かないで浮いたとか思って，

(A: [H][H]₂₈)

(19) B: *tsukatchau₂₉ kara.₃₀*

(19) 使っちゃうから。

(20) (A: *Un.*)

(20) （うん。）

(21)　A:　*Eeh,'*₃₁ *demo kakaru n da*₃₂ *ne, ni-man-*　(21) えっ, でもかかるんだね,

en mo₃₃ kakaru n da ne.　二万円もかかるんだね。

(22)　(B:　[H] *Un.*)　(22)（うん。）
(23)　A:　*Takai ne,*　(23) 高いね,
　　(B:　[H][H])
(24)　A:　*yappari ne.*　(24) やっぱりね。

Information Useful for Interpretation:

The style observed here is female casual speech. (See Entries 3 and 39 for information regarding style.)

1. This utterance comments on the previous turn. For the use of interactional aprticle, *nee*, see E-35.
2. *Nan ka* is a filler (E-80).
3. Although it appears singularly, *toka* expresses implied enumeration, meaning 'candy and other things.' (E-29)
4. *N desu* is an extended predicate used to catch the listener's attention (E-74). Tag-question-like verb ending *-desho* is added also (E-41).
5. This is a case of deletion from *Kyandee wa denai no?* (E-14). *No* is a question marker used often in feminine speech style (E-74).
6. An interactional particle *nee* is inserted immediately after the topic is mentioned, to which B responds with her utterance. The point where the interactional particle appears often provides an opportunity for the listener to respond (E-125).
7. An interactional particle appearing within an utterance (E-125).
8. An example of listener response (E-69).
9. The subject marker *ga* marks the noun. *Okashi* is introduced for the first time into the discourse, constituting new information (E-15).
10. *Ichi-do* is a combination of a numeral and a counter, *do*, for frequency (E-28, E-33).
11. *Koto ga nai* is a negation of *koto ga aru* which is an idiomatic use of the nominalizer *koto*, meaning 'have ever experienced . . .' (E-120)
12. In this utterance *hikooki* is postposed. The normally expected order is *hikooki ni notta koto ga nai no*. The speaker refers to the airplane with *are* 'that' earlier, but adds the word *hikooki* again at a postposed position (E-98).
13. In uttering *saitee*, *da* is not mentioned (E-14).
14. The conjunction *demo* is used as an opener and an interactional particle *saa* is added before the main part of the utterance appears (E-56, E-57).

15. *No* nominalizes the preceding clause (E-105).
16. *Ni-kai* is a combination of a numeral and a counter (E-28, E-33).
17. The particle, *gurai*, is used to express quantity in approximation (E-33).
18. An example of a listener response accompanied by a non-verbal sign, nodding (E-69).
19. A *ba*-conditional. B presents a condition without making a personal commitment that she will indeed fulfill the condition (E-92).
20. The particle *toka* is used singularly, but it implies the meaning of enumeration. By implying that travel abroad is not the only choice, B presents her view less domineeringly (E-29).
21. *Ikeru* is a potential form of the verb *iku* (E-75).
22. This interpersonal particle appears independently, and is used as a filler. Immediately preceding is the listener response *un, ikeru ne* uttered by A. B responds to the listener response and fills in the pause between the speaker turns (E-35, E-69, E-80).
23. The conditional phrase *nara* follows the noun *Honkon* (E-92).
24. The adverb *nakanaka* is used in an implied negative context of *nakanaka ikenai*.
25. A's listener response consists of a verbal sign followed by repeated nods (E-69).
26. Connecting clauses with *to* (E-88).
27. For expressing a personal opinion, *to omou* is used. Additionally, in order to express hesitation, the particle *ka* is added (E-102, E-122).
28. An example of a nonverbal listener response (E-69).
29. *Tsukatchau* is a colloquial shortened version of *tsukatte-shimau* (E-54).
30. Conjunction *kara* is used to end the utterance providing the reason relevant to the statement (16) (E-77).
31. *Eeh* is an exclamation expressing surprise (E-100).
32. An extended predicate *n da* is used to express emphasis (E-74).
33. The particle *mo* following quantifier expresses surprise and emphasis when reporting unexpected quantity (E-97).

Translation:
(1) A: That's nice, uhh, they serve candy or something, right?
(2) B: You mean "candy"?
(3) A: They don't serve? You know, I . . .
(4) B: Oh, well, tea and,
(5) (A: Uh huh.)
(6) B: sweets are served.

(7) A: You know, I've never been on board, I mean an airplane.

(8) (B: Really?)

(9) A: Worst . . . (*laugh*)

    (B: (*laugh*))

(10) B: But, uh, if I stop returning to Kyushu a couple of times,

(11) (A: Uh huh.)

(12) B: if I supress (my desire and stop returning), travel abroad or something . . .

(13) (A: Yeah, you can go.)

(14) (B: Yeah[, I could].)

(15) A: If it's Hong Kong, you can (afford to) go, right?

(16) B: But it's difficult,

(17) (A: Yeah.)

(18) B: if I don't go, then because I don't go I have some extra money —that's what I think,

    (A: [*head movement*])

(19) B: and I end up spending it (for other things) anyway.

(20) (A: Uh huh.)

(21) A: Oh boy, it does cost a lot, doesn't it, it costs twenty thousand yen;

(22) (B: Yeah.)

(23) A: it sure is expensive,

    (B: [*head movement*])

(24) A: sure is, after all.

Sample Text 2: ☺ Casual Conversation

(Transcript of casual conversation between two male college students chatting, videotaped in Tokyo, in May 1985.)

Two male friends discuss finding jobs after graduation. In the section to follow, A reports that a friend of a friend visited a company looking for a job. A's and B's concern is that they don't quite understand what happens during such visits. ([H] stands for head nod.)

Vocabulary List:

```
-----------------------------------------------------------
hoomon 訪問          N      visit
kaishahoomon         N      visiting companies
   会社訪問
hatashite はたして Adv     in reality, as a
                            matter of fact
toriaezu とりあえず Adv    first of all, as a
                            first step
mensetsu 面接         N      (job) interview
yowaru   弱る         V      to be troubled, to
                            be perplexed
chokusetsutekini     Adv    directly
   直接的に
tanin 他人            N      other, unrelated
                            person
kuwashiku くわしく Adv     in detail
-----------------------------------------------------------
```

(1) A: *Sooyuu$_1$ koto wakannai$_2$ ne, iku*
         tte yuu$_3$ no$_4$ wa$_5$ sa,$_6$

(1) そういうことわかんないね，
    行くっていうのはさ，

   (B: [H]$_7$)

(2) A: *hoomon, kaishahoomon$_8$ da kara,*
         hoomon-sureba$_9$ ii n da to omou$_{10}$
         kedo,$_{11}$

(2) 訪問，会社訪問だから，訪問
    すればいいんだと思うけど，

(3) (B: [H] *Un.*)

(3) （うん。）

(4) A: *itte$_{12}$ hatashite dare to nani shite-*
         kuru$_{13}$ n daroo$_{14}$ tte no$_{15}$ wa,$_{16}$

(4) 行ってはたして誰と何してく
    るんだろうっていうのは，

(5) (B: *Soo, soo, soo.*₁₇ [H])

(6) (A: *nee.*₁₈)

(B: [H])

(7) A: *Jinji-ka no*₁₉ *hito ni toriaezu au-desho?*₂₀

(5) (そう，そう，そう)

(6) (ねえ。)

(7) 人事課の人にとりあえず会うでしょ？

(8) B: *Soo, soo,*₂₁ *ore*₂₂ *wakannai n da yo ne,*₂₃ *dakara*₂₄ *kuwashiku*₂₅ *kikitai*₂₆ *n da kedo*₂₇ *ne.*

(8) そう，そう，おれわかんないんだよね，だからくわしく聞きたいんだけどね。

(9) A: *Un, un, soo yuu koto wakannee*₂₈ *mon*₂₉ *na.*₃₀ *Gakkoo gawa ja*₃₁ *nani mo*₃₂ *oshiete-kureru, a, oshiete-kureta*₃₃ *no ka,*

(9) うん，うん，そういうことわかんねえもんな。学校側じゃ何も教えてくれる，あ，教えてくれたのか，

(10) (B: *Soo ka na.*₃₄)

(10) (そうかな。)

(11) A: *kono aida no*₃₅ *mensetsu toka.*

(11) この間の面接とか。

(12) B: *Are uketenai*₃₆ *n da, ore.*₃₇

(12) あれ受けてないんだ，おれ。

(13) A: *Soo datta,*₃₈ *ore mo uketenai. Yowatta ne.*

(13) そうだった，おれも受けてない。弱ったね。

(14) B: *Dakara tomodachi no sa,*

(14) だから友だちのさ，

(15) (A: *Un.*)

(15) (うん。)

(16) B: *tomodachi ga itta tte*₃₉ *yuu kara sa,*

(16) 友だちが行ったっていうからさ，

(17) (A: *Un.*)

(17) (うん。)

(18) B: *chokusetsuteki ni wa*₄₀ *shiranai wake*₄₁ *desho? dakara sono hito.*₄₂

(18) 直接的には知らないわけでしょ？ だからその人。

(19) A: *Aa, tanin ka.*

(19) ああ，他人か。

(20) B: *Tanin da*₄₃ *yo.*

(20) 他人だよ。

(21) A: *Tomodachi no tomodachi wa tanin da mon ne.*

(21) 友だちの友だちは他人だもんね。

(22) B: [H][H][H]₄₄ *Dakara, soitsu ga*₄₅ *itta n dattara*₄₆ *kuwashiku kikeru*₄₇

(22) だから，そいつが行ったんだったらくわしく聞ける

(23) (A: *Un.*)

(23) (うん。)

(24) B: *kedo,*₄₈ *ne, doo yuu koto yatte-kita*₄₉ *no ka.*₅₀

(24) けど，ね，どういうことやってきたのか。

(25)　A:　*Un, soo omoetari shite*~51~ . . .　　㉕ うん，そう思えたりして……

(26)　B:　*Dakara kikenai kara sa.*~52~　　㉖ だから聞けないからさ。

Information Useful for Interpretation:

This conversation is in masculine casual speech style. See Entries 3 and 39 for stylistic features.

1.　*Sooyuu* is a demonstrative using the *so-* series. In the immediately preceding discourse, they discuss what *sooyuu* refers to, that is, what students actually do when they visit a potential employer (E-8).

2.　*Wakannai* is a colloquial version of *wakaranai*, the negative of the verb *wakaru* (E-26).

3.　The particle *tte* is a colloquial version of the quotative particle *to* and *tte yuu* is inserted here to connect the explanatory clause with the nominalizer *no* (E-112, E-114).

4.　*No* nominalizes a preceding clause (E-105).

5.　See E-15 and E-16 for the use of topic marker *wa*.

6.　*Sa* is an interactional particle used in very casual situations (E-35).

7.　An example of a nonverbal listener response (E-69).

8.　*Kaishahoomon* is a complex nominal consisting of *kaisha* 'company' and *hoomon* 'visit.'

9.　*Hoomon-suru* takes the conditional *ba*-form, *hoomon-sureba* (E-92).

10.　Expression of personal opinion by *to omou* (E-122).

11.　A conjunction *kedo* marks the end of utterance. See E-57 for conjunctions and E-14 for the non-specification of the main clause.

12.　The [V*te*] form of the verb *iku*, *itte*, is used to connect the clauses (E-81).

13.　*Shite-kuru* expresses the implied direction in that the friend "does" something and "come back" (E-55).

14.　See E-74 for extended predicate, and E-99 for the use of *-daroo* to express speaker's uncertainty and doubt.

15.　The phrase *tte no* is a shortened version of *tte yuu no*—combination of clausal explanation and the nominalizer *no* (E-105, E-114).

16.　The particle *wa* marks what precedes it, as a topic. In this context, the comment is not specified (E-14).

17.　A repetition of *soo* in a listener response (E-69).

18.　The interpersonal particle *nee* is singularly used as a filler (E-35, E-80).

19.　*No* is a linker, making *jinjika no* as a modifier (E-20).

20. The verb *au* 'to see (a person)' takes *ni* as its object marker (E-29). *-Desho* is used as a tag-question-like verb ending, seeking confirmation and/or listener response (E-41).

21. B sends listener response at the beginning of his turn, then he continues his own turn. The expression *soo soo* functions as a listener response as well as an opener here (E-69, E-80).

22. An informal male self reference term *ore* is used here to imply a weak contrast that "I" don't understand (E-12).

23. A case of multiple interactional particles (E-35).

24. See E-56 for conjunctions such as *dakara*.

25. *Kuwashiku* is an adverb, corresponding to the [Adj-*i*], *kuwashii* (E-48).

26. *Kikitai* is a combination of [Vstem + *tai*], expressing desire (E-65).

27. The conjunction *kedo* is used here not to connect clauses, but more generally to end the statement with the effect of trailed ending (E-57).

28. *Wakannee* is a male casual speech (in very casual cases only with an effect of machoism) of *wakaranai* (E-26).

29. *Mon* is a shortened version of *mono*, which signals that the statement provides a reason or cause (E-120).

30. *Na* is a casual interactional particle used frequently by males (E-35).

31. The expression *ja* is a shortened version of *de wa*.

32. See E-36 and E-97 for the use of interrogative words plus *mo*.

33. The verb of giving (giving to self), *kureru*, in *oshiete-kureru* is obligatory here, since teaching directly involves a personal give-and-take relationship (E-73). The sound *a* preceding *oshiete-kureta* is an interjection used to repair one's own speech.

34. *Soo ka na* is a useful commentary to express one's doubt and mild disagreement in a socially preferrable manner (E-69, E-101).

35. *No* is a linker. The phrase *kono aida* 'recently' is used as a noun phrase when modifying the noun linked by *no* (E-20).

36. *Uketenai* is a shortened version of *ukete-inai*; meaning that B has not participated in the interview (E-51).

37. *Ore* is postposed (E-98).

38. *Datta* is an informal past of the verb *da* (E-22).

39. The quotative *to* often becomes *tte* in casual speech (E-112).

40. *Wa* defines the scope of negation, meaning I don't know "directly" implying that "I only know indirectly" (E-26).

41. *Wake* provides explanation, a case of extended predicate (E-74).

42. *Dakara sono hito* is postposed; a more expected order is *dakara sono hito chokusetsutekini wa shiranai wake desho?* (E-98)

43. In male speech, the informal *da* is not deleted as frequently as it is in female speech (E-39).

44. Nonverbal filler, a repetition of nodding (E-69, E-80).
45. Although *soitsu* refers to an individual introduced earlier and recognized by A and B, it takes *ga* (instead of *wa*) here; it appears in a subordinate clause (E-16).
46. See E-93 for the conditional *tara.*
47. *Kikeru* is a potential form of *kiku* (E-75).
48. *Kedo* is grammatically connected to B's previous turn in (22). A gives listener response *un* in between, almost as if anticipating a clausal division and responding a bit earlier (E-69).
49. *Yatte-kita* expresses the direction involved in the friend's action (E-55).
50. *No* is a nominalizer (E-105) and *ka* is added because the clause contains the interrogative word *doo* (E-102). *Dooyuu koto yatte kita no ka* is also postposed (E-98).
51. The enumerative *tari* is used singularly here to imply other possibilities. The utterance also ends with [V*te*] form to make the statement less imposing (E-81).
52. *Kara* is added to end an utterance, not to directly connect the clauses (E-57). *Sa* is a casual interactional particle (E-35).

Translation:
(1)   A: But such a fact, we don't understand it, do we? (Talking about) going,

      (B: [*head movement*])

(2)   A: (well,) visiting, they are visiting companies, so I think it is fine just to visit companies,

(3)   (B: Yeah.)

(4)   A: (but) when they go, what do they actually do; and this (I don't know).

(5)   (B: Yeah, yeah, yeah.)

(6)   (A: Right?)

      (B: [*head movement*])

(7)   A: You first meet the personnel division staff, right?

(8)   B: Yeah, yeah, you know, I'm not quite sure about it, and so I want to ask about it in detail.

(9)   A: Uh-huh, those kinds of facts, we don't quite know about, so . . . The university side, they don't teach you anything . . . uh . . . I guess they did (kindly) teach us . . .

(10) (B: I doubt it . . .)

(11) A: You know, the interviews the other day, (for example),

(12) B: That (interview), I didn't go.

(13) A: That's right, I didn't go either. Quite troublesome . . .

(14) B: So, my friend's, you know,

(15) (A: Yeah.)

(16) B: my friend tells me that his friend went, so . . .

(17) (A: Yeah.)

(18) B: (my friend) doesn't directly know about it, right?, I mean my friend.

(19) A: (Oh you mean he is just) one of them (not related).

(20) B: Yeah, he is not related (meaning a friend).

(21) A: Your friend's friend isn't among us (he's one of others) for sure.

(22) B: So, if my friend went, I could ask (about what happened) from him,

(23) (A: Yeah.)

(24) B: but, you know, (I can't ask about) what the guy actually did there,

(25) A: Yeah, I guess I can think that way (I see your point), too.

(26) B: So since I cannot ask him (about it), so . . .

Sample Text 3: ♦ Short story

(*Wakare no yume*, in *Mirai Isoppu* by Shin'ichi Hoshi. 1982. Tokyo: Shin-chosha, Co. pp. 159-160.)

Vocabulary List:

----

wakare	別れ	N	parting, farewell
yume	夢	N	dream
otoko	男	N	man
atoaji	あと味	N	aftertaste
arawareru	あらわれる	V	to appear
mottomo	最も	Adv	most
shitashii	親しい	Adv	intimate, familiar, close
yuujin	友人	N	friend
sabishigena さびしげな		Adj	lonesome-looking
kanashigena 悲しげな		Adj	sad-looking
hyoojoo	表情	N	expression
kasukana	かすかな	Adj	faint, subtle
koe	声	N	voice
kotaeru	答える	V	to answer
doko e tomo naku どこへともなく		Adv	somewhere (lit. nobody knows where)
kieru	消える	V	to disappear
yokuasa	翌朝	Adv	next morning
me ga sameru 目がさめる		V	to awaken
iyana	いやな	Adj	uncomfortable, distasteful
kibun	気分	N	feeling
nande	なんで	Adv	why
yagate	やがて	Adv	soon
unazuku	うなずく	V	to nod
aitsu	あいつ	N	that guy
okoru	起こる	V	to happen
ryokoochuu 旅行中		N	on the road (being on a journey)

tabisaki	旅先	N	(travel) destination, on a journey
tsugeru	告げる	V	to say, to greet
kinodokuna 気の毒な		Adj	pitiful, regrettable
rusutaku	留守宅	N	home in the absence of its master
moshimoshi もしもし		Int	hello (on the phone)
renraku	連絡	N	communication, message
betsuni	べつに	Adv	(not) especially
hujin	夫人	N	wife
hushigina	ふしぎな	Adv	strange
kotoba o nigosu 言葉をにごす		V	(idiomatic) to speak ambiguously
shiboo-suru 死亡する		V	to die
hanmei-suru 判明する		V	to become clear
sorenara	それなら	Conj	then, if so
gaishutsu-suru 外出する		V	to go out
bon'yarito ぼんやりと		Adv	absent-mindedly
kangaeru	考える	V	to think
huini	ふいに	Adv	suddenly
imi	意味	N	meaning
yahari	やはり	Adv	after all
kizuku	気づく	V	to notice, to realize
mohaya	もはや	Adv	already
teokure	手おくれ	N	being too late, being past remedy
hanetobasu はね飛ばす		V	to hit (by a car)
dooro	道路	N	road
gekitotsu-suru 激突する		V	to crash into, to be crashed against
sunzen	寸前	N	a moment before, immediately before

Text:

Wakare no Yume

(1) Sono otoko wa yume o mita.

(2) Atoaji no yokunai yume.

(3) Kare no mottomo shitashii yuujin ga araware, sabishigena to yuu ka kanashigena to yuu ka, sonna hyoojoo o shi, kasukana koe de itta no da.

(4) "Sayonara."

(5) "Ittai, doo shita to yuu n da."

(6) Yume no naka de otoko wa kiki-kaesu.

(7) Shikashi, yuujin wa sore ni kotaeru koto naku, te o hurinagara doko e tomo naku kieta.

(8) Yokuasa, me ga samete kara mo, otoko wa iyana kibun datta.

(9) Nande anna yume o mita no daroo.

(10) Shikashi, yagate unazuku.

(11) Aitsu ni nani ka okotta no dewa-nai ka.

(12) Aitsu wa ima ryokoochuu no hazu da.

(13) Tabisaki de shinda no ni chigainai.

(14) Soshite mottomo shitashikatta ore no yume ni araware, wakare o tsugeta no daroo.

(15) Kinodokuna koto da.

(16) Otoko wa yuujin no rusutaku ni denwa o kakete-mita.

(17) "Moshimoshi, goshujin kara nani ka renraku wa?"

(18) "Ie, betsuni. Demo, naze desu no?"

(19) Hujin wa hushigisooni kiki-kaeshita.

(20) Otoko wa kotoba o nigoshite denwa o kiru.

別れの夢

(1) その男は夢を見た。

(2) あと味のよくない夢。

(3) 彼の最も親しい友人があらわれ、さびしげなというか悲しげなというか、そんな表情をし、かすかな声で言ったのだ。

(4) 「さよなら」

(5) 「いったい、どうしたというんだ」

(6) 夢のなかで男は聞きかえす。

(7) しかし、友人はそれに答えることなく、手を振りながらどこへともなく消えた。

(8) 翌朝、目がさめてからも、男はいやな気分だった。

(9) なんであんな夢を見たのだろう。

(10) しかし、やがてうなずく。

(11) あいつになにか起こったのではないか。

(12) あいつはいま旅行中のはずだ。

(13) 旅先で死んだのにちがいない。

(14) そして最も親しかったおれの夢にあらわれ、別れを告げたのだろう。

(15) 気の毒なことだ。

(16) 男は友人の留守宅に電話をかけてみた。

(17) 「もしもし、ご主人からなにか連絡は」

(18) 「いえ、べつに。でも、なぜですの」

(19) 夫人はふしぎそうに聞きかえした。

(20) 男は言葉をにごして電話を切る。

(21) Shiboo-shita no nara₃₅ moo hanmei-shite
mo ii hazu na noni,₃₆ sore rashii₃₇ yoosu
wa nakatta.

(22) Sorenara,₃₈ doo yuu koto na₃₉ no daroo.

(23) Otoko wa gaishutsu-shi, bon'yarito
kangaenagara₄₀ aruita.

(24) Sono tochuu, huini yume no imi ga wakat-
ta.₄₁

(25) Are wa yahari, moo ni-do to₄₂ aenai₄₃ to
yuu, wakare o tsugeru₄₄ yume datta no da.

(26) Shikashi, kizuita toki₄₅ wa mohaya
teokure.

(27) Otoko wa kuruma ni hanetobasare,₄₆
dooro ni gekitotsu-shiyoo to suru sunzen₄₇
datta.

(21) 死亡したのならもう判明して
もいいはずなのに，それらし
いようすはなかった。

(22) それなら，どういうことなの
だろう。

(23) 男は外出し，ぼんやりと考え
ながら歩いた。

(24) その途中，不意に夢の意味が
わかった。

(25) あれはやはり，もう二度と会
えないという，別れを告げる
夢だったのだ。

(26) しかし，気づいた時はもはや
手おくれ。

(27) 男は車にはね飛ばされ，道路
に激突しようとする寸前だっ
た。

Information Useful for Interpretation:

1. In a narrative as shown here often the participant of the story is marked by the topic marker *wa*; although the topic consists of brand new information, it is presented as if it is given. This strategy is often used to effectively establish the protagonist as a topic (E-16).

2. Informal ending is used in the written Japanese (E-3).

3. *Atoaji no yokunai* modifies the noun, *yume* 'dream.' *No* represents a case where the subject marker, *ga*, optionally changes to *no* (E-83).

4. The sentence ends with a noun; the *be*-verb is deleted (E-14).

5. The second character in the story is introduced with *ga*, co-occurring with the verb that indicates a new person "appears" within the topic frame already established (E-16).

6. The [Vstem] ending is used for conjoining clauses in the written style (E-56).

7. The structure [Adj-*i* stem + *gena*] adds the meaning of 'giving an impression of,' 'looking as if.' *Sabishigena* means 'appearing sad' or 'giving an impression of being sad.'

8. The phrase *to yuu* marks the clause that modifies the noun—in this case, *sonna hyoojoo* (E-114).

9. This particle *ka* lists alternative(s); the structure here is of [A *ka* B *ka*] (E-29).

10. See E-128 for the extended use of the verb *suru*. *Shi* is a [Vte] form of the verb *suru*.

11. The extended predicate used for pointing out the important information (E-74).

12. See that *sayonara* is used when a person parts for a long time (E-85).

13. *Doo shita* is an idiomatic expression meaning 'what happened?'

14. *To yuu* is used to connect the clause *doo shita* and the nominalizer *n(o)* in the extended predicate pattern (E-114).

15. In direct quotations presented in (4) and (5), a description of who made these utterances, something in the line of "said he," is deleted. This happens frequently in the Japanese narrative.

16. See E-24 for expressions indicating location.

17. *Kiki-kaesu* is a verb compound, meaning 'ask again for clarification' (E-121).

18. *Koto* is a nominalizer (E-105).

19. The verb, *hurinagara*, expresses actions happening simultaneously (E-84).

20. [Vte kara] is a temporal conjunctive phrase meaning 'after' (E-84).

21. The *be*-verb *da* in *otoko wa iyana kibun datta* is used in a broad sense, meaning that the man "had" bad feelings (E-128).

22. *Nande* is an interrogative word functioning similarly to *naze* and *dooshite* (E-21).

23. *Daroo* expresses the speaker's guess, meaning 'I wonder . . .' (E-99).

24. The topic phrase (*otoko wa*) is not mentioned (E-14, E-15). Non-past tense of the verb *unazuku* is used for dramatic effect (as elsewhere in the story).

25. See E-36 and Appendix 6 for the combination of interrogative words and *ka*.

26. *Hazu da* expresses the speaker's feeling that the present state is naturally so-and-so (E-104).

27. *Ni chigainai* expresses the speaker's guess made with confidence (E-108).

28. *Shitashikatta* is an informal past form of the [Adj-*i*], *shitashii* (E-31). *Ore* represents the case where a pronoun is directly modified by an adjectival phrase (E-12).

29. *Kakete-miru* is a verb compound expressing a kind of modality, meaning 'to make a phone call and see' (E-121).

30. *No* is used as a question marker predominantly used by female speakers (E-74).

31. *Hujin* is a descriptive term for a mature married woman.

32. *Sooni* is an adverbial form of *soona* (E-87).

33. *Kiki-kaesu* is a verb compound (E-121).

34. [V*te*] of *nigoshite* conjoins the preceding clause with the following (E-76).
35. See E-92 for *nara* conditional.
36. *Noni* is a conjunction meaning 'despite' (E-56).
37. *Rashii* expresses non-committing speculation (E-91).
38. *Sorenara* 'if so,' 'then' is a conjunction similar to *soredewa* (E-56).
39. *Doo yuu koto da* is an idiomatic expression meaning 'what happened?' or 'what does that mean?'
40. See E-84 for the expression using *nagara*.
41. See E-53 to review how the particle *ga* co-occurs with *wakaru*.
42. *Ni-do* is a combination of a numeral and the counter for frequency (E-28, E-33). *To* in *ni-do to* is used for emphatic negation.
43. *Aenai* is a negative of the potential form of the verb *au* (E-75).
44. The clause *wakare o tsugeru* explains about the noun *yume* (E-114).
45. *Toki* is a temporal conjunction (E-84).
46. *Hanetobasare* is a passive of *hanetobasu* (E-109).
47. *Shiyoo to suru sunzen* is similar to the pattern *shiyoo to shite-ita tokoro* (E-129). Structurally *shiyoo to suru* modifies the noun *sunzen* 'a moment before.'

Translation:
Title: A Dream of a Farewell
(1) The man had a dream.
(2) A dream that left a bad aftertaste.
(3) His closest friend appeared with a somewhat lonely or sad expression on his face, and said in a faint voice,
(4) "Good bye."
(5) "What happened to you?"
(6) In the dream the man repeatedly asked his friend.
(7) But the friend, without answering the question, disappeared somewhere as he waved his hand.
(8) The next morning, after waking up, he still felt bad.
(9) Why did I dream such a dream?
(10) But soon he nodded.
(11) Isn't it the case that something happened to him?
(12) My friend is supposed to be travelling now.
(13) He must have passed away on the road.
(14) Probably it is that he appeared in my dream, the dream of a person who was the closest friend to him, and said good bye.
(15) How regrettable!
(16) The man called the friend's home (whose master was away).

(17) "Hello, did you hear anything from your husband?"

(18) "No, not specially. But why?"

(19) The wife responded by asking "why," wondering what happened.

(20) The man just mumbled ambiguously and hung up the phone.

(21) If the friend had died, it should have been made known by now, but there was no indication of it.

(22) Then, what does this (whole thing) mean?

(23) The man went out, and walked thinking absent-mindedly.

(24) In the middle of his walk, suddenly he understood the meaning of the dream.

(25) The dream was (indeed) after all a dream in which a person says good bye, meaning that he would not see one's friend again.

(26) But when he realized, it was too late.

(27) The man was hit by a car, and it was one split-second before he was to be crushed against the pavement.

Appendixes

Appendix 1.   Parts of Speech and Definitions of Grammatical Terms

The parts of speech adopted in this book mostly correspond with those in English. The categories nonexistent in English—including two different types of adjectives and the particles—are explained in detail in relevant entries. Although obviously there are some differences between Japanese and English parts of speech, for practical purposes we use most of the grammatical terms across these two languages. Here is a list of parts of speech and grammatical terms (alphabetically ordered) with definitions and examples. Definitions of these and other terms are also given throughout the book.

Active verb:
> A verb describes (dynamic) action. —*taberu* 'to eat'

Active durative verb:
> A verb describing an action whose process is expressed by its progressive form. —*tabete-iru* 'to be eating'

Adjective:
> Any member of a class of words that independently without combination with other words functions as a modifier of a noun. —*atarashii* 'new'

Adverb:
> Any member of a class of words that functions as modifiers of verbs, of adjective, or adverbs or adverbial phrases. —*yukkuri* 'slowly'

Apposition:
> A clause or a phrase which modifies a noun and explains what the modified noun is. —*Tomodachi no Sano-san* 'Ms. Sano, my friend'

Auxiliary adjective:
> An adjective used in combination with the stem form of the preceding verb or an adjective and in combination with the preceding predicates that take [V/Adj pre-Aux] forms. —*tsukai-yasui* 'easy to use,' *oishi-soo da* 'seems delicious'

Auxiliary verb:
> A verb which is used in combination with the [V*te*] or the stem of the preceding verb or an adjective and in combination with the preceding predicates that take [V/Adj pre-Aux] forms. —*otoshite-shimau* 'to drop,' *muzukashi-sugiru* 'too difficult'

Be-verb:

Equivalent to English *be*, a copula. Refers to *da* and its conjugated forms.

Casual colloquial style:

Style used for casual speech among familiar members.

Causative:

A relation in which the actor of the causative action causes or forces someone else to act.

Conditional:

A relation where an event or state is presented as a condition for another event or state to occur.

Conjunction:

A phrase that connects clauses and sentences. —*sorede* 'then'

Controllable verb:

A verb describing an action that its performer can control as to whether the action or state takes place or not. —*oyogu* 'to swim'

Demonstrative:

A word indicating or singling out the thing referred to. —*kono* 'this,' *sono* 'that'

Feminine style:

Style of speech used predominantly by female speakers, often considered soft and other-accommodating.

Formal style:

Style used in formal, often official situations; style used toward those to whom you should show respect in less formal situations; used for formal letter writing.

Informal style:

Style used in casual non-official settings. A superior may use this style toward subordinates in formal situations; often used for writing novels and essays.

Interjection:

A word expressing emotion, distinguished by its usage in grammatical isolation. —*Masaka!* 'No kidding.'

Interrogative:

Of questioning. Interrogative words are those equivalent to English words such as why, what, how, when and so forth.

Intransitive verb:
A verb that describes an action in the framework of "agent-conducts-itself." —*iku* 'to go'

***I*-type adjective:**
Adjectives ending in -*i*. —*atarashii* 'new'

Masculine style:
Style of speech used predominantly by male speakers, often considered blunt.

***Na*-type adjective:**
Adjectives that end with -*na*. —*benrina* 'convenient'

Noun:
A class of words referring to persons, places and things which grammatically become subjects and objects by themselves. —*uchi* 'house,' *pasokon* 'personal computer'

Numeral:
A word or words expressing number and quantity. —*go* 'five,' *roku-man* 'sixty thousand'

Particle:
A group of words typically consisting of a small number of syllables that mark grammatical case relations (grammatical particle) or interpersonal expressions (interpersonal particle). —*wa* (topic marker), *yo* (marker for new information with some emphasis)

Passive:
A sentence which describes an action from the point of view of someone who is influenced or affected by the action.

Predicate:
A group of words that function as one of the main constituents of a simple sentence, the other being subject. It normally contains a verbal element, and the predicate as a whole typically expresses the action performed by or the state attributed to the subject. —*Tomodachi ga ashita kimasu.* 'My friend will come tomorrow.'

Progressive:
A verb form that describes the continuation of action or continuation of state resultant of the action.

Proper noun:
A noun that refers to only specific person(s) or thing(s) that bear the specific name(s). —*Yamada* 'Yamada,' *Nyuuyooku* 'New York'

Proposition:
A statement in which something is affirmed or denied, and which one can judge whether the statement is true or false.

Potential form:
A verb form that describes the performer's potential and ability to do the act. —*kakeru* 'to be able to write'

Spontaneous verb:
A verb which describes the event that spontaneously and naturally occurs without the actor's initiation. —*mieru* 'can be seen'

Subject:
An element within a sentence or an utterance which is in "primary predicate focus," normally marked by *ga*, unless topicalized.

Stative durative verb:
A verb describing a state that can be expressed by its progressive form. —*niru* 'to resemble'

Stative verb:
A verb that describes the state of things. —*aru, iru* 'to be, to exist'

Transitive verb:
A verb that describes an action in the framework of "agent-operates-on-another-entity." —*hon o yomu* 'to read a book'

Topic:
Something which language users are talking about and commenting on.

Verb:
A word that typically expresses action or state. This category includes existential verbs *iru* and *aru*, as well as the *be*-verb *da*. —*utau* 'to sing,' *taberu* 'to eat,' *da* 'to be'

Volitional form:
A verb form that expresses the will of its actor. —*benkyoo-shiyoo* 'will study'

Written style:
Style used primarily and sometimes exclusively for writing.

Appendix 2. Basic Verb and Adjective Conjugation

Basic Verb Conjunction

Verb types	Informal non-past (Basic)	Formal non-past	Informal past	Formal past	Informal non-past negative	Formal non-past negative
U-verb	kaku	kakimasu	kaita	kaki-mashita	kakanai	kaki-masen
RU-verb	taberu	tabemasu	tabeta	tabe-mashita	tabenai	tabe-masen
Irregular verb						
kuru	kuru	kimasu	kita	kima-shita	konai	kimasen
suru	suru	shimasu	shita	shima-shita	shinai	shima-sen
Special verb						
irassharu	irassharu	irasshai-masu	irasshat-ta	iras-shaima-shita	irassha-ranai	irasshai-masen

*Verb stem [Vstem] is obtained by deleting final -masu from formal non-past form of the verb.

Informal past negative	Formal past negative	[V*te*]	Conditional	Volitional	Passive	Causative
kakanakatta	*kaki-masen-deshita*	*kaite*	*kakeba*	*kakoo*	*kaka-reru*	*kakaseru*
tabenakatta	*tabe-masen-deshita*	*tabete*	*tabereba*	*tabeyoo*	*tabe-rareru*	*tabe-saseru*
konakatta	*ki-masen-deshita*	*kite*	*kureba*	*koyoo*	*korare-ru*	*kosaseru*
shinakatta	*shi-masen-deshita*	*shite*	*sureba*	*shiyoo*	*sareru*	*saseru*
irasshatta	*irasshai-masen-deshita*	*iras-shatte*	*irasshareba*			

Basic Adjective Conjugation

Adjective type	Basic	Informal non-past	Formal non-past	Informal past	Formal past	Informal non-past negative
[Adj-*i*]	*atara-shii*	*atarashii*	*atara-shii-desu*	*atarashi-katta*	*atarashi-katta-desu*	*atarashi-ku-nai*
[Adj-*na*]	*benri-na*	*benri da*	*benri desu*	*benri datta*	*benri deshita*	*benri denai* *benri ja-nai*

*Adjective stem [Adj stem] is obtained by deleting the final -*i* from [Adj-*i*] and the final -*na* from [Adj-*na*]. The adjective *yoi* (or *ii*) is an exception to be noted.

> *yoi, ii*
>
> Basic: *yoi, ii*
> Informal non-past: *yoi, ii*
> Formal non-past: *yokunai-desu*
> Informal past: *yokunakatta*
> Formal past: *yokatta-desu*
> Negative informal non-past: *yokunai*
> Negative formal non-past: *yokunai-desu, yokuarimasen*
> Negative informal past: *yokunakatta*
> Negative formal past: *yoku arimasen-deshita, yokunakatta desu*
> [Adj *te*]: *yokute*
> Conditional: *yokereba*

Formal non-past negative	Informal past negative	Formal past negative	[Adj *te*]	Conditional
atarashikunai-desu atarashiku arimasen	atarashiku-nakatta	atarashikuwa-nakatta-desu atarashikuarima-sen-deshita	atarashi-kute	atarashikereba
benri dewa-nai-desu benri dewa-arimasen benri ja-nai-desu benri ja-arimasen	benri dewa-nakatta benri ja-nakatta	benri dewanakatta-desu benri dewa-arimasen-deshita benri ja-nakatta-desu benri ja-arimasen-deshita	benri de	benri nara(ba)

Appendix 3. Verb and Adjective Connecting Forms: Pre-nominal and Pre-Aux Forms

[V/Adj pre-nominal] forms

	Non-past	Past	Non-past negative	Past negative
Verbs	oyogu	oyoida	oyoganai	oyoganakatta
Be-verb	no	datta	dewanai	dewanakatta
[Adj-i]	akai	akakatta	akakunai	akakunakatta
[Adj-na]	benrina	benri	benri	benri dewa
		datta	dewanai	nakatta

[V/Adj pre-Aux] forms

	Non-past	Past	Non-past negative	Past negative
Verbs	oyogu	oyoida	oyoganai	oyoganakatta
Be-verb	(deletion)	datta	dewanai	dewanakatta
[Adj-i]	akai	akakatta	akakunai	akakunakatta
[Adj-na]	benri	benri	benri	benri dewa
		datta	dewanai	nakatta

*Both pre-nominal and pre-Aux forms have only informal forms. The difference between [V/Adj pre-nominal] and [V/Adj pre-Aux] forms are: (1) be-verb: pre-nominal takes *no* while for pre-Aux, *da* is totally deleted, (2) [Adj-na]: pre-nominal takes basic form with *na*, while pre-Aux takes [Adj stem] without *na*.

*Forms that follow pre-nominal forms are:

[Vpre-nominal] + {
hoo ga ii (Entry 64, Entry 118) —excluding past negative
nouns (clausal modification) (Entry 83)
nouns (clausal explanation) (Entry 114)
}

[V/Adj pre-nominal] + {
no da/waka da (Entry 74)
tame ni (cause) (Entry 77)
toki, koro (Entry 84)
aida ni (Entry 84)
yoona (Entry 89)
tsumori (Entry 103) —excluding [Vnon-past]
hazu (Entry 104)
koto, no (Entry 105)
koto ga aru (occurs occasionally) (Entry 120) —with [V/Adj pre-nominal non-past] only
mono da (surprise) (Entry 120)
}

*Specially noted cases where [N + *da*] changes to [N + *na*]:

[N + *na*] + {
n(o) da (Entry 74)
node, noni (Entry 77)
no (Entry 105) —Also note that when preceding *koto*, [N + *da*] changes to [N + *da to yuu*].
}

*Forms that follow pre-Aux forms:

[V/Adj pre-Aux] + {
-daroo/-deshoo (Entry 41)
mitaina (Entry 89)
rashii (Entry 91)
nara(ba) (Entry 92)
kashira (Entry 99)
ka na (Entry 99)
kamoshirenai (Entry 99)
ni chigainai (Entry 108)
}

Appendix 4. Verb and Adjective Connecting Forms: [Vstem], [V*te*] and others

Those that follow [Vbasic]:

[Vbasic] +
- *tame ni* (goal) (Entry 62)
- *koto ga dekiru* (Entry 75)
- *mae ni* (Entry 84)
- *to* (Entry 88)
- *beki* (Entry 106)
- *bakari da* (be ready to) (Entry 119)
- *koto wa nai* (Entry 120)
- *mono da* (mild command) (Entry 120)
- *tokoro da* (about to happen) (Entry 129)

Those that follow [Vinformal non-past]:

[Vinformal non-past] +
- *tsumori* (intention) (Entry 103)
- *yotei, keikaku* (Entry 103)
- *koto ni suru* (Entry 120)
- *koto ni naru* (Entry 120)

Those that follow [Vinformal past]:

[Vinformal past affirmative] +
- *ato de* (Entry 84)
- *bakari da* (just did) (Entry 119)
- *tokoro da* (just happened) (Entry 129)

Those that follow [V/Adj informal]:

[V/Adj informal] +
- *to yuu, to omou* (indirect quotation) (Entry 112)
- *soo da* (Entry 115)

Those that follow [V/Adj informal past]:

[V/Adj informal past] +
- *ri* (Entry 81)
- *ra* (Entry 93)
- *mono da* (reflection) (Entry 120)
- *koto ga aru* (past experience) (Entry 120)

Those that follow [V/Adj informal non-past]:

[V/Adj informal non-past] +
- *yori* (Entry 64)
- *hoo* (Entry 64)

Those that follow [Vstem]:

[Vstem] +
$$\begin{cases} \textit{-mashoo} \text{ (Entry 44)} \\ \textit{ni iku, ni kuru} \text{ (Entry 62)} \\ \textit{-tai, -tagaru} \text{ (Entry 65)} \\ \textit{-nasai} \text{ (Entry 79)} \\ \textit{-nagara} \text{ (Entry 84)} \\ \textit{-naosu/-kaesu} \text{ (Entry 121)} \\ \textit{-kakeru} \text{ (Entry 121)} \\ \textit{-hajimeru, -dasu} \text{ (Entry 121)} \\ \textit{-yasui, -nikui} \text{ (Entry 123)} \end{cases}$$

Special cases of [Vstem]:

o + [Vstem] +
$$\begin{cases} \textit{suru} \text{ (Entry 86)} \\ \textit{ni naru} \text{ (Entry 86)} \end{cases}$$

Those that follow [V/Adj stem]:

[V/Adj stem] +
$$\begin{cases} \textit{soona} \text{ (Entry 87)} \\ \textit{-sugiru} \text{ (Entry 121)} \end{cases}$$

Those that follow [V te]:

[V te] +
$$\begin{cases} \textit{-kudasai} \text{ (Entry 40)} \\ \textit{-iru} \text{ (Entry 51)} \\ \textit{-shimau} \text{ (Entry 54)} \\ \textit{-iku, -kuru} \text{ (Entry 55)} \\ \textit{hoshii} \text{ (Entry 65)} \\ \textit{-ageru, -kureru, -morau} \text{ (Entry 73)} \\ \textit{-kara} \text{ (Entry 84)} \\ \textit{-aru, -oku} \text{ (Entry 95)} \\ \textit{-miru} \text{ (Entry 121)} \end{cases}$$

Those that follow [V/Adj te]:

[V/Adj te] +
$$\begin{cases} \textit{mo} \text{ (Entry 97)} \\ \textit{mo ii} \text{ (Entry 110)} \\ \textit{wa ikenai} \text{ (Entry 111)} \end{cases}$$

* Specially noted are Entries 119, 120, 121, 128 and 129 in which these and additional idiomatic adjective and verb connecting forms are introduced.

Appendix 5. Predicates for "Reactive" Description

1. **Natural Phenomena**

huru	*Ame ga huru.* 'Rain falls.'
huku	*Kaze ga huku.* 'Wind blows.'

2. **Sense, Perception, Physical Condition**

suru	*Nioi ga suru.* 'It smells.'
suku	*Onaka ga suita.* 'I'm hungry.'
kawaku	*Nodo ga kawaita.* I'm thirsty.'
deru	*Seki ga deru.* 'I cough.'
itai	*Atama ga itai.* 'I have a headache.'

3. **Existence, Possession**

aru	*Ookii tatemono ga aru.*
	'There is a large building.'
	Musume ga aru. 'I have a daughter.'
iru	*Kodomo ga iru.* 'There is a child.'

4. **Emotional Response**

sukina/kiraina	*Ano hito ga suki da.* 'I like that person.'
hoshii	*Okane ga hoshii.* 'I want money.'
-tai	*Oishii mono ga tabe-tai.* 'I want to eat something delicious.'

5. **Spontaneous Occurrence**

mieru	*Umi ga mieru.* 'The ocean can be seen.'
kikoeru	*Ongaku ga kikoeru.* 'The music is heard.'

6. **Potential**

dekiru	*Tenisu ga dekiru.* 'I can play tennis.'
tsukureru	*Kawaii ningyoo ga tsukureru.* 'I can make a cute doll.'
joozuna	*Nihongo ga joozu da.* 'I'm good at Japanese.'
hetana	*Tenisu ga heta da.* 'I'm not a good at tennis.'

7. **Other**

wakaru	*Nihongo ga wakaru.* 'I can understand Japanese.'
kakaru	*Jikan ga kakaru.* 'It takes time.'
iru	*Okane ga iru.* 'Money is needed.'

In all these types of predicates except the first natural phenomena, the experiencer may be added followed by *ga*. For spontaneous and potential predicates the experiencer may be marked by *ni*. Remember that particle *ga* in these patterns may be replaced by *wa* (or possibly *mo*) if it is topicalized.

Appendix 6. Interrogative Words in Combination with *Ka, Mo* and *De mo*

Interrogative words in question	With *ka* in affirmation	With *mo* in affirmation	With *mo* in negation	With *de mo*
ikura how much	*ikura-ka* some amount	*ikura-mo* plenty as much as	*ikura-mo* not much	*ikura de mo* any amount
itsu when	*itsu-ka* sometime some day	*itsu-mo* always	*itsu-mo* never	*itsu de mo* any time
dare who	*dare-ka* somebody	*dare-mo* everybody	*dare-mo* nobody	*dare de mo* anybody
doko where	*doko-ka* somewhere	*doko-mo* everywhere	*doko-mo* nowhere	*doko de mo* anywhere
dochira which (one of the two)	*dochira-ka* either one	*dochira-mo* both	*dochira-mo* neither	*dochira de mo* either
dore which (among more than two)	*dore-ka* some (one)	*dore-mo* every one	*dore-mo* none	*dore de mo* any one
nani what	*nani-ka* something	—	*nani-mo* nothing	*nan de mo* any thing

References for Sample Texts

Abe, Kobo. 1981. *Suna no Onna.* Tokyo: Shinchosha. Shincho Bunko.

Hoshi, Shin'ichi. 1972. *Kimagure Robotto.* Tokyo: Kadokawa Shoten. Kadokawa Bunko.

———. 1982. *Wakare no Yume.* In *Mirai Isoppu.* Tokyo: Shinchosha. Shincho Bunko.

Kawabata, Yasunari. 1950. *Izu no Odoriko.* Tokyo: Shinchosha. Shincho Bunko.

———. 1966. *Yukiguni.* Tokyo: Obunsha. Obunsha Bunko.

Kondo, Ineko. 1968. *Kokoro.* Translation of *Kororo* by Soseki Natsume. Tokyo: Kenkyusha.

Matsumoto, Seicho. 1982. *Kami to Yajuu no Hi.* Tokyo: Kodansha. Kodansha Bunko.

Natsume, Soseki. 1951. *Kokoro.* Tokyo: Kadokawa Shoten. Kadokawa Bunko.

Nishimura, Kyotaro. 1986. *Ikisaki no nai Kippu.* Tokyo: Futabasha. Futaba Bunko.

Saunders, E. Dale. 1967. *The Woman in the Dunes.* Translation of *Suna no Onna* by Kobo Abe. Tokyo: Charles E. Tuttle Co.

Seidensticker, Edward. 1956. *Snow Country.* Translation of *Yukiguni* by Yasunari Kawabata. New York: Berkley Publishing.

———. 1974. *The Izu Dancer.* Translation of *Izu no Odoriko* by Yasunari Kawabata. Rutland, Vermont and Tokyo, Japan: Charles E. Tuttle Co.

Tanikawa, Shuntaro. 1982. *Pe.* Tokyo: Kodansha. Kodansha Bunko.

Terayama, Shuji. 1973. *Dare ka Kokyoo o Omowazaru.* Tokyo: Kadokawa Shoten. Kadokawa Bunko.

Yuki, Shoji. 1977, *Shisha-tachi no Yoru.* Tokyo: Kadokawa Shoten. Kadokawa Bunko.

Bibliography

Alfonso, Anthony. 1966. *Japanese Language Patterns—A Structural Approach*, Vol. 1 and 2. Tokyo: Sophia University L.L. Center of Applied Linguistics.

Aoki, Haruo, Masayoshi Hirose, Jean Keller and Katsuhiko Sakuma. 1984. *Basic Structures in Japanese*. Tokyo: Taishukan.

Bunkacho. 1973. *Nihongo to Nihongo Kyooiku Bunpoohen*. Kokugo Shiriizu, Bessatsu 2. Tokyo: Okurasho Insatsukyoku.

Chamberlain, Basil Hall. 1888. *A Handbook of Colloquial Japanese*. Tokyo: Hakubunsha.

Doi, Takeo. 1973. *The Anatomy of Dependence*. Translated by John Bester. Tokyo: Kodansha International.

Haga, Yasushi. 1982. *Shintei Nihon Bunpoo Kyooshitsu*. Tokyo: Kyoiku Shuppan.

Henderson, Harold G. 1948. *Handbook of Japanese Grammar*. New York: Houghton Mifflin Co.

Hosoe, Itsuki. 1973. *Dooshi Jisei no Kenkyuu*. Tokyo: Shinozaki Shorin.

Ikegami, Yoshihiko. 1981. *Suru to Naru no Gengogaku*. Tokyo: Taishukan.

Inter-University Center. 1975. *Basic Japanese—A Review Text*. Tokyo: Inter-University Center.

Jorden, Eleanor Harz. 1963. *Beginning Japanese*, Part 1 and 2. New Haven, CT: Yale University Press.

———. 1987, 1988. *Japanese: The Spoken Language*, Part I and II. With Mari Noda. New Haven: Yale University Press.

Kawarazaki, Mikio, Taketoki Yoshikawa and Hideyuki Yoshioka. 1983. *Kyookasho Kaidai*. Kyooshiyoo Nihongo Kyooiku Handobukku, Bessatsu. Tokyo: The Japan Foundation.

Kindaichi, Haruhiko. 1976. *Nihongo Dooshi no Asupekuto*. Tokyo: Mugishobo.

———. 1985. "Nihongo no Kokoro." In *Nihon no Kokoro*. Edited by NHK Kokusaikyoku Bunka Purojekuto. Translated by Don Kenny, 74-89. Tokyo: Kodansha International.

Lebra, Takie Sugiyama. 1976. *Japanese Patterns of Behavior*. Honolulu: University of Hawaii Press.

———. 1987. The Cultural Significance of Silence in Japanese Communication. Paper presented at the 1987 International Pragmatics Conference, at Antwerp, Belgium.

Makino, Seiichi and Michio Tsutsui. 1986. *A Dictionary of Basic Japanese Grammar*. Tokyo: The Japan Times.

Maynard, Senko K. 1981. The Given/New Distinction and the Analysis of the Japanese Particles -*Wa* and -*Ga*. *Papers in Linguistics*, Vol. 14 (1), 109-130.

———. 1984. Functions of -*to* and -*koto-o* in Speech and Thought Representation in Japanese Written Discourse. *Lingua*, Vol. 64, 1-24.

———. 1985. Choice of Predicate and Narrative Manipulation: Functions of *dearu* and *da* in Modern Japanese Fiction. *Poetics*, Vol. 14, 369-385.

———. 1986. On Back-Channel Behavior in Japanese and English Casual Conversation. *Linguistics*, Vol. 24, 1079-1108.

————. 1987. "Thematization as a Staging Device in the Japanese Narrative." In *Perspectives on Topicalization: The Case of Japanese -Wa*. Edited by John Hinds, Senko K. Maynard and Shoichi Iwasaki, 57-82. Amsterdam: John Benjamins.

————. 1989. *Japanese Conversation: Self-contextualization through Structure and Interactional Management*. Norwood, NJ: Ablex.

McClain, Yoko M. 1981. *Handbook of Modern Japanese Grammar*. Tokyo: The Hokuseido Press.

Mikami, Akira. 1960. *Zoo wa Hana ga Nagai*. Tokyo: Kuroshio Shuppan.

————. 1972. *Gendai Gohoo Josetsu*. Tokyo: Kuroshio Shuppan.

Mizutani, Osamu and Nobuko Mizutani. 1977-1986. *Nihongo Notes*, Vol. 1-7. Tokyo: The Japan Times.

————. 1977. *An Introduction to Modern Japanese*. Tokyo: The Japan Times.

Morita, Yoshiyuki. 1977, 1980. *Kiso Nihongo*, Vol. 1 and 2. Kadokawa Shoojiten No. 7 and 8. Tokyo: Kadokawa Shoten.

————. 1981. *Nihongo no Hassoo*. Tokyo: Tojusha.

Nagano, Masaru. 1986. *Bunshooron Soosetsu: Bunpooronteki Koosatsu*. Tokyo: Asakura Shoten.

Nakane, Chie. 1970. *Japanese Society*. Berkeley and Los Angeles: University of California Press.

Okutsu, Keiichiro. 1978. *"Boku wa Unagi da" no Bunpoo*. Tokyo: Kuroshio Shuppan.

Ono, Hideichi. 1973. *Japanese Grammar*. Tokyo: The Hokuseido Press.

Sakuma, Kanae. 1940. *Gendai Nihongohoo no Kenkyuu*. Tokyo: Koseikaku.

————. 1983. *Gendai Nihongo no Hyoogen to Gohoo*. Tokyo: Kuroshio Shuppan.

Soga, Matsuo and Noriko Matsumoto. 1978. *Foundations of Japanese Language*. Tokyo: Taishukan.

Suleski, Ronald and Hiroko Masada. 1982. *Affective Expressions in Japanese*. Tokyo: The Hokuseido Press.

Suzuki, Takao. 1978. *Japanese and the Japanese*. Translated by Akira Miura. Tokyo: Kodansha International.

Tannen, Deborah. 1984. *Conversational Style: Analyzing Talk among Friends*. Norwood, NJ: Ablex.

Teramura, Hideo. 1978. *Nihongo no Bunpoo*, Joo. Tokyo: Kokuritsu Kokugo Kenkyujo.

————. 1981. *Nihongo no Bunpoo*, Ge. Tokyo: Kokuritsu Kokugo Kenkyujo.

————. 1982. *Nihongo no Shintakusu to Imi*, Vol. 1. Tokyo: Kuroshio Shuppan.

————. 1984. *Nihongo no Shintakusu to Imi*, Vol. 2. Tokyo: Kuroshio Shuppan.

Tokieda, Motoki. 1950. *Nihonbunpoo Koogohen*. Tokyo: Iwanami Shoten.

Uyeno, Tazuko. 1971. A Study of Japanese Modality—A Performative Analysis of Sentence Particles. Unpublished dissertation, University of Michigan.

Yamada, Yoshio. 1922. *Nihon Koogohoo Koogi*. Tokyo: Hobunkan.

Subject Index

(For the definition of grammatical terms, see also Appendix 1.)

Vocabulary Lists
(List 1: Japanese-English)

The following list contains Japanese words and phrases appearing in this book in alphabetical order with their English semantic equivalents, or in some cases with a description of their grammatical functions. The number following each item refers to the page where it first appears. Use main or key words to locate phrases consisting of multiple words. The verb types (U, RU, or Irregular) and adjective types (-i, or -na) are indicated in brackets.

*   *   *   *   *

a(a)   oh   324
aa   that way   32
aaa   whew   324
aayuu   such as that   32
achira   that way over there   31
agaru [U]   to rise   322
ageru [RU]   to give   39, 226
    te-ageru   (giving a favorable action to someone)   231
Ahurika   Africa   129
aida   between   86
aida ni   while   272
aisukuriimu   icecream   24
aite   companion   243
aitsu   that guy   431
akarui [-i]   bright   210
akemashite omedetoo gozaimasu   Happy New Year   306
akeru [RU]   to open [transitive]   39, 157
aki   fall   68
akireru [RU]   to be surprised, to be astounded   106
akiru [RU]   to get bored, to get tired of   106
akogareru [RU]   to long for, to pine for   106
aku [U]   to open [intransitive]   38, 157, 169
amaeru [RU]   to be dependent upon   106
amai [-i]   sweet   109
a(n)mari   (not) so much   94, 97
ame   rain   80
Amerika   America (United States of)   24
Ameriaka taishikan   American embassy   371
Amerika-jin   American   26
anata¹   husband [address term]   196
anata²   you   45
ane   elder sister   195
ani   elder brother   195

ano   that   31
ano ne   (for getting attention)   194
anoo   uh, well   123, 193, 259
anta   you   45
apaato   apartment   407
arau [U]   to wash   38, 169
arawareru [RU]   to appear   431
are   that one over there   31
aree   oh my!   324
arigataku choodai itashimasu   I accept your gift with gratitude   230
arigatoo (gozaimsu)   thank you   199, 306
arigatoo gozaimashita   thank you for . . .   199
arihureru [RU]   to be common   172
aru   one   350
aru [U]   there exists   36, 41, 169
arubaito   part-time job   25
aruku [U]   to walk   61, 156
asa   morning   67
asaban   mornings and evenings   183
Asagaya   (a place name in Tokyo)   32
Asagaya Apaato   (a name of an apartment building)   32
asagohan   breakfast   76
asaneboo o suru   to oversleep   186
asatte   the day after tomorrow   67
asebamu [U]   to sweat   381
ashita   tomorrow   57, 67
asobu [U]   to play   38, 169
asoko   over there   31
asu   tomorrow   67
ataeru [RU]   to give   229
atakushi   I [female]   45
atama   head   215
    atama ga itai   to have a headache   215
atarashii [-i]   new   15
atashi   I [female]   45
atatakai [-i]   warm   15

atatakana [-na] warm 131
atatakasa warmth 395
*ato de*¹ after doing 272
*ato de*² later 84, 163
atoaji aftertaste 431
*atsui*¹ [-i] hot 15
*atsui*² [-i] thick, heavy 15
atsumaru [U] to gather 61
atsumeru [RU] to collect 391
atsusa heat 107
au [U] to meet, to see 38
awarena [-na] pitiful 131

-ba if 297, 303, 376
  -ba yokatta I wish I had done so . . . 301
baa bar 25
baagaapan hamburger buns 23
baka fool 291
*bakari*¹ about 120, 381
*bakari*² only 380
  *bakari da*¹ just did 381, 416
  *bakari da*² ready to 381
  bakari de naku . . .mo not only but also 381
-ban (counter for order) 119
banana bananas 221
banshuu late fall 316
basu bus 25
basudai bus fare 395
basukettobooru basketball 25
beki ought to 335, 340
benkyoo(-suru) (to) study 40, 139, 169
benrina [-na] convenient, useful 131
benrisa convenience 395
betsuni (not) especially 432
biiru beer 24
-biki (phonological change of *-hiki*) 119
bin bottle 368
Biru Bill 24
biru building 23
boku I [male] 45
-bon (phonological change of *-hon*) 119
bon'yarito absent-mindedly 432
boonasu bonus 324
booringu bowling 25
booshi hat 262
Bosuton Boston 24
bubun part, section 164
buchoo manager 280
bukka price 322
bunka culture 73
burabura rambling 411
  burabura-suru [Irr] to walk aimlessly 411

Buraun Brown 24
butaniku pork 121
-byoo seconds 103, 119
byooin hospital 76
byooki illness 133, 215
  byooki ni naru to become sick 215

cha (contraction of *te wa*) 357
chau (colloquial version of *te-shimau*) 181
chichi my father 82, 195
chigainai lit. there is no mistake 345
  ni chigainai (guessing with confidence) 345
chigau [U] to differ 169
chiisai [-i] small 15
chikai [-i] near 15
chikaku near 86
chittomo (not) at all 97
chokusetsutekini directly 425
chooshuu audience 356
choppiri very little, a wee bit 97
chosha author 70
*chotto*¹ (for getting attention) 193
*chotto*² a little 97
*chotto*³ uhh . . . 153
  chotto muzukashii naa, sore wa . . . it's a bit too difficult, I'm afraid . . . 253
  sore ga, chotto nee . . . well, it's a bit of a problem 253
Chuugokumuke bound for China, catered to China 395
chuui warning 356
chuukaryoori Chinese cuisine 221
chuushi cancellation 261

da be (am, is, are) 29, 410
dai fare 395
-dai (counter for vehicles etc.) 118
daigaku university 116
daigaku kyooju university professor 28
daigakusei university student 105
daijoobu all right 166, 352
  daijoobu desu I'll be fine 166
daikiraina [-na] abhorring 219
daisukina [-na] favorite 219
dakara and so 186, 409
dake only, just 97
  dake de naku . . .mo not only but also 380
damasu [U] to deceive 349
dame
  nakereba dame must 344
  te wa dame must not 353

ga² (subject marker) 38, 46
ga³ but 113, 187, 190, 409
gabugabu nomu to drink thirstily 175
gaikoku foreign countries 172
gaishutsu-suru [Irr] to go out 432
gakkoo school 59
gakkooyoo for consumption at school 395
gakusei student 28
gakusha scholar 28
gaman-suru [Irr] to suppress 420
ganbaru [U] to do one's best 182
gankona [-na] stubborn 131
garasu glass 368
-gatsu (indicating month) 103
gekitotsu-suru [Irr] to crash into 432
gengo language 414
genki? how have you been? 308
(o)genkina [-na] healthy, well 246
gensokuteki ni wa in principle 327
geragera warau to laugh boisterously 175
getsuyoobi Monday 68
ginkoo bank 85
ginkooin banker, bank employee 28
Ginza Ginza 148
go five 100
go- (respectful prefix) 138
go-gatsu May 103
gobusata-shite-orimasu I haven't seen you
    for a long time 306
gochisoosama deshita thank you for the
    delicious food/drink 366
gogo afternoon 67
gohan cooked rice 412
gokazoku family 196
gokuroosama (desu/deshita) thank you for
    your effort 201
gokuroosan thank you for your effort 201
gokyoodai sibling 196
gomen sorry, excuse me 161
gomenkudasai hello, excuse me 194, 365
gomennasai I'm sorry 161
gookei total, sum 336
goranninaru [U] to look 279
goruhu golf 25
goshujin(sama) husband 196
gozenchuu morning, before noon 67
guai wa doo desu ka how are you feeling?
    307
gurai about 120
-guramu gram 118
gutaiteki ni yuu to more concretely 258
guuzen unexpectedly, coincidentally 163

ha tooth 215
    ha ga itai to have a toothache 215

haa? uh? 264
hachi eight 100
hachi-gatsu August 103
hachi-ji eight o'clock 37
hadena [-na] showy 131
hageshii [-i] pouring (rain) 137
haha mother 195
hai yes 115, 221, 253
-hai (counter for liquid) 118
haikensuru [Irr] to look 279
hairu [U] to enter 36, 61
haisha(-san) dentist 344
haishakusuru [Irr] to borrow 279
hajimaru [U] to begin 37
hajimemashite how do you do? 33
-hajimeru something begins to occur 388
hakaru [U] to measure 396
Hakata Hakata 64
hakken-suru [Irr] to discover 339
hakkiri (to) clearly 163
hako box 86
hakobu [U] to carry 61
haku [U] to put on, to wear (shoes) 396
hamueggu ham-and-eggs 59
han thirty minutes 103
hana¹ flower 227
hana² trunk 57
hanashi talk 138
    hanashi chigau kedo to change the
    subject 258
hanasu [U] to talk 210
hanbaagaa hamburger 25
hanbaagu hamburger 25
hanbai(-suru) (to) sell 40
hanbun half 311
hanetobasu [U] to hit (by a car) 432
hankachi handkerchief 23
hanmei-suru [Irr] to become clear 432
hannin criminal 362
happyoo-suru [Irr] to make a presentation
    311
Hara (last name) 28
haradatsu [U] to get angry 107
hareru [RU] to clear up 80
haru spring 68
hashiru [U] to run 169, 181
hatarakimono hard worker 44
hataraku [U] to work 37, 39
hatashite in reality, as a matter of fact
    425
hate na? I wonder 324
hatsuka 20th [date] 102
hayai [-i] early, quick 16
hayaku early 68
hazu be supposed to 335
hee is that right, really! 324

-mashoo ka shall I . . .? 165
masukomi mass communication 52
mata addtionally 192
mata doozo please come again 308
mata wa or 409
mata yoosu o mite to yuu koto de we will see what happens 327
matsu [U] to wait 39, 169
Matsumoto (last name) 28
matsuri festival 273
mawari surrounding 289
mayonaka midnight 67
mayou [U] to be puzzled 107
mazu first 341
mazui [-i] with bad taste 16
mazushii [-i] poor 182
me eye 172
   me ga mawaru to feel giddy 215
   me ga sameru to awaken 431
-meetoru meter 118
megane glasses 268
meishi business card 34
memai ga suru to feel dizzy 215
memo memo 204
mensetsu (job) interview 425
meron melon 90
meshiagaru [U] to eat 279
mezamashidokei alarm clock 250
mi (nominalizing suffix) 395
michi road 109
midori green 350
mieru [RU] to be seen 217
mijikai [-i] short 16
mikakeru [RU] to see in passing 238
mikan tangerine 62
mikka 3rd [date] 102
minami south 183
minasama everyone 246
minasan you all 314
minna¹ everyone 146
minna² everything 242
miru [RU] to see 39
miruku milk 24
mise store 62
misoshiru miso soup 412
mitaina it seems 291
mitsukaru [U] to be found 157
mitsukeru [RU] to find 157
mittsu three 100
(o)miyage small gift 230
mizu water 37
mo also, in addition (topic marker) 57, 105, 263, 316
moderu (fashion) model 28
modoru [U] to return, to come back 267
mohaya already 432

mokuyoobi Thursday 68
mondai question 131
mono¹ thing(s) 106, 383, 394
   mono da¹ (expressing surprise) 384
   mono da² (to convey mild, indirect command) 385
   mono da³ used to do 383
mono² (to add explanation in written style) 384
   n da mono (pointing out reason [colloquial]) 383
   [Vstem] + mono (nominal compound) 394
monoreeru monorail 25
moo already, more 82, 163
   moo ichido onegai-shimasu could you repeat it one more time? 265
   moo nidoto never 267
moo sukoshi a little more 163
   moo sukoshi matte-kudasai please wait a little longer 353
   moo sukoshi yukkuri onegai-shimasu could you speak a little more slowly? 265
mooshiageru [RU] to say 279
mooshiwake arimasen I'm sorry 161
moosu [U] to say 279
morau [U] to receive 39, 226
   te-moraitai (expressing request) 252
   te-morau (receiving a favorable action) 231
moshika shitara if it should be 321
moshika suruto if it is 321
moshimoshi hello (on the phone) 432
motomeru [RU] to seek 360
motsu [U] to possess, to carry, to hold 39, 166
motte-iru to have 197
motte-kuru to bring 183
motto more 163
   motto wakai younger 304
mottomo most 163, 208
mudazukai wasteful spending 229
muika 6th [date] 102
mujitsu innocent 359
mukaeru [RU] to welcome 203
mukashi once upon a time 44
muke bound for, catered toward 395
mukoo beyond 86
mukoo gishi the other side 64
mura village 359
murina [-na] unreasonable 254
   murina onegai da to wa omoimasu ga although I think it is an unreasonable request to grant 253
musuko(san) son 196

480

Vocabulary Lists
(List 2: English-Japanese)

The following list contains English words and phrases appearing in this book as English semantic equivalents of Japanese. The number following each item refers to the page where it first appears. Note that grammatical functions are not listed here; for these, see Subject Index.

*   *   *   *   *

a few   *sukoshi*   97
   sukunai [-*i*]   15
a little   *chotto, sukoshi*   97
   just a little   *honno sukoshi*   230
   very little   *choppiri*   97
a lot   *yoku*   81
a moment before   *sunzen*   432
a wee bit   *choppiri*   97
abhorring   *daikiraina* [-*na*]   219
about   *bakari*   120, 381
   hodo, kurai, gurai, yaku   120
   ni tsuite   327
   be about to   *tokoro da*   415
   was about to do   *to shite-ita tokoro da*   415
(to be) absent   *yasumu* [*U*]   57
absent-mindedly   *bon'yarito*   432
accept
   I accept your gift with gratitude
   arigataku choodai itashimasu   230
(to) accumulate   *tamaru* [*U*]   303
accurate   *seikakuna* [-*na*]   137
achiever   *yarite*   192
(to) add   *tasu* [*U*]   285
additionally   *mata*   192
   ni   105
address   *juusho*   154
admission fee   *nyuujooryoo*   395
advertisement   *kookoku*   281
Africa   *Ahurika*   129
after all   *doose*   224
   kekkyoku   188
   yahari   411
after doing   *ato de*   272
   te kara   270
afternoon   *gogo*   67
aftertaste   *atoaji*   431
agreement   *sansei*   327
ahead   *saki*   86
air conditioning   *reiboo*   312
airplane   *hikooki*   182

airplane ticket   *kookuuken*   312
airport   *kuukoo*   110
alarm clock   *mezamashidokei*   250
all   *subete*   359
all day long   *ichinichijuu*   81
all night   *hitobanjuu*   334
all right   *daijoobu*   166, 352
   kamaimasen   352
already   *mohaya*   432
   moo   82, 163
also (topic marker)   *mo*   57, 105, 263, 316
although   *kedo*   187, 376
   [Adj] + *tokoro*   415
always   *itsumo*   67, 163
America (United States of)   *Amerika*   24
American   *Amerika-jin*   26
American embassy   *Ameriaka taishikan*   371
and   *dano, toka, yara*   105
   soshite   186, 409
   to   59, 105, 263
   ya   105, 263
and others   *nado*   105
and so   *dakara, desukara, sorede*   186, 409
   node   187, 249
(to be) angry   *okoru* [*U*]   38
   haradatsu [*U*]   107
answer   *kotae*   300
(to) answer   *kotaeru* [*RU*]   39
any one   *dore-mo*   94, 128
any time   *itsu-mo*   128
anyone   *dare de mo*   129
   dare-mo   94, 128
anything   *nani-mo*   94, 128
anyway   *doose*   224
anywhere   *doko e mo*   94
   doko-mo   128
apartment   *apaato*   407
   upscale apartment   *okushon*   26
(to) appear   *arawareru* [*RU*]   431
   deru [*RU*]   359

(to) do   *suru* [Irr]   35, 403, 410
do in excess   *-sugiru*   388
   (to) do one's best   *ganbaru* [U]   182
(to) do [humble]   *itasu* [U]   279
(to) do [respectful]   *nasaru* [U]   279
dog   *inu*   43
dollar   *-doru*   118
don't you? (interactional particle)   *ne(e)*   14,
   125, 222, 377
door   *doa*   155
   to   152
drawer   *hikidashi*   87
dream   *yume*   289
(being) drenched   *zubunure*   350
dress   *yoohuku*   243
dress shirt (solid colored)   *waishatsu*   25
drink   *nomimono*   123
(to) drink   *nomu* [U]   36, 39
   (to) drink (sake)   *sake o nomu*
      262
   (to) drink thirstily   *gabugabu nomu*
      175
(to) drive   *doraibu, doraibu-suru*   23
driver   *untenshu(-san)*   27
(to) drop   *otosu*[U], *ochiru* [RU]   38, 39
drunken driving   *inshuunten*   356
(to) dry   *kawakasu* [U]   157
   (to) be dried up   *kawaku* [U]   157
durable   *joobuna* [-na]   336
duration of hours   *-jikan*   103, 119

each   *zutsu*   198
early   *hayai* [-i]   16
   hayaku   68
early morning   *soochoo*   67
earthquake   *jishin*   44
easy   *yasashii* [-i]   16
   easy to do   *-yasui*   394
(to) eat   *taberu* [RU]   36, 156, 169
   manner of eating   *tabekata*   395
(to) eat [humble]   *itadaku* [U]   279
(to) eat [respectful]   *meshiagaru* [U]   279
economics   *keizaigaku*   173
effort   *doryoku*   385
   with much trouble and effort *sekkaku*
      224
eight   *hachi, yattsu*   100
eight o'clock   *hachi-ji*   37
eighth [date]   *yooka*   102
elder brother   *ani, (o)niisan*   195
elder sister   *ane, (o)neesan*   195
elephant   *zoo*   57
embassy   *taishikan*   371
emergency   *kyuuyoo*   374
(to be) employed   *tsutomeru* [RU]   360

employment   *shokuba*   343
end   *saigo*   275
(to) end   *owaru* [U]   38
endearing   *kawaii* [-i]   208
enemy   *teki*   42
engineer   *enjinia*   28
England   *Igirisu*   24
English   *eigo*   21
English literature   *eibungaku*   173
English person   *Igirisu-jin*   26
(to) enter   *hairu* [U]   36, 61
entrance exam   *nyuugakushiken*   73, 311
(not) especially   *betsuni*   432
Europe   *Yooroppa*   72
even now   *ima de mo*   219
even though   *-tatte, -datte*   318
evening   *yuugata*   67
every day   *mainichi*   67
every month   *maitsuki*   68
every morning   *maiasa*   37
every week   *maishuu*   56, 67
every year   *mainen*   68
everyone   *minasama*   246
   minna   146
everything   *minna*   242
   zenbu   180
examination   *shiken*   73
   entrance exam   *nyuugakushiken*   73,
      311
   (to) make up questions for an exam
      shiken mondai o dasu   269
(to) examine   *shiraberu* [RU]   330
(to) excel   *sugureru* [RU]   172
(to) exclude   *nozoku* [U]   407
excuse me   *gomen, shitsurei*   161
   gomenkudasahi   194, 365
   ojama-shimashita   366
   ojama-shimasu, shitsurei-
      shimasu   365
   excuse me for leaving early   *osakini*
      (shitsurei[-shimasu])   276
   excuse me, but . . .   *sumimasen ga . . .*
      190, 193
(there) exists   *aru* [U]   36, 41, 169
   iru [RU]   36, 39, 41, 169
(there) exists [respectful]   *irassharu* [U]
   279
(to) expand   *hirogaru* [U]   407
expense   *shuppi*   335
expensive   *kookana* [-na]   131
   takai [-i]   15
experience
   I have experienced it   *koto ga aru*   385
(to) explain   *setsumei-suru* [Irr]   192
(to) export   *yushutsu, yushutsu-suru*   40
expression   *hyoojoo*   431

girl *onna no ko* 294
(to) give *ageru [RU]* 39, 226
    ataeru [RU] 229
    please give *kudasai* 110
    someone gives to self *kureru [RU]* 226
(to) give [giver is higher] *yaru [U]* 226
    someone gives to self [giver is higher]
    kudasaru [U] 226
(to) give [giver is lower] *sashiageru [RU]*
    226
glass *garasu* 368
    koppu 161
glasses *megane* 268
(to) go *iku [U]* 202
    go for the purpose of *ni iku* 202
    (to) go out *dekakeru [RU]* 210
    deru [RU] 39
    gaishutsu-suru [Irr] 432
    I will go and return *itte-kimasu, itte-mairimasu* 276
(to) go [humble] *mairu, ukagau [U]* 36,
    279
(to) go [respectful] *oideninaru [U]* 279
(to) go bankrupt *tsubureru [RU]* 188
(to) go on a business trip *shutchoo-suru*
    [Irr] 69
(to) go through hardships *kuroo-suru* [Irr]
    351
(to) go to bed *neru [RU]* 39
the Golden Pavilion *Kinkakuji* 350
golf *goruhu* 25
good *ii, yoi [-i]* 16
    be good at *joozuna [-na]* 55, 131
    it would be better *hoo ga ii* 209, 378
good afternoon *konnichiwa* 12
good evening *konbanwa* 12
good morning *ohayoo (gozaimasu)* 12,
    308
goodbye *sayo(o)nara* 276
government employee *koomuin* 28
grade school student *shoogakusei* 273
gradually *dandan* 182
graduation *sotsugyoo* 138
graduation thesis *sotsuron* 52
gram *-guramu* 118
grandfather *ojiisan* 195
grandfather (one's own) *sohu* 195
grandmother *obaasan* 195
grandmother (one's own) *sobo* 195
great *idaina [-na]* 131
great! *ureshii naa!* 292
green *midori* 350
green tea *ocha* 420
greengrocer *yaoya* 28
(to) greet *tsugeru [RU]* 432

(to) grieve *kanashimu [U]* 293
(to) grill *yaku [U]* 367
    (to) be grilled *yakeru [RU]* 217
(to) grin *niyaniya suru* 175
guest *okyaku-san* 203

Hakata *Hakata* 64
half *hanbun* 311
ham-and-eggs *hamueggu* 59
hamburger *hanbaagaa, hanbaagu* 25
hamburger buns *baagaapan* 23
hand *te* 338
(to) hand (over) *watasu [U]* 303
handkerchief *hankachi* 23
handwriting *ji* 315
hangover *hutsukayoi* 385
(to) happen *okoru [U]* 431
happy
    Happy New Year *akemashite omede-too gozaimasu* 306
    I am happy! *shiawase!* 292
hard *isshookenmei* 37
hat *booshi* 262
(to) have *motte-iru* 197
head *atama* 215
headache *zutsuu* 204
    (to) have a headache *atama ga itai*
    215
healthy *genkina [-na]* 246
    kenkoona [-na] 133
(to) hear *kiku [U]* 38, 170
    (to) be heard *kikoeru [RU]* 217
    I hear *soo da* 370
heat *atsusa* 107
heavy *atsui [-i]* 15
height *takasa* 395
hello *gomenkudasai* 194, 365
hello (on the phone) *moshimoshi* 432
(to) help *tetsudau [U]* 165
    I'll help myself, thank you *itadaki-masu* 366
    with the help from *(no) okage* 314
here *koko* 31
    here's something for you *tsumaranai mono desu ga . . .* 229, 365
hi! *yoo!* 308
high school student *kookoosei* 273
high-rise *koosoo* 407
history *rekishi* 173
(to) hit *nagaru [U]* 232
(to) hit (by a car) *hanetobasu [U]* 432
Hokkaido *Hokkaidoo* 361
(to) hold *motsu [U]* 166
holiday *kyuujitsu* 407

university *daigaku* 116
university professor *daigaku kyooju* 28
university student *daigakusei* 105
unreasonable *murina* [-*na*] 254
   although I think it is an unreasonable request to grant *murina onegai da to wa omoimasu ga* 253
up to *made* 59
upper class *jookyuu* 337
upscale apartment *manshon* 25
use
   for the use by *yoo* 395
   (to) use *riyoo-suru* [Irr] 351
            tsukau [*U*] 146
used to do *mono da* 383
useful *benrina* [-*na*] 131
(to) utilize *riyoo-suru* [Irr] 351

variety *hinshu* 71
various *iroirona* [-*na*] 68
very *totemo* 72
very much *zuibun* 97
vicinity *hukin* 391
village *mura* 359
visit *hoomon* 425
(to) visit *yoru* [*U*] 303
voice *koe* 431

(to) wait *matsu* [*U*] 39, 169
   please wait a little longer *moo sukoshi matte-kudasai* 353
(to) wake *okosu* [*U*] 157
(to) walk *aruku* [*U*] 61, 156
   (to) go for a walk *sanpo-suru* [Irr] 272
   (to) walk aimlessly *burabura-suru* [Irr] 411
wallet *saihu* 254
(to) want *hoshii* [-*i*] 211
   a third person wants *hoshigatte-iru* 211
   a third person wants to -*tagatte-iru* 211
   (to) want to -*tai* 211
warm *atatakai* [-*i*] 15
   atatakana [-*na*] 131
warmth *atatakasa* 395
warning *chuui* 356
(to) wash *arau* [*U*] 38, 169
wasteful spending *mudazukai* 229
watch *tokei* 137
water *mizu* 37
water fee *suidooryookin* 395
(to) wave *huru* [*U*] 338

way
   the way of doing -*kata* 395
(to) wear *kiru* [*RU*] 39, 170
   (to) wear (shoes) *haku* [*U*] 396
   (to) wear clothes *hukusoo o suru* 289
   (to) wear glasses *megane o kakeru* 268
weather *tenki* 94
Wednesday *suiyoobi* 68
week -*shuukan* 119
   the week after next *saraishuu* 67
   the week before last *sensenshuu* 67
weekend *shuumatsu* 189
(to) welcome *mukaeru* [*RU*] 203
   welcome (to our place) *irasshaimase* 308
   you are welcome *doo itashimashite* 199
well[1] *genkina* [-*na*] 246
   yoku 81,163
well[2] *anoo* 123, 193, 259
well . . . *ee, maa . . .* 265
   maa, ano 258
   soo da naa, soo nee 154
   well . . .I'm afraid not *iyaa, chotto . . .* 353
   well, I am not sure *soo desu ka nee . .* 222, 328
   well, let's see . . . *saa* 127, 222
   well, my apologies, but I cannot *soo iwaremashite mo nee . . .* 253
   well, say . . . *maa . . .* 259
Western culture *seiyoo bunka* 73
Western world *seiyoo* 73
what *nani* 75
   what should I say? *nan to iimashoo ka . . .* 259
   what was that? *nan deshita ka* 265
what? *e(e)?* 222, 264, 324
what . . .! *nante/nanto . . .daroo!* 325
   what a disaster! *nante koto da* 325
when -*tara* 301
   itsu 73
   to 285
whenever *to* 285
where *dochira, doko* 31, 75
whether or not *te mo* 318
   ka doo ka 330
whew *aaa* 324
which *dono* 31
which date *nan-nichi* 102
which month *nan-gatsu* 103
which one *dochira, dore* 31, 75, 209
while *aida ni* 272
   nagara 270
   a while ago *sakki* 67,163